TABLE OF CONTENTS

Introduction   **xi**

How This Book Is Organized................... xii

Which Suites Are Covered?................... xii

The Office Applications xiii

PART I: **INTRODUCING MICROSOFT OFFICE 2007**   **1**

Chapter 1:   **What's New in Office 2007?**   **3**

The New User Interface 4

New File Formats 7

New Features and Changes 8

Chapter 2:   **Office Basics**   **11**

Creating a New Document................... 13

Opening Documents 14

Saving Documents 15

Closing Documents 16

Working with Windows 17

Setting the Magnification................... 19

Using the Office Clipboard................... 20

Printing 22

Getting Help............................... 24

Quitting an Office Program.................. 26

PART II: **MICROSOFT WORD**   **27**

Chapter 3:   **Getting Started with Word 2007**   **29**

The Word Interface 30

Working in Different Views................... 33

Managing Windows......................... 35

Setting Show/Hide Options.................. 37

Entering Text............................... 38

Basic Text Editing........................... 39

Using the Proofing Tools 41

Finding and Replacing Text 45

Entering Symbols and Special Characters...... 48

Chapter 4: **Formatting Documents** **49**

Specifying Page Settings 50
Modifying the Background 52
Inserting Breaks 55
Adding a Cover Page or Blank Page 57
Adding Headers or Footers 59
Paragraph Formatting 62
Setting Alignment 63
Setting Indents 64
Creating Lists 66
Between-Paragraph and Line Spacing 70
Character Formatting 72
Working with Styles 75
Merge Formatting 78

Chapter 5: **Creating Outlines** **85**

About Outline View 86
Starting an Outline 87
Reorganizing an Outline 88
Changing Display Settings 90

Chapter 6: **Tables, Charts, and Art** **91**

Inserting Tables 92
Entering Data into a Table 94
Modifying the Table Grid 95
Formatting Table Data 98
Calculations in Tables 99
Creating Charts 101
About Adding Graphics and Objects 102
Adding Pictures 103
Adding Clip Art 104
Adding Shapes 105
Using a Drawing Canvas 106
Adding SmartArt 107
Creating WordArt 108
Adding a Text Box 109
Setting Text Wrap 110
Resizing, Moving, and Rotating Objects 111

Chapter 7: **Sharing Word Documents** **113**

Choosing a File Format 114
Emailing Word Documents 115
Publishing Blog Entries 116
Change Tracking 118
Comparing Documents 120

TABLE OF CONTENTS

Combining Documents. 121
The Document Inspector 122
Protecting a Document. 123

PART III: MICROSOFT EXCEL   125

Chapter 8:   Getting Started with Excel 2007   127
The Excel Interface. 128
Workbooks and Worksheets. 130
Cell and Range Selection 132
Entering Data. 134
Editing Data 136
Reorganizing a Worksheet. 137
Filling Cells 142
Importing Data 144
Finding/Replacing Data 149
Sorting Data 152
Naming Cells and Ranges. 154
Password-Protecting Workbooks 156

Chapter 9:   Formatting Worksheets and Data   159
Setting Column Width and Row Height 160
About Data and Cell Formatting. 162
Character and Paragraph Formatting 163
Fitting Text Within a Cell 164
Number Formatting. 165
Conditional Formatting 166
Adding Cell Borders and Backgrounds 168
Removing, Replacing, and Reusing Formats . . . 170

Chapter 10: Formulas and Functions   173
About Cell References 174
Formula Essentials. 176
Creating Formulas 180
Editing Formulas 182
Troubleshooting Tips 183

Chapter 11: Working with Tables   185
Creating a Table 186
Formatting a Table. 187
Creating Calculated Columns. 188
Adding a Total Row 189
Sorting and Filtering 190
Changing a Table's Size. 192

TABLE OF CONTENTS

Chapter 12: **Creating Charts** **195**

Chart Elements 196
Creating a Chart 197
Changing the Background 198
Adding and Formatting Text 199
Rows vs. Columns. 201
Changing the Layout and Style. 202
Displaying the Data Set. 203
Working with Gridlines 204
Working with the Legend 205
Adding Trendlines 206
Modifying the Axes 207
Changing the Chart Data 208

PART IV: **MICROSOFT POWERPOINT** **209**

Chapter 13: **Getting Started with PowerPoint 2007** **211**

The PowerPoint Interface 212
Working in Different Views. 214
Creating a Presentation 215

Chapter 14: **Creating a Presentation** **217**

Beginning a Presentation. 218
Setting the Theme 220
Adding and Deleting Slides 221
Replacing Placeholders 222
Inserting Other Items 225
Creating a Photo Album. 229
Previewing the Slide Show 231

Chapter 15: **Completing a Presentation** **233**

Animating Objects and Text. 234
Organizing the Slides. 236
Adding Transitions 237
Rehearsing a Presentation 239
Printing Notes and Handouts. 240
Saving a Presentation in Other Formats 242

PART V: **MICROSOFT OUTLOOK** **245**

Chapter 16: **Getting Started with Outlook 2007** **247**

Types of Email Accounts 248
About Email Addresses. 250

Adding Email Accounts 251
Changing Account Settings. 254
Working with Profiles 256
Working with Send/Receive Groups 258
Subscribing to RSS Feeds 261
The Outlook 2007 Window 262
Working Online and Offline 264
Setting Preferences. 265
Getting Help. 266

Chapter 17:   Using the Address Book   267
The Contacts Window 268
Viewing Contact Records. 269
Creating Contact Records 270
Searching for a Contact. 274
Using Business Cards 276
Creating Distribution Lists 278

Chapter 18:   Composing and Sending Mail   281
The Message Window. 282
Creating Messages 283
About Message Formats. 288
Adding Attachments. 292
Inserting Items 293
Correcting Spelling Errors 296
Using Signatures. 298
Other Message Options. 300

Chapter 19:   Receiving Mail   303
Checking for New Mail 304
Reading Messages. 306
Changing the View. 308
Searching for Messages. 309
Working with Attachments 310
Printing Messages. 311

Chapter 20:   Managing the Mail   313
Marking Messages as Read 314
Deleting Messages 316
Copying and Moving Messages 318
Creating Message Folders 319
Categorizing Messages 320
Flagging Messages 323
Handling Junk Mail and Phishing 325
Creating Message Rules 327

TABLE OF CONTENTS

Chapter 21: **Tasks and Appointments** **329**

Calendar Basics 330
Recording an Appointment or Event 331
Creating Recurring Events 332
Responding to Reminders 333
Modifying Events and Appointments 334
Searching for an Event or Appointment 335
Emailing a Calendar 336
Task Basics 338
Creating a Task 339
Modifying Tasks 340

PART VI: **MICROSOFT ONENOTE** **341**

Chapter 22: **Getting Started with OneNote 2007** **343**

The OneNote Interface 344
Notebooks, Sections, and Pages 346
Opening and Closing Notebooks 349
OneNote Integration 350
Getting Help 352

Chapter 23: **Creating Notes** **353**

Typing a Note 354
Recording an Audio Note 355
Recording a Video Note 356
Creating Handwritten Notes 357
Copy-and-Paste and Drag-and-Drop 358
Creating Notes from Outlook Items 360
Notes without OneNote 361

Chapter 24: **Embellishing and Editing Notes** **363**

Using Page Templates 364
Inserting Images from Disk 365
Inserting and Working with Tables 366
Inserting Hyperlinks 369
Editing and Formatting Notes 372
Correcting Spelling Errors 374

Chapter 25: **Managing Notes** **375**

Rearranging Notebooks, Sections, Pages 376
Moving Pages and Sections 377
Creating Section Groups 379
Creating Page Groups 380
Deleting Notes and Objects 381

Adding Section Passwords. 382
Searching for Notes 384
Printing Notes 386

PART VII: MICROSOFT PUBLISHER   **387**

Chapter 26: Getting Started with Publisher 2007   **389**
The Publisher Interface. 390
Creating a Publication. 392
Creating a Business Information Set 394
Replacing Text Placeholders 395
Replacing and Inserting Artwork. 397
Previewing the Publication 398
Making Minor Changes 399
Storing and Reusing Items. 404
Changing the Font or Color Scheme. 406
Changing Templates 407
Addressing the Postcards. 408

Chapter 27: Distributing and Printing Publications   **409**
Running a Prepress Check 410
Creating PDFs 411
Emailing a Publication 414
Publishing to the Web. 417
Printing a Publication 419

Index   **423**

Special Thanks to:

The Peachpit Press editorial and production crew for being so helpful, supportive, and understanding.

INTRODUCTION

Welcome to *Microsoft Office 2007 for Windows: Visual QuickStart Guide*. In the pages that follow, you'll find the information and instructions you need to quickly become productive with the applications in Microsoft Office 2007.

Like other titles in the *Visual QuickStart* series, this book was written primarily as a reference. Unlike a book on a single program, however, this one covers *six* major applications. Rather than discuss every command and procedure in excruciating detail (as you'd expect in a one-program book), the focus of this book is on commands and procedures you're most likely to actually *use*.

How This Book Is Organized

To make it easy for you to find the information you need at any given moment, the book is divided into major sections called *parts*.

◆ Part I provides an introduction to essential Office procedures and describes the changes you'll find in Office 2007.

◆ Parts II through VII are devoted to the individual Office applications—one part for each application.

Which Suites Are Covered?

Microsoft Office 2007 is available in eight configurations (or *suites*), each with a different combination of applications (**Table i.1**). This book covers the following applications in the Basic, Home & Student, Standard, and Small Business suites: Word, Excel, PowerPoint, Outlook, OneNote, and Publisher.

If you purchased one of the other suites (Professional, Ultimate, Professional Plus, or Enterprise), you're still covered—but you'll have to look elsewhere for help with Access, Microsoft's database application.

✔ Notes

■ Only the Ultimate suite includes *all* the programs discussed in this book. Because the other suites are missing one or more of the applications, some of this book's chapters will not apply to you.

■ For a solid primer about the previous version of Access, you might want to pick up a copy of *Microsoft Office Access 2003 for Window: Visual QuickStart Guide*, written by yours truly.

Table i.1

Microsoft Office 2007 Suites

OFFICE APPLICATIONS	Basic	Home & Student	Standard	Small Business	Professional	Ultimate	Professional Plus	Enterprise
Word	◆	◆	◆	◆	◆	◆	◆	◆
Excel	◆	◆	◆	◆	◆	◆	◆	◆
PowerPoint		◆	◆	◆	◆	◆	◆	◆
Outlook	◆		◆				◆	◆
Outlook w/Business Contact Manager				◆	◆	◆		
OneNote		◆				◆		
Publisher				◆	◆	◆	◆	◆
Access					◆	◆	◆	◆

The Office Applications

Whether you're a first-time Office user or an old hand, depending on the Office suite you've purchased, you may find yourself the proud owner of some unfamiliar applications. The following pages provide a quick overview of the programs covered in this book and the tasks for which they're suited.

Microsoft Office Word 2007

Word is a *word-processing* program. You can use it to write letters, memos, contracts, reports, or the Great American Novel. Because Word is so commonly used in the business world, you'll find that most word-processing documents you receive from others will be Word files.

Like other word-processing programs of the past twenty years, Word uses a *WYSIWYG* (What You See Is What You Get) approach to document formatting, layout, and display. That is, the fonts, paragraph formats, margins, and page breaks you see onscreen will precisely match those in the printout.

If your needs go beyond simple text documents, you can embellish them with tables, clip art, and photos. You can also apply stylish, 3-D effects called WordArt to text and embed important titles or bulleted lists in eye-catching SmartArt.

In addition to allowing you to create new documents from scratch, Word provides an array of templates for useful documents and forms. Many can be used as-is or with only minor modification. And if you want to generate personalized mailings, Word has a mail-merge feature.

Microsoft Office Excel 2007

Like Word, Excel is the most widely used *spreadsheet* application around. You use a spreadsheet program to enter, analyze, and summarize large amounts of numerical and text data on a row-and-column grid.

Excel is an excellent tool for performing calculations (via formulas and its built-in functions), as well as for creating colorful, informative graphs. And because so many people use worksheets to record lists, Excel also includes list-management features. To automate repetitive operations, you can create *macros* by recording a series of actions or by using Microsoft Visual Basic.

The days of the drab, colorless, single-font worksheet are over. Excel supports mixed fonts, styles, colors, and rotated text, as well as cell background formatting and conditional formatting. To further embellish any worksheet, you can add clip art, pictures, pre-defined shapes (such as arrows and text balloons), WordArt, and SmartArt.

Microsoft Office PowerPoint 2007

PowerPoint is Office's "best in class" program for creating *presentations*: slide shows with between-slide transition effects, within-slide animations, recorded audio narration, presenter notes, and handouts.

To give your slides a consistent, professional look, you can select from the included themes or download additional ones from Microsoft Online. You can also create and save templates that include designs and other key elements, such as a company logo or address information.

After you've rehearsed and set the timing for your presentation, it can be played on a computer, professionally output to slides, or used to generate a Web-based presentation.

Microsoft Office Outlook 2007

Outlook's primary function is that of an *email client*. Outlook can send, receive, and manage email for all types of accounts (including certain Web-based ones, such as MSN HotMail accounts). Outlook 2007 can also be configured to receive Really Simple Syndication (RSS) message feeds.

In addition to its email capabilities, Outlook can serve as your business and home calendar (allowing you to record and schedule reminders for upcoming appointments, meetings, and other events), handle your to-do list, and manage all your work and personal contacts.

Microsoft Office OneNote 2007

OneNote is a free-form *notebook* application. Much like a scrapbook, each notebook page can contain any combination of text, graphics, video or audio clips, and *hyperlinks* (Web page links), arranged in any manner you like.

To impart organization to your material, each notebook is divided into sections and pages. A variety of tools are provided that simplify the process of adding material to a notebook by extracting information and images from Outlook email messages, Web pages, and screen clippings.

Microsoft Office Publisher 2007

Microsoft Office Publisher 2007 is a *desktop publishing* program. You can use it to quickly create an impressive business card, flyer, brochure, or newsletter, for example. The end result of a Publisher project is often a document you'll turn over to a service bureau to have professionally printed. However, you can also do the printing yourself using any available laser or inkjet printer.

Unlike high-end desktop publishing applications, such as InDesign or QuarkXPress, Publisher is known more for its "fill in the placeholders" approach to publication creation than it is for designing documents from scratch. To this end, Publisher comes with a huge assortment of publication templates that simplify the creation process by setting the fonts, colors, and design elements for you.

THE OFFICE APPLICATIONS

Part I: Introducing Microsoft Office 2007

Chapter 1 What's New in Office 2007?...................3

Chapter 2 Office Basics..11

WHAT'S NEW IN OFFICE 2007?

In this chapter, you'll receive a brief overview of the new features and changes introduced in Office 2007—changes in each application, as well as a few *major* changes that affect all applications and all Office 2007 users.

As mentioned in the introduction, not all new features mentioned in this chapter will be covered in this book (although many of them will). Changes that affect the *typical* user will be found in the application chapters.

The New User Interface

Not since the introduction of toolbars has Office's interface received a more dramatic face lift—one that will so profoundly affect users. In the key Office applications (Word, Excel, PowerPoint, Outlook, and Access), Microsoft has eliminated the menus in favor of new interface elements collectively referred to as the *Ribbon* (**Figure 1.1**).

The new interface components consist of these elements for formatting documents, inserting items (such as tables and graphics), and performing common tasks:

◆ Ribbon

◆ Office Button

◆ Quick Access Toolbar

◆ Enhanced ToolTips

◆ Contextual tabs

◆ Live preview

◆ Mini toolbar

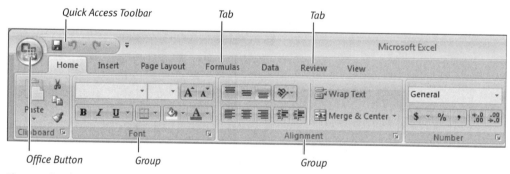

Figure 1.1 A portion of the Ribbon in Microsoft Office Excel 2007.

Office Button

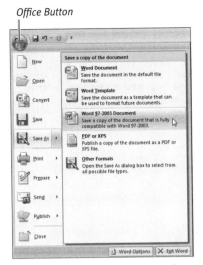

Figure 1.2 Click the Office Button, and choose a command.

ToolTip

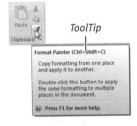

Figure 1.3 ToolTips often provide detailed information about commands, tools, and interface elements.

Click to open the Customize menu

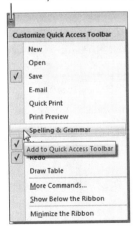

Figure 1.4 Add commands to the Quick Access Toolbar by choosing them from this drop-down menu.

Office Button

The Office Button hides the few menus that remain in many of the Office programs. Click the Office Button to reveal the file- and print-related functions (**Figure 1.2**).

Ribbon

The *Ribbon* (see Figure 1.1) is the interface for every Word, Excel, and PowerPoint document, found at the top of the document window. (In Outlook, the Ribbon is available only in document windows. The main window containing the folder and message lists is still driven by the familiar menus of previous versions.)

To use the Ribbon, click the tab containing the command you want to perform. Within each tab, related commands are organized into *groups*, such as a Font group that presents text-formatting commands and tools.

Enhanced ToolTips

Rest the cursor over a Ribbon item or other application element to see a ToolTip that explains the item's purpose, how it works, and its keyboard shortcut, if any (**Figure 1.3**).

Quick Access Toolbar

Click an icon in the Quick Access Toolbar (see Figure 1.1) to perform a common function, such as saving the current document.

✔ Tips

- You can customize the Quick Access Toolbar by adding command icons to it. Click the down arrow to the right of the toolbar, and choose the commands you'd like the toolbar to display (**Figure 1.4**). Choose More Commands if there's an unlisted command you'd like to add to the toolbar.

- You can hide the Ribbon by pressing Ctrl F1 or double-clicking a Ribbon tab.

Contextual tabs

When working with certain kinds of items in a document, such as an image or table, a highlighted tab appears above the other Ribbon tabs (**Figure 1.5**). Click it to replace the current Ribbon elements with ones relevant to the selected material. Note that some contextual tabs, such as Table Tools in Word (**Figure 1.6**), may be divided into *several* tabs.

When you're done using a contextual tab's tools, you can dismiss it by selecting a different object in the document or by clicking one of the standard Ribbon tabs.

Live preview

When choosing text or object formatting and styles from a gallery (**Figure 1.7**), some Ribbon elements provide a *live preview* of what the selected material in the document will look like if the format, style, or option is applied. Thus, you can quickly try out a variety of options without committing to them.

Mini toolbar

You're probably familiar with the context menus (called *shortcut menus* in Office 2007) that appear when you right-click an object or selected text. Office 2007 improves on them by introducing a pop-up command gallery known as the *Mini toolbar*.

To see the Mini toolbar, select text you'd like to format and then move the cursor upward. The ghostly Mini toolbar solidifies (**Figure 1.8**), enabling you to easily apply common character or paragraph formatting to the selected text. When you're finished, move the cursor down to dismiss the Mini toolbar.

✔ Tip

- When you right-click selected text, *both* the Mini toolbar and the shortcut menu appear.

Picture Tools contextual tab

Figure 1.5 When an image in the document is selected, the Picture Tools contextual tab appears. Click it to display image-editing tools in the Ribbon.

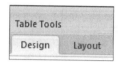

Figure 1.6 The Table Tools contextual tab has two tabs: Design and Layout.

Selected table   *Table Styles gallery*

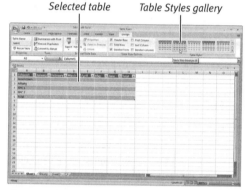

Figure 1.7 When a feature supports live preview, you can rest the cursor over any gallery option to see how it will affect the selected material in the document.

Mini toolbar

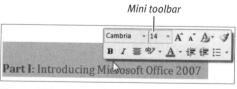

Figure 1.8 You can use the new Mini toolbar to format text rather than mousing all the way up to the Ribbon or typing hard-to-memorize keyboard shortcuts.

Office Button

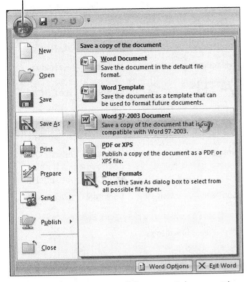

Figure 1.9 To save a copy of the current document in a format that other Office users can read, click the Office Button and select the 97-2003 Document format from the Save As submenu.

New File Formats

Office 2007 introduces a new file format for the three core applications: Word, Excel, and PowerPoint. Based on *Extensible Markup Language* (XML), it results in smaller files and improved security. To easily distinguish the new file types from the originals, each now has a four-character extension (**Table 1.1**): the original extension, plus an *x* or an *m*. When an *m* is appended to the extension, it signifies that the file contains macros.

As you'd expect, the Office 2007 applications can read files created in earlier versions of Office. However, as you might also expect, owners of earlier versions will *not* be able to open your XML-based Word, Excel, or PowerPoint files. There are two solutions to this file-sharing problem:

◆ Save a copy of the document in the application's old file format (**Figure 1.9**).

◆ Instruct the person to install a *converter* that enables Office 2000, XP, or 2003 to read Office 2007 files.

✔ Tips

■ To ensure that recipients of your Office 2007 documents can *read* (but not edit) the files, you can install an add-in that enables you to save Office documents as PDF (Adobe Reader) files. Go to http://office.microsoft.com. Click the Downloads tab, 2007 Office System, 2007 Microsoft Office System, and then Add-Ins. Download and install the Microsoft Save As PDF or XPS add-in.

■ Users of earlier versions of Office should visit http://office.microsoft.com, click the Downloads tab, and search for *Office 2007 compatibility*. In the search results, click the link for Microsoft Office Compatibility Pack for Word, Excel, and PowerPoint 2007 File Formats.

Table 1.1

Office 2007 File Extensions

APPLICATION	ORIGINAL EXTENSION	OFFICE 2007 EXTENSIONS
Word	.doc	.docx and .docm
Excel	.xls	.xlsx and .xlsm
PowerPoint	.ppt	.pptx and .pptm

NEW FILE FORMATS

New Features and Changes

In this section, you'll find application-specific lists of the new features and changes introduced in Office 2007. While these are not *all* the new features and changes, they *are* the ones that the Office development and marketing teams felt were the most significant.

New in Word

◆ New user interface

◆ Quick Styles (**Figure 1.10**) and document themes

◆ Charting and diagramming features

◆ Compare document versions

◆ Resolve revisions and comments

◆ Document Inspector (**Figure 1.11**)

◆ Separate macro file format (.docm)

New in Excel

◆ New user interface

◆ Larger worksheets; support for more memory and dual processors

◆ Longer formulas

◆ Themes and styles; more colors

◆ Structured references

◆ Calculated columns

◆ Improved sorting and filtering

◆ Named ranges centralized

◆ Conditional formatting

◆ Function AutoComplete

◆ OLAP formulas and cube functions

◆ Shared charting with other Office programs

◆ Page Layout view

◆ Sharing via the Web

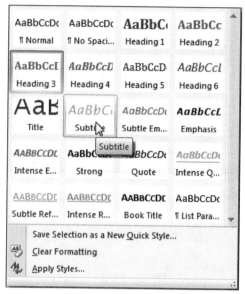

Figure 1.10 You can quickly apply an attractive, colorful format to Word text by choosing a Quick Style.

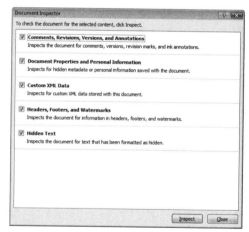

Figure 1.11 Before emailing or distributing a Word document, you can run the Document Inspector to ensure there's no hidden personal data in the file.

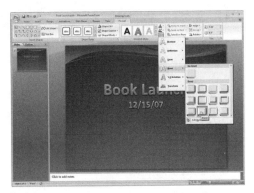

Figure 1.12 You can apply designer-quality effects to selected text, shapes, objects, and SmartArt.

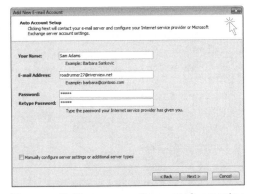

Figure 1.13 Setting up an email account often requires only that you enter your email address and password.

New in PowerPoint

◆ New user interface

◆ New themes, layouts, and Quick Styles

◆ Custom layouts

◆ SmartArt graphics

◆ Improved effects for text and objects (**Figure 1.12**)

◆ Additional character and paragraph formatting options

◆ Presenter View (for dual monitors)

New in Outlook

General changes

◆ New user interface (displayed only when creating or opening an item)

◆ Instant Search

◆ Color categories

◆ To-Do Bar

◆ RSS feed support

Email changes

◆ Auto Account Setup (**Figure 1.13**)

◆ Attachment previewing

◆ Outlook Email Postmark

◆ Phishing protection

Calendar changes

◆ Task integration in Calendar

◆ Calendar overlays

◆ Mailable Calendar snapshots

New in OneNote

- New file format
- Multiple notebooks, notebook templates, and shared notebooks
- Improved search capabilities
- Synchronization with Outlook tasks
- Email message export from Outlook to OneNote (**Figure 1.14**)
- Ability to send Web pages to OneNote
- File attachments on pages (optionally inserted as print images)
- Hyperlinks between notes
- Text recognition within pictures
- Tables
- Drawing tools
- Lasso selection
- Calculator
- Audio search

New in Publisher

- Reusable content stored in the Content Library (**Figure 1.15**)
- Preflight check for printing problems
- Improved Pack and Go Wizard packs all files for printer
- PANTONE support
- Personalized hyperlinks
- Improved list management

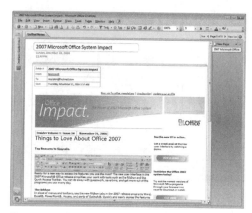

Figure 1.14 Using the Send to OneNote command, you can instantly create a new OneNote page from an Outlook email message.

Figure 1.15 To make important content (such as logos, design elements, and boilerplate text) available to all new publications, you can store it in the Content Library.

OFFICE BASICS

2

Although the applications in the various Office suites aren't heavily integrated with one another, they do share some basic similarities. For example, saving files, working with windows, printing, and other basic operations vary little from one Office application to the next. In this chapter, you'll become acquainted with these "Office essentials." Once you understand how these procedures work in general, you'll have a better ability to grasp the specifics when they're discussed in depth in later chapters.

Launching Office Applications

You launch Office applications (such as Word or Excel) in the same manner as any other Windows application.

To launch an Office application:

1. Click the Start button, All Programs, and the Microsoft Office folder (**Figure 2.1**).

   The Microsoft Office folder expands, showing all installed Office 2007 applications.

2. Click the Office program you want to run. The selected program launches.

✔ Tips

■ You can also launch an Office application by doing any of the following:

▲ If you recently ran the application, you can select its name from the list in the Start panel.

▲ If you've created them, you can click a Desktop or Quick Launch shortcut icon for the application or any of its documents.

▲ Open an Office document by clicking (or double-clicking) its file icon. The document opens in the appropriate Office application.

▲ Choose a recently opened Office document from Windows Vista's Start > Recent Items submenu (**Figure 2.2**).

■ Although the Start menus in Windows Vista and XP look different, they work similarly. In XP, click the Start button. Then move the cursor over All Programs and the Microsoft Office folder. Click the Office application you want to launch.

■ You can also open the Start menu by pressing the Windows logo key on your keyboard.

Start button

Figure 2.1 A common way to launch programs is to choose them from the Start menu (Windows Vista shown).

Word doc

Figure 2.2 You can open a document you've recently worked on by choosing it from Recent Items.

Templates list *Preview of selected template*

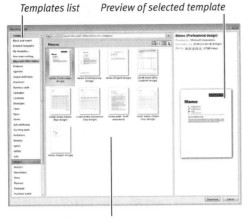

Templates in category

Figure 2.3 Pick a category from the Templates list, select a template, and click Create or Download (depending on whether the template is on your computer or is available from Microsoft Office Online).

Creating a New Document

By default, document-based Office programs (Word, Excel, and PowerPoint, for example) automatically create a new, blank document each time you launch the program. To create additional new documents when an Office program is running, perform the steps below.

To create a new document:

◆ *Do either of the following:*

▲ Click the Office Button and choose New. Select the type of document you want to create from the dialog box that appears (**Figure 2.3**). Click the Create (or Download) button.

▲ To skip the New Document, Worksheet, or Presentation dialog box and create a standard document, press Ctrl N.

✔ Tips

■ To create a standard document in Word, Excel, or PowerPoint, select Blank and recent from the Templates list, and then select Blank document, Blank worksheet, or Blank presentation, respectively. Select this same Templates category to base the document on a recently used template.

■ Office has two kinds of templates: those installed on your computer and ones you can download as needed from Microsoft. To use one of the former, select Installed Templates. For a downloadable template, select a category from the Microsoft Office Online section of the Templates list.

■ To base a new document on one of your own documents, select New from existing in the Templates list.

■ Publisher does not have the new interface sported by the major Office applications. To create a new document, choose File > New, click the New toolbar icon, or press Ctrl N.

Single- vs. Double-Clicking

Whether it requires a single or double click to open a folder, document, or program on your computer depends on a Folder Options control panel setting:

1. In Windows Vista or XP, click the Start button and choose Control Panel.

2. Open the Folder Options control panel.

3. In the Click items as follows section of the control panel, select the Single-click or Double-click radio button.

4. Click OK to save the new setting.

Opening Documents

In addition to creating new documents, you can open existing documents—to view, print, or revise them. You can open documents from within the appropriate Office application or from the Desktop (simultaneously launching the creating program, if it isn't already running).

To open an existing document from within an Office application:

1. *Do one of the following:*
   - ▲ **Word, Excel, PowerPoint.** Click the Office Button, and choose Open.
   - ▲ **Publisher.** Choose File > Open.
   - ▲ **Any program.** Press Ctrl O.

   The Open dialog box appears (**Figure 2.4**).

2. Navigate to the drive and folder that contains the document you want to open.

3. Select the document, and click Open.

   If Folder Options have been set on your PC to open items by single-clicking them (see the sidebar on page 13), the selected document may open without having to click Open.

To open an existing Office document from the Desktop:

1. Locate the Office document file on the Desktop or in the folder where it's stored.

2. *Do either of the following:*
   - ▲ Click (or double-click) the file icon.
   - ▲ Right-click the file icon, and choose Open from the pop-up menu that appears (**Figure 2.5**).

   The appropriate Office program launches (if it isn't already running), and the document opens.

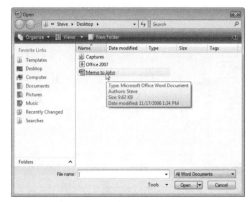

Figure 2.4 Select an Office document in the Open dialog box, and click Open (Windows Vista shown).

Figure 2.5 You can also open an Office document by right-clicking its file icon and choosing Open.

✔ Tip

■ In Word, Excel, and PowerPoint, you can also open documents by clicking the Office Button and choosing a file from the Recent Documents list. In Publisher, recently opened documents are listed as choices at the bottom of the File menu.

OPENING DOCUMENTS

Figure 2.6 Use the Save As dialog box to save a new document. You also use it to save an edited document with a new name, format, or disk location. (To aid in selecting a folder or drive, click the Browse button.)

Saving in Outlook 2007

In general use, you seldom need to issue a Save command in Outlook. Unless you've disabled the option to Save copies of messages in the Sent Items folder (in the E-mail Options dialog box), all messages you create and send are automatically saved. And incoming messages are stored in each account's Inbox (or another folder you've designated via a message rule).

The only times you have to manually save an email message are when you want to:

◆ Store a draft of a message you aren't ready to send

◆ Save a copy of a message to disk

If you close a message without sending it, a dialog box appears in which you're offered the option of saving it. Click Yes to save the message in the Drafts folder. You can also store a message in progress in the Drafts folder by choosing File > Save (Ctrl S). (Drafts can be opened, edited, and sent whenever it's convenient.)

To save a message in a folder or on another disk, choose File > Save As, choose a format, and click Save. You can use Save As to save a copy of *any* message—whether a draft, sent, or received item.

Saving Documents

Until you save a document to disk, it exists only in your PC's memory. If you close the document or quit the application without saving, the document is gone forever.

To save a new document:

1. *Do one of the following:*

   ▲ **Word, Excel, PowerPoint.** Click the Save icon on the Quick Access Toolbar, click the Office Button and choose Save, or click the Office Button and choose Save As > *file format.*

   ▲ **Publisher.** Choose File > Save or File > Save As, or click the Save toolbar icon.

   ▲ **Any program.** Press Ctrl S.

   The Save As dialog box opens (**Figure 2.6**).

2. Enter a name in the File name box, navigate to the desired disk and folder, choose a file format from the Save as type drop-down menu, and click Save.

To save an edited document:

◆ *Do either of the following:*

   ▲ To replace the current Word, Excel, or PowerPoint file with the edited version, click the Save icon in the Quick Access Toolbar, click the Office Button and choose Save, or press Ctrl S. In Publisher, choose File > Save, click the Save toolbar icon, or press Ctrl S.

   ▲ You can save a *copy* of the edited document using a new name, in a different file format, and/or to a new disk location. In Word, Excel, or PowerPoint, click the Office Button and choose Save As > *format.* In Publisher, choose File > Save As. The Save As dialog box appears (see Figure 2.6). Specify a filename, format, and location, and click Save.

Closing Documents

It isn't necessary to quit an Office application just to work with another document. When you're done working with a document, you can close it. Closing documents frees up memory for working on other documents.

To close a document:

1. Make the document active that you want to close by doing one of the following:
   - ▲ **Any Office application.** Click the document's taskbar icon (**Figure 2.7**) at the bottom of the screen.
   - ▲ **Word, Excel, PowerPoint.** Click the View tab, and select the document name from the Switch Windows icon in the Window group (**Figure 2.8**).
   - ▲ **Publisher.** Choose the document's name from the Window menu (**Figure 2.9**).

2. *Do one of the following:*
   - ▲ Click the Office Button, and choose Close.
   - ▲ Click the close box (X) in the upper-right corner of the application window (**Figure 2.10**). If this is the *only* open document, the application quits.

   The document closes. If the document has never been saved or contains unsaved edits, you're given an opportunity to save it.

✔ Tips

- ■ Quitting an application automatically closes all open documents. If any of them contain unsaved edits, you're given an opportunity to save each one.

- ■ When you have several Excel worksheets open, each has its own close box (found beneath the application's close box).

Figure 2.7 The taskbar displays an icon for each open document and application.

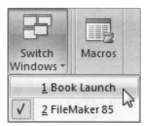

Figure 2.8 You can switch to any open document by selecting its name from the Switch Windows drop-down list.

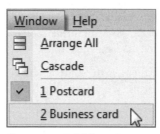

Figure 2.9 In Publisher, all open documents are listed in the Window menu.

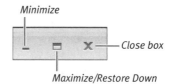

Figure 2.10 You can close a document in any program by clicking its close box.

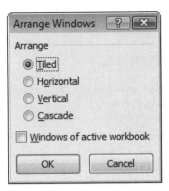

Figure 2.11 In Excel, you have great flexibility in arranging open workbook windows.

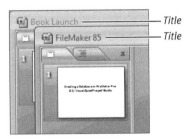

Figure 2.12 When you cascade documents, you can see the corner and title of each one.

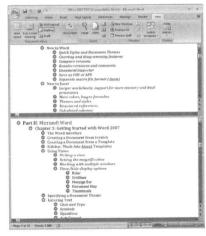

Figure 2.13 Split the window to simultaneously work in two sections of a document.

Working with Windows

If you occasionally have several documents open, you can arrange and manipulate their windows using Office commands. In Word, Excel, and PowerPoint, window management commands can be found in the Ribbon's Window group. In other Office applications, check the Window menu. (Note that the availability, location, and implementation of these commands varies from one Office program to the next.)

New Window. The New Window command creates a new instance of the current document. Use this command to view and work in two sections of a document at once.

Arrange All. This command simultaneously displays all open documents in an application. In Word, the documents are displayed one above the other. In PowerPoint, they're arranged side-by-side. In Excel, you can specify the arrangement of open documents in the dialog box that appears when you click Arrange All (**Figure 2.11**).

Cascade. Arranging documents in cascade fashion displays the upper-left corner of each one, enabling you to quickly switch documents by clicking an exposed corner (**Figure 2.12**). In PowerPoint, Cascade is an icon in the Ribbon's Window group. In Excel, select this option in the Arrange Windows dialog box (see Figure 2.11).

Split. Use this command to split the current document into halves (**Figure 2.13**), enabling you to work in two sections at the same time. In Excel, the split appears above the current cell. In Word, a split bar appears that you position by clicking. You can reposition a split by clicking and dragging the split bar. To remove a split in Excel, click the Split icon. In Word, click the Remove Split icon.

continues on next page

WORKING WITH WINDOWS

Save Workspace. This command in the Window group of Excel's Ribbon saves the current arrangement of worksheets so you can restore it later. (To restore a saved workspace, open it as you would a worksheet.)

Every Office application also supports standard Windows controls and techniques for manipulating windows.

To use standard Windows controls:

◆ *Do any of the following:*

▲ Click the Minimize button (see Figure 2.10) to minimize a window to the taskbar. (Click its taskbar icon to restore the window to its original onscreen position and size.)

▲ The Maximize/Restore Down button has two states (**Figure 2.14**). When it's shown as a box, you can click it to *maximize* the window—filling the screen. When a window is maximized, the button displays a pair of boxes. Click it to restore the window to its original size and position (before you maximized the window).

▲ To move a window to a new location, drag it by its title bar.

▲ To manually resize a window, move the cursor over any edge or corner. When the cursor changes to a double arrow, click and drag to change the window's size.

✔ Tips

■ In Publisher, the Arrange All and Cascade commands are found in the Window menu (**Figure 2.15**).

■ OneNote is generally run in a single window, so most window-related commands are unnecessary. However, you can create a second instance of the main window by choosing Window > New Window or pressing Ctrl M.

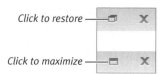

Figure 2.14 The Maximize/Restore Down button changes, depending on the window's current state.

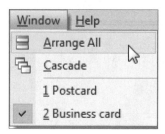

Figure 2.15 Publisher's window commands can be chosen from the Window menu.

WORKING WITH WINDOWS

Figure 2.16 The zoom control provides three ways for you to change the magnification.

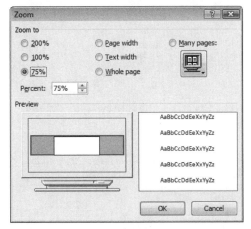

Figure 2.17 Use the Zoom dialog box to set a specific or page-related magnification. Outlook's Zoom dialog box (shown in Figure 2.18) has similar options.

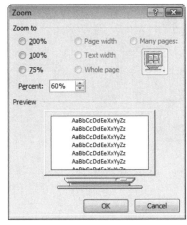

Figure 2.18 Outlook's Zoom dialog box.

✔ Tip

■ You must set magnification separately for each open document in an application.

Setting the Magnification

If you're having difficulty reading a Word document because the type is too tiny or you want a bird's-eye view of a PowerPoint presentation, you can change the document window's magnification (or *zoom*).

To set the magnification in Word, Excel, or PowerPoint:

◆ Use the zoom control (**Figure 2.16**) in the bottom-right corner of the document or application window in any of these ways:

▲ Drag the slider to a specific magnification percentage.

▲ Click the – or + button to decrease or increase magnification by 10 percent.

▲ Click the current zoom number to open the Zoom dialog box (**Figure 2.17**).

◆ In the Zoom group of the View tab, you can do either of the following:

▲ Click Zoom to open the Zoom dialog box (see Figure 2.17).

▲ Click 100% to zoom the document to its normal size.

To set the magnification in other Office applications:

◆ **Publisher.** Choose a zoom level from the View > Zoom submenu or from the Zoom drop-down menu on the toolbar, or click the Zoom Out or Zoom In toolbar icon.

◆ **OneNote.** Choose a magnification from the Zoom drop-down menu on the toolbar.

◆ **Outlook.** In the window for an existing message, choose Zoom from the Other Actions drop-down menu in the Actions group. In a message you're writing, click the Zoom icon in the Zoom group, set a magnification level in the Zoom dialog box (**Figure 2.18**), and click OK.

Using the Office Clipboard

In Windows, the *Clipboard* is an area in memory that stores the last item you copied or cut. When you paste an item, it's drawn from the Clipboard. If you copy or cut a new item, it takes the place of the current item stored in the Clipboard. Using the Clipboard, you can insert items into the current document, into a different document, or even into the documents of other applications.

While working in Office, you can continue to use the Windows Clipboard as you always have. In addition, you can use the *Office Clipboard*, a dedicated clipboard for sharing data among all open Office documents and programs. Unlike the Windows Clipboard, the Office Clipboard can store up to 24 items.

To open the Office Clipboard:

◆ **Word, Excel, PowerPoint.** Switch to the Home tab. In the Clipboard group, click the Clipboard dialog box launcher (**Figure 2.19**).

◆ **Outlook, Publisher.** Choose Edit > Office Clipboard.

The Office Clipboard appears (**Figure 2.20**).

To insert items from the Office Clipboard into a document:

1. Select the spot in the Office document where you want to paste the item(s).

2. *Do either of the following:*

   ▲ To paste a single item, click the item in the Office Clipboard scrolling list.

   ▲ To simultaneously paste all items stored in the Office Clipboard, click the Paste All button.

The item (or items) are added to the document.

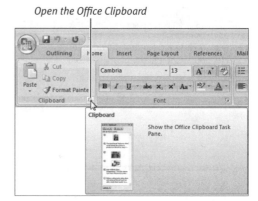

Open the Office Clipboard

Figure 2.19 Click here to open the Office Clipboard.

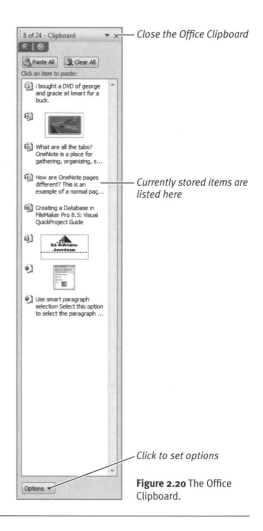

Close the Office Clipboard

Currently stored items are listed here

Click to set options

Figure 2.20 The Office Clipboard.

USING THE OFFICE CLIPBOARD

Figure 2.21 Select Delete from the drop-down menu.

To clear items from the Office Clipboard:

◆ *Do either of the following:*

▲ To remove a single item, move the cursor over the item, click the arrow that appears, and choose Delete from the drop-down menu (**Figure 2.21**).

▲ To remove all current items from the Office Clipboard, click the Clear All button (see Figure 2.20).

To close the Office Clipboard:

◆ *Do the following:*

▲ **Word, Excel, PowerPoint.** Click the Office Clipboard's close box (X) or click the Clipboard dialog box launcher.

▲ **Publisher.** Click the Office Clipboard's close box (X).

▲ **Outlook.** Click the Office Clipboard's close box (X) or choose Edit > Office Clipboard.

✔ Tips

■ You can't open the Office Clipboard in OneNote. However, items copied or cut in OneNote *are* added to the Office Clipboard, and they can be pasted into other Office documents.

■ If you add more than 24 items to the Office Clipboard, the oldest item is automatically deleted to make room for the new item.

■ Use the normal Paste command (choose Edit > Paste, click the Paste toolbar icon, or press Ctrl V) to paste an item from the Windows Clipboard rather than from the Office Clipboard.

■ The last item copied or cut also becomes the current item in the Windows Clipboard.

■ Items remain in the Office Clipboard until you exit from all Office programs.

Printing

The process of printing a document varies little from one Office application to the next. The biggest difference lies in the options you can set. For information on application-specific Print options, refer to the appropriate chapter on that application.

You can also request an onscreen *preview* of a print job prior to sending it to the printer. Using Print Preview is an excellent way to avoid paper waste.

To print a document in Word, Excel, or PowerPoint:

1. Open the document you want to print.

2. Click the Office Button, and choose Print > Print (**Figure 2.22**).

   The Print dialog box appears (**Figure 2.23**).

3. Select the destination printer from the Name drop-down list.

4. *Optional:* To set or review printer-specific settings (such as print quality), click the Properties button.

5. Set any other desired options in the Print dialog box.

6. Ensure that the printer is on and ready to print, and then click OK.

   The print job is sent to the selected printer.

To print a document in Outlook, OneNote, or Publisher:

1. Open the document you want to print.

   In Outlook, it's sufficient to *select* the item (such as an email message) in its list.

2. Choose File > Print.

   The Print dialog box appears (refer to Figure 2.23).

3. Perform Steps 3–6 from the previous task.

   The print job is sent to the selected printer.

Figure 2.22 For a standard print job, choose Print from the Print submenu.

Selected printer

Figure 2.23 The Print dialog box presents standard print options (such as number of copies and page range), as well as program-specific options.

PRINTING

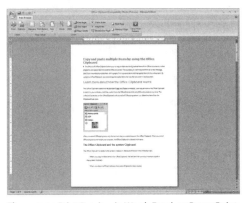

Figure 2.24 Print Preview in Word, Excel, or PowerPoint.

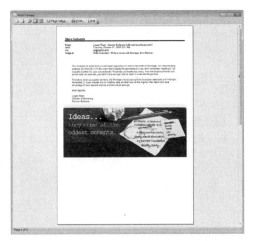

Figure 2.25 Print Preview in Outlook or Publisher.

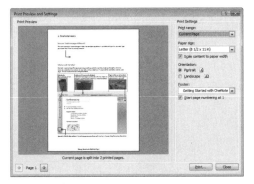

Figure 2.26 Print Preview in OneNote.

To request a print preview:

1. Open the document you want to print.

   In Outlook, it's sufficient to *select* the item (such as an email message) in its list.

2. *Do one of the following:*

   ▲ **Word, Excel, PowerPoint.** Click the Office Button, and choose Print > Print Preview (see Figure 2.22).

   ▲ **Outlook, OneNote, Publisher.** Choose File > Print Preview.

   A Print Preview window appears, displaying the document formatted for your default printer (**Figures 2.24–2.26**).

3. Review the document.

4. *Optional:* Alter the print settings using controls in the Print Preview window.

5. *Optional:* Click the Print button to print the document as shown.

6. Click the Close button or the close box (X).

   The Print Preview window closes and your original document reappears.

✔ Tips

- To bypass the Print dialog box and use the default print settings, do the following:

  ▲ **Word, Excel, PowerPoint.** Click the Office Button, and choose Print > Quick Print (see Figure 2.22).

  ▲ **Outlook, OneNote, Publisher.** Click the Print toolbar icon.

- Not only can you print to a printer that's directly connected to your PC, you may also be able to print to network printers—if you're on a network and have permission to use the networked printer.

- If the desired printer isn't listed in the Print dialog box, you can install it using the Printers and Faxes (XP) or Printers (Vista) control panel.

PRINTING

Getting Help

Office applications can draw help information from Help files stored on your computer, as well as from Office Online (using an active Internet connection). Simple help is provided by means of *ToolTips*, tiny pop-up windows.

To view a ToolTip:

◆ Rest the cursor over a command or control. A ToolTip (including a keyboard shortcut, if there is one) appears (**Figures 2.27–2.28**).

To get help with an Office application:

◆ *Do one of the following:*

▲ **Word, Excel, PowerPoint.** Click the Microsoft Office Help icon (**Figure 2.29**) or press F1 .

▲ **Outlook, Publisher.** Choose Help > Microsoft Office *program name* Help, click the Microsoft Office *program name* Help toolbar icon, type a text string in the Help search box (**Figure 2.30**), or press F1 .

▲ **OneNote.** Choose Help > Microsoft Office OneNote Help or press F1 .

A Help window appears (**Figure 2.31**).

Figure 2.27 ToolTips in Word, Excel, and PowerPoint often provide extensive information.

Figure 2.28 ToolTips in the other Office applications are more terse.

Figure 2.29 Summon help in Word, Excel, or PowerPoint by clicking this icon.

Figure 2.30 In Outlook or Publisher, you can request help on a specific topic by entering a search string in this box.

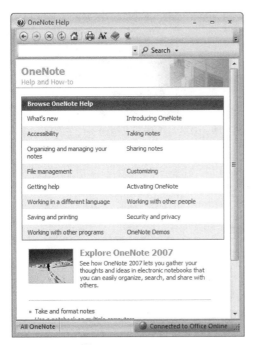

Figure 2.31 An Office Help window.

Figure 2.32 Click the text in the corner of the Help window to choose help text to use.

Figure 2.33 You can also print selected text from a Help topic.

To work in an Office Help window:

1. *Do any of the following:*

   ▲ To view the main Help page, click the Home (house) icon at the top of the Help window.

   ▲ To display/hide Help's content list, click the Table of Contents (book) icon.

   ▲ To read information on a topic, click its blue *link text*. (When you move the cursor over link text, an underline appears beneath the text.)

   ▲ To search Help for a particular topic, type search text in the box and click the Search icon.

   ▲ To go backward or forward among pages you've viewed, click the Back or Forward icon.

   ▲ To print the current help topic, click the Print (printer) icon.

   ▲ To switch between offline and online help information, click the drop-down menu in the lower-right corner of the Help window (**Figure 2.32**) and choose an option.

2. When you're done using Help, click the Help window's close box (X).

✔ Tips

■ You can copy help text and paste it into other documents, such as those of Word or OneNote. Select the text (including images, if you like) and press Ctrl C. The selected material is copied to the system Clipboard. If the Office Clipboard is active, it's also stored there.

■ To print a partial Help topic, select the desired text and click the Print icon. In the Print dialog box, set Page Range to Selection (**Figure 2.33**), and click OK.

Quitting an Office Program

As when working with other Windows programs, when you're done using an Office application, you *exit* from it.

To quit an Office application:

1. *Do one of the following:*

   ▲ **Word, Excel, PowerPoint.** Click the Office Button, and then click Exit *program name* (**Figure 2.34**).

   ▲ **Outlook, Publisher, OneNote.** Choose File > Exit.

   ▲ **Any Office program.** Press ⎡Alt⎤⎡F4⎤.

2. If an open document contains unsaved changes, a dialog box appears (**Figure 2.35**). Otherwise, the program quits immediately.

 — *Exit*

Figure 2.34 Click the Exit button to quit from Word, Excel, or PowerPoint.

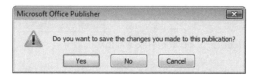

Figure 2.35 When you exit from a program, you get an opportunity to save any edited documents.

Setting Application Preferences

Although the default behaviors of most commands and procedures are designed to meet the needs of most users, you can customize the way any Office application operates.

◆ **Word, Excel, PowerPoint.** Click the Office Button, followed by the *program* Options button.

◆ **Outlook, Publisher, OneNote.** Choose Tools > Options.

Part II: Microsoft Word

Chapter 3   Getting Started with Word 2007.......29

Chapter 4   Formatting Documents.........................49

Chapter 5   Creating Outlines....................................85

Chapter 6   Tables, Charts, and Art.........................91

Chapter 7   Sharing Word Documents 113

GETTING STARTED WITH WORD 2007

Microsoft Office Word is a word-processing application—perhaps the most widely used word-processing application in existence. You can use Word to write letters, memos, reports, and essays. Because it is so pervasive and allows you to save in a variety of file formats, there's an excellent chance you can create a version of a given Word document that can be opened by almost any recipient.

In this introductory chapter, you'll learn about the Word interface, working in different views, and entering and editing text. For information on launching and quitting Word, as well as performing basic document-related tasks, such as creating, opening, saving, and closing documents, see Chapter 2.

✔ Tip

- Every Word document—whether new or opened from disk—opens in its own window. Clicking a document's close box (X) closes only that document. To close *all* documents and quit Word, you must individually close every open document or click the Office Button and click Exit Word.

The Word Interface

Figure 3.1 (bottom) shows the interface elements you'll use when creating Word documents. Many, such as the Ribbon, Office Button, and Quick Access Toolbar, can also be found in Excel, PowerPoint, and Outlook.

Office Button. Click this button to perform file-related activities (**Figure 3.2**), such as creating, opening, saving, and printing. Click Word Options to set preferences. To open a document you've recently worked on, click its name in the Recent Documents list. The Exit command can also be found here.

Quick Access Toolbar. Icons for common commands (such as Save, Undo, and Redo) are found on this customizable toolbar.

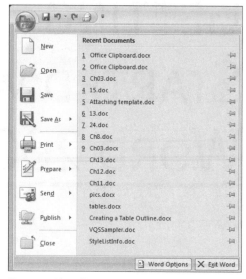

Figure 3.2 The Office Button window.

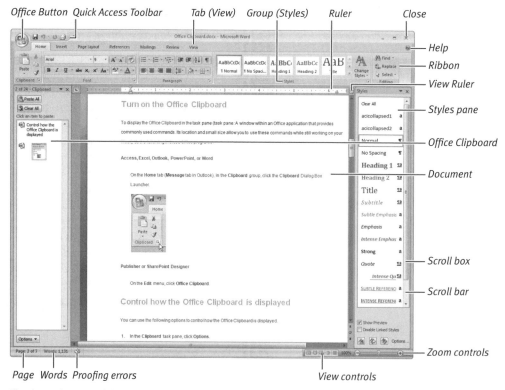

Figure 3.1 Elements of the Word 2007 interface.

Table of Contents   *Links*

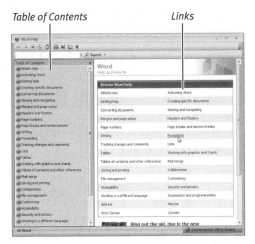

Figure 3.3 Click text links in Word Help to view help topics. Click the close box (X) or quit Word to dismiss Word Help.

Help. Click this icon or press F1 to open the Word Help window (**Figure 3.3**).

Ribbon. The Ribbon is Office 2007's replacement for program menus. Similar commands and procedures are listed together on a *tab*, such as Insert or View. Within each tab, procedures are further divided into *groups*, based on similarity of function. To perform a command, you switch to the appropriate tab by clicking its name, and then click the command's icon or control.

Rulers. Click the View Ruler icon to hide or show the horizontal and vertical rulers. Use the controls on the horizontal ruler to set or change tab stops and indents for the currently selected paragraph(s). The vertical ruler is visible only on the document page that contains the text insertion mark.

Styles pane. To make it easier to apply a Word character or paragraph *style* to selected text, you can display the Styles pane by clicking the tiny icon at the bottom of the Styles group on the Home tab. Click a style name to apply it.

Office Clipboard. The Office Clipboard is shared between major Office applications and allows you to copy and paste multiple items within a document, between documents, and even between applications. To show the Office Clipboard pane, click the icon at the bottom of the Clipboard group on the Home tab. Click the close box (X) to dismiss it.

Document. Most of Word's window is reserved for the open word-processing document. Hide the Office Clipboard and other panes to increase the display area for the document.

Scroll bar and scroll box. You can click in the scroll bar or drag the scroll box to navigate through the document's pages.

Page indicator. This indicator displays the current page number, as well as the total number of pages in the document. Click the indicator to open the Find and Replace dialog box to the Go To tab (**Figure 3.4**).

Words indicator. This indicator shows the word count for the document. If text is selected, it shows the number of words in the selection. Click the indicator to open the Word Count dialog box (**Figure 3.5**).

Proofing indicator. This indicator shows whether there are proofing errors that need to be addressed, such as misspellings, repeated words, or extra spaces between words. Click the indicator to move from one suspected error to the next.

View controls. Click an icon to switch views (**Figure 3.6**). You can also switch views by clicking the View tab and then clicking an icon in the Document Views group.

Zoom controls. Change the current magnification by dragging the slider or by clicking + (increase), – (decrease), or the zoom percentage icon.

Close. Click the close box (X) to close an open document or to quit Word. (When the current document is the only one that's open, clicking the close box quits Word.) You can also close the active document by choosing Close in the Office Button window (see Figure 3.2).

Figure 3.4 On the Go To tab, you can go to a particular page by entering a page number and clicking Go To.

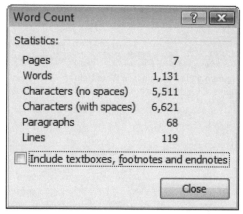

Figure 3.5 For more detailed word count information, open the Word Count dialog box.

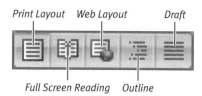

Figure 3.6 You can quickly change views by clicking an icon in the status bar.

Figure 3.7 The Document Views group contains the same five view icons as the ones in the status bar.

Misc. controls   *Page control*   *View Options*

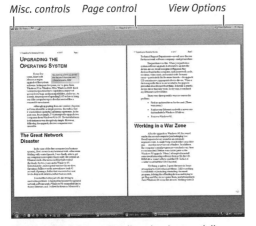

Figure 3.8 Full Screen Reading view is especially useful for proofing documents, as well as reading ones you download or receive as email attachments.

Figure 3.9 View Options menu.

Working in Different Views

Depending on what you currently want to do with a document, you can work in any of Word's *views*: Print Layout, Full Screen Reading, Web Layout, Outline, and Draft. Each view serves a particular purpose, as described below. To switch views, you can click an icon in the status bar (see Figures 3.1 and 3.6) or click an icon in the Document Views group of the View tab (**Figure 3.7**).

Print Layout view

Standard documents, such as letters, memos, and reports, are often written and edited in Print Layout view. One advantage of working in this view is its adherence to *WYSIWYG* (what you see is what you get). The margins, headers, and footers correspond to the printed output. Pages are shown as equivalent pieces of paper with physical breaks between pages.

Full Screen Reading view

If want to read or review a document, Full Screen Reading view (**Figure 3.8**) can simplify the task.

To control Full Screen Reading view:

1. *Do any of the following:*
   - ▲ To show single pages or pairs of facing pages, choose Show One Page or Show Two Pages from the View Options menu (**Figure 13.9**).
   - ▲ To preview the pages as they'll print, choose Show Printed Page from the View Options menu.
   - ▲ To change the text magnification, choose Increase Text Size or Decrease Text Size from the View Options menu.
   - ▲ To enable or disable editing, choose Allow Typing from the View Options menu. (The command is a toggle.)

continues on next page

▲ To change pages, click an arrow button at the bottom of any page; click the left or right arrow icon in the Page controls; or press an arrow key, Page Down, or Page Up.

▲ To go directly to a page, click the Page control and choose a command from its menu, such as Go to First Page, Go to Last Page, or Go To (**Figure 3.10**).

▲ If you're reviewing a document, you can choose Track Changes commands from the bottom of the View Options menu (see Figure 3.9) and click icons in the upper-left corner of the screen (**Figure 3.11**).

2. When you're done reading, you can exit from Full Screen Reading view by clicking the close box (X) in the upper-right corner of the screen.

Web Layout view

Use Web Layout view to create, view, and edit pages as they'll appear online when opened in a browser. By choosing the Office Button's Save As > Other Formats command, you can save pages in a Web format (**Figure 3.12**).

Outline view

Use Outline view to create, view, and edit outlines. (The initial table of contents for this book was created in Outline view.) For information about working in Outline view, see Chapter 5.

Draft view

Work in Draft view when speed is of primary importance. In Print Layout view, physical pages and breaks are drawn. Draft view displays a document as a continuous text scroll; page breaks are denoted by dashed lines. Because repagination occurs almost instantly as you compose, this is an ideal view if you have an older, slower computer.

Figure 3.10 Navigation commands can be chosen from the Page control.

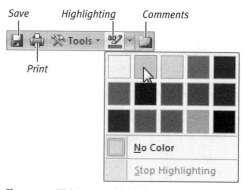

Figure 3.11 Click icons to highlight selected text, open the Comments pane, save changes, or print.

Figure 3.12 You can choose a Web format from the Save as type drop-down list in the Save As dialog box.

Figure 3.14 You can make any open document active by choosing it from the Switch Windows icon's menu.

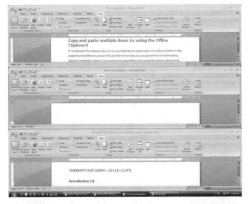

Figure 3.15 Arrange All enables you to see and work with multiple open documents.

Managing Windows

When you create a new Word document or open an existing document, each one opens in a separate window. Because it's common to work with several documents at a time, Word provides window-management commands in the Window group of the View tab (**Figure 3.13, bottom**).

To manage open document windows:

◆ *Do any of the following:*

▲ To create another instance of the current document, click the New Window icon. Edits made in any instance window affect the original document.

Each new instance has the same name as the original, followed by a colon and a number. For instance, a new instance of memo.docx would be named memo.docx:2.

▲ To bring a document to the front (making it the *active* document), choose its name from the Switch Windows menu (**Figure 3.14**).

Because every open Word document is represented by a taskbar button, you can also switch documents by clicking the taskbar button.

▲ To view all open documents at the same time, click Arrange All. The documents are displayed in a stack (**Figure 3.15**) or side by side. To work in one of the windows, click in the document to make it active.

continues on next page

Figure 3.13 The Window group (View tab).

MANAGING WINDOWS

▲ To work with a pair of open documents, click View Side by Side. If more than two documents are open, the Compare Side by Side dialog box appears (**Figure 3.16**). Select the second document and click OK.

▲ When working in View Side by Side mode, you can make the two documents scroll together by clicking the Synchronous Scrolling icon. This feature is useful for comparing two versions of the same document.

▲ To close the active Word document, click its close box (X), press ⸢Alt⸣⸢F4⸣ or ⸢Ctrl⸣⸢W⸣, or click the Office Button and choose Close.

▲ To close a Word document (regardless of whether it's the active document), you can right-click its taskbar button and choose Close from the pop-up menu that appears (**Figure 3.17**).

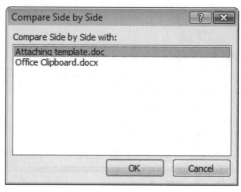

Figure 3.16 After clicking the View Side by Side icon in the first document window, you'll be asked to select the comparison document (if more than two documents are open).

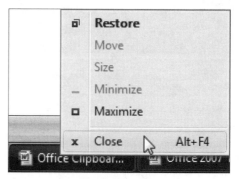

Figure 3.17 You can close any document or application in the taskbar by right-clicking its button and choosing Close from the pop-up menu.

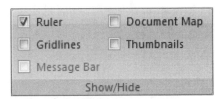

Figure 3.18 Set display options by clicking check boxes in the Show/Hide group of the View tab.

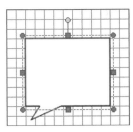

Figure 3.19 Gridlines can make it simpler to place objects.

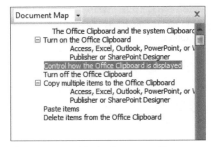

Figure 3.20 Enable the Document Map to display text links to important sections of the document.

Figure 3.21 When thumbnails are enabled, each document page is shown as a tiny graphic representation of the page.

Setting Show/Hide Options

In addition to using the zoom controls to change the magnification (see "Setting the Magnification" in Chapter 2), you can show or hide the following elements in the document window by clicking check boxes in the Show/Hide group (**Figure 3.18**):

◆ **Ruler.** Use the ruler to position objects, set paragraph indents, and set tab stops.

◆ **Gridlines.** When enabled, each page is overlaid with a visible grid (**Figure 3.19**). Placed objects automatically snap to the nearest grid intersection.

◆ **Document Map.** Pages in the document are presented as an outline (**Figure 3.20**). Click text in the Document Map to go to that spot in the document.

◆ **Thumbnails.** Each page is represented by a tiny icon (**Figure 3.21**). Click an icon to go to that page.

To enable/disable rulers:

◆ *Do either of the following:*
   ▲ On the View tab in the Show/Hide group, click the Ruler check box.
   ▲ Click the View Ruler icon at the top of the vertical scroll bar (see Figure 3.1).

To enable/disable gridlines:

◆ On the View tab in the Show/Hide group, click the Gridlines check box.

To display thumbnails or the Document Map:

◆ On the View tab in the Show/Hide group, click the Thumbnails or Document Map check box. (Only one can be active at a time.) To switch between the two, choose an option from the drop-down menu above the pane (see Figures 3.20 and 3.21).

SETTING SHOW/HIDE OPTIONS

Entering Text

If you've previously used a word-processing program, you're already familiar with the basics of entering text. On the other hand, if you're *new* to word processing, here's what you need to know.

To enter text:

1. Create a new document or open an existing document.

2. *Do one of the following:*

   ▲ **New document.** The text insertion mark is automatically positioned at the top of the first document page (**Figure 3.22**).

   ▲ **Existing document.** The text insertion mark is set at the beginning of the document. Scroll to the page where you want to begin entering new text, such as the end of the last page. Click to set the text insertion mark.

3. Type your text.

   Entered text appears at the text insertion mark. In a new document, the text is formatted with the default font and the paragraphs are left-aligned.

4. As you type, text automatically wraps as needed to fit within the current paragraph's margins. When you want to begin a new paragraph, press Enter.

✔ Tips

■ For information on changing character or paragraph formatting (such as applying a different font or centering title text), see Chapter 4.

■ You can add text copied from other documents to a Word document by clicking the Paste icon in the Clipboard group of the Home tab (**Figure 3.23**) or by pressing Ctrl V.

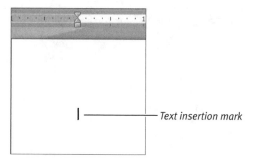

Text insertion mark

Figure 3.22 In a new (shown here) or opened document, the text insertion mark is set at the beginning of the document.

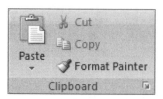

Figure 3.23 To paste copied text from the Clipboard, click the Paste icon.

Using Click-and-Type

If you're more comfortable working with a typewriter than with a word-processing program, you can use Word's *click-and-type* to approximate a typewriter feature.

Instead of typing from the text insertion mark at the top of a new document or the bottom of an opened document, you can double-click any blank spot below either of these points. Word sets the text insertion mark at the double-clicked spot and automatically adds sufficient paragraph returns to fill in the gap above.

ENTERING TEXT

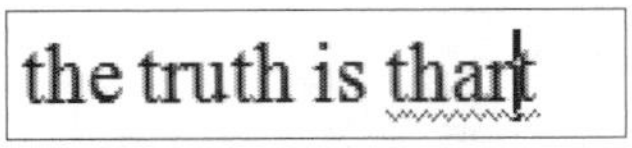

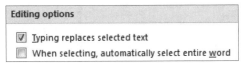

Figure 3.24 Set the text insertion mark to the right or left of the text you want to correct.

Selected text

• Find an updated driver for the card. (There were none.)

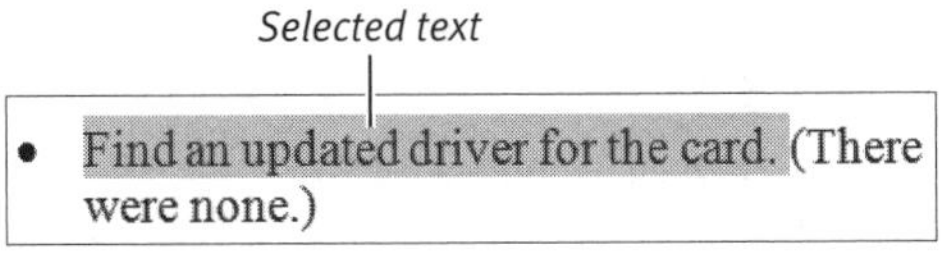

Figure 3.25 Selected text is highlighted like this.

Editing options

☑ Typing replaces selected text
☐ When selecting, automatically select entire word

Figure 3.26 To simplify text selection, remove the check mark from the second option.

Selecting Partial Words

If you find that you're frequently (and automatically) selecting entire words when trying to select partial words, the reason is that a Word Options setting is getting in the way.

To change this setting, click the Office Button, and then click the Word Options button. In the Word Options dialog box, select the Advanced category and remove the check mark from When selecting, automatically select entire word (**Figure 3.26**). Click OK to save the new setting.

Basic Text Editing

You can use any of the following techniques to correct errors in a document and make other desired changes. The techniques vary, depending on whether you are changing unselected or selected text.

To delete unselected text:

1. Position the text insertion mark immediately to the right or left of the text you want to correct or remove (**Figure 3.24**).

2. *Do one of the following:*
   ▲ To delete the *previous* character (the one to the left), press Backspace.
   ▲ To delete the *next* character (the one to the right), press Del or Delete.
   To delete additional characters, continue pressing Backspace, Del, or Delete.

3. If necessary, replace the deleted text by typing new characters.

To delete or replace selected text:

1. To select the text (**Figure 3.25**) to be deleted or replaced, *do one of the following:*
   ▲ Set the text insertion mark at one end of the text to be selected, and then drag to or Shift-click the opposite end.
   ▲ Set the text insertion mark at one end of the text to be selected, and then— while holding down Shift—press arrow keys to move to the end of the text.
   ▲ Double-click to select a word or triple-click to select a paragraph.

2. *Do one of the following:*
   ▲ To delete the selected text, press Backspace, Del, or Delete.
   ▲ To replace the selected text, type the replacement text. When you begin typing, the original text is deleted.

To insert new text:

1. Position the text insertion mark where you want to add the new text.

You can insert new text anywhere in a document.

2. *Do either of the following:*

▲ Type the new text.

▲ Paste the new text by clicking the Paste icon in the Clipboard group of the Home tab or by pressing Ctrl V.

✔ Tips

■ You can also delete text by cutting it. Unlike a normal deletion, cut text is stored in the Clipboard (and the Office Clipboard), where it's available for pasting. To cut selected text, click the Cut icon in the Clipboard group of the Home tab or press Ctrl X.

■ You can use *drag-and-drop* to move selected text from one location to another—either within the document or between two Word documents. This is equivalent to performing a cut-and-paste.

■ If you want a drag-and-drop to leave the original text intact (working as a copy-and-paste rather than as a cut-and-paste), drag the selected text using the *right* mouse button. In the pop-up menu that appears at the destination (**Figure 3.27**), choose Copy Here.

■ To undo the most recent edit, immediately click the Undo icon in the Quick Access Toolbar or press Ctrl Z. (Note that you can undo multiple actions by clicking the Undo icon's down arrow.)

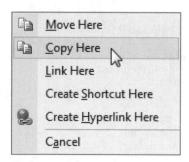

Figure 3.27 When right-dragging text, you can elect to perform a copy instead of a move.

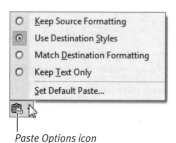

Paste Options icon

Figure 3.28 Choose a formatting method from the Paste Options drop-down menu.

Controlling Paste Formatting

When you paste text into a Word document, its formatting is determined by preference settings in the Advanced section of the Word Options dialog box. Depending on the text's source and whether the styles conflict, either the original formatting is retained or the text is reformatted to match the surrounding text at the destination. However, you can override the default Paste formatting.

When pasting, the Paste Options icon appears at the end of or beneath the pasted text (**Figure 3.28**). Click the icon to choose a formatting option.

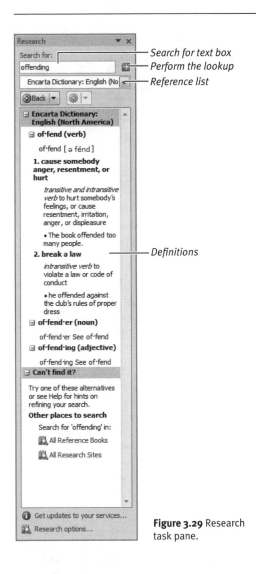

Search for text box
Perform the lookup
Reference list

Definitions

Figure 3.29 Research task pane.

Figure 3.30 To use a synonym in the current document, click its down arrow.

Using the Proofing Tools

Word includes a dictionary, thesaurus, and spelling/grammar checker you can use to help with writing and editing. Spelling and grammar can be checked *on the fly* (as you type) or run as a traditional full-document or selected-text check.

To look up a word's definition:

◆ *Do either of the following:*

▲ If the word is in the current document, select it, right-click it, and choose Look Up from the pop-up menu that appears.

▲ Switch to the Review tab, and click the Research icon in the Proofing group. In the Research task pane (**Figure 3.29**), type or paste the word into the Search for box, select Encarta Dictionary from the drop-down list, and click the green arrow button.

The word's definition is displayed in the task pane.

To find a synonym for a word:

◆ *Do either of the following:*

▲ If the word is in the current document, select it, right-click it, and open the Synonyms submenu in the pop-up menu that appears. To replace the selected word, choose a synonym from the list.

▲ Switch to the Review tab, and click the Research icon in the Proofing group. In the Research task pane (see Figure 3.29), type or paste the word into the Search for box, select Thesaurus from the drop-down list, and click the green arrow button. To use a listed synonym in your document, click the arrow beside it and choose an option from the drop-down menu (**Figure 3.30**).

To check spelling/grammar as you type:

1. When the "check as you type" preferences are enabled (see the Tip at the end of this section), each suspected spelling or grammatical error is marked with a wavy, colored underline.

2. To correct or dismiss a marked spelling error, right-click the underlined text. Choose one of these options from the pop-up menu that appears (**Figure 3.31**):

   ▲ To accept a suggested correction (if any are listed), choose a replacement spelling from the words listed at the top of the pop-up menu.

   ▲ Choose Ignore to skip this instance of the word, leaving it unchanged.

   ▲ Choose Ignore All to ignore all instances of the flagged spelling in the document.

   ▲ If the spelling is correct, choose Add to Dictionary to ensure that the word is never flagged again—in this or any other document.

3. To correct or dismiss a marked grammar error, right-click the underlined text. Choose one of these options from the pop-up menu that appears (**Figure 3.32**):

   ▲ Choose the suggested fix to allow Word to make the correction.

   ▲ Choose Ignore if you believe the grammar is correct or if you want to manually make the correction.

Potential spelling error   *Mini toolbar*

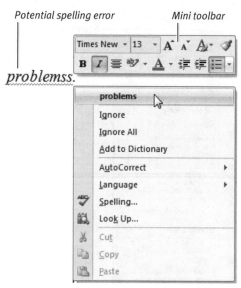

Figure 3.31 Right-click a marked spelling error and choose a handling option from the pop-up menu.

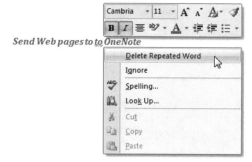

Figure 3.32 Marked grammar errors can be handled by accepting a proposed correction or by choosing Ignore.

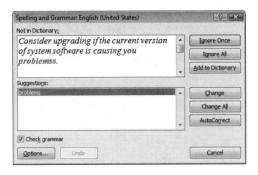

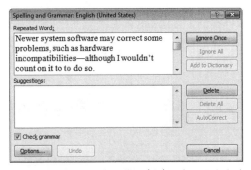

Figure 3.33 Suspected spelling (top) and grammatical (bottom) errors are marked in red and shown in context in the top of the dialog box.

To check spelling/grammar for selected text or an entire document:

1. *Optional:* To restrict the check to a specific portion of the document, select the text to be checked.

2. *Do one of the following:*
   - ▲ On the Review tab, click the Spelling & Grammar icon in the Proofing group.
   - ▲ Press F7.

   If suspected errors are identified, the Spelling and Grammar dialog box appears (**Figure 3.33**).

3. **Spelling.** To handle a suspected spelling error, *do one of the following:*
   - ▲ To accept a suggested correction (if any are listed), select it in the list and click Change.
   - ▲ To accept a suggested correction and apply it throughout the document, select it in the list and click Change All.
   - ▲ Edit the misspelled word in the Not in Dictionary box and click Change or Change All.
   - ▲ To accept the flagged word as spelled correctly, click Ignore Once to ignore this instance of the word or click Ignore All to ignore all instances of this word found in the document.
   - ▲ To accept the flagged word as spelled correctly and to add it to the Office user dictionary (so it isn't flagged in later checks), click Add to Dictionary.
   - ▲ If the flagged word is one that you routinely misspell this way, select the correct spelling in the Suggestions list and click AutoCorrect. (The misspelling is added to the AutoCorrect list and will automatically be corrected as you type in later writing sessions.)

continues on next page

USING THE PROOFING TOOLS

4. Grammar. To handle a suspected grammatical error, *do one of the following*:

▲ Click the button labeled with the correction, such as Delete or Change, if one is presented.

▲ If you believe the grammar is correct or you intend to rewrite the text, click Ignore Once to ignore the flagged error.

▲ Rewrite the text in the top half of the dialog box and click Change.

✔ Tips

■ To set spelling/grammar checking preferences, click the Office Button and then click Word Options. In the Word Options dialog box, select the Proofing category (**Figure 3.34**), make any desired changes, and click OK.

■ You can go directly to the Proofing section of the Word Options dialog box by clicking the Options button in the Spelling and Grammar dialog box.

■ If you choose Ignore or Ignore All for a suspected spelling or grammar error, the error will not reappear in subsequent spelling/grammar checks. To reconsider such errors, click the Recheck Document button in the Proofing section of the Word Options dialog box (see Figure 3.34).

■ The AutoCorrect feature automatically corrects common typos and misspellings as you type. To view or edit the current AutoCorrect word list (**Figure 3.35**), click the AutoCorrect Options button in the Proofing section of the Word Options dialog box (see Figure 3.34).

Figure 3.34 Set preferences for the proofing tools in the Proofing section of the Word Options dialog box.

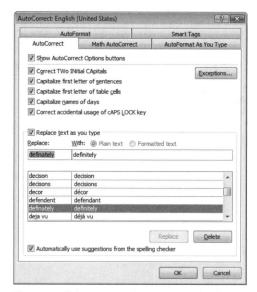

Figure 3.35 If there are words you commonly misspell, you can add them to the AutoCorrect list.

Find tab　　*Search string*

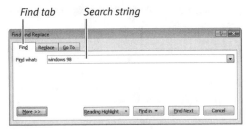

Figure 3.36 To perform a simple search, enter a search string in the Find what box and click Find Next.

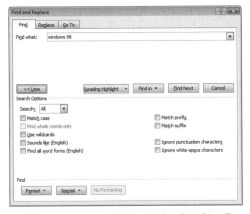

Figure 3.37 You can expand the Find and Replace dialog box to set additional Find options.

Finding and Replacing Text

You use the Find and Replace commands to find a designated text string and optionally replace it with another. In addition to performing standard text searches, you can search for and replace special items, such as paragraph characters (¶) and graphics, or text formatted in a particular manner.

To perform a Find:

1. *Do one of the following:*
   - ▲ On the Home tab, click the Find icon in the Editing group, or click the Find icon and choose Find from the drop-down menu.
   - ▲ Press Ctrl F.

   The Find and Replace dialog box appears, open to the Find tab (**Figure 3.36**).

2. Enter a search string in the Find what box.

3. *Optional:* To set additional options and criteria, click the More >> button. The dialog box expands (**Figure 3.37**):
   - ▲ To perform a more precise search, set options in the Search Options area, such as ensuring that text exactly matches the letter case of the search string (Match case) or specifying the search direction (Search drop-down menu).
   - ▲ To search for a special character (such as a tab), insert it into the Find what box by choosing the character from the Special button's menu.
   - ▲ To find only text with certain formatting (such as a particular font), choose an option from the Format button's menu.

   continues on next page

4. To begin the search, *do one of the following*:

▲ Click Find Next.

▲ Choose an option from the Find in button's menu to restrict the search to a particular document component.

Word highlights the first match, if one is found.

5. *Do either of the following*:

▲ To search for the next match, click Find Next. Repeat as necessary.

▲ When you're finished, click Cancel or click the close box (X).

To perform a Find/Replace:

1. On the Home tab, click the Replace icon in the Editing group (Ctrl H).

The Find and Replace dialog box appears, open to the Replace tab (**Figure 3.38**).

2. Enter a search string in the Find what box and a replacement string in the Replace with box.

3. *Optional:* To set additional options and criteria, click the More >> button. The dialog box expands (**Figure 3.39**).

4. *Do either of the following*:

▲ To simultaneously replace every matching instance, click Replace All.

▲ To selectively replace text after examining each possible match, click Find Next. Word highlights the first match, if one is found. Click Replace if you want to make the replacement, or click Find Next to skip this instance and go to the next match. Continue as necessary.

5. When you're finished, click Cancel or click the close box (X).

Show additional options

Figure 3.38 Enter Find what and Replace with strings.

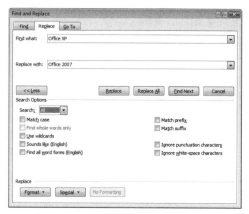

Figure 3.39 Additional Replace options appear when you expand the dialog box.

FINDING AND REPLACING TEXT

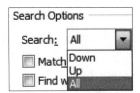

Figure 3.40 Specify a search direction by choosing an option from the Search menu.

✔ Tips

■ Regardless of the command you use to open the Find and Replace dialog box, you can switch between Finds and Replaces by clicking the appropriate tab.

■ To restrict a Find or Replace to only *part* of a document, select the text before you issue the Find or Replace command.

■ The initial direction and scope of a search are determined by the text insertion mark and your choice in the Search drop-down menu (**Figure 3.40**) in the bottom half of the Find and Replace dialog box. A search starts from the text insertion mark and proceeds in the direction specified in the Search drop-down menu, as follows:

▲ If Down or Up is chosen from the Search menu, the search proceeds to the bottom or top of the document or selection. When the bottom or top is reached, a dialog box asks if you'd like to search the rest of the document.

▲ If All is chosen from the Search menu, the search starts from the text insertion mark, continues downward until the end is reached, and then wraps around to the beginning in order to complete the search.

■ When you replace text without checking Match case (see Figure 3.39), capitalization of the replacement text (Replace with) will match that of the replaced text (Find what).

■ It's sometimes important to check Find whole words only (see Figure 3.39) when performing a Replace. For example, when attempting to replace every instance of John with Mike, checking Find whole words only will prevent Johnson from being changed to Mikeson.

FINDING AND REPLACING TEXT

Entering Symbols and Special Characters

Some characters—especially symbols, such as copyright (©)—can be extremely difficult to type. Using the Symbol drop-down gallery or the Symbol dialog box, you can insert any symbol or other character from any font that's installed on your computer.

To insert a symbol or other character:

1. Set the text insertion mark at the spot in your text where you want to insert the symbol or other character.

2. In the Symbol group on the Insert tab, click the Symbol icon.

3. *Do either of the following:*

   ▲ Choose the character from the Symbol drop-down gallery (**Figure 3.41**). The character is inserted into the text.

   ▲ Choose More Symbols to open the Symbol dialog box (**Figure 3.42**). To insert a character, double-click it or select it and click Insert. Click the Close button or the close box (X) to dismiss the dialog box.

✔ Tips

- When inserting a character, Word uses the font at the text insertion mark. To use a different font (Webdings, for example, contains unusual characters not found in other fonts), choose it from the Font drop-down menu in the Symbol dialog box.

- To insert a special character throughout a document, insert it once, select the character, copy it (Ctrl C), and then paste the character wherever it's needed (Ctrl V).

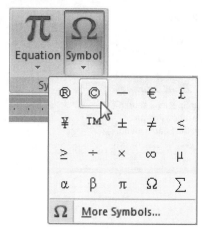

Figure 3.41 Many commonly used symbols can be chosen from the drop-down gallery.

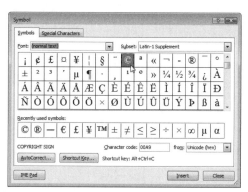

Figure 3.42 All characters in the current font are displayed in the Symbol dialog box.

FORMATTING DOCUMENTS

4

Writing text is only part of what you'll do in Word. (If your main interest is in generating a lot of text with as few interruptions as possible, you can probably do it faster using a simple text editor, such as Notepad.) In order to create documents that are attractive and pleasant to read, you must add *formatting*.

Word supports three main kinds of formatting:

◆ *Document formatting* affects the entire document and is primarily related to page settings, such as paper size, margins, orientation, sections, and columns. Other document formatting commands enable you to insert page, section, and column breaks; insert blank and cover pages; and add headers and footers.

◆ *Paragraph formatting* applies to entire paragraphs and is used to set alignment, indents, and line spacing. You can also create numbered or bulleted lists.

◆ *Character formatting* can be applied to selected words, sentences, or paragraphs and includes attributes such as font, size, color, and style.

To simplify the process of consistently applying paragraph and character formatting to material in a document, you can define *styles*.

Specifying Page Settings

To set basic document formatting, you choose options from the drop-down menus in the Page Setup group on the Page Layout tab (**Figure 4.1**). These settings normally affect the entire document.

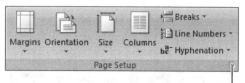

Page Setup Dialog Box Launcher

Figure 4.1 Specify page settings by choosing options from the Page Setup group on the Page Layout tab.

To set paper size and orientation:

◆ **Paper size.** Click the Size icon, and choose a standard paper size from the drop-down menu.

If you want to use a special paper size, choose More Paper Sizes. On the Paper tab of the Page Setup dialog box, select Custom size from the Paper size drop-down list, specify the paper's width and height, and click OK.

◆ **Orientation.** Pages can be laid out and printed in normal fashion (*portrait*) or sideways (*landscape*). Choose Portrait or Landscape from the Orientation drop-down menu.

◆ **Columns.** Certain types of documents look best and are easier to read when arranged in multiple columns. To format a new document or reformat an existing one in this manner, choose the number of columns or a two-column layout (Left or Right) from the Columns drop-down menu (**Figure 4.2**).

◆ **Margins.** Set margins for the document by choosing an option from the Margins drop-down menu (**Figure 4.3**). To set margins that differ from the ones listed, choose Custom Margins, and enter the desired margin settings in the Page Setup dialog box.

Figure 4.2 Choose a number or type of column.

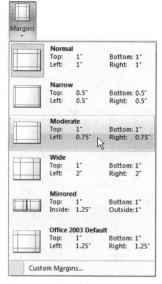

Figure 4.3 Choose margins from the Margins drop-down menu.

Figure 4.4 In the ruler, drag a column's right margin to change its width.

Tabs

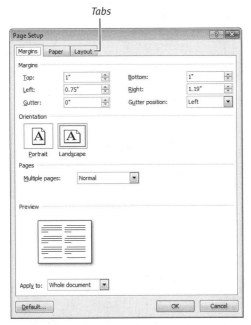

Figure 4.5 You can also specify page settings on the tabs of the Page Setup dialog box.

✔ Tips

- To change a column's width, drag the right margin of the column in the horizontal ruler (**Figure 4.4**).

- To restore a multicolumn document to a single column, choose One from the Columns drop-down menu.

- Although it's uncommon, you can change page settings in mid-document (switching from portrait to landscape mode or setting new margins, for instance). Click the Page Setup Dialog Box Launcher (see Figure 4.1). On the appropriate tab of the Page Setup dialog box (**Figure 4.5**), set new options, choose This point forward from the Apply to drop-down menu, and click OK.

- You can also use the Page Setup dialog box to apply new settings to the *entire* document. Choose Whole document from the Apply to drop-down menu.

- Although you may be tempted, it's usually inappropriate to set left or right margins of zero (0). First, many printers cannot print from edge to edge. Laser printers, for instance, often have a *no-print zone* of 0.2–0.25" on each margin. Second, documents with tiny margins are often difficult to read because so much text is crammed into each line.

- You can specify page settings at any time: before you begin writing, after you've finished, or at any point in between.

Modifying the Background

You can choose options from the Page Background group (**Figure 4.6**) on the Page Layout tab to add color, a watermark/rubber stamp, or a border to every document page.

In general, however, you should apply background settings sparingly and only to special documents. Colors and borders, for example, are best reserved for party invitations, ads, and flyers. On the other hand, a watermark can be extremely useful when applied to certain business documents, marking them as drafts or confidential.

To add a background color to each page:

◆ Click the Page Color icon, and *do one of the following*:

▲ Select a color from the Theme Colors or the Standard Colors palette (**Figure 4.7**).

▲ To select from all possible colors, choose More Colors. Select a color in the Colors dialog box and click OK.

▲ To apply a color gradient, texture, pattern, or picture to the background, choose Fill Effects. Select an option from the tabs in the Fill Effects dialog box (**Figure 4.8**) and click OK.

▲ Remove a previously applied color by choosing No Color.

✔ Tip

■ Document text may be easier to read on certain color, gradient, texture, pattern, and picture backgrounds than on others. For instance, if you choose a dark color, it may be necessary to change the text color to one that contrasts better with the background.

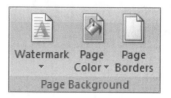

Figure 4.6 Change the page background by choosing options from icons in this group.

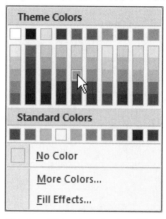

Figure 4.7 The selected color will be applied to every document page.

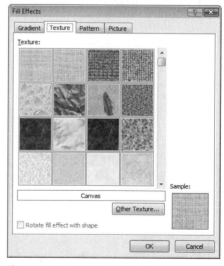

Figure 4.8 The Fill Effects dialog box.

MODIFYING THE BACKGROUND

Figure 4.9 To add a watermark to each page, choose Custom Watermark.

Figure 4.10 Creating a text watermark.

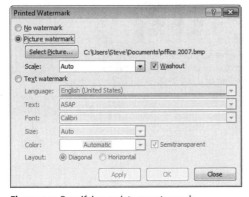

Figure 4.11 Specifying a picture watermark.

To apply a watermark to each page:

1. Click the Watermark icon, and choose Custom Watermark from the drop-down menu (**Figure 4.9**).

   The Printed Watermark dialog box appears.

2. *Do one of the following:*

   ▲ To remove an existing watermark from the document, select No watermark.

   ▲ To use a text string as the watermark, select Text watermark (**Figure 4.10**), and choose settings for the language, text, font, size, color, and layout. For a fainter watermark, ensure that Semitransparent is checked.

   ▲ To use an image as the watermark, select Picture watermark (**Figure 4.11**). Click the Select Picture button to select the image file from your hard disk. You can choose a magnification for the image from the Scale drop-down menu or leave it set to Auto for the optimal size that will fit on the document page without cropping. Click the Washout check box for a fainter image.

3. Click Apply to add the watermark to the document pages. If you don't like its appearance, you can change settings and click Apply again.

4. When you're satisfied with the watermark, click OK. The dialog box closes.

✔ Tips

■ As shown in Figure 4.9, you can also remove a watermark by choosing Remove Watermark from the drop-down menu.

■ You can apply a text watermark *or* a picture watermark—not both. If you switch types, the current watermark is automatically replaced.

■ Check the watermark's appearance with and without Semitransparent or Washout.

MODIFYING THE BACKGROUND

To add borders around each page:

1. Click the Page Borders icon.

   The Borders and Shading dialog box appears (**Figure 4.12**), open to the Page Border tab.

2. Click an icon in the Setting list to specify the type of border you want to create.

3. Specify line properties by choosing options from the drop-down menus.

   Your choices are reflected in the Preview area of the dialog box.

4. From the Apply to drop-down menu, indicate the pages of the document to which the border will be applied.

5. Click OK.

✔ Tips

- To remove an existing page border or to begin designing one from scratch, click None in the Setting list.

- To remove individual lines from the border or to add a line, click that side of the box in the Preview area.

- Rather than create a line border, you can use artwork (such as pencils or Christmas trees) as the border by choosing an image from the Art drop-down menu (**Figure 4.13**).

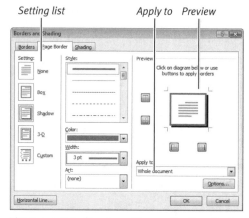

Setting list   Apply to   Preview

Figure 4.12 Select border settings on the Page Border tab of the Borders and Shading dialog box.

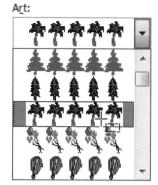

Figure 4.13 Use artwork to add a festive or eye-catching border to a flyer or party invitation.

Automatic page break

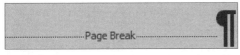

> I learned several valuable lessons from these experiences:
>
> • *Upgrade if you truly need the new system*

Figure 4.14 In Draft view, automatic page breaks are displayed as dotted lines.

.................................Page Break................................ ¶

Figure 4.15 When invisible characters are made visible, manually page breaks are clearly marked.

Avoiding Widows and Orphans

In word processing, a single line at the end of a page is referred to as a *widow*; a single line at the beginning of a page (normally, the final line of a paragraph that began on the previous page) is called an *orphan*. Layout rules indicate that both look amateurish and should be avoided.

If you carefully define and use paragraph styles (see "Working with Styles" in this chapter), you can automatically avoid widows and orphans. For example, when specifying the style for a header, you can enable a combination of Widow/Orphan control, Keep with next, and Keep lines together. For body text paragraphs, Widow/Orphan control will suffice.

Inserting Breaks

Word adds an *automatic page break* wherever it's needed, based on the margins and the style setting of the paragraph that will be broken or moved to the next page. As you add or delete text, the automatic breaks are adjusted as needed; that is, Word repaginates as you type. In Print Layout and Full Screen Reading views, breaks are shown as new physical pages. In Draft view, they're indicated by dotted lines (**Figure 4.14**).

Occasionally, breaks appear in spots where you'd prefer they not occur. For example, a key quote may be split between two pages. You can prevent this by inserting a *manual break* wherever it's needed. In addition to page breaks, you can also insert column and section breaks.

To insert a manual page break:

1. Set the text insertion mark at the beginning of the line on which you want to start the new page.

2. *Do one of the following:*
   ▲ On the Insert tab, click the Page Break icon in the Pages group.
   ▲ On the Page Layout tab, click the Breaks icon in the Page Setup group and choose Page.
   ▲ Press Ctrl Enter.
   A page break is created at the text insertion mark.

✔ Tips

■ The safest time to insert page breaks is after you're finished writing and editing.

■ To remove a manual page break, select it and press Backspace, Delete, or Del. It's easier to do when the breaks are visible (**Figure 4.15**). Click the Show/Hide ¶ icon in the Home tab's Paragraph group.

To insert other types of manual breaks:

1. Set the text insertion mark at the beginning of the line where you want to insert the break.

2. On the Page Layout tab, click the Breaks icon in the Page Setup group. From the drop-down menu that appears (**Figure 4.16**), *choose one of the following:*

   ▲ Choose Column to break the current column in a multicolumn layout. The text following the text insertion mark will begin in the next column.

   ▲ Choose a command from the Section Breaks part of the menu to create or indicate the start of a new section.

   The column or section break is inserted.

✔ Tip

■ Unless you're writing a lengthy or complex report, it's unlikely you'll divide the document into sections. (I suspect that most Word users don't even know this feature exists.) Use sections when you want to use chapter-relative page numbering or dramatically change formatting in the middle of a document (switching between a single- and a multicolumn layout, for example).

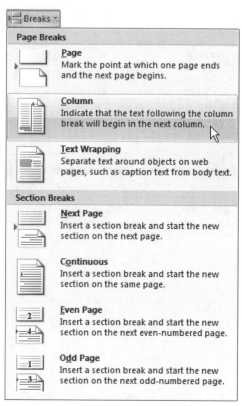

Figure 4.16 You can insert manual breaks for new pages, columns, or sections by choosing a command from the Breaks drop-down menu.

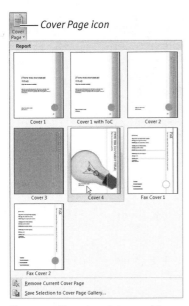
Cover Page icon

Figure 4.17 Some templates provide a gallery of cover pages.

Placeholders

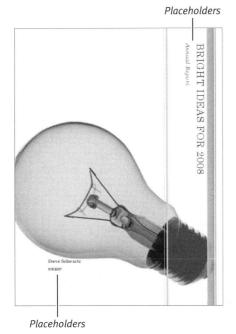

BRIGHT IDEAS FOR 2008
Annual Report

Steve Schwartz

Placeholders

Figure 4.18 Replace the placeholder text to complete the cover page.

Adding a Cover Page or Blank Page

You can add a preformatted *cover page* (or title page) to some documents. A cover page is especially useful for reports. When added, a cover page is automatically placed at the beginning of the document and contains placeholders for important text elements, such as the title, author, and date. Only one cover page is allowed in a document. If you add another, it replaces the current one.

When writing a report or book that will be bound on the left edge, it's tradition to begin each new section or chapter on a right-hand page. As such, if there's no material for the facing page (on the left), the page must be blank. In addition, you can insert blank pages anywhere else you wish.

To add a cover page:

1. On the Insert tab, click the Cover Page icon in the Pages group.

   If the template on which the document was based includes cover pages, a gallery appears (**Figure 4.17**).

2. Select a cover page style by clicking it.

   The cover page is added as the first page.

3. Replace the placeholder text with your own text (**Figure 4.18**).

✔ Tips

- Not all Word 2007 templates offer cover pages. Similarly, if you create a blank, new document rather than basing it on a template, a cover page can't be added.

- You can't attach a cover page to documents created in earlier versions of Word. Cover pages are a Word 2007 feature.

- When cover pages aren't provided or supported, you can create your own by placing graphics and text.

To insert a blank page:

1. Set the text insertion mark where you want to add a new page.

2. On the Insert tab, click the Blank Page icon in the Pages group (**Figure 4.19**).

   A blank page is added at the text insertion mark by adding two page breaks (**Figure 4.20**). As necessary, text is reflowed around—but not into—the blank page.

✔ Tips

- An inserted blank page can be left blank or you can type text onto it.

- To remove a blank page, delete the two manual page breaks and the blank paragraphs that were inserted. It's easiest to select and delete these items in Draft view.

Figure 4.19 Click the Blank Page icon to add a blank page at the text insertion mark.

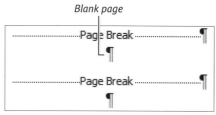

Figure 4.20 To create a blank page, Word inserts a new paragraph surrounded by a pair of manual page breaks.

Adding Headers or Footers

Headers and footers are reserved areas at the top and bottom of each page, respectively, in which you can display important text, such as a page number, date, filename, or text string (*Confidential*, for example).

To create or edit a header or footer:

1. *Optional:* Header and footer elements are aligned using tab stops. To see them, click the Show/Hide ¶ icon in the Paragraph group on the Home tab.

2. *Do either of the following:*

   ▲ In the Header & Footer group on the Insert tab, click the Header or Footer icon and choose Edit Header or Edit Footer.

   ▲ In Print Layout view, double-click in the header or footer area.

   The cursor appears in the header or footer in Print Layout view (**Figure 4.21**).

continues on next page

Footer area

Header & Footer Tools contextual tab

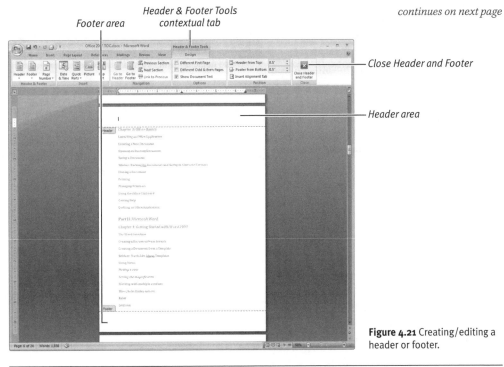

Close Header and Footer

Header area

Figure 4.21 Creating/editing a header or footer.

3. To insert a header or footer element, *do any of the following:*

▲ Type a text string, such as the file-name or document title.

▲ To insert the current date, time, or both, click the Date & Time icon in the Insert group. Select a format from the Date and Time dialog box (**Figure 4.22**). To display the current date and time each time you open the document, click the Update automatically check box. Otherwise, the date/time entered at this moment will be treated as static text. Click OK.

▲ To insert a page number that will automatically reflect each document page, click the Quick Parts icon in the Insert group and choose Field. In the Field dialog box (**Figure 4.23**), select Page from the Field names list, select a number format from the Format list, and click OK.

4. To insert another element, set the text insertion mark before or after an element, press [Tab], and add the new element. Repeat for a third element, if desired.

By default, an element on the left side of the page is left-aligned with the left margin, an element in the center is center-aligned between both margins, and an element on the right side is right-aligned with the right margin (**Figure 4.24**).

5. When you're done entering and editing elements in the header or footer area, *do either of the following:*

▲ Edit the other area by clicking in it. Or click the Header or Footer icon in the Header & Footer group and choose Edit Header or Edit Footer.

▲ Click anywhere in the document to resume writing and editing, or click the Close Header and Footer icon in the Close group (**Figure 4.25**).

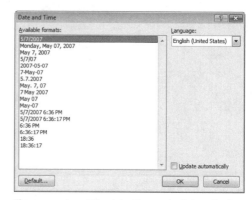

Figure 4.22 Insert the date, time, or both by selecting a format from the Date and Time dialog box.

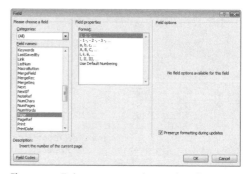

Figure 4.23 To insert page numbers, select the Page field name and specify a display format.

Figure 4.24 In a three-item header/footer, an element would precede each tab. In this example, the lone element is right-aligned by preceding it with two tabs.

Figure 4.25 Click this icon to resume writing and editing.

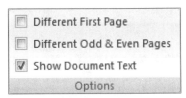

Figure 4.26 The Options group.

Figure 4.27 Templates may provide formatted headers and footers that you can use.

Figure 4.28 You can change the distance of the header or footer from the edge of the page.

- You can reposition the header or footer by entering new settings in the Header from Top or Footer from Bottom boxes in the Position group (**Figure 4.28**).

- For additional control over header and footer tabs, such as adding leader characters, click the Insert Alignment Tab icon (see Figure 4.28).

✔ Tips

- If you find the document text distracting, you can hide it by removing the check mark from Show Document Text in the Options group (**Figure 4.26**). When you finish creating or editing the header and footer, the document text will reappear.

- You can also add graphics to a header or footer, such as a logo or a horizontal rule.

- A Page field can be preceded by text, such as the word *Page*. Position the text insertion mark before the page number in the header or footer, and then type Page and a space.

- If you base a document on a Word template rather than creating it from scratch, you should note that some templates contain a header and footer gallery from which you can choose preformatted headers and footers (**Figure 4.27**).

- Text in a header or footer can be formatted as you like. Select a header or footer element or the entire header or footer. Choose formatting commands from the Mini toolbar or from the Font group on the Home tab.

- Page 1 of certain documents (such as a report with a title or cover page) should contain no header/footer; or the header/footer may need to contain special text. Click the Different First Page check box in the Options group (see Figure 4.26). You can then leave the page 1 header and footer blank or create a *different* page 1 header and/or footer.

- To create different headers and footers on even/left and odd/right pages (as is often done for books and other publications with facing-page spreads), click the Different Odd & Even Pages check box.

ADDING HEADERS OR FOOTERS

Paragraph Formatting

In Word, a *paragraph* (**Figure 4.29**) is any amount of text (a word, a line, a sentence, or multiple sentences) that ends with a paragraph mark (¶). You finish a paragraph and begin a new one by pressing ⏎Enter. This action inserts the paragraph mark.

Generally, the new paragraph will have the same formatting as the previous one. (The exception is when the *style* assigned to the current paragraph is designed to be followed by a paragraph of a different style. For instance, a heading style is typically followed by a body text style.)

Paragraph formatting, such as alignment or indents, can be applied to a selected paragraph by choosing options from the Paragraph group on the Home tab (**Figure 4.30**), the Mini toolbar, or the Paragraph dialog box. You can also apply formatting by choosing a *paragraph style* (discussed later in this chapter).

Paragraph formatting has nothing to do with font, size, style, or color. It is concerned solely with alignment, spacing between lines, indents from one or both margins, and so on.

✔ Tips

■ Normally, paragraph marks are invisible, but you can show them by clicking the Show/Hide ¶ icon in the Paragraph group on the Home tab. Doing so also displays other normally hidden characters, such as spaces, tabs, and line breaks.

■ You can force certain characters (such as paragraph marks) to *always* display. Click the Office Button, and then click Word Options. In the Word Options dialog box, select the Display category, click check boxes of the items you always want to show (**Figure 4.31**), and click OK.

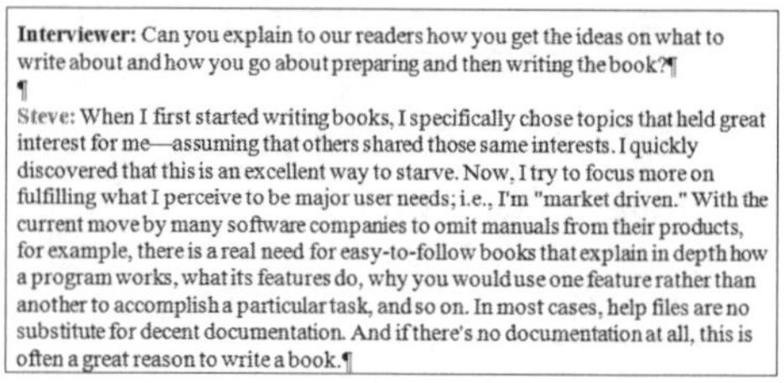

Interviewer: Can you explain to our readers how you get the ideas on what to write about and how you go about preparing and then writing the book?¶
¶
Steve: When I first started writing books, I specifically chose topics that held great interest for me—assuming that others shared those same interests. I quickly discovered that this is an excellent way to starve. Now, I try to focus more on fulfilling what I perceive to be major user needs; i.e., I'm "market driven." With the current move by many software companies to omit manuals from their products, for example, there is a real need for easy-to-follow books that explain in depth how a program works, what its features do, why you would use one feature rather than another to accomplish a particular task, and so on. In most cases, help files are no substitute for decent documentation. And if there's no documentation at all, this is often a great reason to write a book.¶

Figure 4.29 There are three paragraphs here—each ending with a paragraph mark. The middle one is a blank paragraph.

Paragraph Dialog Box Launcher

Figure 4.30 The Paragraph group has icons for common paragraph-formatting options.

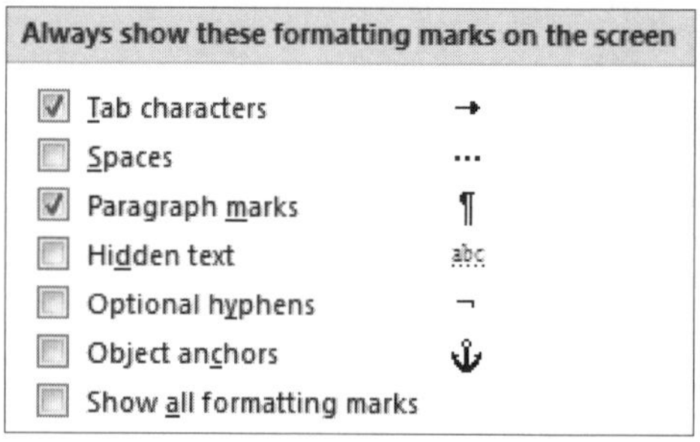

Always show these formatting marks on the screen

☑ <u>T</u>ab characters →
☐ <u>S</u>paces ...
☑ Paragraph <u>m</u>arks ¶
☐ Hi<u>d</u>den text a̲b̲c̲
☐ Optional h<u>y</u>phens ¬
☐ Object an<u>c</u>hors ⚓
☐ Show <u>a</u>ll formatting marks

Figure 4.31 Check the items that will always be displayed, regardless of the status of Show/Hide ¶.

PARAGRAPH FORMATTING

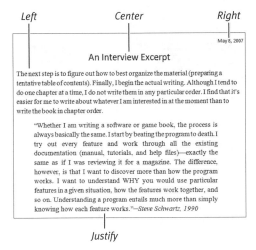

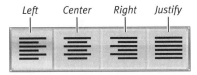

Figure 4.32 No matter how short or long, every paragraph has an alignment.

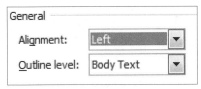

Figure 4.33 Click an alignment icon in the Paragraph group.

Figure 4.34 In the Paragraph dialog box, you can choose an option from the Alignment drop-down menu.

Setting Alignment

A paragraph's *alignment* determines its positioning in relation to the margins. Every paragraph must have one of the following alignments (**Figure 4.32**):

◆ **Left.** The left edge of the paragraph is flush with the left margin and the right edge is ragged. Body text of most documents is left-aligned.

◆ **Right.** The right edge of the paragraph is flush with the right margin and the left edge is ragged.

◆ **Center.** Each line of the paragraph is automatically centered between the two margins. Center alignment is sometimes applied to titles and other headings.

◆ **Justify.** Both edges of the paragraph are flush with a margin. As necessary, Word adjusts the spacing between words to enable each line to be flush with the margins. Magazine copy and block quotations are often justified.

To set paragraph alignment:

1. Select one or more paragraphs.

   To select a single paragraph, it's sufficient to set the text insertion mark in it. To select multiple paragraphs, drag a selection through at least part of each one.

2. *Do one of the following:*

   ▲ On the Home tab, click an alignment icon in the Paragraph group (**Figure 4.33**).

   ▲ Press an alignment keyboard shortcut: Left Ctrl L, Center Ctrl E, Right Ctrl R, or Justify Ctrl J.

   ▲ In the Paragraph dialog box, click the Indents and Spacing tab, choose an alignment (**Figure 4.34**), and click OK.

   ▲ Click the Center alignment icon on the Mini toolbar.

Setting Indents

Every paragraph has three indents that you set to specify the distance from the text to the left and right margins:

◆ **Left.** Distance from the left margin.

◆ **Right.** Distance from the right margin.

◆ **First line.** Distance from the left margin that applies only to the first line of text.

Indents are automatically set for bulleted and numbered lists (hanging indents). You can set equal left and right indents of 0.5" or 1" to format a block quote. Indents can be set on the horizontal ruler or in the Paragraph dialog box. Any or all indents can be set to 0.

To set indents:

◆ *Do any of the following:*

▲ **Paragraph group (Home tab).**
To increase or decrease the selected paragraph's left indent in increments of 0.5", click the Increase Indent or Decrease Indent icon in the Paragraph group (**Figure 4.35**) or on the Mini toolbar.

▲ **Paragraph group (Page Layout tab).**
Enter numbers (in inches) in the Left and/or Right box (**Figure 4.36**).

▲ **Paragraph dialog box.** You can set exact indents on the Indents and Spacing tab (**Figure 4.37**). To create a first-line indent (similar to starting each paragraph by pressing Tab), choose First line from the Special drop-down menu and set the indent. To create a hanging indent for a bulleted or numbered list, choose Hanging from the Special drop-down menu.

▲ **Horizontal ruler.** You can also set indents by dragging markers on the horizontal ruler (**Figure 4.38**).

Decrease Indent

Increase Indent

Figure 4.35 Click an icon to decrease or increase the left indent by half an inch.

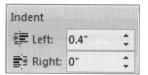

Figure 4.36 You can specify a precise left and right indent.

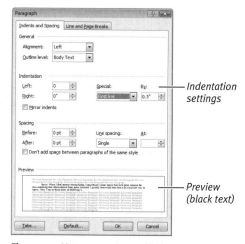

Indentation settings

Preview (black text)

Figure 4.37 You can create any kind of indent in the Paragraph dialog box.

First Hanging   *Right*

Left

✓ **Steve:** When I first started writing books, I specifically chose topics that held great interest for me—assuming

Figure 4.38 By dragging the first line indent marker to the left of the margin, this outdent was created.

✔ Tips

- You can use the Paragraph dialog box to create an *outdent* (extending to the left of the left margin) by entering a negative number for the left indent.

- When setting indents on the ruler, you'll note the following behaviors:

  - ▲ The first-line and right indent markers move independently of other markers.

  - ▲ The left and hanging indent markers move as a pair.

  - ▲ When you drag the left indent marker, it and the hanging indent marker maintain their current distance from the first-line indent marker.

  - ▲ Drag the hanging indent marker to change its distance (and that of the left indent marker) from the first-line indent marker.

Working with Tabs

The ability to set indents and create tables in Word has virtually eliminated the need to uses tabs in most documents. However, if you *do* need them to create a column of numbers aligned on the decimal point, for example, here's what you should know:

- ◆ By default, you can press Tab at the start of or within a paragraph to space to the next 0.5" increment on the ruler.

- ◆ To set a left tab for selected paragraphs, click the desired spot on the horizontal ruler.

- ◆ To create other types of tab stops (right, center, decimal, or bar), modify existing tab stops, or specify a *leader character* (such as a string of periods), double-click a tab icon on the ruler. The Tabs dialog box opens.

- ◆ Change a tab-stop position by dragging its icon or by entering a new position in the Tabs dialog box.

- ◆ You can remove a tab stop by dragging its icon from the ruler onto the document page.

SETTING INDENTS

Creating Lists

Bulleted and numbered lists are special kinds of hanging-indent paragraphs. The hanging portion is either a bullet character (such as a filled or empty circle, diamond, or check mark) or a sequential number. You can create such lists *automatically* (depending on settings in Word Options) or *manually* (by applying a bullet or number format to a set of paragraphs).

You can also create lists with multiple levels of indents. These *multilevel lists* can contain sublists beneath any list item.

To enable automatic bulleted and numbered lists:

1. Open the Word Options dialog box by clicking the Office Button, followed by the Word Options button.

2. Select the Proofing category.

3. Click the AutoCorrect Options button near the top of the dialog box.

4. In the AutoCorrect Options dialog box, select the AutoFormat As You Type tab.

5. In the Apply as you type section (**Figure 4.39**), enable Automatic bulleted lists and Automatic numbered lists.

6. Click OK to close the AutoCorrect Options dialog box.

7. Click OK to close the Word Options dialog box.

✔ Tip

■ This is a one-time procedure. You'll have to revisit it only if you want to stop automatically creating one or both list types.

Figure 4.39 Enable the automatic creation of bulleted and numbered lists by clicking these check boxes.

Before, During, or After?

It's important to understand that paragraph and character formatting can be applied at *any* time: before you begin typing a paragraph or text block, as you type it, or after you've written and edited it.

And there's no single best approach—it depends on your writing style. For example, if you're making a numbered list, you can start a new paragraph, apply the number format, and then type the first item. For each additional paragraph you create, the numbering increments. On the other hand, it's just as easy to write the entire list, select it, and *then* apply the numbered paragraph format.

Bulleted list

Buy the following fresh fruit at the grocery store:

- Apples
- Pears
- Bananas
- Pineapple

Prepare the fruit as follows:

1. Peel and chop the fresh fruit into tiny, bite-sized pieces.
2. Place in a large mixing bowl.
3. Call mom for other ingredients and instructions. ☺
4. Refrigerate.

Numbered list

Figure 4.40 Examples of an automatic bulleted list and a numbered list.

Bullets Numbering

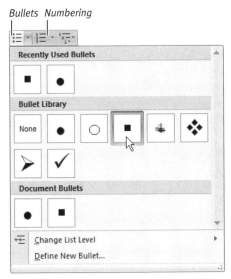

Figure 4.41 You can create a bulleted or numbered list by clicking an icon or by choosing a style from a drop-down gallery.

To automatically create a list:

1. At the beginning of a new paragraph, *do one of the following:*
   - ▲ **Bulleted list.** To create the first item, type an asterisk (*) and a space. The asterisk is converted into a bullet.
   - ▲ **Numbered list.** To create the first item, type 1. and a space. This item becomes the first in a numbered list.

2. Finish the item paragraph and press Enter. Additional consecutive paragraphs you create by pressing Enter will continue the bullets or numbering.

3. To complete the final list item (**Figure 4.40**), press Enter twice.
   The new bullet or number is removed.

To manually create a list:

1. *Do either of the following:*
   - ▲ To create the default bulleted or numbered list, click the Bullets or Numbering icon in the Paragraph group of the Home tab (**Figure 4.41**) or on the Mini toolbar.
   - ▲ Select a bullet or numbering style from the galleries (see Figure 4.41).

2. Finish the item paragraph and press Enter. Additional consecutive paragraphs you create by pressing Enter will continue the bullets or numbering.

3. To complete the final list item, press Enter twice.
   The new bullet or number is removed.

CREATING LISTS

✔ Tips

■ You can also end a bulleted or numbered list by clicking the Bullets or Numbering icon in the Paragraph group (see Figure 4.41).

■ There are other characters you can type (followed by a period and a space) to automatically start a numbered list with a different numbering format, such as a., A., i., and I.

■ To type additional text directly beneath a bulleted or numbered point without interrupting the bullets or numbering (**Figure 4.42**), end the previous line by pressing Shift Enter. (This creates a *line break*.) Type the additional text on the new line. When you press Enter to end the line or paragraph, the bullets or numbering will resume.

■ You can change the bullet or numbering style for an existing list. Select all bulleted or numbered points, and then select a style from the Bullets or Numbering drop-down gallery (see Figure 4.41).

■ To change a list from bullets to numbers or vice versa, click the other icon in the Paragraph group of the Home tab (see Figure 4.41) or on the Mini toolbar.

■ You can sort a bulleted list alphabetically, numerically, or in date order. Select the items, click the Sort icon in the Paragraph group on the Home tab, and set options in the Sort Text dialog box (**Figure 4.43**).

■ You can change the formatting of all bullets and numbers in a list. Click one of them to select them all. Apply character formatting (such as a new font, boldface, or a color) by choosing options from the Font group on the Home tab or from the Mini toolbar.

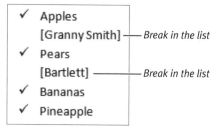

Figure 4.42 You can interrupt a list without ending it.

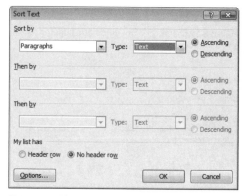

Figure 4.43 These settings can be used to alphabetically sort a bulleted list.

CREATING LISTS

Decrease Indent

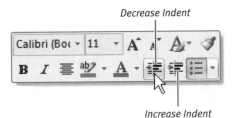

Increase Indent

Figure 4.44 To set or change an item's level, click the Decrease Indent or Increase Indent icon.

Figure 4.45 The Multilevel List drop-down gallery.

❖ Bananas
❖ Pears
   ➤ Anjou
      ■ Red
      ■ Green
   ➤ Bosc
   ➤ Bartlett
      ■ Yellow
      ■ Red
❖ Pineapple

Figure 4.46 A multi-level bulleted list.

To create a multilevel list:

1. Begin an automatic or manual list by following the previous task instructions.

2. To enter an item at a new level, click the Increase Indent icon in the Paragraph group of the Home tab or on the Mini toolbar (**Figure 4.44**).

   Additional items created at the same indent level by pressing ⌈Enter⌉ will have the same bullet or number style.

3. To convert an item to a higher level, click the Decrease Indent icon in the Paragraph group of the Home tab or on the Mini toolbar (see Figure 4.44).

4. To specify the bullet or number format to be applied to each level, click the Multilevel List icon in the Paragraph group of the Home tab and select a style from the gallery (**Figure 4.45**).

   Your list is reformatted to match the gallery selection (**Figure 4.46**).

✔ Tips

■ To select all items at a particular level in a bulleted or numbered list, click the bullet or number for any item at that level.

■ You can substitute other bullets for the ones in the gallery. Click the down arrow beside the Bullets icon in the Paragraph group of the Home tab (see Figure 4.41) or on the Mini toolbar, and choose Define New Bullet. In the Define New Bullet dialog box, click Symbol or Picture to select a character from an installed font or to use an image file, respectively.

CREATING LISTS

Between-Paragraph and Line Spacing

Paragraph attributes also include the space between lines, as well as the space before and after the paragraph. Although line and between-paragraph spacing are defined as part of every paragraph style, there are times when you'll want to change these settings. For instance, if a document is a few lines too long, you can make it fit in fewer pages by reducing the line spacing. Similarly, if an instructor insists on *double-spaced text* (a typewriter term), you can approximate it on a computer by increasing the line spacing of all paragraphs.

To change line spacing for paragraphs:

1. Select the paragraph or paragraphs that will be affected by the new setting.

2. Click the Line Spacing icon in the Paragraph group of the Home tab.

3. *Choose one of the following* from the Line Spacing drop-down menu (**Figure 4.47**):

   ▲ A number, representing the space between each pair of lines. (Double-spacing is 2.0, for example.)

   ▲ Line Spacing Options. The Paragraph dialog box opens. On the Indents and Spacing tab, set the line spacing (**Figure 4.48**), and click OK.

   The selected paragraphs are reformatted.

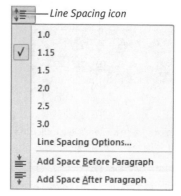

Figure 4.47 The Line Spacing drop-down list.

Figure 4.48 You can select a line-spacing option from this drop-down list.

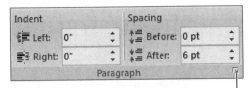

Paragraph Dialog Box Launcher

Figure 4.49 Enter numbers in the Spacing boxes to set the before and after spacing.

Between-paragraph spacing

Spacing
Before: 12 pt
After: 0 pt
Line spacing: Single
At:
☐ Don't add space between paragraphs of the same style

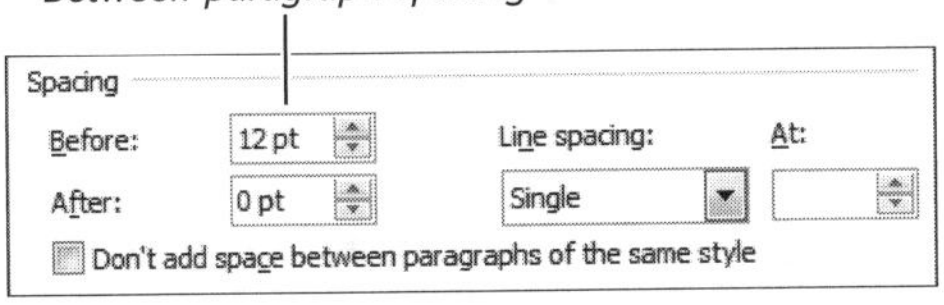

Figure 4.50 Set the before and after spacing (in points), and then click OK.

- In general, it's best to avoid applying new spacing settings directly to paragraphs. Unless you're very consistent, you may end up with an ugly document. Instead, modify the document's paragraph styles. Doing so will ensure consistency because all paragraphs to which you've assigned a given style will automatically update to reflect the new settings.

To change the before or after spacing for selected paragraphs:

1. Select the paragraph or paragraphs that will be affected by the new settings.

2. *Do one of the following:*
   - ▲ In the Paragraph group on the Page Layout tab (**Figure 4.49**), enter numbers (in points) in the Before and/or After boxes.

   - ▲ At the bottom of the Paragraph group on the Home or Page Layout tab, click the Paragraph Dialog Box Launcher (see Figure 4.49). On the Indents and Spacing tab of the Paragraph dialog box, enter numbers (in points) in the Before and/or After boxes (**Figure 4.50**). Click OK to close the dialog box.

   - ▲ In the Paragraph group of the Home tab, click the Line Spacing icon. Choose Add/Remove Space Before Paragraph or Add/Remove Space After Paragraph (see Figure 4.47) to add a 12-point space or remove the current space.

   The new before/after spacing is applied to the selected paragraphs.

✔ Tips

- To set line spacing in *points* (72 per inch), choose Exactly from the Line spacing drop-down menu (see Figure 4.48).

- New line spacing and before/after settings affect only the selected paragraphs. To apply these settings to an entire document, set the text insertion mark and press Ctrl A. Or click the Select icon in the Editing group of the Home tab, and choose Select All.

- If a paragraph or paragraph style is set for no (0) space before and after, it may be difficult to distinguish from the surrounding paragraphs.

Character Formatting

Character formatting is formatting that you can selectively apply to words, phrases, lines, sentences, or paragraphs. To make a phrase stand out in its sentence, you might format it as italic, boldface, blue, or underlined. If the sentence containing the phrase was formatted with the Arial font, you might apply a variation of the font, such as Arial Narrow or Arial Black.

If you're applying a character format as you type (rather than by selecting existing text), you can think of the formatting as an on/off sequence. You turn the formatting feature on, type the new text, and then turn the feature off when you want to return to the original formatting.

Finally, if you want to easily reapply complex character formatting to additional text in the same document, you can use the Format Painter tool.

To apply formatting as you type:

1. To switch to a different character formatting, *do one of the following:*

   ▲ Choose character-formatting options from the Font group on the Home tab (**Figure 4.51**).

   ▲ Choose character-formatting options from the Mini toolbar (**Figure 4.52**).

   ▲ Click the Font Dialog Box Launcher (see Figure 4.51). Choose settings in the Font dialog box (**Figure 4.53**), and click OK.

2. Type the text you want to format with the chosen attribute(s).

3. Disable the attributes chosen in Step 1 by clicking their icons again. If you changed fonts, you can revert to the original font by choosing its name from any Font drop-down menu or scrolling list.

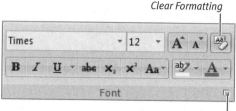

Clear Formatting

Font Dialog Box Launcher

Figure 4.51 You can choose common character-formatting attributes from the Font group.

Figure 4.52 The Mini toolbar provides only basic character-formatting options.

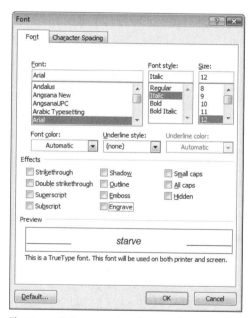

Figure 4.53 Every supported character-formatting attribute is available in the Font dialog box.

To apply formatting to existing text:

1. Select the text to which you want to apply a different character formatting.

2. *Do any of the following:*
   ▲ Choose character-formatting options from the Font group on the Home tab (see Figure 4.51).

   Rest the cursor over any icon to see a ToolTip description of its function.

   ▲ Choose character-formatting options from the Mini toolbar (see Figure 4.52).

   ▲ Click the Font Dialog Box Launcher (see Figure 4.51). Choose settings in the Font dialog box (see Figure 4.53), and click OK.

To remove character formatting:

1. Select the text from which you want to remove character formatting.

2. *Do any of the following:*
   ▲ To remove *all* character formatting (leaving only plain text), click the Clear Formatting icon in the Font group of the Home tab (see Figure 4.51).

   ▲ To selectively remove formatting (when you've applied multiple attributes to the selected text), click icons of the formats you want to remove in the Font group or Mini toolbar.

   ▲ Click the Font Dialog Box Launcher (see Figure 4.51). Choose new settings in the Font dialog box (see Figure 4.53), and click OK.

Changing the Default Font

Whenever you create a new, blank Word document and begin typing, the font used is the *default font*. You can easily change this to a different font, if you prefer:

1. Open the Font dialog box.
   The font, style, size, and other attributes of the currently selected text are shown.

2. To specify attributes other than those of the selected text, select a font and other attributes from the drop-down lists and check boxes.

3. Click Default. Click Yes in the confirmation dialog box that appears.

4. Click OK to close the Font dialog box.

CHARACTER FORMATTING

To use the Format Painter to duplicate formatting:

1. Select some of the text you want to duplicate or position the text insertion mark within that text.

2. Click the Format Painter icon in the Clipboard group of the Home tab (**Figure 4.54**). The Format Painter cursor appears.

3. Drag to select the destination text (**Figure 4.55**).

   The copied character formatting is applied to the destination text.

✔ Tips

- You also can open the Font dialog box by pressing Ctrl D.

- Many character-formatting commands have keyboard shortcuts. You can apply or remove their formatting by pressing the keys listed in **Table 4.1**.

- You can use the Format Painter to duplicate character *and* paragraph formatting. Select the entire paragraph before clicking the Format Painter icon.

- You can apply copied character attributes to *multiple* selections by double-clicking the Format Painter icon. One by one, drag-select each destination text string. When you're finished, click the Format Painter icon again.

- You can easily apply new attributes to multiple text strings that currently share the same formatting. Select any one of the text strings and switch to the Home tab. Click the Select drop-down menu in the Editing group, and choose Select Text with Similar Formatting (**Figure 4.56**). As you choose new character formatting, it'll be applied to *all* the text selections.

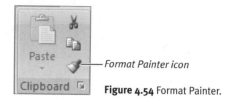

Format Painter icon

Figure 4.54 Format Painter.

Format Painter cursor

Figure 4.55 Using the Format Painter, it's easy to duplicate text formatting.

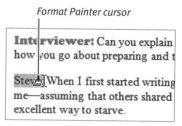

Figure 4.56 You can select text that matches the current formatting.

Table 4.1

Character-Formatting Keyboard Shortcuts	
KEYPRESS	DEFINITION
Ctrl B	Boldface
Ctrl I	Italic
Ctrl U	Underline (single)
Ctrl Shift D	Underline (double)
Ctrl Shift W	Underline words but not spaces
Ctrl Shift K	Small capital letters (caps)
Ctrl =	Subscript
Ctrl +	Superscript
Ctrl <	Decrease font size
Ctrl >	Increase font size
Shift F3	Change letter case
Ctrl Spacebar	Remove manual character formatting

Quick Styles gallery   Change Styles icon

Figure 4.57 Choose a new Quick Style set from the Style Set submenu.

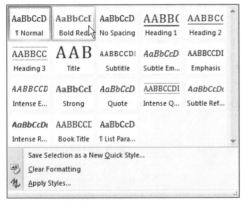

Figure 4.58 A Quick Style set's gallery.

What's a Style?

A *style* is a set of formatting instructions you can apply to selected paragraphs or text. By applying styles rather than manually formatting a document, you can ensure that the formatting is consistent throughout—resulting in a document with a professional appearance.

Working with Styles

The *Quick Styles gallery* (found in the Style group on the Home tab) is a new Word 2007 feature in which a subset of all defined styles for the current document is presented in a drop-down gallery. Designed to help you easily apply the most common paragraph and character styles to selected text, Quick Styles encourage users who have previously ignored Word styles to start using them.

If you create a document from scratch, you can choose from several Quick Style sets, each designed to convey a certain style and tone. If you create a document from a template, a Quick Style set may be included with the template. You can customize the active Quick Style set by adding new styles and removing unwanted ones.

To switch Quick Style sets:

1. Click the Change Styles icon in the Styles group of the Home tab.

2. From the Style Set submenu, choose a new style set (**Figure 4.57**). The current Quick Style set is replaced by the new set.

   As you drag the cursor over each set name, a live preview of the resulting style changes is applied to all visible text.

To apply a style:

1. Select a text string or a paragraph to which you want to apply a new style.

2. Open the Quick Style gallery. Move the cursor over a style icon (**Figure 4.58**).

   A preview of the style is displayed on the text.

3. If this is the correct style, click its icon to apply it to the text. Otherwise, repeat Steps 2 and 3 to find the desired style.

To add a style to the current set:

1. You create new Quick Styles from formatted text or paragraphs in the current document. Begin by applying the desired character formatting to some text or by applying paragraph formatting to a paragraph.

2. Select the formatted word, text string, or paragraph.

3. Right-click the selected text. Choose Styles > Save Selection as a New Quick Style from the pop-up menu (**Figure 4.59**). The Create New Style from Formatting dialog box appears (**Figure 4.60**).

4. Name the new style, and click Modify. A new dialog box appears (**Figure 4.61**).

5. Make any additional formatting changes that are required. Ensure that the setting for Style type matches the type of style you want to create: Character, Paragraph, or Linked (paragraph and character). Click the Format button to view other options. Click OK to return to the previous dialog box.

6. Click OK.

   An icon for the style appears in the Quick Styles gallery and the style definition is added to the document's style list.

To modify a style by example:

1. Make the desired changes to a text string or paragraph that is formatted with the style you want to modify.

2. Select the modified text or paragraph, right-click the selection, and choose Styles > Update *style name* to Match Selection.

   You can also choose this command from the pop-up menu that appears when you right-click the style icon in the Quick Style gallery.

Selected text

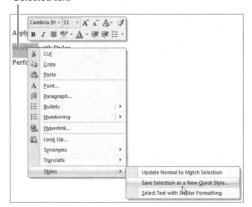

Figure 4.59 Format a paragraph or text string as desired, and select it. Right-click the selection, and choose Save Selection as a New Quick Style.

Style name

Figure 4.60 Name the new style.

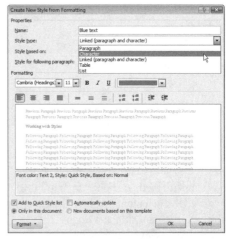

Figure 4.61 Make necessary changes and click OK.

Figure 4.62 The Styles window lists all defined styles for the document. To open the window, click the Styles Dialog Box Launcher at the bottom of the Styles group.

- To apply a different style to all text/paragraphs previously assigned a given style, click the down-arrow beside the style in the Styles window and choose Select All Instances. Reformat the selected material by clicking a new style or by choosing formatting options from the Home tab.

- As an alternative to the Styles window, you can open a floating window from which styles can be chosen to format selected text. Choose Apply Styles from the bottom of the Quick Style gallery (see Figure 4.58).

To modify a style using a dialog box:

1. *Do either of the following:*
    - ▲ Right-click the style icon in the Quick Style gallery and choose Modify.
    - ▲ In the Styles window (**Figure 4.62**), click the down-arrow beside the style name and choose Modify.

    A Modify Style dialog box appears, identical to the dialog box shown in Figure 4.61.

2. Make any desired changes. (You can choose additional options by clicking the Format button.) Click OK.

    The modified style definition is stored. Text or paragraphs formatted with the style automatically update to conform to the new definition.

✔ Tips

- To add a previously defined (but unlisted) style to the current Quick Style set, click the style's down-arrow in the Styles window. Choose Add to Quick Style Gallery.

- To remove a style from the current set, right-click its icon in the gallery and choose Remove from Quick Style Gallery. (Note that this only removes the style from the gallery. It does *not* delete the style from the document's style definitions.)

- To *delete* a style (permanently removing it from a document's style list), click the down-arrow beside the style name in the Styles window and choose Delete *style name* (see Figure 4.62). Text or paragraphs formatted with the style revert to the default formatting.

- Another way to open or close the Styles window is by pressing (Alt)(Ctrl)(Shift)(S).

- To remove all formatting applied by choosing a particular style, click the down-arrow beside the style's name in the Styles window and choose Clear Formatting.

WORKING WITH STYLES

Merge Formatting

By adding specially formatted placeholder text (called *mail merge fields*) to a document and combining it with data from a second document created in Word, Excel, Outlook, or another application, you can *merge* the two documents—creating a separate, customized version of the Word document for each data record. For example, by inserting name and address placeholders in the main document, you could create a mail merge. A personalized letter containing their address and using their first name in the greeting line would be generated for every person.

The easiest way to learn how to perform a merge is to use the Mail Merge Wizard to walk you through the process. As an example, you'll generate a series of personalized letters. To follow along, create an Excel worksheet similar to the one in **Figure 4.63**. Each row is a data record. Be sure to create at least three or four records.

	A	B	C	D	E	F	G
1	First	Last	Address	City	State	Zip	Donation
2	Amy	Fredericks	3226 State Street	Menlo Park	CA	94025	$ 25
3	Dave	Johnson	2480 Christina Lane	Walnut Creek	CA	94596	$ 5
4	Mike	Smith	35 James Rd.	Cocoa	FL	32926	$ 125
5	Steve	Anderson	677 Lillian Ave	Sudbury	MA	01776	$ 5
6	James	Barr	4125 Leeway Trail	Ormond Beach	FL	32174	$ 2
7	Douglas	Simons	299 NW 72nd Circle	Vancouver	WA	98665	$ 10
8	Josiah	Jefferson	13267 Skyline Dr.	Golden Valley	MN	55422	$ 20
9	Andrea	Harrison	3645 Michael St.	Carson City	NV	89703	$ 25
10	Sheri	Slainee	79879 E. Prince Dr., #42	Scottsdale	AZ	85255	$ 5
11	James	Kern	332 Sea Island Dr	Dana Point	CA	92629	$ 50
12	Josh	Kimes	2171 Skipper Lane	Lake Havasu City	AZ	86403	$ 100
13	Jill	Nelson	20 Archway Drive	Slingerlands	NY	12159	$ 50
14	Robert	Eliason	5310 Henderson Street	Duluth	MN	55804-1111	$ 10
15	Russ	Sanders	4000 Wildrose	Flagstaff	AZ	86001	$ 10

donation list.xlsx — Sheet1 / Sheet2 / Sheet3

Figure 4.63 Data in this worksheet will be merged with a Word form letter.

Figure 4.65 Step 1 of the Mail Merge Wizard.

To perform a merge using the Mail Merge Wizard:

1. In Word, create a document similar to the one shown in **Figure 4.64, bottom**. Leave space for the mail merge fields.

2. To open the Mail Merge Wizard task pane, switch to the Mailings tab, click the Start Mail Merge icon in the Start Mail Merge group, and choose Step by Step Mail Merge Wizard.

   The Mail Merge task pane appears on the right side of the window (**Figure 4.65**).

continues on next page

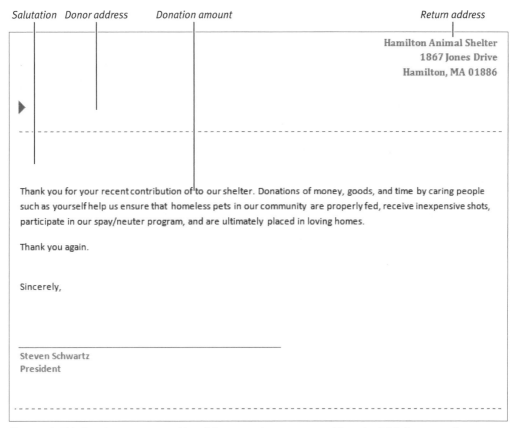

Figure 4.64 This form letter was created by editing a new document created from the Origin Letter template.

MERGE FORMATTING

3. Click the Letters radio button, and then click Next: Starting document (at the bottom of the task pane).

Step 2 of 6 appears in the task pane.

4. *Select one of the following:*

▲ **Use the current document.** If the document is open and onscreen, select this option.

▲ **Start from template.** If you haven't created the document, select this option. Click the Select template text that appears, and then pick the Origin Letter template.

▲ **Start from existing document.** If you've already created the document but it isn't open, select this option, select the document from the list that appears, and click the Open button.

5. At the bottom of the task pane, click Next: Select recipients.

Step 3 of 6 appears in the task pane.

6. Select Use an existing list, and click Browse.

The Select Data Source dialog box appears.

7. Navigate to the drive and folder in which you saved the Excel data file, select the file, and click Open.

The Select Table dialog box appears (**Figure 4.66**).

8. Select the first sheet (Sheet1$), ensure that First row of data contains column headers is checked, and click OK.

The Mail Merge Recipients dialog box appears (**Figure 4.67**).

9. *Optional:* You can skip a recipient by removing the check mark before his or her last name. Click OK when you're ready to continue.

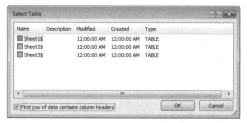

Figure 4.66 Select the first sheet in the workbook. Because the first row of the sheet contains the merge field names, ensure that the check box is checked.

Include/exclude check boxes

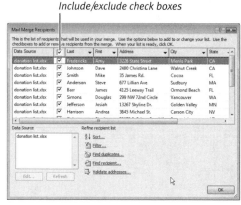

Figure 4.67 Review the data, ensure that it looks correct, and specify the records to include.

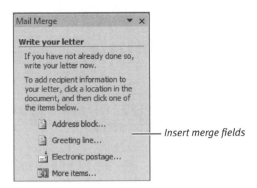

Figure 4.68 Insert merge fields into the letter.

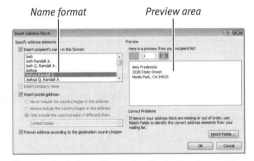

Figure 4.69 Select a format for displaying the recipient's name in the address block.

Figure 4.70 A merge field is surrounded by « and » characters.

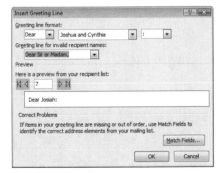

Figure 4.71 The Insert Greeting Line dialog box.

10. At the bottom of the task pane, click Next: Write your letter.

Step 4 of 6 (**Figure 4.68**) appears.

11. In the form letter, click to the right of the triangle to select the spot for the recipient's address, and click the Address block... text in the task pane.

The Insert Address Block dialog box appears (**Figure 4.69**).

12. Select a format for displaying the person's name. Click the arrows above the preview area to ensure that the names and addresses are displayed correctly. Click OK.

The Address Block merge field is inserted into the letter (**Figure 4.70**).

13. Click to set the text insertion mark where the greeting line ("Dear ...") will appear. Click the Greeting line... text in the task pane.

The Insert Greeting Line dialog box appears (**Figure 4.71**).

14. Select options from the drop-down lists to format the greeting line. Click the arrows above the preview area to see how the greeting line looks when filled with your data. Click OK to continue.

continues on next page

MERGE FORMATTING

15. Now you'll add a placeholder for the donation amount. In the first line of the letter, set the text insertion mark after "...contribution of..." and click More items... in the task pane.

The Insert Merge Field dialog box appears (**Figure 4.72**).

16. Select the Donation field, and click Insert.

The Donation merge field is inserted into the letter.

17. Close the dialog box by clicking Close.

18. The Donation merge field must be preceded by and followed by a space. If either space is missing, add it.

19. Type a dollar sign ($) immediately to the left of the merge field (**Figure 4.73**).

When the merge procedure extracts your Excel data, the dollar sign will be ignored. But you can add it to the document.

20. At the bottom of the task pane, click Next: Preview your letters.

Step 5 of 6 appears, displaying a merge letter (**Figure 4.74**).

Figure 4.72 Select a merge field to add at the text insertion mark.

Donation merge field

Figure 4.73 Add a $ immediately before the Donation merge field.

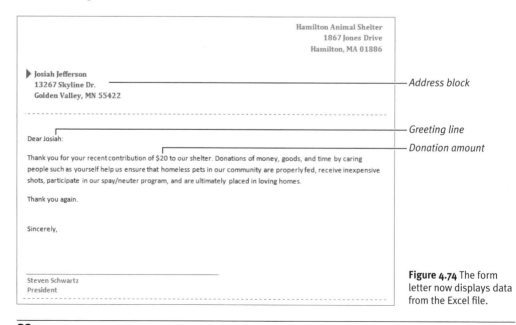

Figure 4.74 The form letter now displays data from the Excel file.

MERGE FORMATTING

Figure 4.75 You can merge directly to a printer or to a new document.

Figure 4.76 In a merge involving a large number of records, error reporting can be helpful.

■ You can format merge fields. Be sure to select the entire field, including the surrounding bracket characters.

21. Click the arrow buttons to examine the letters for other recipients. If you see a person whom you don't want to include in the merge, click Exclude this recipient.

22. At the bottom of the task pane, click Next: Complete the merge.

Step 6 of 6 appears (**Figure 4.75**).

23. *Do either of the following:*

▲ Click Print… to merge directly to a connected printer. A separate letter will be printed for each recipient.

▲ Click Edit individual letters… to generate a new document as the merge output.

✔ Tips

■ As indicated in Step 1 of the wizard (see Figure 4.65), you can use a merge to produce mailing labels and envelopes. And if your email account provides Messaging Application Programming Interface (*MAPI*) support (common in corporate environments), you can merge to email.

■ In the final task pane (see Figure 4.75), the option to Edit individual letters serves several important needs. First, it allows you to individually edit—or delete—the letters. Second, because this option generates an ordinary Word document, you can save the file on disk as documentation of the mailing. Finally, after scanning the letters and making any necessary edits, printing this document is the same as choosing the Print… option. A letter is produced for each recipient.

■ In the final step, you can further control the output by clicking icons on the Mailing tab. In particular, if you click Auto Check for Errors in the Preview Results group, additional options are presented in a dialog box (**Figure 4.76**).

MERGE FORMATTING

83

CREATING OUTLINES

If you remember high school or college, you should also remember *outlines* (lists of key points organized into headings and sub-headings). To demonstrate that you had a thoroughly thought-out plan, teachers often required you to create an outline before starting a paper or report.

Even after you've left school, you may find that writing an outline is an excellent way to get organized. Whether you're about to write an important report, preparing to give a presentation or lecture, or planning a complicated home renovation, you can create an outline to ensure you've hit the important points or steps in the proper order.

Although dedicated outlining applications may be easier to use or have more features, many users will find Word's Outline View sufficient for handling basic outlining tasks.

About Outline View

As far as Word is concerned, a document is a document. Nothing distinguishes an outline from any other Word document. Outline is merely a *view* you can work in—just like Print Layout View. The only real difference is that Outline View provides special tools for working with outlines.

Figure 5.1 Click Outline to switch to Outline View.

To work in Outline View:

1. Click the View tab on the Ribbon.

2. Click the Outline icon in the Document Views group (**Figure 5.1**).

   The current document is displayed in Outline View (**Figure 5.2**). The Outlining tab appears and is automatically selected.

✔ Tips

- Outline View isn't only for outlines. Because Outline View has some unique tools, such as the ability to collapse sections and easily reorganize paragraphs, it's sometimes helpful to use this view to polish a normal document.

- While working in Outline View, you can freely switch tabs to apply formatting, insert objects and WordArt, change layout settings, and the like.

- To exit from Outline View, click the Close Outline View icon on the Outlining tab of the Ribbon.

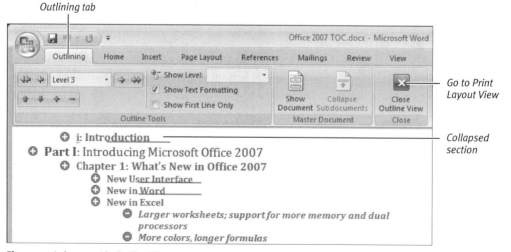

Figure 5.2 A document in Outline View.

Level 1 point   Level 2 point

Figure 5.3 The level of each point is indicated by its indentation and (typically) its formatting. Each paragraph is considered a separate point.

Promote to Level 1   Demote to Body Text

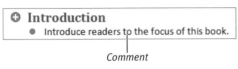

Promote   Outline Level menu   Demote

Figure 5.4 To set or change a point's level, use these tools.

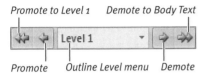

Comment

Figure 5.5 A comment is preceded by a solid bullet symbol, rather than a plus (+) or minus (-).

Starting an Outline

A Word outline consists of outline points and, optionally, comments. Each point is assigned a *level* (**Figure 5.3**); the higher the level, the more important the point. For example, the outline for this book consists of parts, chapters, main headings, and secondary headings, assigned Levels 1, 2, 3, and 4.

To create an outline:

1. In a new document, click the View tab. Click the Outline icon in the Document Views group (see Figure 5.1).

   A plus (+) symbol appears, ready for you to enter the first point.

2. Type the first point, and press (Enter). The cursor moves to the new line.

3. *Do one of the following:*

   ▲ To treat this point as Level 1, enter the text for the point and press (Enter).

   ▲ Use the tools in the Outline Tools group (**Figure 5.4**) to demote this to a Level 2 point by choosing Level 2 from the Outline Level drop-down menu, clicking the Demote icon, or pressing (Alt)(Shift)(→).

   ▲ To treat the new text as a *comment* (**Figure 5.5**) rather than a point, choose Body Text from the Outline Level drop-down menu or click the Demote to Body Text icon.

4. Continue entering outline points. By default, when you press (Enter) to create a new point, the level of the point matches that of the one immediately above it.

✔ Tip

■ You can *promote* a point by choosing a higher level from the Outline Level drop-down menu, clicking Promote to Level 1, or clicking Promote (or pressing (Alt)(Shift)(←)) to raise the level by one.

STARTING AN OUTLINE

Reorganizing an Outline

Creating an outline generally involves a certain amount of reorganizing: changing point levels, adding and deleting points, and moving points and sections to new places. Other than when you're adding a new point, the first step is always to select the point or points you want to manipulate.

To select outline points:

◆ *Do one of the following:*

▲ **Single point or comment.** Click to the left of the point or comment.

▲ **Point and its subordinate points.** Double-click to the left of the main point (**Figure 5.6**).

▲ **Contiguous series of points.** Click to the left of the first point and drag down.

▲ **Noncontiguous series of points.** Ctrl-click to the left of each point.

✔ Tip

■ Selecting a collapsed point also selects its subordinate points.

To add a new point:

1. Click at the end of the point immediately before where you want to insert the new point, and then press Enter.

   A line for a new point appears (**Figure 5.7**), set to the same level as the point above it.

2. *Optional:* You can change the new point's level by using a tool in the Outline Tools group (see Figure 5.4).

To delete one or more points:

◆ Select the point or points, and press Del, Delete, or Backspace.

✔ Tip

■ Deleting a collapsed point also deletes its subordinate points.

Figure 5.6 Double-click to the left of a point to select the point and its subordinate points, if any.

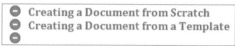

Figure 5.7 To make room for a new point, I clicked to the right of "Template" and pressed Enter.

Level Formatting

If you don't care for the fonts, color, or other aspects of the default level formatting applied to your outline, you're free to change it:

◆ *To change the formatting of selected words or entire points,* use normal formatting techniques: Set options on the Home tab, use the Mini toolbar, or select text and then right-click it.

◆ *To change the formatting for a level throughout the outline,* format a single point for that level, right-click it, and then choose Styles > Update Heading *number* to Match Selection. (The style names for Levels 1–6 are Heading 1–6; comments use the Normal style.)

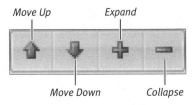

Figure 5.8 Click a Move icon to move the selected point(s) one line at a time.

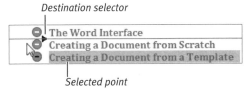

Figure 5.9 You can drag selected points up or down in the outline.

Figure 5.10 You can promote or demote selected points by dragging to the left or right.

To move points up or down:

◆ *Do one of the following:*

▲ Click the Move Up or Move Down icon in the Outline Tools group (**Figure 5.8**). Each click moves the selected point(s) up or down one line.

▲ Cut the selected point(s) by pressing Ctrl X, click to set the text insertion mark where you want to insert the point(s), and then paste by pressing Ctrl V.

▲ Click the expand/collapse icon that precedes the point or group of points you want to move, and then drag up or down to the destination (**Figure 5.9**). When you release the mouse button, the dragged point(s) are moved to the new location.

To promote or demote points:

◆ *Do one of the following:*

▲ Use the tools in the Outline Tools group (see Figure 5.4) to promote or demote the selected point(s).

▲ Drag the expand/collapse icon of a point (and its subordinates, if any) to the left or right (**Figure 5.10**). Release the mouse button to set the new level.

✔ Tip

■ When moving, promoting, or demoting points, mistakes are commonplace. To correct a move that goes awry, click the Undo icon in the Quick Access Toolbar or press Ctrl Z. To undo *multiple* actions, click the down arrow beside the Undo icon and choose the last action you want to correct. The selected action and all the actions above it in the drop-down list are undone.

REORGANIZING AN OUTLINE

Changing Display Settings

Word provides viewing features and tools (**Figure 5.11**) to make it easier to work with outlines. You can collapse sections to focus on the rest of the outline, hide less-significant levels so only important details are visible, and remove level formatting to make it simpler to read the outline.

To change display settings:

◆ *Do any of the following:*

▲ **Collapse sections.** To collapse a section, double-click the symbol (+ or −) that precedes the section's main point. Or with the section's main point selected, click the Collapse icon in the Outline Tools group (see Figure 5.8) or press Alt Shift −. The section and all of its subordinate sections and points collapse (**Figure 5.12**).

▲ **Expand sections.** To expand a collapsed section, double-click the symbol (+ or −) that precedes the section's main point. Or with the section's main point selected, click the Expand icon in the Outline Tools group (see Figure 5.8) or press Alt Shift +. The section and its subordinate sections expand.

▲ **Show Level.** To focus on higher-level points, you can choose a level number from the Show Level drop-down menu (**Figure 5.13**). Only points at that level or higher are then displayed; lower-level points are collapsed. To restore the entire outline, choose All Levels from the drop-down menu.

▲ **Hide formatting.** Remove the check mark from Show Text Formatting to display the entire outline in a single font, size, and style.

▲ **Show First Line Only.** Click this check box to hide additional lines of text beyond the first for each outline point.

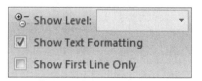

Figure 5.11 View options are set in this section of the Option Tools group.

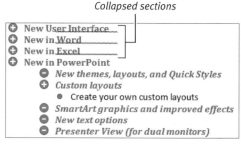

Figure 5.12 Collapsed sections are denoted by a squiggly underline. To expand collapsed points, double-click the symbol beside their section heading.

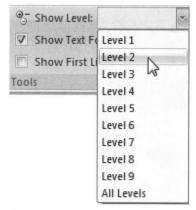

Figure 5.13 Choose the lowest level to display from this drop-down menu.

✔ Tip

■ To print an outline, click the Office Button and choose Print > Print. Note that collapsed points won't print. If Show Text Formatting isn't checked, the output will be in a single font.

Tables, Charts, and Art

6

Although many documents consist solely of page after page of text, you don't *have* to use Word like a typewriter. Any Word document can also contain tables, charts, images, and special Office objects, such as WordArt and SmartArt.

In this chapter, you'll learn how to insert these items into your documents, embellish art by adding color, 3-D effects, and rotation, and set text wrap to enable surrounding text to form around these items.

Inserting Tables

The old way to add a table to a document mimicked using a typewriter. Using tab stops, text and data were carefully aligned in columns. Word avoids this rigmarole by allowing you to place a spreadsheet-style row-and-column table wherever you like.

As shown in **Figure 6.1**, you can insert or create a table in any of the following ways:

◆ Specify the number of rows and columns (visually or by entering numbers in a dialog box).

◆ Manually draw the table grid.

◆ Convert existing text into a table.

◆ Import part of an Excel spreadsheet.

◆ Select a Quick Table template and replace its data with your own.

To insert a table:

1. Set the insertion mark at the spot in the document where you want to insert the table.

2. On the Ribbon's Insert tab, click the Table icon to reveal the drop-down menu (see Figure 6.1).

3. *Do one of the following:*

  ▲ **Insert table by highlighting.** In the top section of the drop-down menu, highlight squares to specify the table's dimensions, such as 4 x 5. To place the table, click the lower-right square of the highlighted selection.

  ▲ **Insert table via dialog box.** Choose Insert Table. In the Insert Table dialog box (**Figure 6.2**), specify the number of rows and columns, select an AutoFit behavior, and click OK.

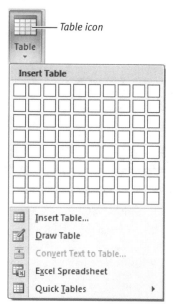

Figure 6.1 Click the Table icon, and choose a table insertion method.

Figure 6.2 For additional precision when creating a table, use the Insert Table command.

Open the Borders and Shading dialog box

Figure 6.3 These tools are available to you when drawing a table.

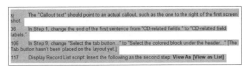

Figure 6.4 Select the text to convert into a table. (For Word to determine how to arrange the text, it should normally be delimited with Returns, tabs, or commas.)

Figure 6.5 Set conversion options, and click OK to create the table.

Figure 6.6 If you need the full capabilities of Excel to manipulate your data, you can embed a worksheet in your document.

▲ **Create table by drawing.** Choose Draw Table. Use the pencil tool to draw the table's line segments. Other Table Tools (**Figure 6.3**) can be used to remove lines (Eraser), change the line width or color, add or remove cell borders, and apply cell shading.

▲ **Convert existing text into a table.** Select the text to convert (**Figure 6.4**), and choose Convert Text to Table. In the Convert Text to Table dialog box (**Figure 6.5**), verify the number of columns and rows, select an AutoFit behavior, ensure that the correct text separator is specified, and click OK.

▲ **Insert a worksheet.** Choose Excel Spreadsheet to embed a worksheet in the current document. Use Excel procedures to enter data, create formulas, and format cells (**Figure 6.6**).

▲ **Insert a Quick Table.** Choose a table from the Quick Tables submenu to insert a fully formatted table into the document. Replace the sample titles and data with your own information.

✔ Tips

■ When using the Insert Table dialog box, the default behavior is to create fixed-width columns. If you select AutoFit to contents, each column will automatically expand as needed to fully display the longest text string in the column.

■ If you switch to a cell-formatting tool (Shading or Borders) while drawing a table, you are taken out of drawing mode. To resume drawing, click the Draw Table icon.

■ You can use the Table Tools to modify *any* table. Click the Draw Table icon in the Draw Borders group (see Figure 6.3). Click the icon again when you're done modifying the table.

Entering Data into a Table

Unless you converted existing text into a table or inserted a Quick Table, you're now staring at an empty grid. Table cells can contain virtually anything that might be found on a Word document page, such as text, numeric data, images, and charts.

To enter data into a table:

1. Click in the first cell in which you want to enter data. (In most newly created tables, the top-left cell is automatically selected.)

2. *Do one of the following:*

   ▲ Type or paste text into the cell.

   If the cell is fixed width, text will wrap within the cell, as required. If an AutoFit option has been applied, the entire column will expand to fit the longest character string in the column.

   ▲ On the Insert tab, select an item from the Illustrations group to insert (**Figure 6.7**), such as a picture, clip art image, or shape.

   ▲ Paste a copied object (such as a photo) into the cell.

3. To enter additional data, *do any of the following:*

   ▲ Press Tab to move to the next cell or Shift Tab to move to the previous cell (**Figure 6.8**). Note that if you Tab out of the bottom-right cell, an additional row is automatically created.

   ▲ Click in the cell in which you want to enter data.

✔ Tip

■ Whenever you're working in a table, the Table Tools contextual tab appears at the top of the Ribbon, along with its Design and Layout tabs.

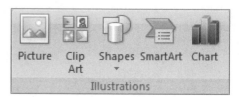

Figure 6.7 Other than pasting, you can insert images and objects by choosing an option from the Illustrations group on the Insert tab.

Figure 6.8 Tabbing from cell to cell (as indicated by the arrows) works as it does in a spreadsheet application, such as Excel.

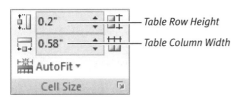

Table Row Height
Table Column Width

Figure 6.9 To precisely set row or column sizes, enter numbers in these boxes.

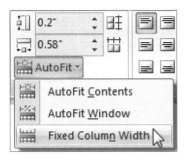

Figure 6.10 Choose an option from the AutoFit drop-down menu to set a table to fixed column widths or to AutoFit to match cell contents.

Modifying the Table Grid

Unless you plan *very* carefully when initially creating a table, you'll usually find that the table grid requires some modification to fit the data, such as changing the size of the entire table, setting new row heights or column widths, coloring or changing line widths, and coloring individual cells or the entire table.

To change the size of table elements:

◆ *Do any of the following:*

 ▲ To change the table size, move the cursor over the table's lower-right corner, and click and drag. To resize proportionately, hold down (Shift) as you drag.

 ▲ To manually change a column width, move the cursor over the column's right edge until it turns into a double arrow. Drag to the left or right to resize the column.

 ▲ To manually change a row height, move the cursor over the row's bottom edge until it turns into a double arrow. Drag up or down to resize the row.

 ▲ To precisely set column widths or row heights, select the columns or rows, and click the Layout tab. Then enter a number (in inches) into the Table Row Height or the Table Column Width box in the Cell Size group (**Figure 6.9**).

 ▲ To change a table from AutoFit to fixed-width columns (or vice versa), click the Layout tab, and choose an option from the AutoFit drop-down menu in the Cell Size group (**Figure 6.10**).

MODIFYING THE TABLE GRID

To remove or add rows or columns:

◆ *Do any of the following:*

   ▲ To delete rows or columns, click the Layout tab, select the rows or columns, and choose an option from the Delete drop-down menu in the Rows & Columns group (**Figure 6.11**).

   ▲ To insert rows or columns, select the cell above or below which you want to insert rows or to the right or left of which you want to insert columns. Click an Insert icon (Insert Below, Left, or Right) in the Rows & Columns group (see Figure 6.11). To insert more rows or columns, click the icon once for each additional row or column.

To merge or split cells:

1. Make the table active, and then click the Layout tab in the Ribbon.

2. *Do one of the following:*

   ▲ To merge cells into a single cell (to create a title row, for example), select the cells and click the Merge Cells icon in the Merge group (**Figure 6.12**).

   ▲ To reverse a merge or split a single cell into multiple cells, select the cell, click the Split Cells icon, and set options in the Split Cells dialog box (**Figure 6.13**).

   ▲ To divide a table into two tables, select a cell and click the Split Table icon. The rows above the selected cell become the first table; the selected row and the rows beneath it become the second table.

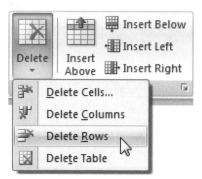

Figure 6.11 Delete selected rows, columns, or an entire table by making a choice from the Delete drop-down menu.

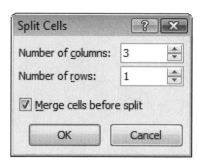

Figure 6.12 Click an icon in the Merge group to merge selected cells, split one cell into several, or split a table into two tables.

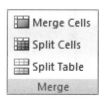

Figure 6.13 You can split a cell into multiple cells.

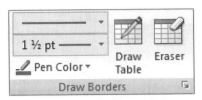

Figure 6.14 Set line properties by choosing options in the Draw Borders group.

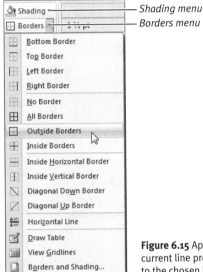

— *Shading menu*
— *Borders menu*

Figure 6.15 Apply the current line properties to the chosen borders.

✔ Tips

■ For help selecting table elements, you can choose commands from the Select icon in the Table group of the Layout tab.

■ The Cell Size, Rows & Columns, and Draw Borders groups each offer a dialog box you can use to modify multiple elements at the same time.

■ You don't have to select *entire* rows or columns. Just select enough cells so Word knows what to do. For instance, when modifying one row or column, you can click in a single cell in that row or column. To modify two columns, you can drag-select across two adjacent cells.

To change line properties:

1. To modify one or more lines (*borders*) of one or more table cells, begin by selecting the cells.

2. In the Draw Borders group on the Design tab, choose a line style, width, and pen color to apply to the selected cell borders (**Figure 6.14**).

3. Open the Borders drop-down menu (**Figure 6.15**) in the Table Styles group and choose the border or borders to affect. The chosen line style, width, and color are applied to the specified borders.

4. If desired, repeat Step 3 to apply the current line properties to other borders of the selected cells.

To apply cell shading:

1. Select the cells to which you want to apply a background color.

2. Open the Shading menu (see Figure 6.15) in the Table Styles group. The Shading menu provides a live preview of any color over which the cursor is hovered. Click to choose a color.

To apply a table style to a table:

1. Make the table active by clicking in a cell.

2. On the Design tab, select a Table Style. If the desired style isn't shown, click the down arrow to the right of the visible styles to reveal the entire list. Click a style to apply it to the table.
   Note that a live preview is shown for any style over which the cursor is hovered.

3. *Optional:* Check options in the Table Style Options group to modify the chosen table style, such as formatting a bottom row differently because it contains totals.

MODIFYING THE TABLE GRID

Formatting Table Data

Like other text in a Word document, you can apply character and paragraph formatting to cell contents.

To apply formatting to cells:

1. Select the words, sentences, or cells to which the formatting will be applied.

2. To apply paragraph formatting to the selection, *do any of the following:*

    ▲ In the Alignment group (**Figure 6.16**) of the Layout tab, click an icon to set the paragraph alignment.

    ▲ In the Paragraph group (**Figure 6.17**) of the Home tab, you can click icons to set alignment, decrease or increase the indent, change line spacing, or apply a bullet, number, or multilevel list format.

    ▲ In the Styles group of the Home tab, you can apply a defined style to the selected text.

    ▲ Move the cursor up or right-click the selected text to reveal the Mini toolbar (**Figure 6.18**). By clicking icons on the toolbar, you can center-align paragraphs, decrease or increase the indent, or apply a bullet format.

3. To apply character formatting to the selection, *do any of the following:*

    ▲ In the Font group (**Figure 6.19**) of the Home tab, you can change the font, size, style, color, and highlighting of the selected text.

    ▲ In the Styles group of the Home tab, you can apply a defined style to the selected text.

    ▲ Move the cursor up or right-click the selected text to reveal the Mini toolbar. Apply formatting changes by selecting from the options provided.

Figure 6.16 Select an alignment by clicking an icon in the Alignment group.

Figure 6.17 In addition to setting the alignment, you can apply bullet and number formats by clicking icons in the Paragraph group.

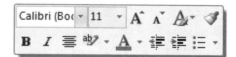

Figure 6.18 The Mini toolbar.

Figure 6.19 Use the controls in the Font group to apply character formatting to selected text.

✔ Tips

■ If a cell contains several paragraphs, each one can have a different paragraph format.

■ You can also use keyboard shortcuts to apply character and paragraph formatting.

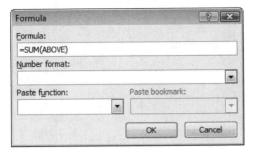

Figure 6.20 Create the formula in this dialog box.

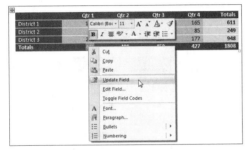

Figure 6.21 To recalculate a formula, right-click the formula cell and choose Update Field.

Calculations in Tables

Word allows you to include simple row- or column-based formulas in tables to compute sums and averages, for example. You can also sort an entire table or individual columns numerically or alphabetically.

To enter a formula in a cell:

1. Click in the cell that will contain the formula.

   Generally, the cell will be in the bottom row or the right-most column.

2. On the Layout tab, click the Formula icon in the Data group.

   The Formula dialog box appears (**Figure 6.20**).

3. Type an Excel-style formula in this form:

   =*function*(LEFT/RIGHT/ABOVE/BELOW)

   The word in parentheses determines the cells that are included in the calculation. For example, to total the cells above the current cell, you'd use =SUM(ABOVE).

4. *Optional:* Select a format for the result from the Number format drop-down list.

5. Click OK.

   The calculation is performed and the results are displayed.

✔ Tips

- When performing complex calculations, it's better to insert an Excel worksheet than to create formulas in a standard table.

- To copy a supported function into the Formula box, select the function name from the Paste function drop-down list.

- If the data on which a formula is based changes, the result does not automatically update. To force a recalculation, right-click the formula cell and choose Update Field (**Figure 6.21**).

To sort a table:

1. Select the table you want to sort.

2. In the Data group on the Layout tab, click the Sort icon.

    The Sort dialog box appears (**Figure 6.22**).

3. Select a sort field from the Sort by drop-down list, a data Type (Text, Number, or Date), and a sort order (Ascending or Descending).

4. *Optional:* To sort by more columns, repeat Step 3 for additional Then by sections.

5. For My list has, click a radio button to indicate whether the table has a *header row* (a row of column labels).

6. Click OK to perform the sort (**Figure 6.23**).

✔ Tip

■ Sorting a Word table works the same as sorting a range in Excel. As shown in Figure 6.23, information in each table row is treated as a *record*. When you specify a column by which to sort, data in other columns of each record remains associated with the data in the Sort by column.

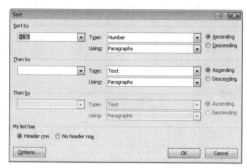

Figure 6.22 Set options in the Sort dialog box, and then click OK.

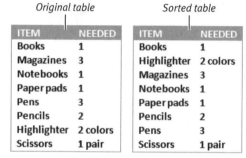

Figure 6.23 To sort this table alphabetically by the first column, the options set were Sort by: ITEM column, Type: Text, Ascending, Header row.

CALCULATIONS IN TABLES

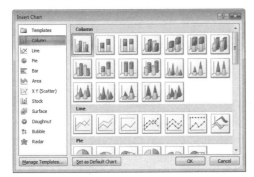

Figure 6.24 Select a chart type from the left column, select a style icon, and click OK.

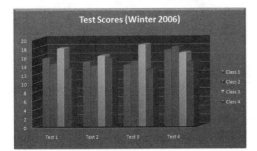

Figure 6.25 In the Excel worksheet that appears, replace the sample chart data with your own data.

Test Scores (Winter 2006)

Figure 6.26 You can change any element in the initial chart, such as adding a title, selecting new fonts, and picking a flashier background.

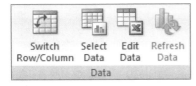

Figure 6.27 The Data group.

Creating Charts

Excel's charting tools also enable you to create charts in PowerPoint and Word. The chart is embedded in your document, and its data is automatically stored in an Excel worksheet.

To create a chart in Word:

1. On the Insert tab, click the Chart icon in the Illustrations group.

   The Insert Chart dialog box appears (**Figure 6.24**).

2. Select the type of chart you want to create, and click OK.

   An Excel worksheet appears, containing sample data.

3. Type or paste to replace the sample data with your data and labels (**Figure 6.25**).

   The chart is constructed as you enter your data.

4. If your data's range doesn't match the sample's range, drag the bounding box's lower-right corner so the range matches that of your data.

   In some cases, Excel will automatically adjust the bounding box for you.

5. *Optional*: Embellish and modify the chart by choosing options from the Design, Layout, and Format tabs (**Figure 6.26**).

✔ Tips

- For more information on creating and modifying charts, see Chapter 12.

- You can copy a chart in an Excel worksheet and paste it into Word. Click the Paste Options icon to indicate whether the chart will be linked to the data or be treated as an embedded picture.

- The Data group on the Design tab has commands for swapping axes, selecting other data, and editing (**Figure 6.27**).

About Adding Graphics and Objects

By clicking icons on the Insert tab (**Figure 6.28**), you can add many common types of images and objects to your Word documents. Word also has features that help you create your own graphics, such as WordArt, SmartArt, and common shapes.

An image can be placed *inline* with text or as a floating *object* that text wraps around. Images can be loaded from disk, copied from open documents in other programs, or dragged directly into your document from an open document in certain programs.

Word also provides tools for modifying and embellishing graphics. For instance, you can do the following:

◆ Crop an image, removing unwanted parts

◆ Change an image's brightness or contrast

◆ Recolor a picture by adding a color cast

◆ Add a border in any combination of color, line width, and line style

◆ Apply special effects, such as bevel, glow, 3-D rotation, and shadow (**Figure 6.29**)

◆ Set text-wrap instructions for the image

✔ Tip

■ In Internet Explorer, if an image is also a clickable link and you attempt to place it in your document via drag-and-drop, the link appears in the document rather than the image. You *can*, however, use copy-and-paste to add such an image to a document.

Figure 6.28 You can click icons in the Illustrations and Text groups to add images and objects to a document.

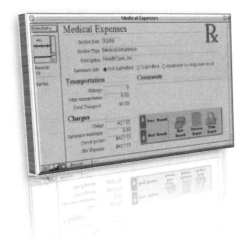

Figure 6.29 Using the Picture tools, you can convert any image into impressive artwork.

Figure 6.30 Select a picture, and then click Insert.

Figure 6.31 The image appears in the document.

Figure 6.32 Click the arrow beside the Insert button to specify file linking or embedding.

Adding Pictures

You can insert almost any photo or drawing from your hard disk into a Word document.

To insert a picture:

1. On the Insert tab, click the Picture icon in the Illustrations group.

   The Insert Picture dialog box appears (**Figure 6.30**).

2. Navigate to the drive and folder that contain the picture. Select the picture, and click the Insert button.

   The picture appears in the document (**Figure 6.31**).

✔ Tips

- You can click and drag a handle on any corner or edge of a placed picture to change its size. Drag a corner handle to proportionately resize the image.

- The Insert button also has a drop-down menu (**Figure 6.32**). Your menu choice determines whether a *copy* of the image is embedded in the document (Insert) or the image is merely *linked* to the file (Link to File) on your hard disk. Use Insert when a document will be shared with others. Use Link to keep a document's file size small.

- You can also insert a picture via *copy-and-paste*. Open the picture or the document in which it's embedded, select the picture, and choose Edit > Copy (Ctrl C). Switch to your Word document, position the text insertion mark, and choose Edit > Paste (Ctrl V).

- You can add a descriptive *figure caption* to a photo or picture by right-clicking the image and choosing Insert Caption from the pop-up menu that appears.

Adding Clip Art

Clip art images are simple drawings and photos (sans background) that you can use to embellish flyers, memos, brochures, party invitations, and the like. Office 2007 includes a healthy selection of clip art, supplemented by additional downloadable online images.

To insert clip art:

1. On the Insert tab, click the Clip Art icon in the Illustrations group.

   The Clip Art panel appears (**Figure 6.33**).

2. Click the down arrow beside the Search in box and specify where to search.

   Click the Everywhere check box at the top of the drop-down list to search all Office, personal, and Office Online collections. Otherwise, click the check boxes of the specific collections to search.

3. Click the down arrow beside the Results should be box and specify the acceptable type(s) of media.

4. Type a search string in the Search for box, and click Go.

   Icons for matching media appear in the results area of the Clip Art panel.

5. To insert a found image into the document, *do one of the following:*

   ▲ Double-click the image icon.

   ▲ Click the icon and drag the image onto the document.

   ▲ Select the icon, click the down arrow that appears beside the icon, and choose Insert from the drop-down menu (**Figure 6.34**).

✔ Tip

■ To learn more about an item (such as its size or file type), choose Preview/Properties from the icon's drop-down menu (see Figure 6.34).

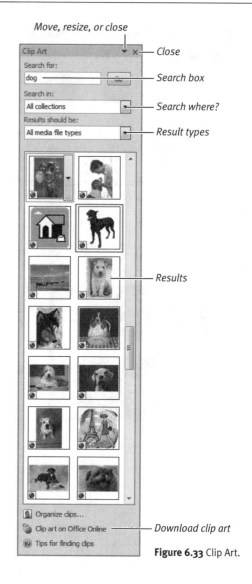

Move, resize, or close — *Close*

Search box

Search where?

Result types

Results

Download clip art

Figure 6.33 Clip Art.

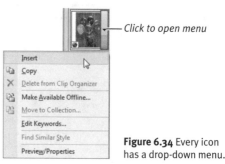

Click to open menu

Figure 6.34 Every icon has a drop-down menu.

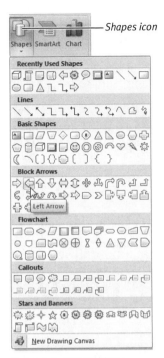

Shapes icon

Figure 6.35 Select a shape.

Figure 6.36 You can create a cartoon balloon, apply a color or gradient fill, and then enter and format text.

✔ Tip

- Text can be added to most shapes. Some require only that you click in them and type. Right-click other shapes, and choose Add Text from the pop-up menu that appears. You can apply standard character and paragraph formatting to the text.

Adding Shapes

Word includes a variety of predefined shapes (such as cubes, arrows, cartoon balloons, and flowchart elements) that you can insert into documents. A shape can optionally be assigned a color, a shadow, and 3-D effects. You can also insert text into shapes.

To insert a shape:

1. On the Insert tab, click the Shapes icon in the Illustrations group and select a shape (**Figure 6.35**).

   A plus (+) drawing cursor appears.

2. Click and drag in the document to create the shape.

   To draw a uniform shape (a circle or square rather than an ellipse or rectangle, for example), press (Shift) as you draw.

3. Release the mouse button to complete the shape.

4. *Optional:* Apply color (**Figure 6.36**) to the selected shape by doing the following:

   ▲ **Apply a Quick Style.** On the Format tab, choose a style from the Text Box Styles or Shape Styles group. (The particular Style group displayed depends upon the shape type.)

   ▲ **Apply a solid, gradient, picture, or pattern fill.** On the Format tab, click the Shape Fill icon in the Text Box Styles or Shape Styles group. Choose an option from the drop-down menu.

   ▲ **Apply a complex style.** Click the Advanced Tools icon in the lower-right corner of the Text Box Styles or Shape Styles group bar. The Format AutoShape dialog box appears, enabling you to set color, line, size, and text-wrap options for the shape.

5. *Optional:* Change the size or rotation of the shape by dragging its handles.

Using a Drawing Canvas

If a drawing will require multiple shapes, you may find it easier to work in a special area called a *drawing canvas*.

To create and use a drawing canvas:

1. Each drawing canvas is created as an inline graphic. Position the text insertion mark where you want the drawing canvas to appear.

2. On the Insert tab, click the Shapes icon in the Illustrations group, and choose New Drawing Canvas from the menu.

   A drawing canvas appears (**Figure 6.37**).

3. When working on a drawing canvas, use the tools on the Format tab to insert and modify shapes. Use the commands in the Arrange group (**Figure 6.38**) to group objects, align objects with one another, and set layering.

✔ Tips

- You can create as many drawing canvases as you need.

- To resize a drawing canvas, drag any black side or corner handle (see Figure 6.37).

- A drawing canvas is also an object. By clicking icons on the Format tab, you can specify a text wrap for a drawing canvas, fill it with color or a gradient, add a shadow, or apply 3-D effects.

- When you're done drawing, you can resize the canvas to fit tightly around the drawn shapes (**Figure 6.39**). Right-click the drawing canvas, and choose Fit from the drop-down menu.

- You can drag elements off the drawing canvas into other areas of the document.

- To delete a drawing canvas, right-click it and choose Cut from the pop-up menu.

Figure 6.37 A new drawing canvas.

Corner handle

Edge handle

Corner handle

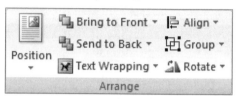

Figure 6.38 Commands in the Arrange group are useful for arranging and grouping drawing elements.

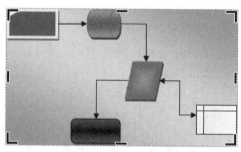

Figure 6.39 Apply the Fit command to resize a drawing canvas to the smallest possible size that encloses all elements.

The Little Yellow Dot

When you select an inserted shape, you may see a tiny yellow dot around the outside or within the shape. You can click and drag the dot to modify a property of the shape. For example, when you drag this dot in the cartoon balloon shown in Figure 6.36, you can change the direction and length of the balloon's handle.

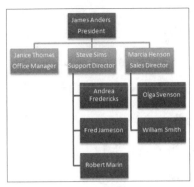

Figure 6.40 This organizational chart was quickly created using a hierarchy SmartArt graphic.

Categories   *Preview*

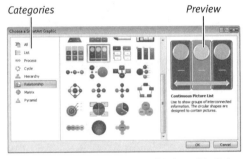

Figure 6.41 Select a SmartArt graphic from this dialog box, and click OK to insert it into the document.

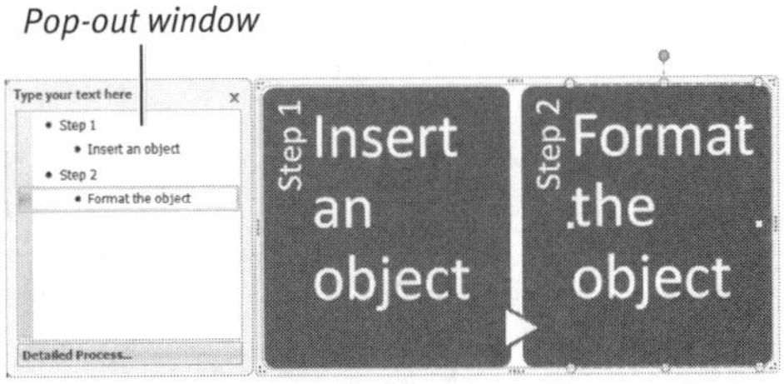

Pop-out window

Figure 6.42 It may be easier to type text into the pop-out window than to enter it directly into the elements.

■ To delete an unneeded element, select it and press ⌐Del⌐. To create more elements, select an element at the same level in the pop-out window and press ⌐Enter⌐.

Adding SmartArt

A *SmartArt* object is a ready-made combination of shapes and text. You can use SmartArt to create bullet lists and organizational charts (**Figure 6.40**), show processes, and illustrate relationships.

To insert SmartArt:

1. On the Insert tab, click the SmartArt icon in the Illustrations group.

    The Choose a SmartArt Graphic dialog box appears (**Figure 6.41**).

2. Select a graphic category from the list on the left side of the dialog box.

3. SmartArt graphics for the selected category are shown in the center of the dialog box. Click to select one.

    A preview and explanation for the selected graphic are presented on the right side of the dialog box.

4. To insert the selected SmartArt graphic into the document, click OK.

5. To replace text and picture placeholders with your own material, *do the following:*

    ▲ **Text.** Click a text placeholder and type. Or click the arrows on the left edge of the SmartArt graphic's border, and enter text in the pop-out window that appears (**Figure 6.42**).

    ▲ **Picture.** Double-click a picture placeholder. The Select Picture dialog box appears. Select an image on disk, and click Insert.

6. *Optional:* Format the elements, and resize the SmartArt object's bounding box.

✔ Tips

■ To format several objects the same way, select the objects (drag a selection rectangle around them or ⌐Ctrl⌐-click each one), and then apply the formatting.

Creating WordArt

WordArt is a decorative inline or floating text object, created by applying a special effect to text and then optionally stylizing it using object-formatting commands. Although WordArt is too flashy for most business and school documents, it's great for flyer, brochure, and party invitation headlines.

CREATING WORDART

To create WordArt:

1. *Optional:* Select text in the document that you want to convert into WordArt.

   WordArt can be created from existing text or specified in the Edit WordArt Text dialog box.

2. On the Insert tab, click the WordArt icon in the Text group, and select a WordArt style (**Figure 6.43**).

   The Edit WordArt Text dialog box appears (**Figure 6.44**).

3. If the text box contains a placeholder (Your Text Here), replace it with your own text.

4. Set font, size, and style options. Click OK.

   The text is converted to a WordArt object (**Figure 6.45**).

✔ Tips

- WordArt is created as inline text. To change it into a floating object, set a different text-wrap option for it. (On the Format tab, click the Text Wrapping icon in the Arrange group.)

- For a very interesting effect, try formatting WordArt with a picture background. On the Format tab in the WordArt Styles group, click the Shape Fill icon and choose Picture.

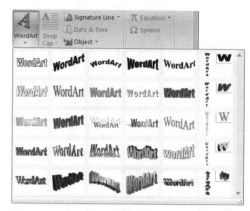

Figure 6.43 Select a style from the WordArt gallery.

Figure 6.44 Enter the text string (if it isn't already displayed). Select a font, size, and style, and click OK.

Figure 6.45 An example of WordArt.

> See a penny, pick it up, and all the day you'll have one cent.
> —*Steve Schwartz, 1963*

Figure 6.46 This is an example of a text box formatted with a gradient fill.

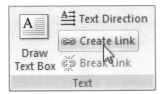

Figure 6.47 Click icons in the Text group to establish or break links and to draw additional text boxes.

Linking Text Boxes

You can also use text boxes to create complex documents (such as newsletters) that are normally tackled with a desktop publishing program. To facilitate this use, text boxes can be *linked* to allow text to automatically flow from one into the next:

1. Create the initial text box, and type or paste your text into it.

2. Create a second text box, but leave it empty. (You can only create a link to an empty text box.)

3. Select the first text box or set the text insertion mark inside of it.

4. On the Format tab, click the Create Link icon (**Figure 6.47**) in the Text group. Click the empty text box to establish the link.

Adding a Text Box

A *text box* is a rectangular object that contains text. Text boxes are commonly used to set off important snippets of text (such as the quote shown in **Figure 6.46**) from the main text. Magazines often use text boxes (without the surrounding border or background) to print blurbs that summarize and draw attention to the article in which they're embedded.

To create a text box:

1. On the Insert tab, click the Text Box icon in the Text group and choose Draw Text Box from the drop-down menu.

   A drawing cursor (+) appears.

2. Click and drag to draw the box.

   When you release the mouse button to complete the box, a text insertion mark appears inside the box.

3. Type or paste text into the box.

4. Format the text using commands on the Mini toolbar or the Home tab. If necessary, you can resize the box to fit the final text by dragging a side or corner handle.

5. *Optional:* Format the box using tools on the Format tab.

6. *Optional:* The initial text-wrap setting for a text box is In Front of Text. If you'd prefer that text wrap around the box, choose another option from the Text Wrapping drop-down menu (found in the Arrange group of the Format tab).

7. Drag the box into the desired position.

   To drag a text box, move the cursor over any edge until it becomes a plus symbol with arrowheads. You can then drag the box to a new location.

✔ Tip

■ To delete a text box, select it and press Del.

Setting Text Wrap

Whether you're placing photos, charts, clip art, WordArt, SmartArt, text boxes, or any other type of object on your document pages, each object must have a *text wrap* setting. This setting determines how surrounding text interacts with the object—whether it wraps around the object or enables the object to be placed under or on top of the text.

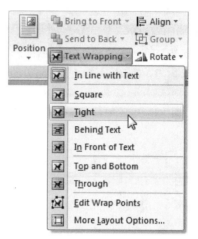

Figure 6.48 Choose a wrapping option from the drop-down menu.

To set text wrap for an object:

1. Select the object.

2. On the Format tab of the Arrange group, choose an option from the Text Wrapping drop-down menu (**Figure 6.48**).

3. *Do any of the following:*

   ▲ Drag the object into position.

   ▲ Choose a command from the Position drop-down menu in the Arrange group (**Figure 6.49**).

   The surrounding text wraps around the object as specified.

✔ Tips

- You also use the Text Wrapping drop-down menu (see Figure 6.48) to switch an object from inline to floating (and vice versa):

  ▲ To convert a floating object to an inline object, choose In Line with Text.

  ▲ To convert an inline object to a floating object, choose any command *other* than In Line with Text.

- You can add a watermark or stamp to a page, such as Confidential or Not for Distribution. Create a text box with large type (72 pt., for example), set the text color to a light gray, and then choose Behind Text as the Text Wrapping setting.

Figure 6.49 If the object must appear in a specific location on the page, choose it from the Position drop-down menu.

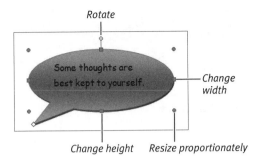

Rotate

Change width

Change height   Resize proportionately

Figure 6.50 Drag a handle to resize a selected object.

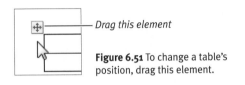

Drag this element

Figure 6.51 To change a table's position, drag this element.

About Layers

Any page of a Word document can consist of multiple layers. A page that contains only text or a single object, such as a chart, has a single layer. However, when you create or place *additional* objects on a page, each object can be either on the same layer as the other material or on its own layer—on top of or beneath other objects and text.

To change a selected object's layer, choose a command from the Bring to Front or Send to Back drop-down menu in the Arrange group on the Format tab. Ensure that In Line with Text is *not* the Text Wrapping setting (see previous page).

Resizing, Moving, and Rotating Objects

Using the handles that surround any selected object, you can manually resize, move, or rotate the object.

To change an object's size:

1. Select the object.

   Handles appear around the object (**Figure 6.50**).

2. *Do either of the following:*

   ▲ To change only an object's height or width, click and drag an edge handle. Resizing an object in this manner does *not* maintain the original proportions.

   ▲ To proportionately change both the object's height and width, click and drag a corner handle.

To move an object:

1. Select the object.

2. Move the cursor over the object until the cursor changes to a plus symbol with arrowheads:

   ▲ In drawn objects, photos, and clip art, click anywhere inside the object and drag.

   ▲ In a text box, drag any edge of the box.

   ▲ In a table, move the cursor over the upper-left corner and drag the element that appears (**Figure 6.51**).

3. Release the mouse button when the object is in the desired position.

To rotate an object:

1. Select the object.

   Handles appear around the object (see Figure 6.50).

2. To rotate the object, click the green ball, and drag to the left or right.

✔ Tips

- Some objects, such as tables, can't be rotated.

- You can also change the size or rotation of objects by specifying exact amounts:

  - ▲ **Size.** Type a number or click an arrow in the Shape Height or Shape Width box in the Size group on the Format tab (**Figure 6.52**).

  - ▲ **Rotation.** Click the Rotate icon in the Arrange group on the Format tab (**Figure 6.53**), and choose an option from the drop-down menu. To set a specific rotation angle, choose More Rotation Options.

- When entering dimensions into boxes in the Size group, resizing affects only the selected dimension or occurs proportionately, depending on a setting in the Format AutoShape dialog box. To open the dialog box, click the icon at the bottom of the Size group (see Figure 6.52). To specify a resizing behavior, add or remove the check mark from Lock aspect ratio (**Figure 6.54**), and click OK.

- If you've carefully placed several objects and now want to move them, it's easier if you *group* them first. Select all the objects, and choose Group from the Group drop-down menu (see Figure 6.53). To later separate the objects (enabling you to work with them individually again), choose Ungroup from the Group menu.

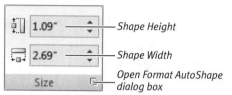

Figure 6.52 The Size group.

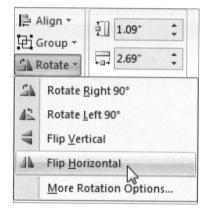

Figure 6.53 Choose a rotation option. The top four commands provide a live preview.

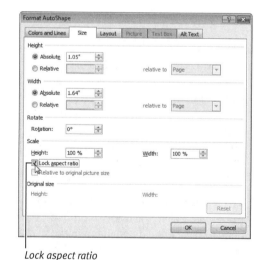

Figure 6.54 The behavior of the Size boxes is determined by the Lock aspect ratio setting.

RESIZING, MOVING, AND ROTATING OBJECTS

SHARING
WORD DOCUMENTS

7

Some documents are destined never to leave your hard disk. You might mail a printout of selected documents as letters, but the actual *files* are meant for your use only.

Other Word documents, however, are meant to make the rounds. You may intend to email them to a friend, share them on the company network, put them out for review by members of a workgroup, or post them for download on the Web. In this chapter, you'll learn about Word tools for sharing and protecting such documents.

Choosing a File Format

The most straightforward way to share Word documents is to provide the file—on disk, by email, or via a download link on your Web site. However, the decision concerning which *file format* to use (**Figure 7.1**) depends on the recipient's software and whether the document needs to be editable. Options include:

◆ **Word 2007 XML (.docx)**. These native Word 2007 files can be read and edited only by owners of Word 2007 or by people who have installed the converter software for Office 2000, XP, or 2003.

◆ **Word 97–2003 (.doc)**. This binary file format is the one used by Word 97–2003 documents. Recipients with any recent version of Word (including 2007) can read and edit .doc files.

◆ **Adobe Acrobat (.pdf)**. This is the most common format for the Web distribution of read-only documents that remain true to their original formatting. The files can be opened with Adobe Reader (free from www.adobe.com).

◆ **Rich Text Format (.rtf) and Plain Text (.txt)**. Rich Text Format is a good choice for files that must retain their formatting but can be opened by many word-processing applications or WordPad. Plain Text files can be read and edited by *all* word-processing programs and text editors, but all formatting is eliminated.

✔ Tip

■ See Chapter 1 for information about the free converter for Office 2000, XP, and 2003 (Microsoft Office Compatibility Pack for Word, Excel, and PowerPoint 2007 File Formats), as well as the Save As PDF or XPS add-in.

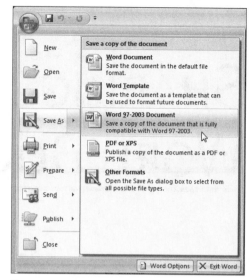

Figure 7.1 To save a copy of a Word document in a different format, click the Office Button and choose a format from the Save As submenu. (Choose Other Formats to save as Plain Text or Rich Text Format.)

Emailing a Document as the Message Body

In addition to emailing documents as attachments, you can send them as the *body* of a message. To do so, you must add a command to the Quick Access Toolbar:

1. Click the Office Button, followed by the Word Options button.

2. Click Customize in the Word Options dialog box.

3. Select All Commands from the Choose commands from drop-down list.

4. Select Sent to Mail Recipient, click the Add button, and then click OK.

To email any active Word document as the message body, click the new Send to Mail Recipient icon, enter recipients, and click the Send a Copy toolbar icon.

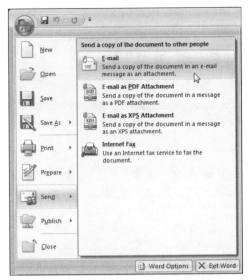

Figure 7.2 To email a document from within Word, click the Office Button and choose an option from the Send submenu.

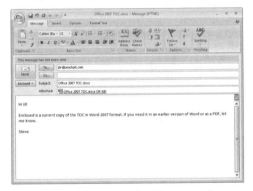

Figure 7.3 You can easily enclose the current document in an email message—without leaving Word.

✔ Tip

■ Like other file types, XPS files can only be opened by certain programs. One such program is Internet Explorer 7.

Emailing Word Documents

As explained in Chapter 19, *any* kind of document (including Word files) can be sent as an attachment to an email message. In addition to attaching the file within Outlook or another email client, you can attach Word documents to messages from within Word.

To send a Word file in or as a message:

1. In Word, open the document you want to send via email. Ensure that any recent changes have been saved.

2. *Optional:* To send the document as Word 97–2003, Rich Text Format, or Plain Text format, click the Office Button, choose Save As, and save a copy of the document in the desired format.

   The document in the new format becomes the active document.

3. Click the Office Button, and choose one of the following commands from the Send submenu (**Figure 7.2**):

   ▲ **E-mail.** A message window opens with the current document attached as a Word file (**Figure 7.3**). Enter recipients, type the message text, and click Send.

   ▲ **E-mail as PDF Attachment, E-mail as XPS Attachment.** A message window opens with the current document attached as an Adobe Acrobat (PDF) or XML Paper Specification (XPS) file. Enter recipients, type the message text, and click Send. (This option requires the Save As PDF or XPS add-in.)

   ▲ **Internet Fax.** The current document is transmitted as a fax using an Internet Fax service. If you don't already have a fax service provider, you can enroll with one after choosing this option.

   The document is transmitted via the chosen method.

Publishing Blog Entries

Another way to share written information is to publish it to a Web log (*blog*). Blog journals can be viewed in any Web browser. To create your own blog, you must register with a blog service provider, such as Blogger (`www.blogger.com`) or Windows Live Spaces (`http://spaces.msn.com`). Many providers host blogs without charge.

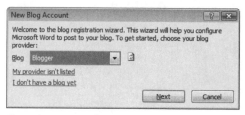

Figure 7.4 Select your blog service, and click Next.

To configure Word for blog work:

1. If you haven't registered with a blog service, do so before proceeding.

2. The first time you issue a blog-related command in Word, the Register a Blog Account dialog box appears. Click Register Now.

3. In the New Blog Account dialog box (**Figure 7.4**), select your blog service from the drop-down list, and click Next.

4. In the New *service* Account dialog box (**Figure 7.5**), enter the user name and password for your blog account. Click the Remember Password check box.

5. Click the Picture Options button.

   The Picture Options dialog box appears (**Figure 7.6**).

6. Select your blog service from the Picture provider drop-down list, and click OK.

   If your blog service isn't listed or your blog posts won't contain images, select None - Don't upload pictures.

7. Click OK to close the New *service* Account dialog box.

✔ Tip

■ If the Picture Options dialog box doesn't list your service, you may still be able to upload pictures to your blog. For instructions, see the service's Help pages.

Figure 7.5 To enable Word to transmit new blog posts to your account, enter your user name and password.

Figure 7.6 Select the blog's picture-hosting service from the drop-down list.

Entry title   Entry text

Figure 7.8 Type a title for the entry, and write the text.

Figure 7.9 Here's how the new blog entry (on the left) looks when viewed in a Web browser.

- To view your blog, click Home Page. To register a new blog account or change an existing one, click Manage Accounts.

- To edit a published blog entry, click Open Existing, select the entry you want to edit, and click OK. Make the changes, and then publish it as you did before.

- To delete a blog entry, use the tools provided by the blog service.

To create and publish a blog entry:

1. Click the Office Button, and choose New. The New Document window appears.

2. Select Blank and recent in the Templates list, select the New blog post icon, and click Create.

   A blog post template appears. The Ribbon tabs and icons (**Figure 7.7**, page bottom) provide the tools to write, format, and post your blog entry.

3. Create your new blog entry. Replace the title placeholder with a title for the entry, and type the entry text (**Figure 7.8**).

4. When you're satisfied with the entry, click the Publish icon and choose Publish from the drop-down menu that appears.

   The new entry is posted to your blog (**Figure 7.9**).

✔ Tips

- You can also publish an existing Word document as a blog entry, rather than starting from the template. Click the Office Button, and choose Publish > Blog. The placeholder for the entry title and the vertical rule (see Figure 7.7) appear above the current document's text. When you're satisfied with the entry, click the Publish icon and choose Publish from the drop-down menu that appears.

PUBLISHING BLOG ENTRIES

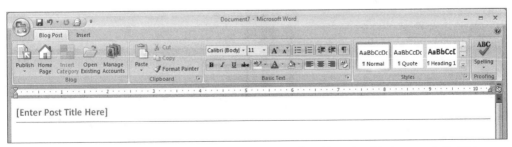

Figure 7.7 When creating a blog entry using the New blog post template, blog-related tools appear in the Ribbon.

Change Tracking

When multiple people will be working on, reviewing, or commenting on a document, you can use Word's *change tracking* features to simplify and coordinate the process.

When change tracking is enabled, you can see every modification made to a document: deletions, insertions, and formatting changes. If multiple people are editing the document, each person's changes are differentiated from everyone else's. During the writing and editing or at the tail end of the process, the document's author can finalize the document, accepting or rejecting each suggested change.

To enable/disable change tracking:

♦ *Do either of the following:*

▲ Click the Review tab, click the Track Changes icon in the Tracking group, and choose Track Changes.

▲ Press Ctrl Shift E.

When enabled, the Track Changes icon is colored orange (**Figure 7.10**).

To set tracking options:

1. Click the Review tab, click the Track Changes icon in the Tracking group, and choose Change Tracking Options.

   The Track Changes Options dialog box appears (**Figure 7.11**).

2. Make any desired changes, and click OK.

To set the view for change tracking:

1. On the Review tab, choose an option from the Display for Review drop-down menu (**Figure 7.12**).

   Original refers to the original document, prior to any edits. *Final* displays the document as if all changes have been accepted.

2. Click the Balloons icon, and choose a method for displaying revisions.

Track Changes enabled   Display for Review menu

Figure 7.10 Change tracking and its options are set in the Tracking group of the Review tab.

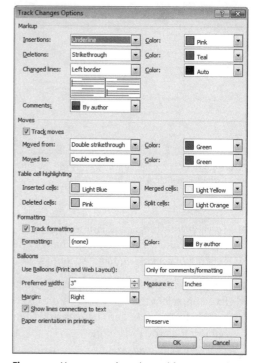

Figure 7.11 You can set the color and formatting of various edits in the Track Changes Options dialog box.

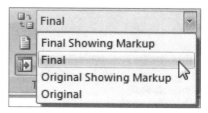

Figure 7.12 Choose a display option for the document from this drop-down menu.

Reviewing Pane (vertical)

Figure 7.13 The Reviewing Pane presents all edits in a scrolling list. Double-click any entry to scroll the document directly to that edit.

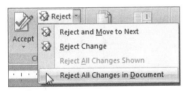

Figure 7.14 Process revisions by clicking these Changes icons.

Figure 7.15 You can simultaneously accept or reject all revisions.

■ To accept or reject *all* edits, choose Accept All Changes in Document or Reject All Changes in Document from the Accept or Reject icon's menu (**Figure 7.15**).

■ If you mistakenly accept or reject an edit, you can reverse your action by immediately clicking the Undo icon in the Quick Access Toolbar or by pressing Ctrl Z.

To process document revisions:

1. *Optional:* Open the Reviewing Pane (**Figure 7.13**) by clicking the Reviewing Pane icon and choosing a display option: vertical or horizontal.

2. Click in the document at the point where you wish to start and, using the icons in the Changes group (**Figure 7.14**), do the following for each revision:

   ▲ To accept the current revision, click the Accept icon or choose an option from the icon's drop-down menu. (Accepting a revision incorporates the edit into the text.)

   ▲ To reject the current revision, click the Reject icon or choose an option from the icon's drop-down menu. (Rejecting a revision removes the edit.)

   ▲ Temporarily skip a revision by clicking the Next or Previous icon.

✔ Tips

■ You don't have to share a document to use change tracking. You can use it to track and manage your own edits, too.

■ Another way to view the content of edits and comments is to move the cursor over them in the body of the document. A pop-up box will appear.

■ You can close the Reviewing Pane by clicking its icon or the pane's close box.

■ Any reviewer can insert comments in the text. Comments can be used for any purpose, such as explaining the reason for an edit or pointing out material that needs to be rewritten. To insert a comment, set the insertion mark or select the text to which the comment refers, click the New Comment icon in the Comments group, and type the comment. Comments are identified by the reviewer's initials, followed by a number, such as [SS3].

CHANGE TRACKING

Comparing Documents

Whether you're working alone on an important document or with others, it can be helpful to compare two versions to see what's been changed. (This assumes, of course, that you've saved multiple versions of the document or, at least, an original and a current version.)

To compare two versions of a document:

1. On the Review tab, click the Compare icon (in the Compare group) and choose Compare from the drop-down menu.

   The Compare Documents dialog box appears.

2. Select the original and revised documents from the drop-down lists (**Figure 7.16**).

   If a document isn't listed, click its Browse icon to locate the document on disk.

3. If the bottom half of the dialog box is hidden, click the More button to reveal the document-comparison options.

4. Review and set options, and then click OK.

   The comparison document is created and displayed (**Figure 7.17**).

✔ Tips

■ You can compare *any* two versions of the same document—not just the first and last or the previous and current versions.

■ Each pane in the comparison document has its own close box.

■ If a document has undergone multiple revisions, you'll find it more manageable to compare the last two versions than to compare the original and final.

Show/hide options   Browse

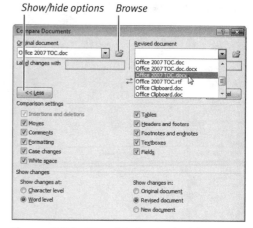

Figure 7.16 Select the original and revised documents, set options, and click OK.

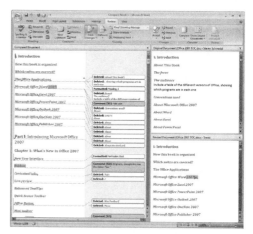

Figure 7.17 Word creates a comparison document. You can customize the display by choosing commands from icon drop-down menus, such as Balloons, Reviewing Pane, and Show Source Documents.

Show/hide options

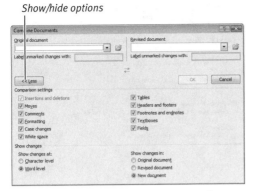

Figure 7.18 Select the two documents, set options, and click OK.

Reviewing Pane   *Original document*

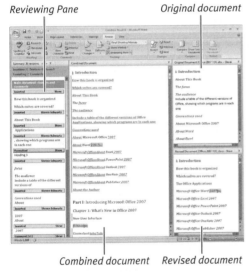

Combined document *Revised document*

Figure 7.19 The combined document appears in a new window. You can enable the Reviewing Pane to process the revisions.

✔ Tip

■ Creating a combined document does *not* save it to disk. If you'd like a permanent copy of the combined document, remember to save!

Combining Documents

If multiple reviewers are independently reviewing the same document, you can use the Combine command to merge their edits and comments (two documents at a time) into a single, master document. Then the author or group leader can process the revisions, as explained earlier in this chapter.

To merge two documents:

1. On the Review tab, click the Compare icon (in the Compare group) and choose Combine from the drop-down menu.

   The Combine Documents dialog box appears (**Figure 7.18**).

2. Select the two documents from the drop-down lists.

   If a document isn't listed, click its Browse icon to locate the document.

3. If the bottom half of the dialog box is hidden, click the More button to reveal the procedure options.

4. At the bottom of the dialog box, select Show changes in: New document. Review the other options, and click OK.

   The combined document is created and displayed (**Figure 7.19**).

5. Click the Office Button, choose Save As > Word Document, and save the combined document.

6. If additional documents need to be merged with the new, combined document, repeat Steps 1–5, but specify the combined document saved in Step 5 as one of the documents.

7. *Optional:* To process the revisions, open the Reviewing Pane (see Figure 7.19) by clicking the Reviewing Pane icon and choosing a display option: vertical or horizontal.

COMBINING DOCUMENTS

The Document Inspector

Before giving a Word document to someone, you should be aware that it can contain data you might prefer *not* to provide. Examples include comments and revision marks, as well as *invisible data* (such as personal information and text formatted as hidden). You can run the Document Inspector to find and remove this material.

To run the Document Inspector:

1. Open the document.

2. Click the Office Button, and choose Prepare > Inspect Document.

   The Document Inspector appears (**Figure 7.20**).

3. Uncheck any element you don't want to examine, and click Inspect.

   The document is examined, and the results are presented (**Figure 7.21**).

4. To eliminate a found element from the document, click its Remove All button.

5. Click Close to dismiss the Document Inspector.

6. *Do one of the following:*

   ▲ To incorporate the Document Inspector changes into the original document, click the Office Button and choose File > Save, click the Save icon in the Quick Access Toolbar, or press Ctrl S.

   ▲ Save the Document Inspector changes in a *new* file. Click the Office Button, choose File > Save As, and save the revised document using a new name. Send this copy to the recipient rather than the original document.

✔ Tip

■ Think carefully before saving the changes to the original document. You can't Undo a Save.

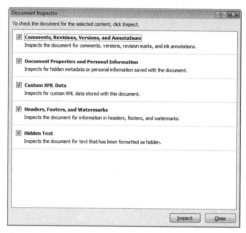

Figure 7.20 Remove check marks from items you want to ignore (if any), and click Inspect.

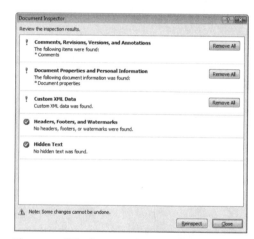

Figure 7.21 If the Document Inspector finds material, it is marked with an exclamation point (!). Click the Remove All button to eliminate it from the document.

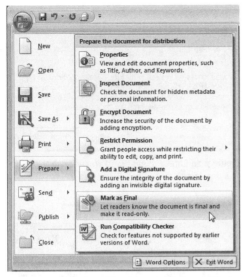

Figure 7.22 Click the Office Button and choose Mark as Final from the Prepare submenu.

Figure 7.23 Click OK to continue.

Identify Yourself

To automatically use your name as the author of your Office documents, you must *personalize* your copy of Office. This information is also used when you're reviewing Office documents to identify your edits and comments:

1. Click the Office Button, followed by the Word Options button.

2. In the Popular section of the Word Options dialog box, enter your user name and initials. Click OK.

Protecting a Document

Whether a document will be distributed to others in your office or school, will be sent around the world (via the Web), or will never leave your PC, Word offers several ways for you to protect the document. The two simplest options are:

♦ Mark the document as final, changing it to read-only to prevent additional changes

♦ Encrypt the document, requiring a password to open and work with it

To mark a document as final:

1. Click the Office Button, and choose Prepare > Mark as Final (**Figure 7.22**). A dialog box appears (**Figure 7.23**).

2. Click OK.
   The document is marked as final and saved. An explanatory dialog box appears.

3. Click OK to dismiss the dialog box.
   The document is now read-only. When it's opened, any user (including you) will be prevented from editing or proofing the document.

✔ Tip

■ Mark as Final is not a *secure* means of protecting a document because of the following:

   ▲ When opened in an earlier version of Word, the document is no longer read-only and can be freely edited.

   ▲ To change it back to a normal document in Word 2007, all you have to do is issue the Mark as Final command again.

To encrypt a document:

1. With the document open in Word, click the Office Button, and choose Prepare > Encrypt Document.

   The Encrypt Document dialog box appears (**Figure 7.24**).

2. Enter the password you will use to open the file, and click OK.

3. Reenter the password in the Confirm Password dialog box, and click OK.

4. When you're done working with the document, save the changes. Saving also saves the new encryption and password protection.

   When you or another user attempt to open the document, a Password dialog box will appear (**Figure 7.25**). Unless the correct password is entered, the document will refuse to open.

✔ Tips

- To remove encryption and password protection from a document, issue the Encrypt Document command again and *delete* the password that's shown. (You must first open the document by supplying the password before you can remove the password.)

- If you forget a document's password, you will not be able to open it. It's a good idea to keep a record of the password in a secure place or retain an unencrypted copy of the document.

- Digital signatures and restricted permissions are two other protection features supported by Word, but they require that you enroll in optional services.

Figure 7.24 Enter the password you will use to open this document.

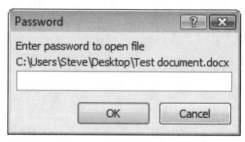

Figure 7.25 A password dialog box appears whenever anyone tries open to the document. (The dialog box may be different in other versions of Word.)

Part III: Microsoft Excel

Chapter 8   Getting Started with Excel 2007 127

Chapter 9   Formatting Worksheets and Data .. 159

Chapter 10 Formulas and Functions 173

Chapter 11 Working with Tables 185

Chapter 12 Creating Charts 195

GETTING STARTED WITH EXCEL 2007

Excel is Office 2007's spreadsheet program. You use Excel to create, analyze, and manage documents called *workbooks* that contain text and numeric data. Workbooks can contain simple lists (such as address books, club rosters, and collections) or complex calculations (such as those found in bookkeeping systems, sales and expense tracking analyses, engineering computations, and manufacturing measurements).

To get you started, this chapter presents the following essential Excel topics:

- ◆ Working with the Excel interface
- ◆ Understanding workbooks and worksheets
- ◆ Selecting cells and ranges
- ◆ Entering and editing data
- ◆ Reorganizing a workbook
- ◆ Filling cells
- ◆ Importing data
- ◆ Finding and replacing data
- ◆ Sorting data
- ◆ Naming cells and ranges
- ◆ Password-protecting workbooks

The Excel Interface

Before we jump into learning to use Excel, take a moment to examine **Figure 8.1** (bottom). It shows many of the interface components you'll be using. You'll note that several elements, such as the Ribbon, Office Button, and Quick Access Toolbar, can also be found in Word, PowerPoint, and Outlook.

Office Button. Click this button to perform file-related actions (**Figure 8.2**), such as creating, opening, saving, and printing documents. Click Excel Options to set preferences. To open a document you've recently worked on, click its name in the Recent Documents list. The Exit command can also be found here.

Quick Access Toolbar. Common commands are found here, such as Save, Undo, and Redo.

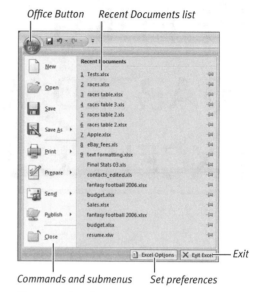

Office Button *Recent Documents list*

Commands and submenus *Set preferences* *Exit*

Figure 8.2 The Office Button window.

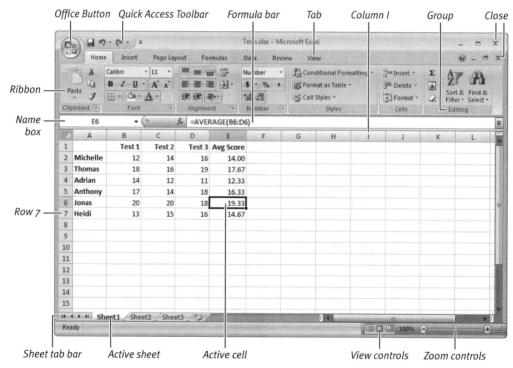

Office Button *Quick Access Toolbar* *Formula bar* *Tab* *Column I* *Group* *Close*

Ribbon

Name box

Row 7

Sheet tab bar *Active sheet* *Active cell* *View controls* *Zoom controls*

Figure 8.1 Elements of the Excel 2007 interface.

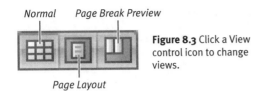

Normal   Page Break Preview

Page Layout

Figure 8.3 Click a View control icon to change views.

Ribbon. The Ribbon is Office 2007's replacement for program menus. Similar commands and procedures are listed together on a *tab*, such as Insert or View. Within each tab, procedures are further divided into *groups*, based on similarity of function. To perform a command, you switch to the appropriate tab by clicking its name, and then click the command's icon.

Sheet tab bar. A workbook can contain multiple worksheets (or sheets). This area of the document window displays the names of all worksheets in the current workbook. To switch worksheets, click the sheet's name.

Active sheet. This is the worksheet you're currently viewing and/or editing.

Columns and rows. Columns are designated using letters and rows are numbered. A *column* consists of all cells directly beneath a column letter. A *row* is the string of cells to the right of a row number.

Active cell. This is the currently selected cell (indicated by a heavy black border), named by combining the intersection of column and row. For example, E6 is in column E, row 6. The active cell name is shown in the name box, and the cell's column letter and row number are highlighted.

Name box. The name box performs a variety of functions, including displaying the name of the active cell and creating *names* (a descriptive name for a cell or range, such as SalesTax or Budget). Names are also referred to as *range names* and *named ranges*.

View controls. Click an icon to switch views (**Figure 8.3**). You can also change views by selecting the View tab and clicking an icon in the Worksheet Views group.

Zoom controls. Change the current magnification by dragging the slider, clicking + (increase) or – (decrease), or clicking the zoom percentage number.

Formula bar. Data and formulas can be entered in the formula bar or directly into the active cell. The formula bar displays any formula contained in the active cell.

Close. Workbooks and Excel each contain a close box you can click to close an open workbook or to quit Excel, respectively.

THE EXCEL INTERFACE

Workbooks and Worksheets

An Excel document consists of a single workbook containing one or more worksheets. A *worksheet* (or sheet) has numbered rows and lettered columns that form a grid. The intersection of a row and column is called a *cell* (**Figure 8.4**). You can enter text data, numeric data, or formulas into the cells. Unlike documents in other programs you've used, you don't have to enter data from the top down, left to right. You can use any cells that you want, leaving blank rows and columns as best suits your data.

An Options setting (**Figure 8.5**) determines the initial number of worksheets in a new workbook. Depending on the data you're entering and analyzing, you can ignore all worksheets but the first, or use the others for a completely different type of data or related data. Because Excel lets you perform calculations across worksheets within a workbook, you can also use one sheet to consolidate the data in other sheets. For example, in a bookkeeping workbook, you might collect each month's data in separate sheet and use another sheet to calculate annual figures, based on the contents of the monthly sheets.

Worksheets are managed using the *Sheet tab bar*, found in the bottom-left corner of every workbook window (**Figure 8.6**). To make a different worksheet active, you click its name. You can add, delete, and change the order of the sheets. You can also rename any sheet to make it easier to identify.

To rename a worksheet:

◆ Right-click the tab of the worksheet you want to rename, and choose Rename from the pop-up menu that appears (**Figure 8.7**). Type a new name, and press (Enter).

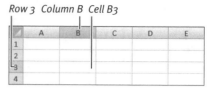

Row 3   Column B   Cell B3

Figure 8.4 A worksheet is a grid composed of rows and columns.

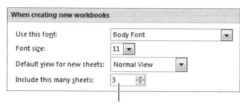

Number of sheets per workbook

Figure 8.5 To set Excel preferences (such as the number of sheets per workbook), click the Office Button and then click Excel Options.

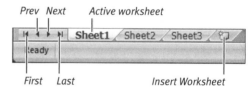

Prev Next   Active worksheet

First   Last   Insert Worksheet

Figure 8.6 You use the Sheet tab bar to make a worksheet active and to manage your worksheets. Each worksheet is represented by a named tab. Click the arrow icons to show additional sheets.

Figure 8.7 Right-click a worksheet name to reveal this pop-up menu.

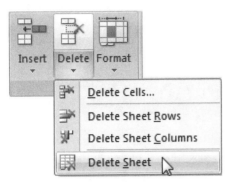

Figure 8.8 You can delete or insert worksheets by choosing a command from the Delete or Insert icon.

Worksheet icon

Figure 8.9 To insert a new worksheet, ensure that Worksheet is selected and click OK.

Creating New Workbooks

Although you can continue to add sheets to a workbook, you'll want to create a *new* workbook whenever you begin a project:

◆ To immediately create a new workbook, press Ctrl N.

◆ To create a specific type of workbook, click the Office Button, and click New. In the New Workbook window, select Blank Workbook, a template, or an existing workbook, and click Create.

To delete a worksheet:

◆ *Do either of the following:*

▲ Right-click the sheet tab of the worksheet you want to delete, and choose Delete from the pop-up menu that appears (see Figure 8.7).

▲ Switch to the Home tab, click the worksheet's name in the Sheet tab bar (to make the worksheet active), and choose Delete Sheet from the Delete drop-down menu in the Cells group (**Figure 8.8**).

If the worksheet contains data, a warning dialog box appears. Otherwise, the worksheet is immediately deleted.

To insert a new worksheet:

◆ *Do one of the following:*

▲ Click the Insert Worksheet icon in the Sheet tab bar (see Figure 8.6). The new worksheet appears at the end of the sheet list.

▲ Right-click a worksheet name in the Sheet tab bar, and choose Insert from the pop-up menu that appears. On the General tab of the Insert dialog box (**Figure 8.9**), select Worksheet and click OK. The new sheet is inserted before the right-clicked sheet name.

▲ Select a worksheet name in the Sheet tab bar, switch to the Home tab, and choose Insert Sheet from the Insert drop-down menu in the Cells group. The new worksheet is inserted before the active worksheet.

To change the order of worksheets:

◆ Drag the worksheet name to a new position in the Sheet tab bar (see Figure 8.6). As you drag, a tiny triangle shows the sheet's position. Release the mouse button to complete the move.

Cell and Range Selection

Whether you're preparing to enter, edit, or format data, the first step is to select a cell or cell range. Following are some cell-selection techniques.

To select cells:

◆ **Single cell.** *Do one of the following:*

▲ Scroll to bring the cell into view, and then click the cell.

▲ Press a navigation key, such as ⟵, ⟶, ⟰, ⟱, Tab, Shift Tab, Enter, Shift Enter, to move into the cell. See the Tips on the following page for other useful key combinations.

▲ On the Home tab, choose Go To from the Find & Select icon's drop-down menu in the Editing group (**Figure 8.10**), or press Ctrl G.

In the Go To dialog box (**Figure 8.11**), select or type the cell address or name (if a name has been assigned to the cell). Click OK.

▲ Type the cell address or name into the name box (**Figure 8.12**) and press Enter.

▲ To find a cell based on its contents, choose Find from the Find & Select icon's drop-down menu (see Figure 8.10). In the Find dialog box, enter the text, number, date, or time contained in the cell and click Find Next. When the desired cell is selected, click Close. See "Finding/Replacing Data," later in this chapter, for additional options.

CELL AND RANGE SELECTION

Figure 8.10 To go to a cell address or range, choose Go To from the Find & Select drop-down menu.

Figure 8.11 To specify a destination, enter an address, range, or name in the Reference box, or select a recently visited address, range, or name.

Figure 8.12 Enter an address, range, or name in the name box.

Anchor (B2)

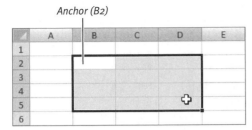

Figure 8.13 To select a range, click a cell in one corner of the range and drag to the opposite corner.

Click to select entire worksheet

Selected column (A)

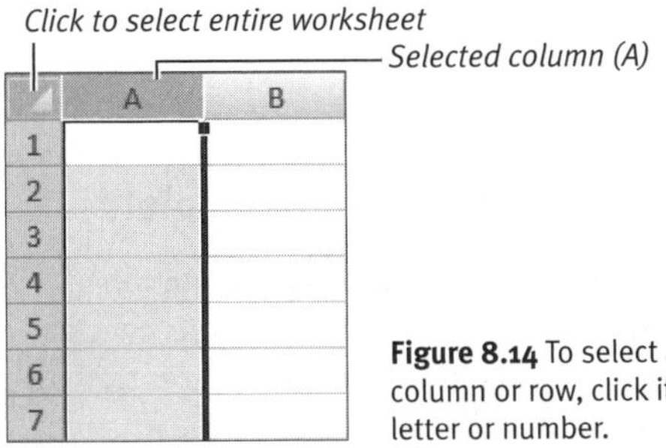

Figure 8.14 To select a column or row, click its letter or number.

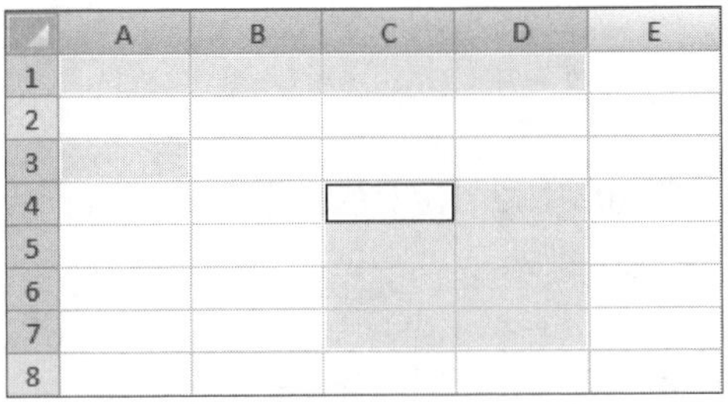

Figure 8.15 You can also select any combination of cells, ranges, rows, and columns (marked with light blue highlighting).

- Press (Ctrl) and an arrow key to move to the next filled cell in the specified direction. If there are no other filled cells, the first or last cell in the row or column will be selected.

- Press (Ctrl)(End) to select the last cell in the active area of the worksheet, (Home) to move to the first cell in the current row, or (Ctrl)(Home) to move to cell A1.

◆ **Contiguous cell range.** *Do one of the following:*

▲ Click a cell in any corner of the range (called the *anchor*) and drag to the opposite corner to select the additional cells (**Figure 8.13**).

▲ To select an entire column or row, click its letter or number (**Figure 8.14**).

▲ To select the entire worksheet, click the intersection of the column and row headings (see Figure 8.14).

▲ On the Home tab, choose Go To from the Find & Select icon's drop-down menu in the Editing Group (see Figure 8.10) or press (Ctrl)(G). In the Go To dialog box (see Figure 8.11), enter the cell range in the form

    start cell:end cell

such as a1:d4. If you've named the range (see "Naming Cells and Ranges," later in this chapter), you can enter its name rather than the range. Click OK.

▲ Enter the cell range or its name into the name box (see Figure 8.12) and press (Enter).

◆ **Noncontiguous cell ranges.** While pressing (Ctrl), click or click and drag to select the cells, ranges, columns, and/or rows (**Figure 8.15**).

✔ Tips

■ If you need to regularly return to a cell or range, naming it will enable you to easily do so using the Go To command or the name box (see "Naming Cells and Ranges," later in the chapter).

■ You can speed the entry of new data by preselecting the destination range. After each entry, pressing (Tab) or (Enter) will move you through the range in left-to-right or top-to-bottom fashion, respectively.

Entering Data

A cell can contain one or more lines of text, a number, a date, a time, or a formula that results in one of these data types. To enter data into a cell, follow the instructions below. (Formulas are discussed in Chapter 10.)

To enter data into a cell:

1. Select the cell into which you want to enter data, making it the active cell.

   You can select a cell by clicking in it. For other cell-selection options, see the previous section.

2. *Do one of the following:*

   ▲ **Text.** Type or paste the text.

   ▲ **Number.** Type the number.

   ▲ **Date.** Type a date in a recognizable format, such as 9-12-06, 09/12/2006, or 12-Sep-06. Date components must be separated by a slash (/) or hyphen (–) character.

   ▲ **Time.** Type a time in a recognizable format, such as 4:, 4:07, 4:07:53, 4:07 p, 4 pm, or 16:07. Time components must be separated by a colon (:).

   When a 12-hour time is entered, such as 10:43, it is assumed to be AM. To indicate PM, you must enter the time in military (24-hour) format or follow the time with p or pm, such as 6:15 p or 6:15 pm. Similarly, AM times can be followed by an a or am, such as 7:15 a or 7:15 am.

3. To complete the entry, click another cell or press a navigation key, such as [Enter] or [Tab]. See **Table 8.1** for options.

Table 8.1

Keystrokes to Complete a Cell Entry

KEYSTROKE	DIRECTION
[Tab], [→]	Right
[Shift][Tab], [←]	Left
[Enter], [↓]	Down
[Shift][Enter], [↑]	Up

Using Entry AutoComplete

When you enter text or a combination of text and numbers into a cell, Excel checks the current column for matching entries. If one is found, Excel proposes it. To accept this AutoComplete entry, press [Enter]. To ignore it, continue typing.

Changing the Behavior of [Enter]

Normally, pressing [Enter] when you finish entering data into a cell causes the cursor to move down, selecting the cell directly beneath the current cell. However, if you like, you can change the behavior of the [Enter] key:

1. Click the Office Button, and then click Excel Options.

2. In the Excel Options dialog box, select the Advanced category.

3. Select a cursor-movement direction from the Direction drop-down list (found at the top of the dialog box).

4. Click OK.

1957 Birchmont Dr.
Apt. 4
Boston, MA 01706

Figure 8.16 You can force line breaks within a cell.

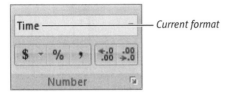

Time ———————— — *Current format*

Figure 8.17 You can see the formatting for the active cell in the Number group.

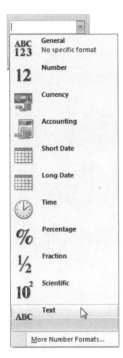

Figure 8.18 You can format any data as text by choosing Text from the Number Format drop-down menu.

✔ Tips

- If a cell shows a string of # characters (#####), it means that the number in the cell is too large to display. To display the complete number, widen the column (see Chapter 9).

- To enter multiple lines of text, numbers, dates, or times into a cell (**Figure 8.16**), press Alt Enter to insert a line break between each pair of lines.

- To enter today's date into a cell, press Ctrl ;. To enter the current time, press Ctrl Shift ;.

- If you want the data to display differently, select the cell and apply formatting (see Chapter 9). Current formatting for the active cell is displayed in the Number group on the Home tab (**Figure 8.17**).

- If you enter a number that begins with one or more zeros, Excel discards the zeros. This presents a problem with certain ZIP codes, for example. To force Excel to retain the zeros, choose Text from the drop-down Number Format menu (**Figure 8.18**) before entering the data.

- Excel distinguishes between data *display* (determined by formatting) and what is *stored*. When performing calculations, Excel uses the stored data, regardless of what's shown in the cells. For example, when calculating a sales tax of 7.75% on a $12.50 purchase, the result is 0.9675. When formatted as Currency, the number displays as $0.97, the result rounded to two decimal places. If you create a formula in another cell that adds the sale amount ($12.48) to the sales tax, the result is 13.46875—*not* $13.47.

Editing Data

As you create and work with a worksheet, you can correct errors, update data with new values, and revise formulas.

To edit the contents of a cell:

1. Select the cell whose contents you wish to change.

2. You can edit in the formula bar or in the cell itself. To set the insertion mark and begin editing, click in the formula bar or double-click in the cell.

   If the cell contains a formula, the formula appears (**Figure 8.19**). Otherwise, the data is shown.

3. Make the desired changes.

4. To finish the edits, *do one of the following:*

   ▲ Press a navigation key to move to another cell (see Table 8.1).

   ▲ Click another cell.

✔ Tips

■ You can use the same editing techniques you use when modifying other kinds of Windows documents. For example, press Backspace to delete the character to the left, press Del or Delete to delete the character to the right, or press any of these keys to delete selected text. To replace a string, select it and type the replacement or delete the string and then type.

■ The cursor keys are active while editing. Press ← or → to move one character in the desired direction; press Ctrl ← or Ctrl → to move one string at a time.

■ To rearrange data within a cell, you can cut (Ctrl X) selected data, set the insertion mark where you want to move the data, and then paste (Ctrl V).

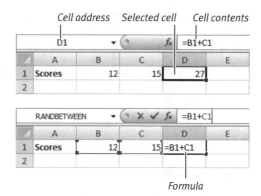

Cell address   Selected cell   Cell contents

Formula

Figure 8.19 When you select a cell (top), its contents are shown in the formula bar. When you set the insertion mark for editing (bottom), the result is replaced by the actual formula in the cell.

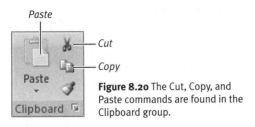

Figure 8.20 The Cut, Copy, and Paste commands are found in the Clipboard group.

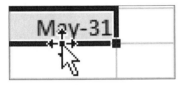

Figure 8.21 When the cursor changes to this symbol, you can drag the selected cells to a new location.

Figure 8.22 To undo your last action, click the Undo icon. To undo multiple actions, choose an action from the Undo icon's drop-down menu.

Reorganizing a Worksheet

In addition to editing cell contents, you can also rearrange the data. You can move cells to other locations, add or delete cells (automatically shifting the affected surrounding cells), and insert or delete rows and columns.

To move cells to another location:

1. Select the cell or range you want to move.

2. *Do one of the following:*

   ▲ Cut the cell/range by pressing $\boxed{Ctrl}\boxed{X}$ or by clicking the Cut icon in the Clipboard group on the Home tab (**Figure 8.20**). Select the destination cell or the cell in the upper-left corner of the destination range. Press $\boxed{Enter}$, press $\boxed{Ctrl}\boxed{V}$, or click the Paste icon in the Clipboard group.

   ▲ Move the cursor over the border of the selected cell or range (**Figure 8.21**). Drag the selected cell to the destination cell or the selected range to the cell that will serve as the upper-left corner of the destination range. Release the mouse button to complete the move.

   Neither procedure *deletes* the original cells. The data in the cells is simply moved to a new location.

✔ Tips

■ Whether performed by cut-and-paste or drag-and-drop, cell/range moves are *destructive*. If you select a destination that already contains data, the old data will be replaced by the moved data. If this happens unintentionally, immediately click the Undo icon in the Quick Access Toolbar (**Figure 8.22**) or press $\boxed{Ctrl}\boxed{Z}$.

■ To move data between worksheets, use cut-and-paste.

To copy cells to another location:

1. Select the cell or range you want to copy.

2. *Do one of the following:*

   ▲ Copy the cell/range by pressing Ctrl C or by clicking the Copy icon in the Clipboard group on the Home tab (see Figure 8.20). Select the destination cell or the cell in the upper-left corner of the destination range. Press Enter, press Ctrl V, or click the Paste icon in the Clipboard group on the Home tab.

   ▲ While pressing Ctrl, move the cursor over the border of the selected cell or range. A tiny plus symbol is added to the cursor (**Figure 8.23**). Drag the cell/range to the destination cell or to the cell in the upper-left corner of the destination range.

To insert cells:

1. Select the cell or range where you want to insert new, blank cells.

2. *Do one of the following:*

   ▲ On the Home tab, click the Insert icon in the Cells group, and choose Insert Cells from the drop-down menu (**Figure 8.24**).

   ▲ Right-click the cell or range, and choose Insert from the pop-up menu.

3. In the Insert dialog box (**Figure 8.25**), select Shift cells right or Shift cells down, and then click OK.

   Surrounding cells affected by the insertion are shifted to make room for the inserted cell(s).

Figure 8.23 You can copy material to another location by Ctrl-dragging.

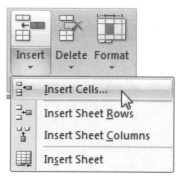

Figure 8.24 Choose Insert Cell from the Insert icon's drop-down menu.

Figure 8.25 When inserting new cells, you must specify how other cells will be affected.

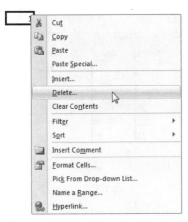

Figure 8.26 Right-click a selected cell or range, and then choose Delete.

Figure 8.27 Specify how surrounding cells will shift in response to the cell deletion.

	A	B	C	D	E	F	G
		Post					
1	Position	Name	Last Race	Post	Finish	Time	Odds
2	1	Flying Stone	Jun-15	4	1	2:03	5.0
3	2	Lady Chris Time	Jun-12	2	5	2:00	32.5
4	3	Black Bart	Jun-13	7	2	2:00	24.6
5	4	Shadrack	Jun-08	5	5	2:02	3.9
6	5	Sundust Prince	Jun-18	4	5	2:01	15.1
7	6	J.J.'s Ferro	Jun-15	3	4	2:04	1.0
8	7	Pat's Comedian	May-31	4	8	2:01	8.1
9							

Figure 8.28 To insert two blank rows at 6 and 7, start by selecting the current rows 6 and 7.

To delete cells:

1. Select the cell or range you want to delete.

2. *Do one of the following:*

   ▲ On the Home tab, click the Delete icon in the Cells group, and choose Delete Cells from the drop-down menu.

   ▲ Right-click the cell or range, and choose Delete from the pop-up menu (**Figure 8.26**).

3. In the Delete dialog box (**Figure 8.27**), select Shift cells left or Shift cells up, and then click OK.

   Surrounding cells affected by the deletion are shifted to close up the space left by the deleted cell(s).

To insert rows:

1. Select the row where you want to insert a new row.

2. *Do one of the following:*

   ▲ On the Home tab, click the Insert icon in the Cells group (see Figure 8.24).

   ▲ Right-click any cell in the selected row, and choose Insert from the pop-up menu (see Figure 8.26).

   The new row appears. The rows affected by the insertion shift down.

✔ Tips

■ You can also select a single cell in the row where you want to insert a new row. However, you must then choose Insert Sheet Rows from the Insert icon's drop-down menu or select Entire row from the Insert dialog box (see Figure 8.25).

■ To insert *multiple* rows, select as many rows as you want new rows (**Figure 8.28**). Then click the Insert icon, or right-click any cell in the selected rows and choose Insert from the pop-up menu (see Figure 8.26).

REORGANIZING A WORKSHEET

139

To insert columns:

1. Select the column where you want to insert a new column.

2. *Do one of the following:*
   - ▲ On the Home tab, click the Insert icon in the Cells group (see Figure 8.24).
   - ▲ Right-click any cell in the selected column, and choose Insert from the pop-up menu (see Figure 8.26).

   The new column appears. The columns affected by the insertion shift to the right (**Figure 8.29**).

✔ Tips

- ■ You can also select a single cell in the column where you want to insert the new column. However, you must then choose Insert Sheet Columns from the Insert icon's drop-down menu or select Entire column from the Insert dialog box (see Figure 8.25).

- ■ To insert *multiple* columns, select the columns (or a cell in each column) where you want to insert new columns in Step 1 (**Figure 8.30**).

To delete rows:

1. Select the row or rows you want to delete.

2. *Do one of the following:*
   - ▲ On the Home tab, click the Delete icon in the Cells group.
   - ▲ Right-click any cell in the selected row, and choose Delete (see Figure 8.26).

   The row(s) are deleted. The rows affected by the deletion shift up to close the space.

Original worksheet   *Selected column (C)*

▲	A	B	C	D
1		Test 1	Test 2	Test 3
2	Michelle	12	14	16
3	Thomas	18	16	19
4	Adrian	14	12	11
5	Anthony	17	14	18
6	Jonas	20	20	18
7	Heidi	13	15	16

Modified worksheet   *Inserted column*

▲	A	B	C	D	E
1		Test 1		Test 2	Test 3
2	Michelle	12		14	16
3	Thomas	18		16	19
4	Adrian	14		12	11
5	Anthony	17		14	18
6	Jonas	20		20	18
7	Heidi	13		15	16

Figure 8.29 Suppose you forgot to record a quiz between Tests 1 and 2. When you select column C and issue the Insert command. original columns C and D are shifted to the right to become columns D and E.

Selected cell in column C, row 3

▲	A	B	C	D
1		Test 1	Test 2	Test 3
2	Michelle	12	14	16
3	Thomas	18	16	19
4	Adrian	14	12	11
5	Anthony	17	14	18
6	Jonas	20	20	18
7	Heidi	13	15	16

Figure 8.30 You can also begin a column or row insertion by selecting a single cell in the column or row.

Insertion/Deletion Considerations

When inserting or deleting cells, rows, or columns, you must consider the impact on your worksheet. Insertions and deletions often cause other data to move:

- When inserting a cell, the current cell must either move to the right or down. Other cells to the right or below the inserted cell will also shift to the right or down.

- When deleting a cell, all cells directly below or to the right of the deleted cell must shift up or left to fill the hole created by the deletion.

- When inserting a new row, the current row automatically moves down to make room for the new row. Rows below the current row also move down one row.

- When inserting a column, the current column and all columns to its right shift one column to the right.

The impact of an insertion or deletion on data *elsewhere* in the worksheet must be considered. For instance, if a worksheet contains a single data array or table, such as an address book, inserting or deleting a row or column will have little impact. And if you discover that you entered the same data in two cells in a row (causing the row to have an extra entry), deleting a duplicate and choosing Shift cells left quickly fixes the problem.

But if the worksheet is complex and contains multiple data arrays, an insertion or deletion is liable to create problems elsewhere. If such is the case, the safest approach is to move affected data, rearranging the worksheet as needed.

✔ Tips

- Deleting cells, rows, and columns are destructive processes. Because every row and column extends to the end or bottom of the worksheet, be sure not to accidentally delete data that isn't in view.

- You can also select a cell in the row you want to delete. However, you must then choose Delete Sheet Rows from the Delete icon or select Entire row from the Delete dialog box (see Figure 8.27).

- To delete *multiple* rows, select the rows (or a cell in each row) that you want to delete in Step 1.

To delete columns:

1. Select the column you want to delete.

2. *Do one of the following:*
   - ▲ On the Home tab, click the Delete icon in the Cells group.
   - ▲ Right-click any cell in the selected column, and choose Delete from the pop-up menu (see Figure 8.26).

   The column is deleted, and all columns to its right shift to the left.

✔ Tips

- You can also select a single cell in the column you want to delete. However, you must then choose Delete Sheet Columns from the Delete icon or select Entire column from the Delete dialog box (see Figure 8.27).

- To delete multiple columns, select the columns (or a cell in each column) that you want to delete in Step 1.

- Deleting cells, rows, or columns isn't the same as clearing their contents. To clear selected cells, switch to the Home tab and choose a command from the Clear icon's drop-down menu in the Editing group.

REORGANIZING A WORKSHEET

Filling Cells

Two situations occur in worksheet creation that can be simplified using the Fill feature:

◆ You have a text constant, numeric constant, or formula you want to repeat several times in the current row or column.

◆ You have or are creating a series of cell entries in the current row or column that you want to extend.

To fill adjacent cells with a constant:

◆ *Do either of the following:*

▲ Select the cell that contains the text or numeric constant. Move the cursor over the lower-right corner of the cell, click the *fill handle* (**Figure 8.31**), and drag in the direction you want to fill (**Figure 8.32**).

▲ Select the cell with the text or numeric constant, as well as the cells you want to fill. On the Home tab, choose the fill direction from the Fill icon's drop-down menu in the Editing group (**Figure 8.33**).

The cells fill with the constant.

✔ Tips

■ To duplicate a cell regardless of the type of data it contains (text, number, date, or time), select the cell immediately to the right or below it and press Ctrl R or Ctrl D, respectively.

■ You can perform a drag fill in *any* direction: right, left, down, or up.

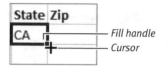

Figure 8.31 You can fill cells by dragging.

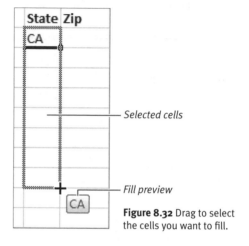

Figure 8.32 Drag to select the cells you want to fill.

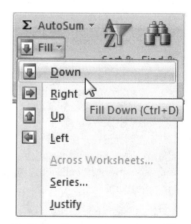

Figure 8.33 You can also perform a fill by choosing a direction from the Fill drop-down menu.

FILLING CELLS

Formula in E2

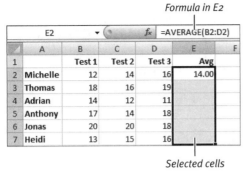

Selected cells

Figure 8.34 Select the cell that contains the formula (E2), as well as the cells you want to fill (E3:E7).

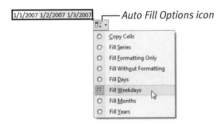

Figure 8.35 This series expands in 14-day increments.

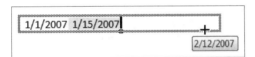

— *Auto Fill Options icon*

Figure 8.36 The Auto Fill Options menu.

✔ Tips

■ When expanding certain series, such as dates, an Auto Fill Options icon appears (**Figure 8.36**). Click it to set a fill specification for the series. If you drag-extend the series using the *right* mouse button, similar options appear in a pop-up menu.

■ When continuing a series, select enough data so Excel can discern the nature of the series. In some cases, such as a month name, day name, or numbered text (such as Quarter 1, Score 1, Team 1), *one* item is often sufficient.

To fill adjacent cells with a formula:

◆ *Do either of the following:*

▲ Select the cell with the formula. Click the fill handle, and drag in the direction you want to fill (see Figures 8.31 and 8.32).

▲ Select the cell with the formula, as well as the cells you want to fill (**Figure 8.34**). On the Home tab, click the Fill icon in the Editing group and choose a fill direction: Down, Right, Up, or Left (see Figure 8.33).

The cells fill with the formula. Note that *relative cell references* (see Chapter 10) in the formula are automatically adjusted in the filled cells.

To continue a series into adjacent cells:

1. If the series doesn't already exist, begin it by typing at least two adjacent entries in a row or column.

For example, for invoice numbers starting with 1050, you would enter 1050 and 1051. For company divisions, you could type Div1 and Div2, Div. 1 and Div. 2, or Division 1 and Division 2. For days of the week, you could enter Sunday and Monday, or Sun and Mon.

2. *Do either of the following:*

▲ Select two or more adjacent cells containing members of the series. Drag the fill handle of the right-most or lowest cell in the direction you want to fill (**Figure 8.35**). As you drag, Excel shows the data each cell will contain.

▲ Select two or more adjacent cells containing members of the series, as well as the cells you want to fill. On the Home tab, click the Fill icon in the Editing group and choose the fill direction: Down, Right, Up, or Left (see Figure 8.33).

New members of the series fill the cells.

FILLING CELLS

Importing Data

You don't have to manually enter the data in every worksheet. If the data exists elsewhere, such as in a table on the Web, in another program, or in a properly formatted text file, you can *import* the data into a new or existing worksheet. Following are examples of common data-importing scenarios.

To import data from a Web table:

1. Switch to the Data tab, and click the From Web icon in the Get External Data group.

   A New Web Query dialog box appears.

2. In the Address box (**Figure 8.37**), type or paste the URL for the Web page that contains the data, and click Go. (If you recently viewed the page, you may be able to select its URL from the Address box's drop-down menu.)

   The Web page is fetched from the Internet and displayed in the dialog box.

3. Each table on the page is marked with a yellow box. Click the box for each table that you want to import (**Figure 8.38**), and click Import.

   The Import Data dialog box appears (**Figure 8.39**), asking where you want to import the data. By default, the active cell on the current worksheet is proposed.

4. *Select one of the following:*
   - ▲ **Existing worksheet.** Specify the starting cell to receive the imported data by typing its address into the box or by clicking the cell on the sheet.
   - ▲ **New worksheet.** Excel will create a new worksheet in the current workbook and import the data into a range beginning with cell A1.

5. Click OK.

   The table(s) are imported (**Figure 8.40**).

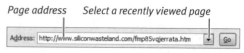

Page address   Select a recently viewed page

Figure 8.37 Enter a page address in the Address box at the top of the New Web Query dialog box.

Table-selection icon   Go   Options

Figure 8.38 Click the icon beside each table you want to import.

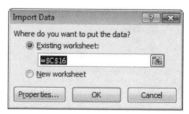

Figure 8.39 Specify a destination for the imported data and click OK.

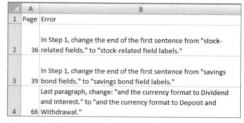

Figure 8.40 Here's the imported data (after applying text-wrap formatting to the data in column B).

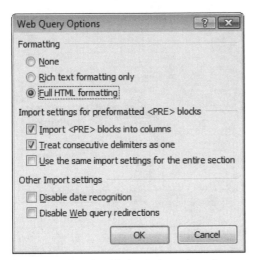

Figure 8.41 To retain table formatting, select a Formatting option in the Web Query Options dialog box..

✔ Tips

- After entering a URL in the Address box (see Figures 8.37–8.38), you can interact with the fetched page. You can follow links by clicking them; enter your user name and password (for sites that require a login); and click buttons at the top of the dialog box to go backward and forward, refresh the page, or stop.

- To import data with its original formatting intact (rather than the Plain Text result shown in Figure 8.40), click the Options button at the top of the New Web Query dialog box (see Figure 8.38). In the Formatting section of the Web Query Options dialog box (**Figure 8.41**), select Rich text formatting only or Full HTML formatting, and then click OK.

- Another way to retain a Web table's formatting is to open the page in a Web browser, drag to select the table, and copy (Ctrl C) the data. Select a destination cell in the worksheet, and paste (Ctrl V). See **Figure 8.42** for an example.

- When working in Internet Explorer 7, you can drag-and-drop a selected table directly into an Excel 2007 worksheet.

- Additional options for a Web import can be viewed by clicking the Properties button in the Import Data dialog box (see Figure 8.39).

IMPORTING DATA

10	Page	Error
11	36	In Step 1, change the end of the first sentence from "stock-related fields." to "stock-related field **labels**."
12	39	In Step 1, change the end of the first sentence from "savings bond fields." to "savings bond field **labels**."
13	66	Last paragraph, change: "and the currency format to Dividend and Interest." to "and the currency format to **Deposit** and **Withdrawal**."

Figure 8.42 When moved into a worksheet via copy-and-paste, a Web table retains its fonts, styles, colors, and cell shadings. This can also be achieved by selecting Full HTML formatting in the Web Query Options dialog box.

To export data from another program in Excel format:

1. Open the document in its creating application, such as a database, a spreadsheet, or an address book utility.

2. *Optional:* Select the records (or portion of the document) you want to use in Excel. If possible, rearrange the data fields to match the order you want them to appear in the worksheet.

3. Use the program's Export, Save As, or equivalent command to save a copy of the data as an Excel (.xls or .xlsx) worksheet file (**Figure 8.43**).

   Note, however, that not all programs offer this capability.

4. In Excel, click the Office Button, click Open, and open the exported data file (**Figure 8.44**).

✔ Tips

■ The exported data may require cleanup in Excel. For instance, you may need to add or edit column heads, rearrange the columns and change their widths, and add appropriate number and date formatting.

■ Most Export and Save As procedures do not export formulas. In general, the *results* of such calculations are exported. If you intend to work with and extend the data in Excel, you'll probably want to recreate the formulas. On the other hand, if the reason you exported the data was so you could use Excel to analyze or chart it, working with the export as-is may suffice.

Export filename

Specify Excel as the file type

Figure 8.43 In FileMaker Pro 8.5 (Mac version shown), a database can be exported as an Excel file.

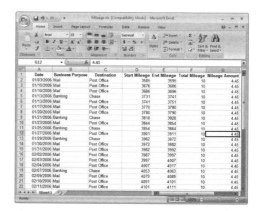

Figure 8.44 Here's the exported FileMaker Pro database opened in Excel.

Display these file types

Figure 8.45 Select the exported data file from the files in the Import Text File dialog box.

Field-arrangement description

Preview of the data

Figure 8.46 Examine the data in the Preview area and ensure that the correct field-export description is selected.

To export data from another program as a text file:

1. Open the document in its creating application, such as a database, a spreadsheet, or an address book utility.

2. *Optional:* Select the records (or portion of the document) you want to use in Excel. If possible, rearrange the data fields to match the order you want them to appear in the worksheet.

3. Use the program's Export, Save As, or equivalent command to save a copy of the data as a tab-delimited or comma-delimited text file.

   The program may also refer to these text file types as *tab-separated* and *comma-separated*.

4. In Excel, switch to the Data tab, and click the From Text icon in the Get External Data group.

   The Import Text File dialog box appears (**Figure 8.45**).

5. Navigate to the drive/folder that contains the exported data file.

6. *Do one of the following:*
   ▲ If the exported data file appears in the Open dialog box's file list, select it and click Open (or Import).
   ▲ If the export file is *not* present in the file list, select All Files from the drop-down file-type list (see Figure 8.45). Select the export file in the file list, and click Open (or Import).

7. In Step 1 of the Text Import Wizard (**Figure 8.46**), ensure that Delimited is selected and examine the data preview in the bottom of the window, verifying that it is the correct file and displays properly. Click Next to continue.

continues on next page

8. In Step 2 of the wizard (**Figure 8.47**), ensure that the correct data delimiter is checked. (Data in the Data preview section will be correctly divided into fields when the right delimiter is selected.) Click Next to continue.

9. *Optional:* In Step 3 of the wizard (**Figure 8.48**), you can specify a format for the data in any field. Select the field in the Data preview, and click the appropriate Column data format radio button.

   Note that General format is appropriate for most types of data, including dates.

10. If you decide not to import certain fields, select each field in the Data preview and click the Do not import column (skip) radio button. Click Finish.

    The exported data opens as the first sheet of a new workbook.

✔ Tips

- Excel can also open comma-separated value (*CSV*) files *directly*, bypassing the Text Import Wizard. Instead of clicking the From Text icon in Step 4, click the Office Button, click Open, set the file type drop-down list to Text Files, and open your .csv file. The CSV data file opens as the first sheet of a new workbook.

- Excel can also import data from files with *fixed-width fields* (see Figure 8.46). Some programs, especially very old database applications, store data in fixed-width fields. When originally creating the file, you had to specify the maximum number of characters for each field. When entering data, if you failed to use the allotted characters for a field, the program simply padded the field with spaces.

Select the delimiter character

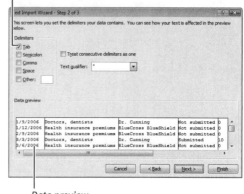

Data preview

Figure 8.47 Select the delimiter character used to separate fields in the export file.

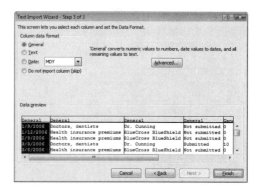

Figure 8.48 Click each column in the Data preview area to ensure that an appropriate format is assigned.

IMPORTING DATA

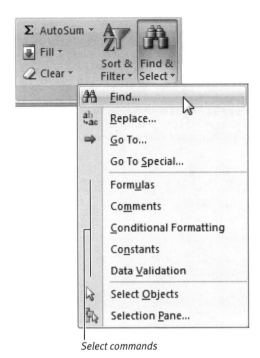

Select commands

Figure 8.49 Find, Replace, Go To, and Select commands can be chosen from the Find & Select menu.

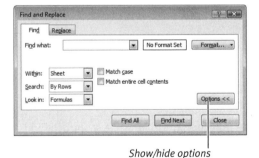

Show/hide options

Figure 8.50 The Find and Replace dialog box (with options displayed).

Finding/Replacing Data

Although you can scroll through a worksheet to find a particular string (such as a label, data, a cell reference, or a formula element), you can use the Find feature to quickly locate the item. You can optionally replace any found string with another string.

To perform a Find:

1. To restrict the search to a range, select the range. Otherwise, click the cell in which you'd like to begin the search.

2. On the Home tab, choose Find from the Find & Select icon's drop-down menu (**Figure 8.49**) in the Editing group or press Ctrl F.
   The Find and Replace dialog box appears (**Figure 8.50**).

3. Enter a search string in the Find what box.
   Unless you check the Match entire cell contents check box, the search string can be found *anywhere* within a cell. For instance, searching for 3 would match 3, 7.23, 1:37, 5/3/2005, A32, and =B7-G23.

4. *Optional:* If the additional search options aren't visible, click the Options button to display them. You can set these options:
   ▲ **Within.** Indicate whether you want to search within the current worksheet or all sheets in the workbook.
   ▲ **Search.** Specify whether the search will proceed across rows and down (By Rows) or down columns and across (By Columns).
   ▲ **Look in.** Specify the cells to be searched. Choose *Formulas* to consider all cells, *Values* to search all cells except those containing a formula, or *Comments* to search only within comments (ignoring cell contents).

continues on next page

▲ **Match case.** When this option is enabled, capitalization within a cell must match that of the search string.

▲ **Match entire cell contents.** When enabled, cell contents must exactly match the search string. For example, searching for Microsoft will find cells that contain Microsoft but ignore Microsoft Corporation.

▲ **Format.** To include formatting in the Find criteria, click the Format button and choose one of these options from the drop-down menu (**Figure 8.51**):

Format. Specify format settings in the Find Format dialog box.

Choose Format From Cell. Click a cell whose formatting will serve as the match criterion using the eyedropper cursor.

Clear Find Format. Choose this option to remove previously chosen formatting as a criterion.

5. *Do one of the following:*

▲ Click Find Next to go to the first instance of the search string (if any are present). Continue clicking Find Next to step through the matches.

▲ Click Find All to display a list of all matches in the bottom of the dialog box (**Figure 8.52**). Click any match to go to that cell.

6. When you're finished, click Close.

✔ Tips

■ To perform a simple search, hide the options in the Find and Replace dialog box by clicking the Options button, and then click Close. Issue the Find command again, enter a search string in the Find and Replace dialog box, and click Find Next or Find All. The search is performed by rows, identifies partial matches, and searches in every cell.

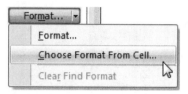

Figure 8.51 To add or remove cell formatting as a match criterion, click the Format button and choose a command.

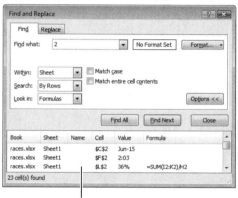

Find All results

Figure 8.52 When you click Find All, matching cells are presented in a scrolling list.

■ Another way to limit the scope of a Find is to first choose a selection command from the Find & Select icon's drop-down menu (see Figure 5.49).

■ The Find and Replace procedures support the use of *wildcards* in the Find what and Replace with boxes. Use the ? wildcard to replace a single character and * to replace multiple (or 0) characters. For example, you could enter ba?k to find back, balk, bank, bark, and bask. Enter John* to find John, Johns, Johnson, and Johnston.

Show/hide other options

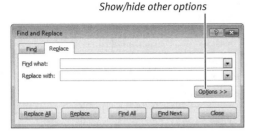

Figure 8.53 The Find and Replace dialog box with options hidden (top) and displayed (bottom).

✔ Tips

■ When the Find and Replace dialog box is open, you can switch freely between its modes by clicking the Find or the Replace tab. In fact, a Replace is frequently preceded by a Find, allowing you to first determine if there is anything to replace.

■ When making a replacement without checking Match entire cell contents, you will only replace the matching portion of a cell's contents. For example, if you search for `corp` with the intent of replacing it with `corporation`, `scorpio` will be replaced by `scorporationio`.

■ You can also use the Find and Replace dialog box to replace formatting without changing cell contents. Leave the Find what and Replace with boxes empty, and set Format options for both.

To perform a Find/Replace:

1. To restrict the Find/Replace to a range, select the range. Otherwise, click the cell in which you'd like to start the search.

2. Open the Find and Replace dialog box by doing one of the following:

   ▲ On the Home tab, choose Replace from the Find & Select icon's drop-down menu (see Figure 8.49) in the Editing group or press Ctrl H.

   ▲ On the Home tab, choose Find from the Find & Select icon's drop-down menu (see Figure 8.49) in the Editing group or press Ctrl F. In the Find and Replace dialog box, click the Replace tab.

   The Find and Replace dialog box is ready to receive search criteria (**Figure 8.53**).

3. Enter criteria by performing Steps 3–4 of the previous procedure. Enter a replacement string in the Replace with box.

   Note that Format can be set separately for the Find and Replace strings.

4. *Do one of the following:*

   ▲ To make the replacement decision individually for each match, click Find Next. Excel moves to the first match, if one is found.

   To replace the matching contents with the Replace with string, click Replace. Or to ignore the current match, click Find Next. Excel selects the next matching cell. Repeat for each additional match.

   ▲ To simultaneously perform all replacements, click Find All. Review the matches in the bottom of the dialog box, and click Replace All. Click OK to close the dialog box and view the results of the Replace All.

5. Click Close.

Sorting Data

To maintain data in a particular order (arranging entries in an address list by last name, phone number, or ZIP code, for example), you can *sort* the data. You can sort any column in ascending or descending order, based on the contents of that column. If surrounding data is related to the data in the selected column (created as records), data in the adjacent columns can also be reorganized to match that of the sorted column.

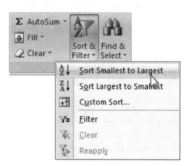

Selected column

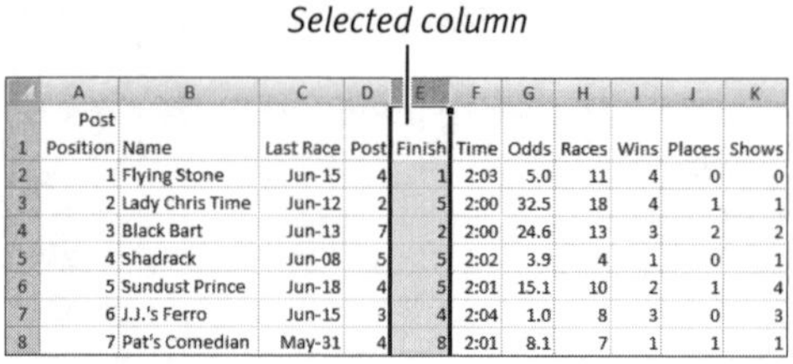

Figure 8.54 Start by selecting the column to sort.

To sort a column or data array:

1. Select the column you want to sort or by which you want to sort all surrounding data (**Figure 8.54**).

2. On the Home tab, click the Sort & Filter icon and choose a sort order, such as Sort A to Z, Sort Smallest to Largest, or Sort Oldest to Newest (**Figure 8.55**).

   The options presented vary with the type of data in the selected column. If there are no adjacent columns on either side of the selected column, the column is sorted as specified.

3. Otherwise, if columns *are* adjacent to the selected column, the Sort Warning dialog box appears (**Figure 8.56**). *Select one of these options:*

   ▲ **Expand the selection.** Treat all contiguous columns (on both sides of the selected column) as a data array.

   ▲ **Continue with the current selection.** Sort only the selected column, leaving any surrounding columns unchanged.

   Click Sort to sort the data as specified.

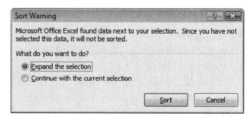

Figure 8.55 Choose a sort order command from the Sort & Find icon's drop-down menu.

Figure 8.56 To clarify your cell selection, indicate whether you want to sort the entire array or only the selected column.

Figure 8.57 Choose Custom Sort to sort on multiple fields, such as this two-way sort. In this example, a trip record data array is sorted first on Date and then—within each date—by Total Mileage.

Consider letter case

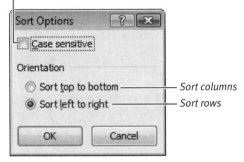

Figure 8.58 Set additional options in the Sort Options dialog box.

■ Another way to analyze a data array is to *filter* it by hiding selected rows (records) or showing only those that satisfy a criterion, such as `after 5/1/06`:

▲ To add filter capabilities to a single column (whether or not it's part of an array), select the column, switch to the Home tab, click the Sort & Filter icon in the Editing group, and choose Filter from the drop-down menu.

▲ To add filter capabilities to all columns in a data array, select the entire array or any individual cell in the array, and choose Filter from the Sort & Filter icon's drop-down menu.

See Chapter 11 for information about applying and using filters.

✔ Tips

■ To perform a more complex sort, choose Custom Sort from the Sort & Filter drop-down menu, and then set options in the Sort dialog box (**Figure 8.57**). Options include sorting on multiple columns (last name *and* first name, for example) and performing sorts based on cell or font color.

To sort by rows (rather than by columns) or to use letter case in a sort, click the Options button in the Sort dialog box. Set options in the Sort Options dialog box (**Figure 8.58**), and then click OK to return to the Sort dialog box.

■ To really simplify the process of sorting a data array, consider defining the array as a *table* (see Chapter 11).

■ A sort can also be initiated using other cell and range selections:

▲ If you select only a cell in the column you want to sort or by which you want to sort all surrounding data, the sort is performed immediately. If there are no adjacent columns, the column is sorted as specified. If there *are* adjacent columns, they are treated as an array. The entire array is sorted based on the data in the sort column.

▲ If you select a range prior to choosing a Sort command, the selected range will be sorted. The first column is automatically treated as the sort-by column. Other adjacent columns and cells outside of the selected range are not changed.

SORTING DATA

Naming Cells and Ranges

In addition to referencing cells and ranges by their addresses (such as G17 and A1:D8), you can assign names to them. There are two reasons to name selected cells and ranges:

◆ It's easier to find important data in the Go To dialog box (see Figure 8.11) using a name because you don't have to memorize the cell's or range's address.

◆ A name can be used in formulas (see Chapter 10) as a replacement for a cell or range address, making the formula easier to create and understand, such as =Total*Tax_Pct.

A name can contain 255 characters: letters, numbers, periods, and underscores (_). The first character must be a letter, underscore, or backslash (\). Although names cannot contain spaces, you can represent a space with a period or underscore, such as Div_1 or Div.1. Names aren't case-sensitive, so Budget, BUDGET, and budget are treated as the same name.

To name a cell or range:

1. Select the cell or range you want to name (**Figure 8.59**).

2. *Do one of the following:*

   ▲ Enter the name in the name box (**Figure 8.60**) and press Enter.

   ▲ On the Formulas tab, click the Define Name icon in the Defined Names group or choose Define Name from the Define name drop-down menu. Complete the information in the New Name dialog box (**Figure 8.61**), and click OK.

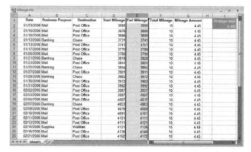

Figure 8.59 Select the cell or range to be named. (In this example, column E is selected.)

Figure 8.60 Enter a name for the selected cell or range in the name box.

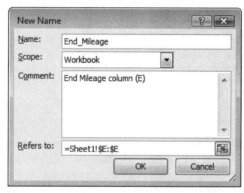

Figure 8.61 Creating a name in the New Name dialog box allows you to set a scope for the name (worksheet or workbook), add an optional comment, and edit the cell or range reference.

Filter the Name list

Figure 8.62 You can create, rename, edit, and delete names in the Name Manager dialog box.

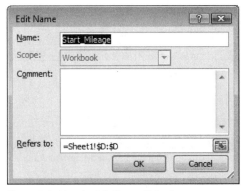

Figure 8.63 Use the Edit Name dialog box to rename a name, add a comment, or change the address or range to which the name refers.

✔ Tip

- To limit listed names to defined names, table names, names scoped to the worksheet or the workbook, or ones with or without errors, click the Filter button and choose an option from the drop-down menu (see Figure 8.62).

✔ Tips

- In previous versions of Excel and in other spreadsheets, a named cell or range was referred to as a *range name* or *named range*.

- If Excel can associate a row or column label with the selected range, it will propose the label as the name.

- Every created name has a *scope*; it can be a specific worksheet or all worksheets in the current workbook. When a name is created in the name box, its scope is automatically set to the workbook. If you create the name in the New Name dialog box (see Figure 8.61), you can set either as the scope.

- Tables can also be named. In fact, when you create a table, a name is assigned to it, based on the number of tables already created in the worksheet (Table1, Table2, and so on).

To rename, delete, or modify a name:

1. On the Formulas tab, click the Name Manager icon in the Defined Names group. The Name Manager dialog box appears (**Figure 8.62**).

2. Select a name from the Name list, and click one of these buttons:
   - ▲ **Delete.** Delete the name. To confirm the deletion, click OK in the dialog box that appears.
   - ▲ **Edit.** Modify the name, add a comment (or edit the current comment), or change the cell or range to which the name refers (**Figure 8.63**). Click OK to close the dialog box, saving your edits.

3. Click Close to dismiss the Name Manager dialog box.

NAMING CELLS AND RANGES

Password-Protecting Workbooks

Excel provides a variety of tools for protecting data. One that you are likely to use is that of adding password protection to a workbook (requiring a password to open and/or modify the contents).

To password-protect a workbook:

1. Click the Office Button, click Save As, and choose a format in which to save the workbook.

   Choose Save As even if the document already exists on disk. You can select the same file format and use the same name, if you like.

2. In the Save As dialog box (**Figure 8.64**), navigate to the drive and folder where you want to store the file (if the correct drive/folder aren't already shown). Enter a filename or accept the proposed one.

3. At the bottom of the dialog box, click the Tools drop-down menu and choose General Options (**Figure 8.65**).

   The General Options dialog box appears (**Figure 8.66**).

4. *Do any of the following:*

   ▲ To prevent unauthorized users from opening the workbook, enter a password in the Password to open box. Excel encrypts the workbook when saving it.

   ▲ To prevent unauthorized users from modifying the workbook but still enable them to view its contents, enter a password in the Password to modify box. No encryption is added.

   Click OK. You'll be asked to reenter the password(s).

5. Click Save to save the file on disk with the specified password or passwords.

Filename   Current folder

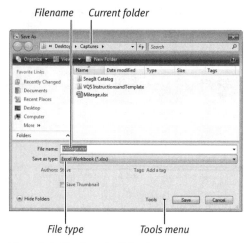

File type   Tools menu

Figure 8.64 The Save As dialog box.

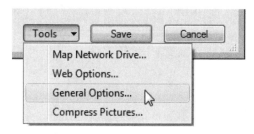

Figure 8.65 To password-protect a workbook, choose General Options from the Tools drop-down menu.

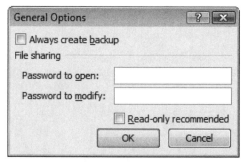

Figure 8.66 Enter one or both passwords in the General Options dialog box, and then click OK.

PASSWORD-PROTECTING WORKBOOKS

Figure 8.67 This dialog box appears when a password to open has been set for a workbook.

Figure 8.68 This dialog box appears when a password to modify has been set for a workbook.

To open a password-protected workbook:

1. Open the file using any of the standard methods.

2. Depending on the password types associated with the file, the following occurs:

   ▲ **Open protection.** A Password dialog box appears (**Figure 8.67**). Enter the password and click OK. If the password is incorrect or Cancel is clicked, the workbook does not open.

   ▲ **Modify protection.** A Password dialog box appears (**Figure 8.68**). Enter the password for permission to modify the workbook or click Read Only for permission to view but not change the workbook.

To remove or change a password:

1. Open the workbook by supplying the password(s). The following occurs:

   ▲ **Open protection.** A Password dialog box appears (see Figure 8.67). Enter the password and click OK. If the password is incorrect or Cancel is clicked, the workbook does not open.

   ▲ **Modify protection.** A Password dialog box appears (see Figure 8.68). Enter the password for permission to modify the workbook or click Read Only for permission to view but not change the workbook.

2. Perform Steps 1–3 of "To password-protect a workbook," culminating in the General Options dialog box opening (see Figure 8.66).

   You can optionally rename the file or select a different save location.

continues on next page

3. *Do one of the following:*

▲ To eliminate a password, delete it.

▲ To change a password, delete the current password and enter a new one.

4. Click OK to close the General Options dialog box, and then click Save.

✔ Tips

■ Save an unprotected, archival copy of the workbook to floppy, CD, or another type of removable media—just in case you forget the password(s).

■ Use the Password to modify option when one or more users need to view a workbook but not change it. Restrict access to the password to those few users (or only yourself) who have permission to change the data.

■ If you assign both passwords to a workbook, use two *different* passwords.

FORMATTING WORKSHEETS AND DATA

Although you're free to accept the default formatting for any worksheet (using the preset column widths, row heights, font, and font size), you're unlikely to do so very often. Simply put, properly formatted worksheets are easier to read.

And if you go to the effort of applying Excel's *attractive* formatting features (such as shading and border styles for cells, and fonts, styles, colors, and alignment for data), you can transform an ordinary worksheet into something worthy of being published in a corporate report.

Setting Column Width and Row Height

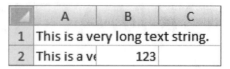

	A	B	C
1	This is a very long text string.		
2	This is a v<	123	

Figure 9.1 Cells A1 and A2 contain the same text string. Because cells B1 and C1 are empty, A1's text can spill into them. But because B2 contains data, the text string in cell A2 is truncated.

Unless you've set a specific width for a column or height for a row, each row and column automatically adjusts to fit the data it contains, as follows:

◆ **Row height** adjusts to the largest font size in any cell within the row.

◆ **Column width** adjusts to the longest number in any cell within the column.

A long text string in a cell (**Figure 9.1**), on the other hand, does *not* result in a column-width adjustment. If adjacent cells are empty, the extra text spills into them. If adjacent cells already contain data, only the text that fits within the current cell width is displayed.

To set a column width:

1. To select the column (or columns), *do one of the following:*

   ▲ **Single column.** Click its letter or select a single cell within the column.

   ▲ **Multiple contiguous columns.** Drag-select the column letters.

   ▲ **Multiple noncontiguous columns.** Ctrl-click each column letter.

2. On the Home tab, click the Format icon in the Cells group. *Do one of the following:*

   ▲ To set a fixed width, choose Column Width from the drop-down menu (**Figure 9.2**). In the Column Width dialog box (**Figure 9.3**), enter a number (representing the approximate number of characters), and click OK.

   ▲ Choose AutoFit Column Width. Excel will continually adjust the column's width to the longest number that appears anywhere in the column.

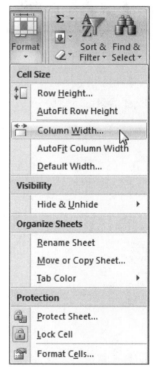

Figure 9.2 Choose a column width or row height command.

Figure 9.3 Enter a new width (in characters), and click OK.

Figure 9.4 Enter a new row height (in points), and click OK.

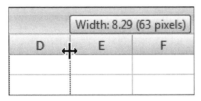

Figure 9.5 Click and drag between column letters to resize the column on the left (in this case, column D).

To set a row height:

1. To select the row(s), *do one of the following*:
   - ▲ **Single row.** Click its number or select a single cell within the row.
   - ▲ **Multiple contiguous rows.** Drag-select the row numbers.
   - ▲ **Multiple noncontiguous rows.** [Ctrl]-click each row number.

2. On the Home tab, click the Format icon in the Cells group. *Do one of the following*:
   - ▲ To set a fixed height, choose Row Height from the drop-down menu (see Figure 9.2). In the Row Height dialog box (**Figure 9.4**), enter a height in *points* (72 points per inch), and click OK.
   - ▲ Choose AutoFit Row Height. Excel will continually adjust the row's height to accommodate the largest font (or text wrap) in the row.

✔ Tips

- ■ You can *manually* adjust column widths and row heights:
  - ▲ **Column width.** Click the right border of the column's letter and drag to the left or right (**Figure 9.5**).
  - ▲ **Row height.** Click the bottom border of the row's number and drag up or down.

- ■ You can simultaneously set a width or height for *multiple* columns or rows. Select the columns or rows, and then manually adjust the width or height of any one of them.

- ■ To instantly make a column wide enough to accommodate the longest number or text string in the column, double-click the column letter's right border. To adjust a row height in the same manner, double-click the row number's bottom border.

About Data and Cell Formatting

If you start a new worksheet by simply entering data, it will all have the same formatting. Every text and number entry will use the same font, size, style, and color. Numbers will be displayed using the General format (as typed, unless the column isn't wide enough to show the entire number). Cells will have no background color and no borders.

However, Excel offers many data- and cell-formatting options. To make any worksheet more attractive and easier to interpret, you can do the following:

◆ Apply different fonts, styles, sizes, and/or colors to data within selected cells.

◆ Set paragraph alignment for individual cells (left-, center-, or right-aligned).

◆ Wrap text within cells or shrink it to fit, rather than let it spill into adjacent cells.

◆ Apply a variety of Number formats to cells that contain numeric data, such as setting the number of decimal places and formatting as currency or percentages.

◆ Use *conditional formatting* to make certain numbers stand out, such as values below the average or values that correspond to a rule of your own creation.

◆ Fill cells with color.

◆ Add *borders* (lines) around cell edges.

✔ Tips

■ If you don't care for the default font used to format worksheets, you can change it. Click the Office Button, and then click the Excel Options button. On the Popular tab of the Excel Options dialog box (**Figure 9.6**), choose a new font and/or size, and click OK.

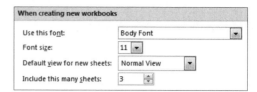

Figure 9.6 You can specify a default font and size for all new worksheets.

■ Displaying the gridlines on any worksheet is traditional—*but optional.* To hide the gridlines, click the View tab and remove the check mark from Gridlines in the Show/Hide group.

Figure 9.7 Character-formatting commands can be found in the Font group.

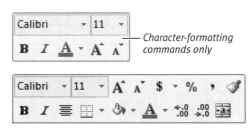

Character-formatting commands only

Figure 9.8 The Mini toolbar displays different formatting commands when text within a cell (top) or the cell itself (bottom) is selected.

Figure 9.9 Choose a style from the Cell Styles gallery to format headings, titles, totals, and good/bad data.

Figure 9.10 Choose paragraph-formatting commands from the Alignment group.

Character and Paragraph Formatting

By choosing commands from the Home tab or the Mini toolbar, you can specify a font for selected text within a cell or the entire cell, as well as change the paragraph alignment.

To set character or paragraph formatting:

1. *Do one of the following:*
   - ▲ To format all text within a cell, select the cell.
   - ▲ To format only certain text within a cell, highlight the text you want to format.

2. To apply character formatting, *do any of the following:*
   - ▲ On the Home tab, choose character-formatting commands from the Font group (**Figure 9.7**).
   - ▲ Right-click the cell or selected text, and choose commands from the Mini toolbar (**Figure 9.8**).
   - ▲ Click the Cell Styles icon in the Styles group, and choose a style from the gallery (**Figure 9.9**).

3. To apply paragraph formatting, choose commands from the Alignment group on the Home tab (**Figure 9.10**).

✔ Tip

- ■ Character and paragraph formatting can also be applied to multiple selected cells simultaneously. Use any of the selection techniques described on pages 160–161 prior to choosing formatting commands.

CHARACTER AND PARAGRAPH FORMATTING

Fitting Text Within a Cell

Occasionally, a cell contains more text than will fit. To fully display the text, you can allow the additional characters to overflow into adjacent cells, widen the column in which the cell is located, or use one of the methods discussed below.

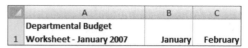

Figure 9.11 Long text, such as the string in cell A1, can be wrapped within its cell.

To enable text wrap:

1. Select the cell or cells in which you want text to wrap.

2. On the Home tab, click the Wrap Text icon in the Alignment group.

   Text within the selected cells wraps. The row height increases as needed in order to accommodate present and future text in the row (**Figure 9.11**).

To shrink text to fit a cell:

1. Select the cell or cells containing text you want to shrink to fit within the cell width.

2. On the Home tab, click the Format icon in the Cells group and choose Format Cells. The Format Cells dialog box appears.

3. On the Alignment tab (**Figure 9.12**), click Shrink to fit and then OK. (Shrink to fit is available only when cells with appropriate data are selected in Step 1.)

   Text in the cells is reduced as needed in order to fit the cell widths.

✔ Tips

■ To eliminate text wrap from selected cells, click the Wrap Text icon again.

■ If you've enabled text wrap, you may also want to set a vertical alignment for the entire row or selected cells within the row (**Figure 9.13**).

■ If you set a specific height for a row, its height will no longer increase to accommodate text wrap.

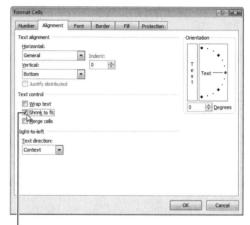

Shrink to fit

Figure 9.12 Click Shrink to fit, and then click OK.

Top, Middle, and Bottom Align icons

Figure 9.13 Bottom Align was set for the column heads in cells B1 and C1 in Figure 9.15 (above).

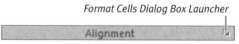

Format Cells Dialog Box Launcher

Figure 9.14 Click this tiny icon to open the dialog box.

■ You can also open the Format Cells dialog box by clicking the Format Cells Dialog Box Launcher on the Font, Number, or Alignment group bar (**Figure 9.14**).

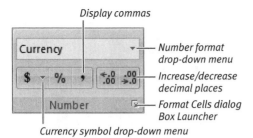

Display commas

Number format drop-down menu

Increase/decrease decimal places

Format Cells dialog Box Launcher

Currency symbol drop-down menu

Figure 9.15 Choose common number formatting options from the Number group.

Category list   *Options*

Figure 9.16 For more complex formatting, as well as date and time formats, use the Format Cells dialog box.

Number Formatting

Like any modern spreadsheet application, Excel 2007 offers a wide variety of formats that you can apply to numeric data. You can format numbers as currency, percentages, fractions, or scientific notation, for example. You can optionally display numbers with commas and a set number of decimal places.

Note that the display options set for a given number do *not* affect the way the number is stored or used in calculations. For instance, if you apply a currency format to a cell containing 28.1225, $28.12 will display. The remaining .0025 isn't gone; it simply isn't shown.

To apply a Number format:

1. Select the cell or cells to which you want to apply a Number format.

2. *Do one of the following:*

   ▲ On the Home tab, choose formatting options from the Number group (**Figure 9.15**).

   ▲ Right-click any selected cell and choose format options from the Mini toolbar (see Figure 9.8).

   ▲ Click the Format Cells Dialog Box Launcher on the Number group bar (see Figure 9.15). Choose formatting options from those on the Number tab (**Figure 9.16**). Click OK to apply the options to the selected cells.

✔ Tip

■ Be sure to thoroughly explore the Number tab of the Format Cells dialog box (see Figure 9.16). It also includes formatting options for dates and times. And if you choose the Special category, you'll find formats for zip codes, phone numbers, and Social Security numbers.

NUMBER FORMATTING

Conditional Formatting

By applying *conditional formatting* (formatting that's applied only when criteria are met), you can make important data stand out from other elements in a data set. You can do any of the following:

- ◆ Overlay every member of the data set with a data bar, color, or icon that indicates its position in the distribution.

- ◆ Apply a color highlight to a specific number of items that are highest, lowest, above average, or below average.

- ◆ Apply a color highlight to items identified by a *rule*, such as bowling averages greater than 200.

Unlike manually applied formatting, conditional formatting updates itself as required. That is, if the data that has been conditionally formatted changes, the items formatted in this manner (highlighted in green, for instance) will automatically change, too.

To apply data bars, color scales, or icon sets to data:

1. Select the cell range to which you want to apply conditional formatting.

2. On the Home tab, click the Conditional Formatting icon in the Styles group.

   A drop-down menu appears (**Figure 9.17**).

3. Choose an option from the Data Bars, Color Scales, or Icon Sets submenu (**Figure 9.18**).

   A live preview is provided for each formatting option.

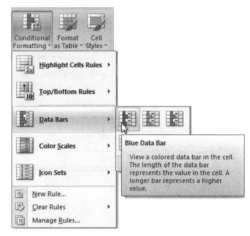

Figure 9.17 Choose conditional formatting from this drop-down menu.

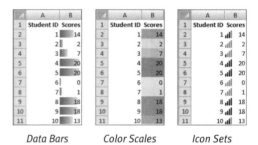

Data Bars   Color Scales   Icon Sets

Figure 9.18 You can show the relative size of every item in a data distribution by formatting with data bars, a color scale, or an icon set.

Custom Conditional Formatting

In addition to the Top/Bottom Rules and Highlight Cells Rules (discussed on page 167), you can create *custom rules*—including rules based on a formula. To create a custom rule, choose New Rule from the Conditional Formatting drop-down menu or More Rules from any of its submenus.

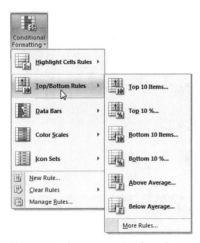

Figure 9.19 Choose an option from the Top/Bottom Rules submenu to select the highest/lowest items or above/below the average for the data set.

Number or percentage *Formatting options*

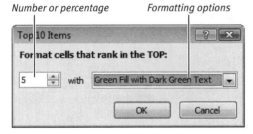

Figure 9.20 Set options for the rule, and click OK.

Figure 9.21 Highlight Cell Rules submenu.

To apply a Top/Bottom Rule to data:

1. Select the cell range to which you want to apply a Top/Bottom Rule.

2. On the Home tab, click the Conditional Formatting icon in the Styles group.

3. From the drop-down menu that appears, choose an option from the Top/Bottom Rules submenu (**Figure 9.19**).

   A live preview is provided for each rule.

4. In the dialog box that appears (**Figure 9.20**), set options:

   ▲ For the Average rules, the dialog box allows you to select fill and text colors.

   ▲ For the Top and Bottom rules, you can also set the cutoff point (as a number or percentage), highlighting only the lowest five scores, for example.

5. Click OK to apply the rule to the selected cell range.

To apply a Highlight Cells Rule to data:

1. Select the cell range to which you want to apply a Highlight Cells Rule.

2. On the Home tab, click the Conditional Formatting icon in the Styles group.

3. From the drop-down menu that appears (see Figure 9.19), choose an option from the Highlight Cells Rules submenu (**Figure 9.21**).

4. In the dialog box that appears, set options and click OK to apply the rule.

✔ Tips

■ You can apply multiple types of conditional formatting to the same range.

■ To remove conditional formatting, select the range, open the Conditional Formatting drop-down menu, and choose Clear Rules > Clear Rules from Selected Cells.

CONDITIONAL FORMATTING

Adding Cell Borders and Backgrounds

In addition to formatting cell content, you can also apply formatting to cell borders and backgrounds. For example, you could create a double-line border beneath a row to visually separate data from a totals row. Or you could make critical cells stand out by applying a light-colored fill to them.

To fill cells with color:

1. Select the cells to which you want to apply a background color.

2. On the Home tab, open the Format Cells dialog box by *doing one of the following:*

   ▲ Click the Format icon in the Cells group, and choose Format Cells from the drop-down menu.

   ▲ Click the Format Cells Dialog Box Launcher on the Font, Alignment, or Number group bar (see Figure 9.14).

   ▲ Right-click one of the selected cells, and choose Format Cells from the pop-up menu that appears.

3. In the Format Cells dialog box, click the Fill tab (**Figure 9.22**).

4. *Do one of the following:*

   ▲ **Fill cells with a solid color.** Click a color icon in the Background Colors section. (To choose a color that isn't displayed, click More Colors.)

   ▲ **Fill cells with a pattern.** Choose a pattern style and color from the drop-down menus.

   ▲ **Fill cells with a gradient.** Click the Fill Effects button. Set options in the dialog box that appears (**Figure 9.23**), and click OK.

5. Click OK to close the Format Cells dialog box.

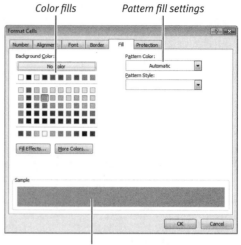

Color fills   *Pattern fill settings*

Preview of color, pattern, or gradient fill

Figure 9.22 Choose Fill options from the Fill tab of the Format Cells dialog box.

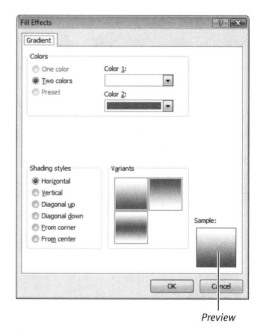

Preview

Figure 9.23 You can apply a custom gradient to cells. Doing so often results in a 3-D background.

Figure 9.24 You can add, remove, or modify borders for currently selected cells.

To add cell borders:

1. Select the cells to which you want to add one or more border lines.

2. On the Home tab, open the Format Cells dialog box by *doing one of the following:*
   ▲ Click the Format icon in the Cells group and choose Format Cells from the drop-down menu.
   ▲ Click the Format Cells Dialog Box Launcher on the Font, Alignment, or Number group bar (see Figure 9.14).
   ▲ Right-click one of the selected cells, and choose Format Cells from the pop-up menu that appears.

3. In the Format Cells dialog box, click the Border tab (**Figure 9.24**).

4. *Do any of the following:*
   ▲ **Add border lines.** Select a line style and color from the left side of the dialog box. To use one of the presets (such as Outline), click its icon. To add a single border line, click its icon or the spot in the sample where you want to add the line.
   ▲ **Remove border lines.** To simultaneously remove *all* border lines from the selected cells, click the None preset. To remove a single border, click its icon or the spot in the sample from which you want to remove the line.
   ▲ **Change border line properties.** To change the style or color of borders, select a new style and/or color, and click the preset or border icon that you want to reformat.

5. Click OK to close the dialog box.

ADDING CELL BORDERS AND BACKGROUNDS

Removing, Replacing, and Reusing Formats

Whether you've applied character, paragraph, number, or conditional formatting, such formatting can be removed or replaced. To simplify the process of applying existing formatting to additional cells or ranges, you can also reuse formatting.

To remove formatting:

1. Select the cell range from which you want to remove formatting. Switch to the Home tab.

2. *Do any of the following:*

   ▲ To remove all character, paragraph, and number formatting, click the Clear icon in the Editing group, and choose Clear Formats from the drop-down menu (**Figure 9.25**).

   ▲ To selectively remove character style formatting (bold, italic, underline, or double underline) from selected cells or selected characters within a cell, reapply the style formatting option.

   ▲ To remove conditional formatting from the selected cells, open the Conditional Formatting drop-down menu, and choose Clear Rules > Clear Rules from Selected Cells.

   ▲ To remove all conditional formatting from the current worksheet, click the Conditional Formatting icon, and choose Clear Rules > Clear Rules from Entire Sheet.

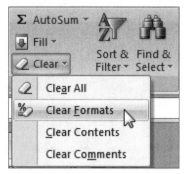

Figure 9.25 Choose Clear Formats to remove all formatting from the selected cells.

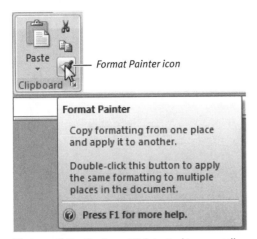

Format Painter icon

Format Painter

Copy formatting from one place and apply it to another.

Double-click this button to apply the same formatting to multiple places in the document.

Press F1 for more help.

Figure 9.26 Use the Format Painter tool to copy cell formatting to a different cell or range.

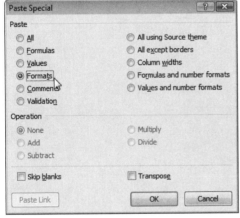

Figure 9.27 Click the Formats radio button to paste the formatting (but not the copied data) into the target cells.

To replace formatting:

1. Select the cell range for which you want to replace or modify the current formatting. Switch to the Home tab.

2. *Do any of the following:*
   - ▲ To alter paragraph formatting, choose options from the Alignment group (see Figure 9.10).
   - ▲ To set a new font or size, choose options from the Font group (see Figure 9.7) or the Mini toolbar (see Figure 9.8).
   - ▲ To replace or modify Number formatting, choose options from the Number group (see Figure 9.15) or the Number tab in the Format Cells dialog box (see Figure 9.16).

To reuse existing formatting:

1. Select a cell that contains the formatting you want to duplicate.

2. On the Home tab, select the Format Painter icon in the Clipboard group (**Figure 9.26**).

3. *Do either of the following:*
   - ▲ Click the cell to which you want to apply the formatting.
   - ▲ Drag-select the cell range to which you want to apply the formatting.

✔ Tips

- You can also reapply existing formatting using copy-and-paste. First, copy ([Ctrl][C]) the cell whose formatting you want to reuse. Next, select the target cells, click the Paste icon, and choose Paste Special from the drop-down menu. In the Paste Special dialog box, click the Formats radio button (**Figure 9.27**), and click OK.

- The Clear Formats command can be used to remove conditional formatting.

- Applying Clear Formats also causes cells to revert to the default font and size.

FORMULAS AND FUNCTIONS

After familiarizing yourself with Excel's list-management features (using it to record mailing lists and membership rosters, for example), you'll want to explore the application's extensive calculation capabilities. By combining the contents of specific cells with each other or constants, you can create *formulas*. For example, you can add two cells' contents, divide the contents of one cell by that of another, or multiply a cell's contents by a constant (such as a sales tax percentage or a commission rate).

You can also use Excel *functions* in your formulas. For instance, rather than laboriously adding the contents of several dozen cells, you can use the SUM function to generate a total for the range. In support of your calculation needs, Excel provides more than 300 built-in functions.

In this chapter, you'll learn the basics of combining cell references, constants, and functions into useful formulas. Techniques for troubleshooting formulas are also presented.

About Cell References

Although a formula can be composed solely of constants, such as =12+5, you'll seldom use Excel to perform such calculations. Almost all formulas include *cell references*, such as =A2+5. This formula is interpreted by Excel as: "Take the current contents of cell A2 and add 5 to it."

A1 reference style

By default, Excel worksheets use *A1 reference style* in which columns are lettered and rows are numbered. Each *cell address* is named for the intersection of the column and row in which the cell is located. For example, G7 is found at the intersection of column G and row 7. A *range* is represented as a pair of addresses separated by a colon (:). For example, B3:B6 means all cells between cells B3 and B6 inclusive—that is, B3, B4, B5, and B6. Refer to **Table 10.1** for some additional examples.

3-D reference style

Excel also provides a *3-D reference style* that allows you to include cells and ranges from other sheets in your formulas, as well as perform calculations across sheets in a workbook:

◆ To include a cell or range from another sheet in a formula, precede the cell or range address with the sheet's name followed by an exclamation point:

=Sheet2!a7-8

In this example, 8 is subtracted from the contents of cell A7 on Sheet2.

◆ To consolidate data across multiple sheets, precede the cell or range address with the sheet range:

=SUM(Sales1:Sales12!G50)

Table 10.1

A1 Reference Style Examples	
EXAMPLE	EXPLANATION
R5	Cell in column R, row 5
B3:E3	Cells B, C, D, and E in row 3
3:3	Row 3
F:F	Column F
5:8	Rows 5, 6, 7, and 8
A:C	Columns A, B, and C
A1:B3	All cells between cells A1 and B3 inclusive (A1, B1, A2, B2, A3, and B3)

H	I	J	K	L
Races	Wins	Places	Shows	In the Money
11	4	0	0	36.4%
18	4	1	1	33.3%
13	3	2	2	53.8%

`=SUM(Table1[[#This Row],[Wins]:[Shows]])/Table1[[#This Row],[Races]]`

Figure 10.1 In Table1 (top), In the Money is a calculated column. When the formula is expressed in structured reference style (bottom), it is identical in every cell in the column. #This Row and column names are used in place of A1 style references.

	1	2	3
1	Date	Business Purpose	Destination
2	01/03/2006	Mail	Post Office
3	01/10/2006	Mail	Post Office

Figure 10.2 In R1C1 reference style, both rows and columns are numbered.

Table 10.2

3-D Reference Style Functions

FUNCTION	DESCRIPTION
AVERAGE	Calculates the average (arithmetic mean)
COUNT	Counts the cells that contain numbers
MAX	Returns the largest value in referenced cells
MIN	Returns the smallest value in referenced cells
PRODUCT	Multiplies numbers in referenced cells
STDEV	Calculates the standard deviation, based on a sample
STDEVP	Calculates the population standard deviation
SUM	Adds numbers in referenced cells
VAR	Calculates the variance, based on a sample
VARP	Calculates the population variance

In this example, monthly sales are recorded in the first 12 sheets, each of which is named Sales, followed by the month number. Consolidating data this way assumes you have laid out the data in the sheets (Sales1–Sales12) in identical fashion; that is, the cell (G50, in this case) contains the appropriate number in each sheet, such as total monthly sales or Janice's monthly commissions.

Structured reference style

Excel 2007 introduces *structured reference style*, a simplified means of addressing table data. When creating a formula in a table (a calculated column, for example), table-based structured references are used rather than specific cell addresses (**Figure 10.1**). In fact, unless you convert a range containing A1 reference style formulas into a table, structured references are *automatically* used.

✔ Tips

- If you prefer, you can use *R1C1 reference style* in which both rows and columns are numbered (**Figure 10.2**). To enable R1C1, click the Office Button followed by the Excel Options button. In the Excel Options dialog box, select the Formulas category, click the R1C1 reference style check box in the Working with formulas section, and then click OK.

- R1C1 reference style is generally used in Excel scripts (called *macros*).

- In 3-D reference style, only 18 functions can be used to consolidate data across sheets. For a list of supported functions, see **Table 10.2**. Supported variants of these functions that can be applied to text and logical values include AVERAGEA, COUNTA, MAXA, MINA, STDEVA, STDEVPA, VARA, and VARPA.

Formula Essentials

This section presents the background information needed to create formulas.

Anatomy of a formula

A basic formula (**Figure 10.3**) consists of a combination of cell references, constants, and operators. (A *constant* is any data entered in a cell, such as text or a number, date, or time.) To distinguish a formula from data, every formula begins with an equal (=) symbol.

Operators

Operators are used to specify the type of calculation to perform, such as addition or multiplication. Operators can be divided into four categories: arithmetic, comparison, text concatenation, and reference.

◆ **Arithmetic operators.** Used to perform mathematical calculations, producing a numerical result.

◆ **Comparison operators.** Used to perform logical comparisons between two values, resulting in either True or False.

◆ **Text concatenation operator.** Used to combine two text values, producing a single text string.

◆ **Reference operators.** Used to specify cell ranges.

See **Tables 10.3–10.6** for a list of supported operators.

Cell reference   Constant

=A3+18

Operator

Figure 10.3 In this simple formula, 18 is added to the data in cell A3. As is the case with all formulas, the result is displayed in the cell containing the formula.

Table 10.3

Arithmetic Operators

OPERATOR	DESCRIPTION	EXAMPLE
+	Addition	A3+5
−	Subtraction	18-B7
−	Negation	-17
*	Multiplication	A6*B6
/	Division	G4/3
%	Percent	35%
^	Exponentiation (raise to a power)	A4^2

Table 10.4

Comparison Operators

OPERATOR	DESCRIPTION	EXAMPLE
=	Equal	A3=B5
>	Greater than	D2>12
<	Less than	E3<E4
>=	Greater than or equal to	A6>=15
<=	Less than or equal to	G4<=3
<>	Not equal to	B7<>5

Table 10.5

Text Concatenation Operator

OPERATOR	DESCRIPTION	EXAMPLE
&	Concatenation	"Phone: "&B5

Table 10.6

Reference Operators

Operator	Description	Example
:	Range	A3:A8 (all cells from A3 to A8)
,	Union	D2,F2:F5 (cells D2 and F2:F5)
[space]	Intersection	C4:D7 D6:D8 (cells D6 and D7)

Table 10.7

Operator Precedence

Operator	Description
:	Colon (range)
[space]	Space (union)
,	Comma (intersection)
–	Negation
%	Percent
^	Exponentiation
*, /	Multiplication and division
+, –	Addition and subtraction
&	Concatenation
=, <>, <=, >=	Comparison operators

Precedence

When calculating the result of a formula, Excel evaluates the elements from left to right. However, this holds true only when all operators are of the same importance (called *precedence*). Every operator has a precedence, as shown in **Table 10.7**. The higher in the table an operator appears, the higher its precedence. Thus, when a formula contains operators of differing precedence, the calculations are performed from highest to lowest precedence. Here are some examples:

4+2+3   [9]

Explanation: All operators have the same precedence, so the formula is evaluated from left to right.

4*2+3   [11]

Explanation: Multiplication has a higher precedence than addition. But because the multiplication occurs first in the formula, the left-to-right order is still followed (8+3).

4+2*3   [10]

Explanation: Multiplication has a higher precedence, so 2*3 is evaluated first (4+6).

In addition, you can change the order of evaluation by enclosing terms in parentheses. Such items are always evaluated first. When multiple sets of parentheses are used, items in the innermost ones are evaluated first.

4*(2+3) [20]

Explanation: Because parentheses surround the last two terms, they are evaluated first (resulting in 5). Without the parentheses, the formula would have been evaluated in left-to-right order: 4*2 (or 8), plus 3, for a result of 11.

FORMULA ESSENTIALS

Relative, absolute, and mixed

Cell references in formulas can be relative, absolute, or mixed. When you enter a reference by typing an address (such as entering =(B2+C2+D2)/3 in cell E2), the references to cells B2, C2, and D2 are *relative* to the location of the formula cell (E2). If the formula is moved or copied to a different cell, Excel adjusts the cell references to point to the correct cells. For example, copying the formula to cells E3:E7 results in the correct formula in each new cell (**Figure 10.4**).

You use an *absolute reference* (preceding both the column and row with dollar signs) for a cell address that must not change when copied or moved. For example, in a business mileage worksheet (**Figure 10.5**), you could create a formula to calculate Mileage Amount: the trip's total mileage multiplied by a fixed mileage rate (found in cell I2). The initial formula in row 2 would be =F2*$I$2 and then repeated in every cell in column G (for example, =F3*$I$2). Unlike relative references, absolute references never change, no matter where on the worksheet the formula is copied or moved.

Finally, Excel also supports *mixed references* in which the column or the row is absolute and the other is relative, such as $A1 (column A is absolute, row 1 is relative) or A$1 (column A is relative, row 1 is absolute).

✔ Tip

- When a formula is copied or moved (**Figure 10.6**), the cell references change as shown in **Table 10.8**:
  - ▲ Relative references change to match the formula's new location, relative to the original location. This also applies to the relative part of a mixed reference.
  - ▲ Absolute references do not change. The absolute portion of a mixed reference also remains unchanged.

Formula copied to E3

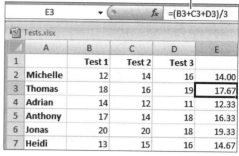

	A	B	C	D	E
1		Test 1	Test 2	Test 3	
2	Michelle	12	14	16	14.00
3	Thomas	18	16	19	17.67
4	Adrian	14	12	11	12.33
5	Anthony	17	14	18	16.33
6	Jonas	20	20	18	19.33
7	Heidi	13	15	16	14.67

Figure 10.4 When copied to cells E3:E7, the relative cell references in the formula automatically adjust to refer to the correct cells, such as =(B3+C3+D3)/3.

F	G	H	I
Total Mileage	Mileage Amount		Mileage Rate
10	4.45		0.445
10	4.45		
10	4.45		

Figure 10.5 The formula in column G uses an absolute reference to point to the fixed mileage rate in cell I2.

	A	B	C	D	E
1	1	4	1		
2	2	5			
3	3	6			
4				D3	
5					

Figure 10.6 If a formula in C1 is copied or moved to cell D3, it changes as described in **Table 10.8**.

Table 10.8

Result of Copying or Moving a Formula

Formula (C1)	Copied/Moved (D3)	Reference Type
=A1	=B3	Relative
=$A$1	=$A$1	Absolute
=$A1	=$A3	Mixed (absolute column)
=A$1	=B$1	Mixed (absolute row)

FORMULA ESSENTIALS

Figure 10.7 The Function Library group organizes the functions by category.

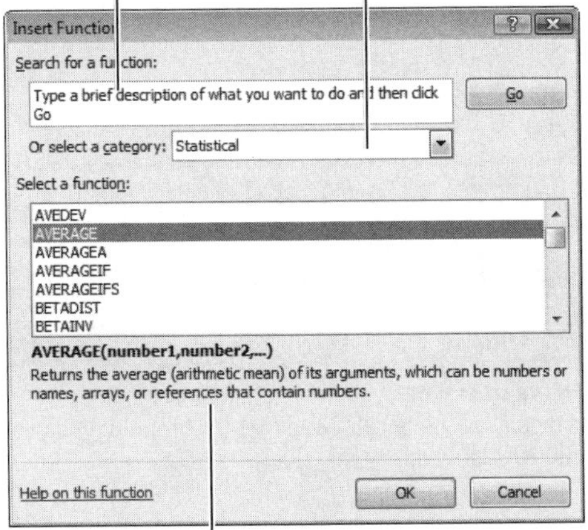

Search for a function   Function categories

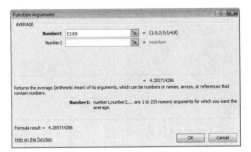

Description of selected function

Figure 10.8 Select a function, and then click OK.

Figure 10.9 You can enter arguments by typing, clicking a cell in the worksheet, or drag-selecting a range.

✔ Tip

■ You can also open the Insert Function dialog box by clicking the *fx* icon in the formula bar.

Functions

Functions are formula helpers—built-in computational routines that you can include in formulas to simplify the creation of complex and special-purpose calculations. For instance, rather than laboriously totaling a string of cells with the formula =A1+A2+A3+A4+A5, you can use the SUM function to add the entire range via the formula =SUM(A1:A5).

All but a few functions require *arguments*, the data on which the function will operate. Arguments are enclosed in parentheses and— if there are multiple arguments—separated by commas. The argument to the SUM function above is the range A1:A5. In addition to operating on a single range, SUM can also be used to total individual cells and constants, as seen in this formula:

=SUM(A1:A5,B7,17)

In this example, the total of cells A1, A2, A3, A4, A5, B7, and 17 is calculated.

When the text insertion mark is at the desired spot in the formula you're creating, you can insert a function in these ways:

◆ Functions for which you know the spelling and syntax can be typed directly into the formula.

◆ On the Formulas tab, you can choose a function by clicking an icon in the Function Library group (**Figure 10.7**).

◆ For guidance in selecting a function, click Insert Function in the Function Library group. In the Insert Function dialog box (**Figure 10.8**), select a function, and then click OK.

In the latter two function-insertion methods, the Function Arguments dialog box appears (**Figure 10.9**). Using the guidance provided, enter the argument(s) and click OK to insert the function into your formula.

FORMULA ESSENTIALS

Creating Formulas

Formulas can be created from any combination of cell contents, constants, and functions. Many common formulas, such as sums or averages of a column or row, can quickly be created using the AutoSum tool.

To create a formula without functions:

1. Select the cell that will contain the formula, and type an equal sign (=).

2. Construct the formula by typing constants, cell references, and operators (**Figure 10.10**). Press [Enter] to complete the formula.

   The formula is replaced in the cell by the calculated result (**Figure 10.11**).

To create a formula with functions:

1. Select the cell that will contain the formula, and type an equal sign (=).

2. A formula can contain a combination of constants, cell references, operators, and functions. To insert a function at the text insertion mark, *do one of the following:*

   ▲ Type the function name, a left parenthesis, the argument(s), and a right parenthesis.

   ▲ Choose a function from the Function Library group (see Figure 10.7). In the Function Arguments dialog box (see Figure 10.9), enter the argument(s) and click OK.

   ▲ Click the Insert Function icon in the Function Library group. In the Insert Function dialog box (see Figure 10.8), select a function, and click OK. In the Function Arguments dialog box (see Figure 10.9), enter the argument(s) and click OK.

3. Press [Enter] to complete the formula.

   The formula is replaced in the cell by the calculated result.

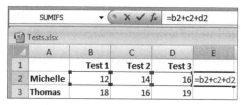

Figure 10.10 The formula in E2 totals Michelle's three test scores. As you select cells or type their addresses, Excel displays handles around each referenced cell.

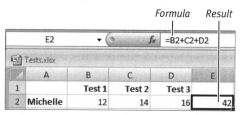

Figure 10.11 When you complete a formula, the result is displayed in the cell. Note that the formula is shown in the formula bar.

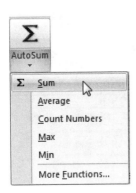

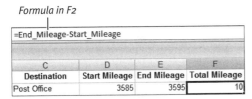

Figure 10.12 Select a function from the drop-down menu.

Figure 10.13 To specify a range for this SUM function, type =SUM(and drag-select the range to be totaled. Type the closing parenthesis to complete the formula.

Formula in F2

=End_Mileage-Start_Mileage

C	D	E	F
Destination	**Start Mileage**	**End Mileage**	**Total Mileage**
Post Office	3585	3595	10

Figure 10.14 Columns D and E have been named Start_Mileage and End_Mileage. To calculate total mileage for any cell in column F, the names can be substituted for the two cell references.

Figure 10.15 Double-click a function name to insert it into the formula.

— *Formula cell*

— *Formula AutoComplete drop-down list*

To create an AutoSum formula:

1. Select the cell at the bottom of a column or end of a row that will contain the formula.

   The cells that will serve as the argument to the selected AutoSum function must be a contiguous string within a single column or row, such as B2:B23.

2. On the Formulas tab, click the AutoSum icon in the Function Library group (**Figure 10.12**). Choose a function from the drop-down menu or click More Functions to pick from all Excel functions.

3. Excel highlights the range it thinks you want to use as the argument to the function. Adjust the range, if necessary.

4. Press Enter to complete the formula.

✔ Tips

- When creating a formula, a cell reference can be typed or added by clicking the cell you want to reference. As an argument to a function, you can type or drag-select a range (**Figure 10.13**).

- Typed cell references can be entered in uppercase or lowercase.

- As explained in Chapter 8, if you've named cells or ranges, you can substitute the names for the addresses and ranges in formulas (**Figure 10.14**).

- If required, a formula can contain multiple functions, as well as functions within functions (called *nested functions*).

- If you can type the first few letters of a function's name when creating a formula, you can use Formula AutoComplete to insert the function (**Figure 10.15**). To select a function, double-click its name in the drop-down list.

- Functions do *not* ignore empty cells within the argument range(s).

Editing Formulas

You can edit existing formulas to correct errors and change cell or range references. Many of the techniques described below are also applicable to editing data.

To edit a formula:

1. Select the cell containing the formula you want to edit.

2. You can edit in the cell or the formula bar, whichever is convenient. *Do one of the following:*

   ▲ Click in the formula bar to set the text insertion mark.

   ▲ Double-click the cell.

3. *Do any of the following:*

   ▲ Use normal text-editing techniques to add, delete, or change the cell contents.

   ▲ To clear the cell, drag-select its contents and press (Backspace), or select the cell and press (Del) or (Delete).

   ▲ To change a cell reference from relative, absolute, or mixed to another reference type, select the address and repeatedly press (F4).

   ▲ To replace a function, select its name in the formula and begin typing the new function's name. Select the desired function from the Formula AutoComplete list by double-clicking its name (see Figure 10.15). You can also replace a selected function name by choosing a new function from the Function Library group (**Figure 10.16**).

4. Press (Enter) to complete the formula.

✔ Tip

■ To make an entry in a cell in multiple worksheets, (Ctrl)-select the sheet names in the Sheet tab bar, select the cell, and then enter the data or formula.

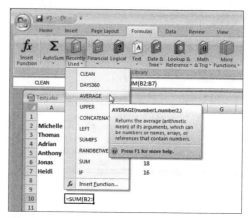

Figure 10.16 Functions can be chosen from the Function Library group. If you regularly use a function, you can often choose it from the Recently Used icon's drop-down menu.

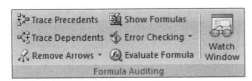

Figure 10.17 Troubleshooting tools are available in the Formula Auditing group.

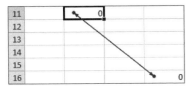

Figure 10.18 This arrow connects a pair of cells that reference each other. The formula in B11 is =D16, and the formula in D16 is =B11+8.

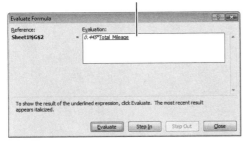

Figure 10.19 Click the Evaluate button to replace the underlined formula element with its data. Click Close when you're finished.

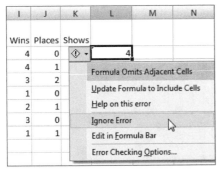

Figure 10.20 Click the icon and choose an option.

Troubleshooting Tips

Following are some techniques for finding and correcting errors in formulas. Start by switching to the Formulas tab to make the icons in the Formula Auditing group (**Figure 10.17**) accessible to you:

◆ **Formulas replaced by data.** To find cells in which you've accidentally replaced a formula with data, click Show Formulas. Any cell containing a formula will now display the formula, rather than the result. Click Show Formulas again to restore the worksheet to its normal state.

◆ **Circular references.** If the formulas in two cells rely on each other, Excel cannot correctly perform the calculations. This is known as a *circular reference* and is denoted on the worksheet by an arrow connecting the two cells (**Figure 10.18**). (You can also find circular references by clicking the Error Checking icon [see Figure 10.17], and choosing any cell listed in the Circular References submenu.) To correct a circular reference, only one of the formulas can refer to the other cell.

◆ **Incorrect result.** If a formula displays an unexpected result, select the cell and click Evaluate Formula (see Figure 10.17). By repeatedly clicking the Evaluate button in the Evaluate Formula dialog box (**Figure 10.19**), you can step through the elements in the formula, displaying the result for each step. Evaluating a formula often makes it easy to find incorrect cell references and identify flaws in the formula's logic.

◆ **Is it an error?** Excel notifies you immediately if it detects a possible formula error—often by displaying a tiny triangle in the cell's upper-left corner. Select the cell (**Figure 10.20**), and choose a handling option from the drop-down menu.

WORKING WITH TABLES

Post Position	Name	Last Race	Post	Finish	Time	Odds	Races	Wins	Places	Shows
1	Flying Stone	Jun-15	4	1	2:03	5.0	11	4	0	0
2	Lady Chris Time	Jun-12	2	5	2:00	32.5	18	4	1	1
3	Black Bart	Jun-13	7	2	2:00	24.6	13	3	2	2
4	Shadrack	Jun-08	5	5	2:02	3.9	4	1	0	1
5	Sundust Prince	Jun-18	4	5	2:01	15.1	10	2	1	4
6	J.J.'s Ferro	Jun-15	3	4	2:04	1.0	8	3	0	3
7	Pat's Comedian	May-31	4	8	2:01	8.1	7	1	1	1

Figure 11.1 Worksheets often contain lists of related data. In this harness racing worksheet, each row is the record for a single horse. Each column is a field, such as post position or horse's name.

Although number-crunching is usually a spreadsheet's purpose, many worksheets are used only to record lists of related data, such as addresses, club memberships, or a course roster. New users quickly discover that a worksheet's row-and-column grid is better for handling lengthy lists than a word-processing document. Such worksheets are simple databases in which each row is a *record* and each column is a *field* (**Figure 11.1**).

Because so many people use worksheets to manage lists, Microsoft added list-related features to Excel 2003. (In Excel 2007, lists are now called *tables*.) Any area of a worksheet can be designated a table, and a worksheet can contain as many tables as you need. Here are some advantages of formatting data as a table rather than using normal Excel formatting and tools to manage your list:

- Quickly sort the table by the contents of any field

- Filter the data to show only certain records or those that match a criterion

- Display a summary statistic for selected columns in an optional *total row*

- Simplify the process of performing a calculation on row data using *calculated columns*

Creating a Table

You can create a table in any blank range or convert existing data into a table.

To create a table:

1. *Do one of the following:*

   ▲ Select a blank range where you want to insert the table.

   ▲ Select a range with data that you want to convert to a table.

2. *Do one of the following:*

   ▲ On the Insert tab, click the Table icon in the Tables group.

   ▲ On the Home tab, click the Format as Table icon in the Styles group, and choose a table format from the gallery (**Figure 11.2**).

   The Format As Table dialog box appears (**Figure 11.3**).

3. If the proposed table range already contains a header row, be sure to check My table has headers.

4. Click OK to create the table (**Figure 11.4**).

✔ Tips

■ The menu icons in each cell of the header row tend to obscure the header text. You may wish to widen the columns and/or apply text wrap to any lengthy headers.

■ To quickly select a table, click in any table cell and then move the cursor over one of the table's top corners. Click when the cursor changes to a plus (+) with arrows.

■ To delete a table, select the entire table and press Del.

■ To change a table back into a normal range, select any table cell. On the Design tab, click the Convert to Range icon in the Tools group. Click Yes in the confirmation dialog box that appears.

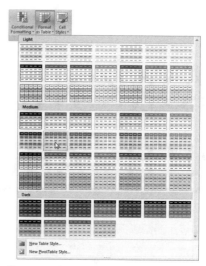

Figure 11.2 One way to create a table is to simply format a cell range as a table.

Figure 11.3 Edit the range (if necessary), indicate whether the range already contains a header row, and then click OK.

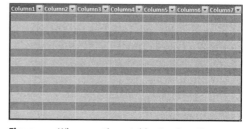

Figure 11.4 When creating a table, Excel applies default formatting to it.

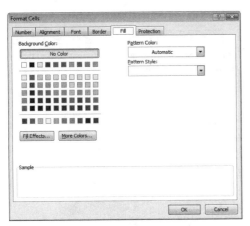

Figure 11.5 A color fill or gradient can be applied to selected table rows, columns, or cells.

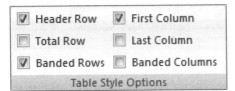

Figure 11.6 Hide, show, and format table components by clicking check boxes in the Table Style Options group.

Printing a Table

You can print a table as part of the current worksheet. On the other hand, there may be instances when you prefer to print *only* the table:

1. Select a cell in the table you wish to print.

2. Click the Office Button, and choose Print > Print.

3. In the Print what section of the Print dialog box, click the Table radio button.

4. Set other print options, and click OK.

Formatting a Table

A table is simply another worksheet range. As such, if you aren't delighted with the default formatting, you can format individual cells, rows, columns, or the entire table any way that pleases you.

To format a table:

◆ **Format the entire table.** Select any cell in the table. On the Design tab, select a new style from the Table Styles gallery.

◆ **Format a row, column, or range.** Select the row, column, or range within the table. On the Home tab, select a cell format from the Cell Styles drop-down menu in the Styles group. Alternatively, you can apply a fill color, gradient, or pattern to selected cells by selecting options on the Fill tab of the Format Cells dialog box (**Figure 11.5**).

◆ **Format the first or last column.** The first column often contains record identifiers, and the last column is frequently used to summarize each record's data. To apply distinctive formatting to these columns (boldface and, in some cases, a background color), switch to the Design tab, and click the First Column and/or Last Column check boxes in the Table Style Options group (**Figure 11.6**).

◆ **Create alternating rows or columns.** On the Design tab, click Banded Rows or Banded Columns in the Table Style Options group (see Figure 11.6).

✔ Tip

■ The effect of selecting First Column and Last Column in the Table Style Options group depends on the table's current formatting. For instance, if the entire table is formatted with a single color, only boldface will be applied to the column.

Creating Calculated Columns

Formulas in a table work differently than ones found elsewhere in the worksheet. If you insert a formula, it's automatically copied to every other cell in the same column. And if you later add rows to the table, the formula is copied to the new cells in the column, too. Any table column that contains a formula is referred to as a *calculated column*.

To create a calculated column:

1. If necessary, insert a new column in the table in which to place the formula.

    To be treated as a calculated column, the column must be empty when you create the formula. If the column contains *any* data, the formula will be applied only to the current cell.

2. Select a cell in the empty column, and type or paste the formula into the cell.

    Many table formulas are automatically converted by Excel to equivalent *structured references* (**Figure 11.7**).

3. Complete the formula by pressing [Enter] or by clicking the Enter icon in the Formula Bar (see Figure 11.7).

    The formula is automatically copied to all other cells in the column (**Figure 11.8**).

✔ Tips

■ If you replace the formula with data in any cell in a calculated column, Excel marks the cell as an *exception*. You can correct an exception by clicking the indicator beside the cell (**Figure 11.9**).

■ As long as a calculated column contains no exceptions, you can replace the formula with a new one. Like the original formula, it will automatically copy itself to every cell in the column.

Enter

Figure 11.7 Some formulas within tables automatically use structured references.

H	I	J
Races ▼	Wins ▼	Win % ▼
11	4	36%
18	4	22%
13	3	23%
4	1	25%
10	2	20%
8	3	38%
7	1	14%

Figure 11.8 The Win % calculated column is based on the formula Wins/Races.

I	J	K	L	M
Wins ▼	Win % ▼	Plac ▼	Sho ▼	
4	36%	0	0	
4	22%	1	1	
3	23%	2	2	
⚠ ▼	75%	0	1	
2	20%	1	4	
	This cell is inconsistent with the column formula.			
1	14%	1	1	

Figure 11.9 An exception cell in a calculated column is denoted by a tiny triangle in the upper-left corner. When you move the cursor over the indicator next to the cell, an explanatory message appears.

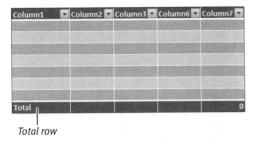

Total row

Figure 11.10 When enabled, the total row appears at the bottom of the table.

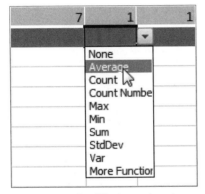

Figure 11.11 Each cell in the total row has a drop-down menu from which you can choose a statistical function.

Adding a Total Row

A table can optionally have a single *total row* at its bottom, enabling you to calculate a summary statistic across all records in the table. Each column can display a different statistic or none at all. For instance, in a donations table, you could compute the total of all donations, the average of the most recent donation (across all donors), and a count of the number of donor records.

To add a total row to a table:

1. Select a cell in the table to make the table active.

2. On the Design tab, click the Total Row check box in the Table Style Options group (see Figure 11.6).

   The total row appears at the bottom of the table (**Figure 11.10**).

3. *Optional:* Edit or delete the *Total* label in the left-most cell of the total row.

4. To display a summary statistic for a column, click the total row cell beneath the column. Click the icon that appears beside the cell, and choose a statistic from the drop-down menu (**Figure 11.11**).

5. Repeat Step 4 for each additional column you want to summarize.

6. Format the total row cells as desired.

✔ Tips

- If the function you need isn't listed in the drop-down menu, choose More Functions.

- To eliminate the summary statistic for a column, choose None from the drop-down menu (see Figure 11.11).

- You can disable and enable the total row as needed. When you re-enable the total row, the statistics previously assigned to the columns reappear.

Sorting and Filtering

Excel provides two tools that simplify viewing and analyzing table data:

- **Sorting.** Sort an entire table based on the contents of one field (column).

- **Filtering.** Restrict visible records (rows) to those that match a criterion. If desired, criteria can be chosen from multiple columns. For instance, you might filter a business table to show June absences of employees paid less than $12 per hour.

To sort a table:

1. *Do one of the following:*

   ▲ In the header row, click the icon in the column by which you want to sort (**Figure 11.12**).

   ▲ Right-click in any cell of the column by which you want to sort, and open the Sort submenu (**Figure 11.13**).

   ▲ Select any cell in the column by which you want to sort. On the Home tab, click the Sort & Filter icon in the Editing group.

2. Choose a sort order (ascending or descending) from the menu.

   The table is sorted as specified.

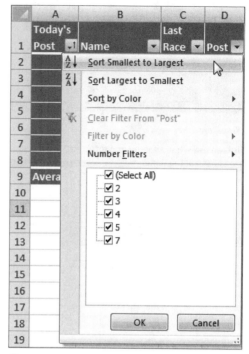

Figure 11.12 Click the icon of the header cell for the column by which you want to sort the table …

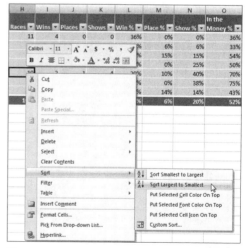

Figure 11.13 … or right-click any cell in the column by which you want to sort, and choose an option from the Sort submenu.

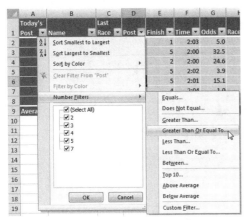

Figure 11.14 There are two ways to set a filter criterion. First, you can clear check boxes to filter out matching data. Second, you can specify a formula-based criterion by choosing a command from the pop-out menu.

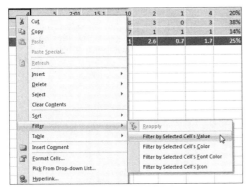

Figure 11.15 You can also filter the data based on a cell's contents, but your options are limited.

Figure 11.16 Sort & Filter icon.

To filter a table:

1. *Do one of the following:*
   - ▲ In the header row, click the icon in the column by which you want to filter the table (**Figure 11.14**).
   - ▲ Right-click in any cell of the column by which you want to filter the table, and open the Filter submenu (**Figure 11.15**).
   - ▲ Select any cell in the column by which you want to filter the table. On the Home tab, click the Sort & Filter icon in the Editing group.

2. Choose or specify a filter criterion.

   Records that do not match the filter criterion are hidden. If present, statistics in the total row are recalculated to reflect only the visible records.

✔ Tips

- To remove all filtering effects from a table (restoring the full record set), click the Sort & Filter icon in the Editing group, and choose Clear from the drop-down menu (**Figure 11.16**).

- To selectively remove one table filter when multiple filters have been applied, click the icon in the column header whose filtering you want to remove and choose Clear Filter From "*field name.*"

- If you've added records to a table, you can reapply the current sort instructions and filter criteria to accommodate the new records. On the Home tab, click the Sort & Filter icon in the Editing group and choose Reapply from the drop-down menu (see Figure 11.16).

Changing a Table's Size

Table contents can change over time. In addition to editing the data, you may want to add or delete fields (columns), as well as add and delete records (rows).

To change a table's size:

◆ **Insert records (rows) within a table.**
Select the row (or a cell in the row) beneath where you want to insert a new row. (To insert multiple rows in the same spot, begin by selecting that number of rows or cells in rows.) On the Home tab, click the Insert icon in the Cells group, and choose Insert Table Rows Above (**Figure 11.17**).

◆ **Insert fields (columns) within a table.**
Select the column (or a cell in the column) to the right of where you want to insert a new column. (To insert multiple columns in the same spot, begin by selecting that number of columns or cells in columns.) On the Home tab, click the Insert icon in the Cells group and choose Insert Table Columns to the Left (see Figure 11.17).

◆ **Increase a table's size by dragging.**
Move the cursor over the lower-right corner of the table. When the cursor changes as shown in **Figure 11.18**, drag to the right to add columns or drag down to add rows.

◆ **Delete records (rows).** Select the row or rows you want to delete. On the Home tab, click the Delete icon in the Cells group and choose Delete Table Rows.

◆ **Delete fields (columns).** Select the column or columns you want to delete. On the Home tab, click the Delete icon in the Cells group and choose Delete Table Columns.

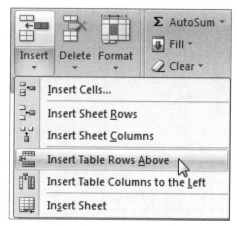

Figure 11.17 To insert or delete table rows or columns, choose a command from the Insert or Delete icon's drop-down menu.

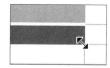

Figure 11.18 You can append rows or columns to a table by dragging the lower-right corner.

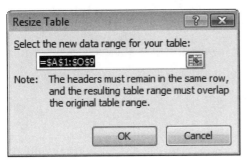

Figure 11.19 Rather than dragging to append new rows or columns to a table, you can type a new range.

✔ Tips

- You can also use the Delete Sheet Rows and Delete Sheet Columns commands in the Delete icon's drop-down menu to modify a table. However, unlike the equivalent Delete Table commands, the Delete Sheet commands also affect data *outside* of the table.

- You can also resize a table by entering a new range. Select a cell in the table, switch to the Design tab, and click the Resize Table icon in the Properties group. Enter a new range in the Resize Table dialog box (**Figure 11.19**) and click OK. Unlike resizing by dragging, the dialog box enables you to add new rows and columns at the same time.

- You can move a table to a new location using cut-and-paste or drag-and-drop. Start by selecting the table (including the header row, if there is one).

  Do one of the following:

  ▲ **Cut-and-paste.** Press Ctrl X or click the Cut icon in the Home tab's Clipboard group. In the destination location, click the cell that will serve as the table's new upper-left corner, and press Enter to perform the paste.

  ▲ **Drag-and-drop.** Move the cursor over a corner of the table. When the cursor changes to a plus symbol with four arrowheads, click and drag the table to the new location.

CREATING CHARTS

In Excel, you can create charts and graphs to display data visually. Although many kinds of charts can be made from tiny data sets, charts are especially useful for presenting and summarizing *large* quantities of data.

An Excel chart is a *floating object*. As such, you can move a chart to any convenient location on the worksheet or change its size by dragging a corner. You can customize almost any part of a chart, such as the title, axis labels, legend, chart wall, or chart floor. You can also choose which optional elements to display and which ones to hide, such as data labels, gridlines, and the data itself. Finally, if you aren't satisfied with the current chart style, you're free to replace it with a variation or a completely different type of chart.

Excel's charting tools are also used to create charts in PowerPoint and Word. Charts in Word and PowerPoint documents can be *embedded* (static objects that are unlinked from the worksheet data) or *linked* (objects that are linked with the data and automatically reflect changes to it).

Chart Elements

Designing a chart is similar to creating art. You can freely add or remove elements, move them to new positions, and change their size, shape, and formatting. (Of course, you are free to accept the default elements and formatting presented in a newly created chart, but it's unlikely you'll do so very often.)

Because you'll spend so much time working with chart elements, it's important for you to be able to *identify* each element. Note that many of the elements shown below (**Figure 12.1**) are optional.

CHART ELEMENTS

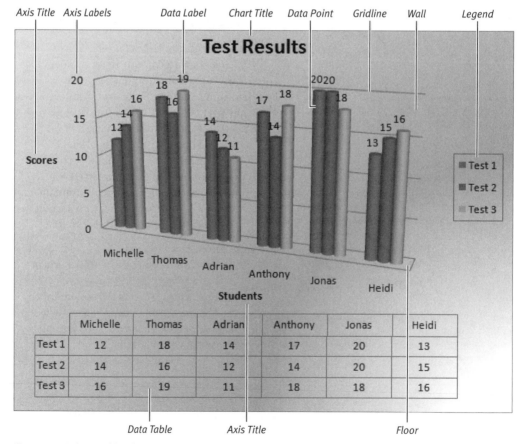

Figure 12.1 A chart and its elements.

	A	B	C	D	E	F	G	H	I	J	K
1	Today's Post	Name	Last Race	Post	Finish	Time	Odds	Races	Wins	Places	Shows
2	4	Shadrack	Jun-08	5	5	2:02	3.9	4	1	0	1
3	7	Pat's Comedian	May-31	4	8	2:01	8.1	7	1	1	1
4	5	Sundust Prince	Jun-18	4	5	2:01	15.1	10	2	1	4
5	3	Black Bart	Jun-13	7	2	2:00	24.6	13	3	2	2
6	6	J.J.'s Ferro	Jun-15	3	4	2:04	1.0	8	3	0	3
7	1	Flying Stone	Jun-15	4	1	2:03	5.0	11	4	0	0
8	2	Lady Chris Time	Jun-12	2	5	2:00	32.5	18	4	1	1

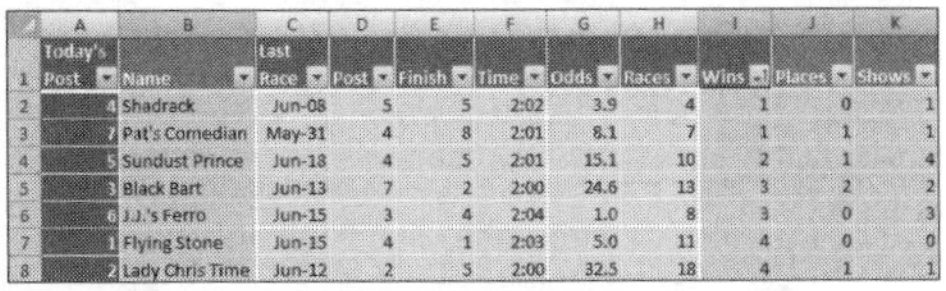

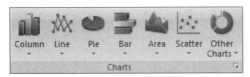

Figure 12.2 In this example, column B (labels) and columns I, J, and K (data) have been selected.

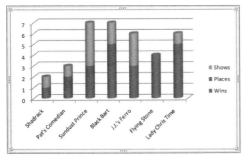

Figure 12.3 Specify the chart type by clicking an icon in the Charts group and choosing a chart from the drop-down menu that appears.

Figure 12.4 Excel adds the chart as a floating object on the worksheet.

Creating a Chart

In many instances, creating a chart is as simple as selecting the labels and data on the worksheet, and then picking a chart type. The chart data can be arranged in columns or rows. However, the columns or rows must be in a specific order for a few types of charts.

To create a chart:

1. If necessary, rearrange the data so it conforms to the chart's requirements.

   For example, to create one type of *stock chart*, the data must be in Date, High, Low, Close order. For other chart requirements, see "Create a chart" in Excel Help.

2. *Optional:* Sort the data to ensure it will appear in the desired order when charted.

3. On the worksheet, select the labels and data from which the chart will be created.

   Remember that the labels and data don't need to be contiguous. For example, in **Figure 12.2**, column B contains the labels and columns I, J, and K contain the data.

4. On the Insert tab, choose a chart type from a Charts group icon's drop-down menu (**Figure 12.3**).

   The new chart appears on the worksheet (**Figure 12.4**).

✔ Tips

- If you select a chart's plot area, the labels and data used to create the chart are highlighted in the worksheet. You can also select the data by switching to the Design tab and clicking the Select Data icon in the Data group.
- To change the chart type or style, select the chart, click the Design tab, and click Change Chart Type in the Type group.
- To delete a chart, select it and press Del.

CREATING A CHART

Changing the Background

If you aren't satisfied with the background formatting on the generated chart, you can change it. You can apply formatting to the entire chart, the plot area, or the legend, as well as to objects you've placed on the chart, such as a title.

To change the background for the chart or a component:

1. Select the chart or component you want to format, such as the plot area, wall, floor, or legend.

2. *Do one of the following:*
   ▲ On the Format tab, choose formatting options from the Shape Styles group (**Figure 12.5**).
   ▲ Right-click the selected area, and choose Format *item* from the pop-up menu. In the Format *item* dialog box (**Figure 12.6**), choose formatting options and click Close.

✔ Tips

■ You can also modify chart formatting by choosing options from the Background group (**Figure 12.7**) on the Layout tab.

■ To easily select a particular chart element, switch to the Layout tab, and choose the element from the drop-down menu at the top of the Current Selection group.

Figure 12.5 You can add an outline, fill, and effects to a selected chart component by choosing options from the Shape Styles group.

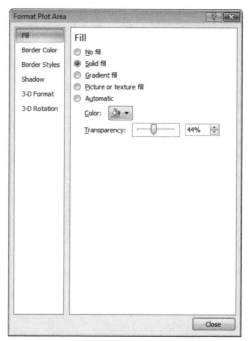

Figure 12.6 To simultaneously modify several formatting options, choose settings in a Format dialog box.

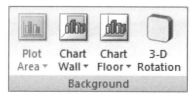

Figure 12.7 To change the wall, floor, or rotation of the plot area, choose options from the Background group.

CHANGING THE BACKGROUND

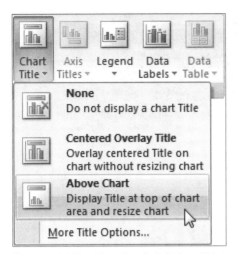

Figure 12.8 Add a title and set its initial position by choosing an option from the Chart Title drop-down menu.

Data label

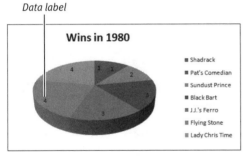

Figure 12.9 Depending on the chart type, it can be useful to display the data on chart elements.

Adding and Formatting Text

Although primarily visual, charts can also include a prodigious amount of text. Text you can add to a chart includes a title, legend, grid division labels, axis labels, data labels, and text boxes.

To add a text item to a chart:

1. Select the chart.

2. *Do any of the following:*

   ▲ **Add a chart title.** Switch to the Layout tab, click Chart Title in the Labels group, and choose an option from the drop-down menu (**Figure 12.8**).

   ▲ **Add an axis title.** Switch to the Layout tab, click Axis Titles in the Labels group, and choose an option from a Horizontal Axis Title or Vertical Axis Title submenu.

   ▲ **Label the data.** Switch to the Layout tab, click Data Labels in the Labels group, and choose an option from the drop-down menu. Labeling options vary by chart type (**Figure 12.9**).

   ▲ **Show chart data.** Switch to the Layout tab, click Data Table in the Labels group, and choose a Show option from the drop-down menu. Doing so displays the chart data in a grid, beneath the plot area.

   ▲ **Add other text.** Switch to the Layout tab, and click Text Box in the Insert group. Click and drag to create a text box on the chart, and then type or paste the text into the text box.

To format chart text:

1. *Do either of the following:*

▲ Select the text object, such as the title, legend, axis label, horizontal or vertical axis, or data labels. (Select an object when you want to apply the same formatting to all text within the object.)

▲ Within a text object, select the specific text to be formatted. (Only certain chart objects allow this, such as a title, axis label, or text box.)

2. *Do any of the following:*

▲ On the Home tab, choose formatting options from the Font group (**Figure 12.10**).

▲ Right-click the selected object or text string, choose Font from the pop-up menu (**Figure 12.11**), select formatting options from the Font dialog box (**Figure 12.12**), and click OK.

▲ With text selected, move the cursor up and choose formatting options from the Mini toolbar (see Figure 12.11).

▲ On the Format tab, choose options from the WordArt Styles group.

✔ Tip

■ To remove most text objects, select the object and press ⌈Del⌋. You can also switch to the Layout tab, click the appropriate icon in the Labels group, and choose None (see Figure 12.8 for an example).

Figure 12.10 You can apply text formatting by choosing commands from the Font group.

Selected object   Mini toolbar

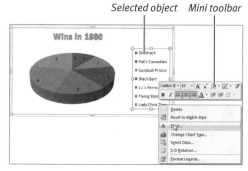

Figure 12.11 You can right-click objects that contain text and choose Font from the pop-up menu.

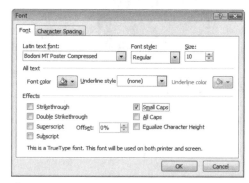

Figure 12.12 For complex text-formatting needs, you may prefer to use the Font dialog box.

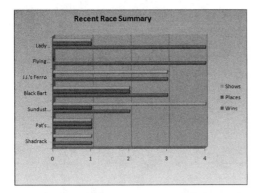

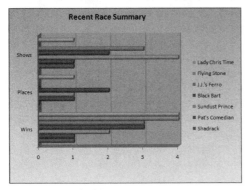

Figure 12.13 By switching rows and columns, you can view the wins, places, and shows for each horse (top) or see how the seven horses compare on number of wins, places, and shows (bottom).

Rows vs. Columns

Regardless of how your data is organized on the worksheet, you can plot it by rows or by columns. With many types of charts, plotting it *both* ways can give you a new perspective on your data.

To switch rows and columns:

1. Select the chart.

2. On the Design tab, click the Switch Row/ Column icon in the Data group.

   The chart is updated to reflect the change (**Figure 12.13**).

Changing the Layout and Style

One of the simplest ways to modify a chart is to specify a new layout or style. *Layout* refers to the elements appearing on the chart and their positions. *Style* refers to the coloring of chart elements, including the data objects, plot walls, and surrounding background.

To specify a new layout:

1. Select the chart.

2. On the Design tab, click an icon in the Chart Layouts group gallery (**Figure 12.14**).

   The chart is modified to match the chosen layout (**Figure 12.15**).

3. If previously undefined text elements appear in the chart (such as a title or axis titles), delete them or replace their text.

To change the chart style:

1. Select the chart.

2. On the Design tab, choose a new style from the Chart Styles group gallery (**Figure 12.16**).

   The chart is modified to match the chosen chart style.

✔ Tips

■ If you've already added an element (such as a chart title) but choose a layout without that element, it is not *deleted*. If you later choose a layout that includes the currently missing element, it reappears.

■ Choosing a new chart style is a destructive process. Elements you've manually formatted, such as specifying colors for gridlines or the background, are replaced with the features specified in the style.

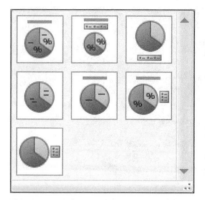

Figure 12.14 Choose a chart layout from the drop-down menu.

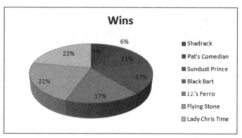

Figure 12.15 The pie chart is modified as necessary to match the chosen layout.

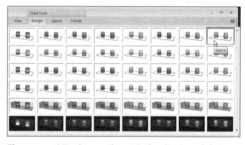

Figure 12.16 To change the style for displayed data elements, choose a new style from the Chart Style gallery.

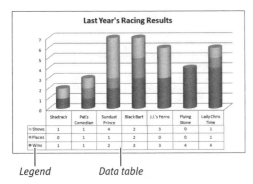

Legend   Data table

Figure 12.17 The data and legend can be combined (shown here), or they can be displayed as separate chart items.

Displaying the Data Set

If a chart is based on a small data set, it can be informative to show the data table on the chart.

To display the data on the chart:

1. Select the chart.

2. *Do one of the following:*

   ▲ On the Layout tab, choose a data display option from the Data Table drop-down menu in the Data group.

   ▲ On the Design tab, choose a layout from the Chart Layouts group that includes the data table.

   The data table is placed on the chart (**Figure 12.17**).

✔ Tips

■ To remove the data table, choose None from the Data Table drop-down menu, or choose a layout from the Chart Layouts group that doesn't includes the data table.

■ Another way to show the data is to place it directly on chart items, such as bars and pie slices. On the Layout tab, choose Show from the Data Labels drop-down menu in the Labels group.

DISPLAYING THE DATA SET

Working with Gridlines

To make it easier to estimate the size of data points, you can display horizontal and/or vertical lines called *gridlines* (**Figure 12.18**) on many kinds of charts. You can modify gridlines by removing them; electing to display major, minor, or both types of gridlines for either axis; and specifying a new color or style for the lines.

To add, remove, or modify gridlines:

1. Select the chart.

2. On the Layout tab, click the Gridlines icon in the Axes group, and choose one of the following options from the Primary Horizontal Gridlines, Primary Vertical Gridlines, or Depth Gridlines submenu (**Figure 12.19**):

    ▲ **None.** Remove all gridlines of the chosen type.

    ▲ **Major Gridlines.** Display major data divisions on the chosen axis, such as 1–5 or integers divisible by 5, 10, or 25 (depending on the size and spread of the data).

    ▲ **Minor Gridlines.** Display subdivisions between major gridlines (whether or not major gridlines are visible).

    ▲ **Major & Minor Gridlines.** Display both major and minor gridlines for the chosen axis.

    ▲ **More Primary Gridline Options.** Open a Format dialog box in which you can set line color, style, or shadow. Select new settings and click Close.

    The chosen option is applied to the chart.

✔ Tips

■ The Depth Gridlines submenu appears only when a true 3-D chart is selected (**Figure 12.20**).

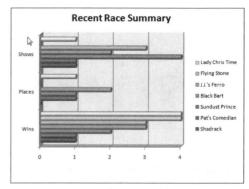

Figure 12.18 Gridlines behind the data make it easier to see or estimate the size of data points.

Figure 12.19 A Gridlines submenu.

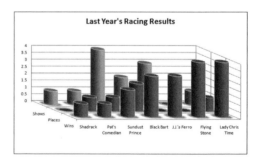

Figure 12.20 A true 3-D chart has depth.

■ You can also remove gridlines by right-clicking them on the chart and choosing Delete from the pop-up menu.

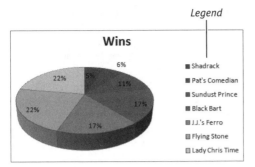

Figure 12.21 The legend serves as a key to the chart. Each element represents a data series.

Figure 12.22 Add, remove, or change the placement of the legend by choosing an option from this menu.

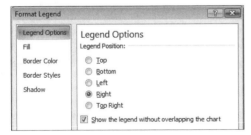

Figure 12.23 You can specify a new location or custom formatting for the legend in the Format Legend dialog box.

Working with the Legend

If you select row or column labels when creating a chart, a *legend* (key to the data series) is generally added to the chart (**Figure 12.21**). You can add or remove the legend, specify its placement in relation to the chart, change its properties (such as fill color and border style), and edit the labels.

To add, remove, or modify the legend:

1. Select the chart.

2. *Do any of the following:*

   ▲ To add, remove, or change the position of the legend, click the Layout tab, and choose an option from Legend drop-down menu in the Labels group (**Figure 12.22**).

   ▲ To manually change the size or position of the legend, drag an edge or the center, respectively.

   ▲ To format the legend, right-click it, choose Format Legend from the pop-up menu, and make the desired changes in the Format Legend dialog box (**Figure 12.23**).

   ▲ To change the properties of a single data series, select that element in the legend, right-click it, choose Format Data Series or Format Legend Entry, and make any desired changes in the Format Data Series or Format Legend Entry dialog box.

   ▲ To modify the text used for legend entries, make the edits in the worksheet cells you used as labels.

✔ Tip

■ You don't have to close the Format dialog box immediately. To format a *different* chart element, select that element in the chart. The Format dialog box changes to one appropriate for the selected element.

Adding Trendlines

If data is gathered over time, you can add lines (called *trendlines*) to the chart that summarize the data and predict future values. Depending on the data set, different trendline types may provide a better *fit* to the data.

To add a trendline:

1. Select the chart.

2. On the Layout tab, click the Trendline icon in the Analysis group, and choose an option from the drop-down menu.

   If the chart includes multiple data series, an Add Trendline dialog box appears. Select the data series to which the trendline will be applied, and click OK.

   The trendline appears on the chart.

3. *Optional:* To modify a trendline's properties or type, select it by clicking one of its ends. Open the Format Trendline dialog box (**Figure 12.24**) by doing one of the following:

   ▲ Right-click the trendline, and choose Format Trendline.

   ▲ Choose More Trendline Options from the Trendline drop-down menu.

   Make the desired changes and click Close. The new settings are reflected on the chart (**Figure 12.25**).

✔ Tips

■ Adding trendlines is cumulative. That is, you can plot multiple types of trendlines on a chart.

■ To remove all trendlines from a chart, choose None from the Trendline drop-down menu. To remove one trendline (when multiple trendlines are displayed), select the trendline on the chart and press ⌐Del⌐.

Figure 12.24 The dialog box offers other options, such as more trendline types and showing predicted values, based on the trendline.

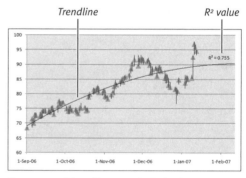

Figure 12.25 A trendline on a stock chart.

■ Explore these other options in the Analysis group:

   ▲ **Lines.** Show high-low marks (especially useful for stock charts) and/or drop lines that extend up from the X axis to each data point.

   ▲ **Error Bars.** Surround each data point with bars showing a confidence interval based on a fixed amount, percentage, standard deviation, standard error, or custom formula.

ADDING TRENDLINES

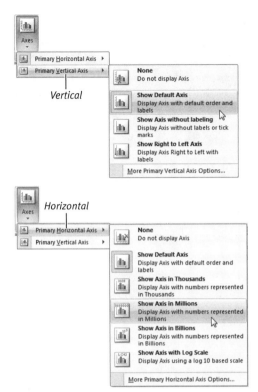

Vertical

Horizontal

Figure 12.26 Because the vertical and horizontal axes serve different purposes, each has different options.

Modifying the Axes

Most charts have a horizontal (X) and a vertical (Y) axis. You can modify either axis by changing its labels or formatting.

To modify an axis:

1. Select the chart.

2. *Do any of the following:*

   ▲ To remove an axis, set the position of the Y axis, or specify numeric units to use for the X axis, click the Layout tab, and choose an option from the Axes drop-down menu in the Axes group (**Figure 12.26**).

   ▲ To change the formatting for an axis, right-click the axis labels on the chart and choose Format Axis, or choose More *axis name* Axis Options from the Axes drop-down menu (see Figure 12.26). Make changes in the Format Axis dialog box, and click Close.

   ▲ To change an axis label, edit the label's text in its worksheet cell. You can also modify axis labels in the Select Data Source dialog box. Click the Design tab, and click the Select Data icon in the Data group.

Changing the Chart Data

Although you've created a chart and carefully formatted it exactly the way you want, a problem sometimes occurs. The data on which the chart is based changes! A column or row in the data source may need to be deleted, data in one or more cells needs to be modified, or you may want to include additional rows or columns.

To modify chart data:

1. Select the chart.

2. *Do any of the following:*

   ▲ **Edit existing data.** If you edit data in the cells on which the chart is based, the chart automatically updates to reflect the edited data.

   ▲ **Delete rows or columns.** If you delete rows or columns within the range(s) used to create the chart, the data is automatically removed from the chart.

   ▲ **Add new rows or columns.** Adding new rows or columns—even within the range of the original chart data— does *not* trigger an update of the chart.

   To add the new data to the chart, switch to the Design tab, and click the Select Data icon in the Data group. The Select Data Source dialog box appears (**Figure 12.27**). Edit the ranges in the dialog box, or select new ranges on the worksheet. Click OK to close the dialog box.

Select Data Source dialog box

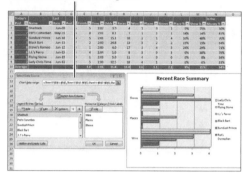

Figure 12.27 To change the ranges on which a chart is based, edit the ranges in the Select Data Source dialog box or select new ranges on the worksheet.

Part IV: Microsoft PowerPoint

Chapter 13 Getting Started with
PowerPoint 2007 211

Chapter 14 Creating a Presentation 217

Chapter 15 Completing a Presentation 233

GETTING STARTED WITH POWERPOINT 2007

You use PowerPoint to create presentations for almost any occasion, such as a business meeting, government forum, school project or lecture, church function, or club fund-raiser. A presentation is designed as a slide show and can be based on one of the included themes, employ a company- or school-provided theme, or be created from scratch.

Presentations can feature within-slide animations (such as flying text) and between-slide transitions (such as dissolves). Slides can include embedded movies and audio clips, as well as recorded narration. You can add notes on each slide to help you present the material and create handouts for the audience.

The resulting slide show can be run on your computer, printed, output to transparencies for viewing on an overhead projector, or saved as HTML for viewing on the Web, an intranet, or a recipient's computer in any current Web browser.

✔ Tip

- When distributing a presentation, your audience doesn't need PowerPoint. They can download PowerPoint Viewer 2007 from Microsoft's site. (When you use the Package a Presentation for CD feature, PowerPoint Viewer is included on the CD.)

The PowerPoint Interface

Figure 13.1, bottom shows the interface elements you'll use when creating presentations. Many of them, such as the Ribbon, Office Button, and Quick Access Toolbar, can be found in Word, Excel, and Outlook.

Office Button. Click this button to perform file-related actions (**Figure 13.2**), such as creating, opening, saving, and printing. Click PowerPoint Options to set preferences. To open a presentation you've recently worked on, click its name in the Recent Documents list. The Exit command can also be found here.

Office Button   *Recent Documents list*

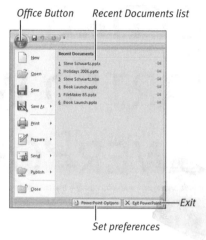

Exit

Set preferences

Figure 13.2 The Office Button window.

Office Button   *Quick Access Toolbar*   *Tab (View)*   *Placeholder*   *Group (Drawing)*   *Close*

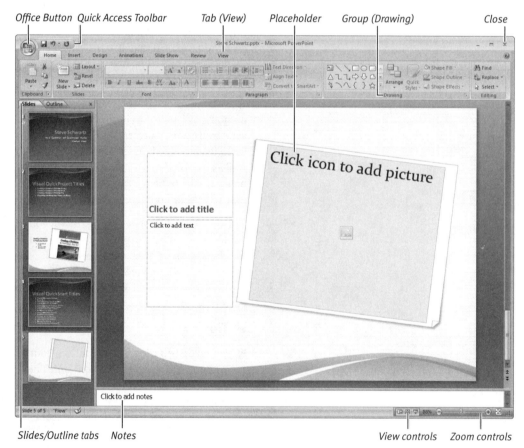

Slides/Outline tabs   *Notes*   *View controls*   *Zoom controls*

Figure 13.1 The PowerPoint 2007 interface.

Current list of Visual QuickProject titles. Discuss how you started writing books in this series, as well as the series' philosophy.

Notes

Figure 13.3 When printed, you can use the note pages to assist you in the presentation or give them out as handouts. Here's a typical slide in Notes Page view.

Normal   *Slide Show*

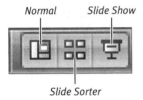

Slide Sorter

Figure 13.4 You can switch to one of these common views by clicking its icon.

Quick Access Toolbar. Icons for common commands are found here, such as Save, Undo, and Redo.

Ribbon. The Ribbon is Office 2007's replacement for program menus. Similar commands and procedures are listed together on a *tab*, such as Insert or View. Within each tab, procedures are further divided into *groups*, based on similarity of function. To perform a command, you switch to the appropriate tab by clicking its name, and then click the command's icon or control.

Slides/Outline tab. When the Slides tab is selected, thumbnails of your slides (in their present order) are displayed. Click a thumbnail to work with that slide. Use the Outline tab to view and work with the presentation in outline mode.

Placeholders. Every PowerPoint theme includes a predefined set of layouts. In each slide layout, placeholders are provided for adding your own formatted text, pictures, and other items.

Notes. To assist with a presentation, you can type notes in this area and print them out, along with a miniature version of the slide to which the notes refer (**Figure 13.3**).

View controls. Click an icon to switch views (**Figure 13.4**). You can also change views by switching to the View tab and clicking an icon in the Presentation Views group.

Zoom controls. Change the current magnification by dragging the slider or by clicking + (increase), – (decrease), the zoom percentage, or the Fit slide to current window icon.

Close. Click the close box to close an open presentation or to quit PowerPoint. (When the current presentation is the only one that's open, clicking the close box quits the program.) You can also close the active presentation by choosing Close in the Office Button window (see Figure 13.2).

Working in Different Views

Figure 13.5 Icons in the Presentation Views group.

Depending on what you want to do at any given moment, you'll work in one of the many PowerPoint *views*. To switch views, you can click an icon in the View controls (see Figures 13.1 and 13.4) or in the Presentation Views groups (**Figure 13.5**) on the Views tab. Because creating a presentation is an interactive process, you'll switch views frequently.

PowerPoint views include the following:

◆ **Normal.** Create, edit, and delete slides (see Figure 13.1).

◆ **Slide Sorter.** Rearrange, delete, and hide slides (**Figure 13.6**).

◆ **Notes Page.** Add and edit notes for each slide in a convenient full-screen format.

◆ **Slide Show.** View the presentation as a full-screen slide show as it will appear to your audience.

◆ **Slide, Handout, and Notes Masters.** Switch to a Master view to create and modify the underlying theme for slides, note pages, and handouts. For instance, changes made to a master slide (such as setting a different font, size, or color for heading text on a title slide) instantly affects all current and new title slides (**Figure 13.7**).

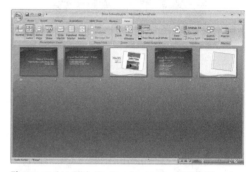

Figure 13.6 In Slide Sorter view, a thumbnail of each slide in the presentation is shown. Rearrange slides by dragging them to new positions.

Figure 13.7 If you don't care for a particular font, change it on its master slide.

Template list

Figure 13.8 When creating a new presentation, you can make one from scratch or start with a template.

Figure 13.9 Pick a theme from Themes group.

New Presentation Tips

◆ To quickly create a Blank Presentation while skipping the New Presentation dialog box, press [Ctrl][N].

◆ Regardless of the format intended for the presentation (such as HTML for display on the Web), save the working version in a native PowerPoint format: PowerPoint Presentation or PowerPoint 97-2003 Presentation.

Creating a Presentation

If you've never made a PowerPoint presentation, the following are the basic steps in the process. Note that many steps—such as creating notes and handouts—are optional. In addition, because presentation design is seldom a linear step-by-step process, you can change the step order as your creative flow dictates.

To create a presentation:

1. **Make an outline.** This step can help you decide what to present and the approximate order in which you intend to cover the material.

   You can use Word's Outline mode (see Chapter 5) for this task.

2. **Create a new PowerPoint presentation.** *Do one of the following:*

   ▲ If you just launched PowerPoint, a new presentation is started for you.

   ▲ If a presentation is open, click the Office Button and choose New. In the New Presentation dialog box (**Figure 13.8**), select Blank Presentation. (If you prefer, you can base the presentation on a template by clicking the appropriate category on the left side of the dialog box.)

3. **Select a theme.** If a theme wasn't set in Step 2, choose a theme from the Themes group on the Design tab (**Figure 13.9**).

   A theme gives a consistent *look* to all slides in the presentation.

4. **Create the slides.** From the New Slide gallery in the Slides group on the Home tab, select a slide style (such as Section Header or Picture with Caption) to add to the presentation. Replace placeholders with appropriate text and pictures.

continues on next page

CREATING A PRESENTATION

5. **Add notes.** If you like, you can add typed comments to the slides to assist you when delivering the presentation. Notes can be entered in Normal or Notes Page view (see Figures 13.1 and 13.3).

6. **Organize the slides.** In Slide Sorter view (see Figure 13.6), arrange the slides in the order you want to present them. Delete or hide unwanted slides.

7. **Add within-slide animations.** You can add motion (fly-in or spin, for example) to slide elements, such as text objects and pictures. With the object selected, choose effects from the Animations group on the Animations tab or from the Custom Animation task pane (**Figure 13.10**).

8. **Add between-slide transitions.** You can also specify visual and/or auditory transition effects that play when you move from one slide to the next. Common transitions include fades, dissolves, and wipes, for instance. By choosing effects from the Transition to This Slide group on the Animations tab (**Figure 13.11**), you can set a different transition for each slide or apply one transition to all slides.

9. **Play and rehearse the presentation.** To play the presentation, switch to Slide Show view or click an icon in the Start Slide Show group on the Slide Show tab. As the show plays, rehearse what you'll say while each slide is onscreen. On the Animations tab, you can specify that each slide will advance in response to a mouse click or be based on the timing established during the rehearsal.

10. **Print notes and handouts, if any.**

11. **Output the show in its final format.** In addition to playing the slide show on a computer, you can have slides professionally made, print transparencies, or output the show in HTML for the Web.

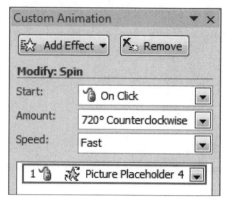

Figure 13.10 Many of the best effects are found in the Custom Animation task pane.

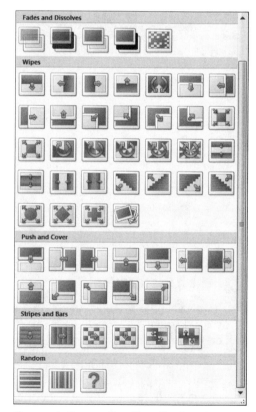

Figure 13.11 Choose a transition effect from the extensive Transition to This Slide gallery.

CREATING A PRESENTATION

In this chapter, you'll learn the mechanics of creating a presentation and the tools used in the process:

◆ Starting a new presentation and choosing a theme

◆ Adding and deleting slides

◆ Replacing slide placeholders with text, images, charts, tables, and objects

◆ Adding other types of items to slides, such as shapes, text boxes, date/time stamps, and slide numbers

◆ Creating a photo album slide show

◆ Previewing a presentation onscreen as a slide show

Beginning a Presentation

As explained in Chapter 13, there are several ways to begin a presentation.

To create a blank presentation (no theme):

◆ *Do one of the following:*

   ▲ Launch PowerPoint 2007. By default, a blank presentation is created.

   ▲ With PowerPoint open, press Ctrl N.

   ▲ Click the Office Button. In the Office Button window, choose New. In the New Presentation dialog box (**Figure 14.1**), select the Blank and recent templates category, click the Blank Presentation icon, and click Create.

To create a presentation based on a template or theme:

1. Click the Office Button.

2. In the Office Button window, choose New. The New Presentation dialog box appears (see Figure 14.1).

3. Select one of the following categories from the Templates list:

   ▲ To base the presentation on a template that's on your hard disk, select Installed Templates or My templates. Select a template and click Create.

   ▲ To base the presentation on an online template, select a category in the Microsoft Office Online section. Select a template and click Download (**Figure 14.2**). The template downloads from Microsoft's site and is added to the My templates category.

   ▲ To base the presentation on the default Blank Presentation but with a theme applied, select Installed Themes. Select a theme icon and click Create.

Blank and recent category

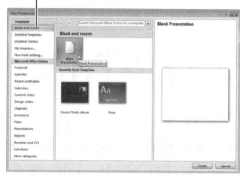

Figure 14.1 To create the same blank presentation that normally appears at startup, click the Blank Presentation icon and click Create.

Microsoft Office Online section   *Preview*

Figure 14.2 Select a template category, review templates available for download, and select a template appropriate for your project.

BEGINNING A PRESENTATION

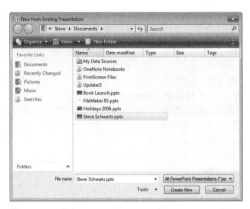

Figure 14.3 Select one of your previous presentations from this dialog box.

Figure 14.4 Click the Save icon to save a new or edited presentation.

Current folder

Filename   *File type*

Figure 14.5 Save the new presentation in the Save As dialog box (Windows Vista shown).

▲ To base the presentation on one of your previous presentations, select New from existing. The New from Existing Presentation dialog box appears (**Figure 14.3**). Navigate to the folder that contains your presentation, select it, and click Create New.

The new presentation opens.

4. Any time after generating the new presentation, you can save it to disk. *Do one of the following:*

   ▲ Click the Save icon in the Quick Access Toolbar (**Figure 14.4**).

   ▲ Press Ctrl S.

   ▲ Click the Office Button and choose Save.

   ▲ Click the Office Button. Choose Save As, followed by a file format (such as PowerPoint Presentation).

   The Save As dialog box appears (**Figure 14.5**).

5. Navigate to the folder in which you want to save the presentation, name the file, select a file type from the Save as type drop-down list, and click Save.

✔ Tips

■ Periodically, you should save the changes made to your presentation. Click the Save icon in the Quick Access Toolbar, click the Office Button and choose Save, or press Ctrl S.

■ If you decide you don't want to use or keep the presentation, close it without saving.

■ Regardless of the presentation-creation method you choose, you can change the *theme* applied to the slides. See the following section for instructions on setting the theme.

BEGINNING A PRESENTATION

Setting the Theme

A *theme* provides a consistent background and fonts to a presentation. Unless your new presentation already has a theme (as it will if the presentation is based on a template or an existing presentation), the first step is to select a theme (**Figure 14.6, bottom**).

To apply a theme to a presentation:

1. Switch to the Design tab.

2. *Do any of the following:*

▲ Choose a theme from the gallery in the Themes group.

▲ Choose a new color scheme for the current theme from the Colors drop-down list (**Figure 14.7**).

▲ Choose a different combination of fonts from the Fonts drop-down list.

▲ Choose a different color or gradient from the Background Styles gallery.

These options all provide a *live preview*. (If you hover the cursor over an option, you can see what it will look like on the current slide.) Click an option to apply it to the entire presentation.

✔ Tips

■ You can change existing themes and theme elements, too. However, the sooner in the design process that you finalize theme choices, the less cleanup work you'll have to do to current slides.

■ Some templates' themes can't be altered.

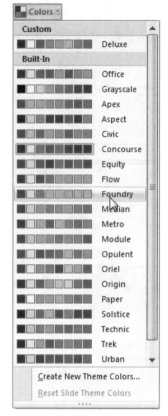

Figure 14.7 You can pick a new color scheme from the Colors drop-down list.

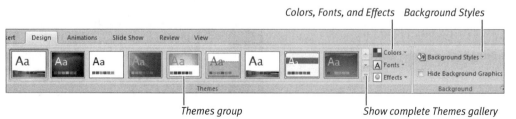

Figure 14.6 Apply theme and theme element changes by choosing options from the Design tab.

SETTING THE THEME

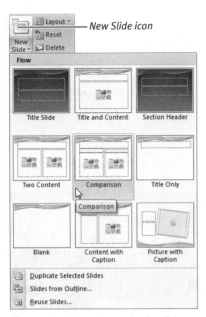

New Slide icon

Figure 14.8 Select a format for the slide you're adding to the presentation.

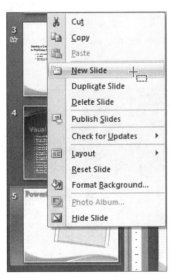

Figure 14.9 You can also add a slide by right-clicking a slide thumbnail.

Adding and Deleting Slides

You can add new slides or delete existing ones in Normal, Slide Sorter, or Notes Page view.

To add a slide to a presentation:

1. Switch to Normal, Slide Sorter, or Notes Page view. Click the Home tab.

2. Select the slide after which you want to insert the new slide.

3. Click the New Slide icon in the Slides group and select the type of slide to insert (**Figure 14.8**).

   The new slide appears after the selected slide.

To delete a slide:

1. Switch to Normal, Slide Sorter, or Notes Page view. Click the Home tab.

2. Click the Delete icon in the Slides group (see Figure 14.8).

   The slide is removed from the presentation.

✔ Tips

- In Normal or Slide Sorter view, you can quickly insert a new slide of the same type as the current slide. Right-click the current slide's thumbnail and choose New Slide from the pop-up menu (**Figure 14.9**).

- In Normal or Slide Sorter view, you can also delete a slide by right-clicking the slide's thumbnail and choosing Delete Slide (see Figure 14.9).

- To modify the layout of an existing slide (changing it from one slide type to another), switch to the Home tab when in Normal or Slide Sorter view and choose an option from the Layout gallery in the Slides group (see Figure 14.8).

ADDING AND DELETING SLIDES

Replacing Placeholders

Most slide layouts contain *placeholders* for text or graphics (**Figure 14.10**). To use the placeholders, you replace them with your own material. Replacing placeholders and other design work is done in Normal view.

To replace a text placeholder:

1. Click a "Click to add title," "Click to add text," or similarly worded placeholder (**Figure 14.11**).

   The placeholder text vanishes.

2. Type your text (**Figure 14.12**). If additional paragraphs are required, press [Enter] to begin each new paragraph.

To replace a picture or movie-clip placeholder:

1. Click the picture or movie-clip placeholder icon (see Figure 14.10).

   An Insert Picture or Insert Movie file dialog box appears, respectively.

2. Navigate to the folder that contains the picture or movie clip, select its file icon, and click Open.

   The picture or movie appears in the placeholder frame.

To replace a clip-art placeholder:

1. Click the clip-art placeholder icon (see Figure 14.10).

   The Clip Art task pane appears on the right side of the PowerPoint window.

2. Follow the procedure in "Adding Clip Art" (Chapter 6) to find, select, and insert a clip-art image.

   After the clip art appears on the slide, close the Clip Art task pane by clicking its close box (X).

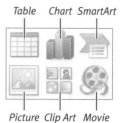

Table   Chart   SmartArt

Picture Clip Art Movie

Figure 14.10 Examples of graphic placeholders.

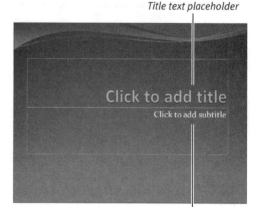

Title text placeholder

Subtitle text placeholder

Figure 14.11 This title slide has two text placeholders.

Figure 14.12 The replacement text takes on the character and paragraph formatting of the placeholder.

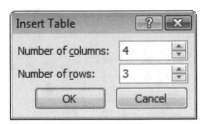

Figure 14.13 Specify the number of columns and rows.

Figure 14.14 A table with the specified number of columns and rows appears in the placeholder area.

Chart categories   *Chart styles*

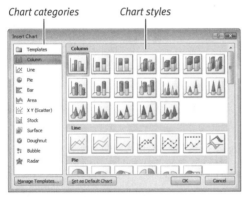

Figure 14.15 Select a chart style from the Insert Chart dialog box, and then click OK.

	A	B	C	D	E	F	G
1		Series 1	Series 2	Series 3			
2	Category 1	4.3	2.4	2			
3	Category 2	2.5	4.4	2			
4	Category 3	3.5	1.8	3			
5	Category 4	4.5	2.8	5			
6							
7							
8		To resize chart data range, drag lower right corner of range.					

Drag to change the chart range

Figure 14.16 Replace the sample data with your data.

To replace a table placeholder:

1. Click the table placeholder icon (see Figure 14.10).

   The Insert Table dialog box appears (**Figure 14.13**).

2. Enter the number of columns and rows for the table, and click OK.

   The new table appears (**Figure 14.14**).

3. Complete the table by entering the appropriate labels and data.

To replace a chart placeholder:

1. Click the chart placeholder icon (see Figure 14.10).

   The Insert Chart dialog box appears (**Figure 14.15**).

2. Select a chart category from the Templates list.

3. Click the icon that represents the chart style you want to create, and click OK.

   Excel launches and opens a worksheet containing sample data (**Figure 14.16**).

4. Replace the chart labels and data with your own information. To add rows or columns to the chart range, drag the lower-right corner of the range. Click the close box (X) for Excel or the worksheet when you're done entering data.

   The chart appears on the slide.

5. *Optional:* With the chart selected on the slide, Chart Tools contextual tabs (Design, Layout, and Format) appear in the Ribbon. Choose commands from these contextual tabs to change the chart type, layout, or formatting.

REPLACING PLACEHOLDERS

223

To replace a SmartArt placeholder:

1. Click the SmartArt placeholder icon (see Figure 14.10).

The Choose a SmartArt Graphic dialog box appears (**Figure 14.17**).

2. Select a graphic category from the list on the left, and select a specific graphic from the center of the dialog box. Click OK.

The SmartArt graphic appears in the image placeholder.

3. Replace the text placeholders in the SmartArt graphic with your own text.

4. *Optional:* Choose options on the Design tab (**Figure 14.18**) to change the colors and style of the graphic (**Figure 14.19**).

✔ Tips

■ To remove an unneeded placeholder from a slide, select it and press (Del).

■ To alter the format, appearance, rotation, size, or position of placeholders and other elements (such as background graphics), make the changes on the master slides. Changes made to a master Title Slide, for example, will automatically be applied to all existing and new Title Slides in the presentation.

Categories   SmartArt graphics   Preview

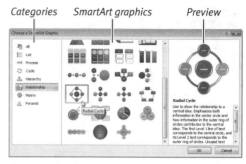

Figure 14.17 Select a SmartArt graphic from the center of the dialog box.

Change Colors

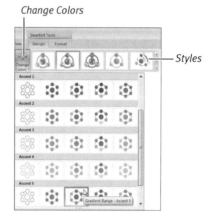

Styles

Figure 14.18 You can change the SmartArt by choosing options from the Design tab.

Figure 14.19 An example of a SmartArt graphic.

Shapes icon

Figure 14.21 Choose a shape from the Shapes drop-down gallery.

Shape Styles group   WordArt Styles group

Figure 14.22 To change the formatting for a shape, choose options from the Shape Styles group. To alter text (standalone or inside an object), choose options from the WordArt Styles group.

Figure 14.23 A formatted shape containing neon text.

Inserting Other Items

In addition to replacing placeholders with an object or text, you can place items *anywhere* on a given slide by choosing options from the Insert tab (**Figure 14.20, bottom**). Position the inserted item by clicking a location on the slide or by dragging the item into position.

To insert a table, picture, clip art, SmartArt, chart, movie, or audio clip, see the instructions in "Replacing Placeholders" on the previous pages.

To insert a shape:

1. Switch to the Insert tab. In the Illustrations group, choose a shape from the Shapes gallery (**Figure 14.21**).

2. Click and drag to draw the shape on the slide. (To maintain the shape's original proportions, press (Shift) as you drag.)

3. *Optional:* To change the shape's color and formatting, choose settings from groups on the Format tab (**Figure 14.22**).

4. *Optional:* To add text inside the shape, *do either of the following:*

    ▲ Right-click the shape and choose Edit Text from the pop-up menu.

    ▲ On the Format tab, click the Text Box icon in the Illustrations group and click inside the shape to set the text insertion mark.

    Type and format the text (**Figure 14.23**).

Figure 14.20 You can add text and objects anywhere on a slide by choosing commands from the Insert tab.

INSERTING OTHER ITEMS

To insert a text box:

1. Switch to the Insert tab. Click the Text Box icon in the Text group (see Figure 14.20).

   A text insertion cursor appears.

2. Click to set the text insertion mark where you want to add the text (**Figure 14.24**).

3. Type the text (**Figure 14.25**). Press ⏎ to begin each additional paragraph.

4. *Optional:* Change the text formatting by performing any of these actions:

   ▲ **Character/Paragraph Format.** Set new character and paragraph formatting by choosing commands from the Font and Paragraph groups on the Home tab or from the Mini toolbar (**Figure 14.26**).

   ▲ **Rotate.** Click the rotation handle (see Figure 14.25) and drag to the left or right to change the text rotation angle.

   ▲ **Stylize.** Choose options from the WordArt Styles group on the Format tab (see Figure 14.22).

   ▲ **Wrap.** Reduce or increase the width of the text box by dragging the center handle on either side. The text within the box will automatically rewrap as required.

5. *Optional:* Reposition the text by moving the cursor over any edge. When a plus cursor with arrowheads appears, you can drag the text box to a new location.

Figure 14.24 This new text box is ready to receive typed or pasted text.

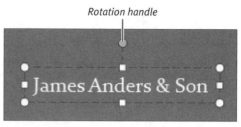

Figure 14.25 The text box automatically expands as you enter the text.

Figure 14.26 If you select text and then move the cursor slightly upward, the Mini toolbar appears.

Duplicating Slides

After you've created several slides, one of the quickest ways to move the creation process along is to duplicate slides and then edit the duplicates, rather than designing every new slide from scratch.

To duplicate a slide, select its thumbnail in the current view, such as Normal or Slide Sorter. Switch to the Home tab, click the New Slide icon in the Slides group, and choose Duplicate Selected Slides from the drop-down menu.

Placement preview

Figure 14.27 Set date/time and numbering options, and then click Apply to All (or Apply).

——— *Inserted date*

Figure 14.28 Date/time appears on the left edge of the footer, numbering appears on the right, and footer text is centered between the two.

To insert a slide number or date/time:

1. Switch to the Insert tab. Click the Header & Footer, Date & Time, or Slide Number icon in the Text group (see Figure 14.20). The Header and Footer dialog box appears (**Figure 14.27**).

2. Click the Slide tab (if it isn't selected).

3. To number the slides consecutively, click the Slide number check box.

4. To display the date, time, or both, click the Date and time check box, and *do one of the following:*
   ▲ To always display the current date and/or time, click Update automatically and select a date/time format from the drop-down list.
   ▲ To stamp the slide(s) with the present date/time, click Fixed and enter the text to display, such as 4/2/2007.

5. *Optional:* To prevent the slide number and date information from being shown on the opening slide, click the Don't show on title slide check box.

6. *Do one of the following:*
   ▲ To add the number and date information to all slides in the presentation (**Figure 14.28**), click Apply to All.
   ▲ To add the number and date information only to the current slide, click Apply.

✔ Tips

■ You can enter *any* text you like in the Fixed text box. You aren't restricted to date/time information.

■ To add text that will be centered in the footer (between the date/time and slide number), click the Footer check box and enter the text you want to display.

✔ Tips

■ Inserted objects can be laid over one another. For example, you can draw a shape around a text box to frame the text or combine shapes to make an illustration. After combining objects, you can *group* them to prevent individual items from accidentally being moved. Select the objects you want to group. On the Home tab, choose Group from the Arrange drop-down menu in the Drawing group.

■ To change the layering of objects, select an object and choose a command (such as Send to Back) from the Arrange group on the Format tab (**Figure 14.29**). Layering commands are also available on the Home tab from the Arrange drop-down menu in the Drawing group (**Figure 14.30**).

■ For assistance in selecting objects, open the Selection and Visibility task pane by clicking the Selection Pane icon (see Figure 14.29) or choosing Selection Pane from the Arrange drop-down menu (see Figure 14.30). Click any item in the task pane to select it on the slide, regardless of the item's layer and whether it's visible or buried under other items.

■ Occasionally, after carefully formatting and adding text to an inserted shape, it just isn't what you want. Rather than create a new shape and add the same text and formatting, you can *replace* the shape with a new one. On the Format tab, click the Edit Shape icon in the Insert Shapes group, choose Change Shape from the drop-down menu, and choose a replacement shape from the gallery.

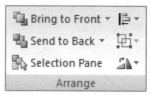

Figure 14.29 You can change the layering of the selected object by choosing a command from the Arrange group icons.

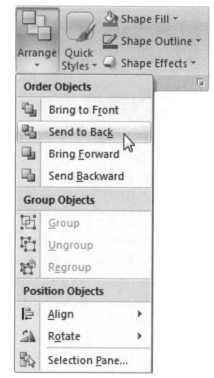

Figure 14.30 You can also choose a layering command from the Arrange drop-down menu.

Select files   Pictures in album   Preview area

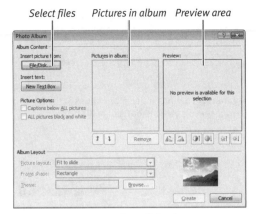

Figure 14.31 The Photo Album dialog box.

Pictures in album   Preview of selected photo

Figure 14.32 Photos are added to Pictures in album in the order in which they're inserted. (In a mass insertion, they're added alphabetically by filename.)

Creating a Photo Album

A *photo album* is a special PowerPoint presentation that enables you to easily present a slide show of personal or business photos.

To create a photo album:

1. On the Insert tab, click Photo Album in the Illustrations group. Choose New Photo Album from the drop-down menu.

   The Photo Album dialog box appears (**Figure 14.31**).

2. To add photos, click the File/Disk button.

   The Insert New Pictures dialog box appears.

3. Navigate to the folder that contains the photos. *Do one of the following:*

   ▲ To add a single photo, click its icon.

   ▲ To simultaneously add multiple photos from the folder, Ctrl-click each photo file.

   ▲ To simultaneously add *all* image files from the folder, press Ctrl A to select them all.

4. If the Insert New Pictures dialog box is still present, click Insert (or Open).

   The selected photo(s) are added to the Pictures in album list (**Figure 14.32**).

5. As necessary, repeat Steps 3 and 4 to add more photos.

6. *Optional:* To remove a photo, select its name in the Pictures in album list and click Remove (see Figure 14.32).

7. *Optional:* The order of photos in the Pictures in album list will match the slide order. To change a photo's position in the list, select it, and click the up or down arrow button beneath the list.

continues on next page

CREATING A PHOTO ALBUM

8. In the Album Layout area of the dialog box (**Figure 14.33**), select a layout from the Picture layout drop-down list.

If you select a "with title" layout, every slide will contain a text placeholder.

9. If you chose any layout other than Fit to slide in Step 8, you can select a frame from the Frame shape drop-down list.

A preview of the selected Picture layout and Frame shape settings is shown to their right (see Figure 14.33).

10. *Optional:* To apply a theme to the slides, click the Browse button. Select a Power-Point theme in the Choose Theme dialog box (**Figure 14.34**) and click Select/Open.

11. *Optional:* In the Picture Options area of the dialog box (**Figure 14.35**), click check boxes to add a caption and/or display the photos in black and white.

By default, each photo's filename is used as its caption. You can edit the captions after the slides have been generated.

12. Click the Create button.

PowerPoint creates a presentation from the selected photos.

13. If you decide to keep the presentation, be sure to save it. Click the Save icon on the Quick Access Toolbar, press Ctrl S, or click the Office Button and choose Save or Save As.

✔ Tips

■ You can treat the photo album as a finished presentation or enliven it by adding PowerPoint features, such as animations, transitions, and audio.

■ After generating the presentation, you can change its settings or add new photos by clicking the Photo Album icon and choosing Edit Photo Album. Make the changes and click Update.

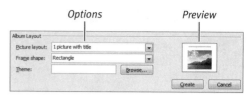

Options   *Preview*

Figure 14.33 Set picture display options in the Album Layout section of the Photo Album dialog box.

Figure 14.34 You can optionally apply a theme to the slides.

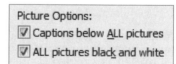

Figure 14.35 Picture Options.

CREATING A PHOTO ALBUM

— From Beginning · From Current Slide · Custom Slide Show ▾ · Start Slide Show

Figure 14.36 If you can't remember the keyboard shortcuts, you can start the show by clicking one of these icons.

Figure 14.37 The slide show runs in full-screen mode.

Previewing the Slide Show

Every slide show is a work in progress. As such, you'll want to periodically preview it onscreen to check the effect of changes, the application of special effects, the addition of new slides, and so on.

To preview a slide show:

1. *Optional:* To begin the slide show with a particular slide (other than the first), select or switch to that slide.

   You can select a slide in Normal, Slide Sorter, or Notes Page view.

2. *Do one of the following:*
   - ▲ To run the show starting with the first slide, click the Slide Show icon on the View tab or press [F5].
   - ▲ To run the show starting with the current slide, press [Shift][F5].
   - ▲ On the Slide Show tab, click the From Beginning or From Current Slide icon in the Start Slide Show group (**Figure 14.36**).

   The show begins (**Figure 14.37**).

3. *Do any of the following:*
   - ▲ To step forward through the slides and within-slide animations (if any), click the mouse or press [n], [Enter], [Page Down], [Spacebar], [→], or [↓].
   - ▲ To move backward through the slides and within-slide animations (if any), [Ctrl]-click the mouse or press [p], [Page Up], [Backspace], [←], or [↑].
   - ▲ To end the show, press [Esc].

✔ Tip

- ■ You can press [Esc] to halt a slide show at *any* time—after the final slide has been displayed or in the middle of the show.

COMPLETING
A PRESENTATION

15

In this chapter, you'll learn about putting the finishing touches on a presentation:

◆ Add within-slide animations, between-slide transitions, and action buttons

◆ Rearrange the slides to match their final order, as well as delete and hide slides

◆ Rehearse the presentation while recording the time spent on each slide and on the total presentation

◆ Print notes, handouts, and other material you'll need for the presentation

◆ Save the presentation in other formats (such as PDF or Web pages) and package its contents on a CD or DVD

✔ Tip

■ To run a finished presentation, follow the steps in "Previewing the Slide Show" in Chapter 14.

Animating Objects and Text

Simple object or text selected

To add motion to a presentation, you can animate any object on a slide, such as text, pictures, charts, and SmartArt. You can animate a selected object by choosing an option from the Animate drop-down menu or by setting options in the Custom Animation task pane.

To apply an animation using the Animate menu:

1. In Normal view, select an object on the current slide to animate.

2. Switch to the Animations tab.

3. Click the Animate icon in the Animations group. The drop-down Animate menu appears (**Figure 15.1**).

   The menu content depends on the type and complexity of the object you're animating. As you hover the cursor over a choice, the animation is previewed on the slide.

4. Choose a command from the menu.

To apply an animation using the Custom Animation task pane:

1. In Normal view, select an object on the current slide to animate.

2. Switch to the Animations tab.

3. Click the Animate icon in the Animations group, and choose Custom Animation from the Animate drop-down menu (see Figure 15.1).

   The Custom Animation task pane appears (**Figure 15.2**). Items that are animated are numbered on the slide and in the pane.

4. Choose an effect from the Add Effect button's submenus (**Figure 15.3**).

5. *Optional:* Modify the settings by choosing options from the pane's drop-down menus.

Chart selected   *SmartArt selected*

Figure 15.1 Animate menu commands depend on the selected object.

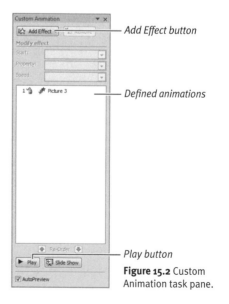

Add Effect button

Defined animations

Play button

Figure 15.2 Custom Animation task pane.

ANIMATING OBJECTS AND TEXT

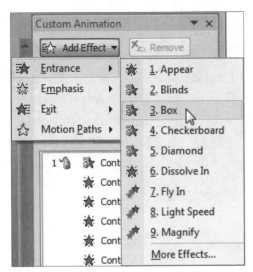

Figure 15.3 Choose an effect from the Add Effect drop-down menu. To see the full list of effects for a submenu, choose More Effects.

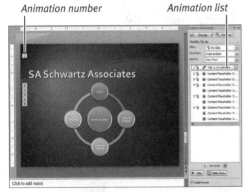

Animation number   *Animation list*

Figure 15.4 To remove, replace, or change the settings for an animation, select the animation by clicking its number on the slide or by selecting it in the animation step list.

✔ Tips

- Only a few basic animations can be chosen from the Animate drop-down menu (see Figure 15.1). You'll usually be better served by setting options in the Custom Animation task pane. The pane contains *many* more effects and offers control over how they execute.

- When animating a *complex object* composed of multiple elements, such as SmartArt or a chart, you can animate it as though it were a single object, one element or item type at a time, and so on.

- Multiple animations can be applied sequentially to a single object.

- Even information in the footer, such as the slide number, can be animated.

- To use the same animation on all slides of a certain type, apply it to the master slide.

- You can view a slide's animations by switching to the Animations tab and clicking the Preview icon in the Preview group. If the Custom Animation task pane is open, you can also click the Play button (see Figure 15.2).

- To remove an animation from a selected object, choose No Animation from the Animate menu. Or, when working in the Custom Animation task pane, select the specific animation you want to remove, and click the Remove button.

- To replace one animation with another, select the animation step in the task pane or on the slide (**Figure 15.4**), click the Change button in the task pane, and choose a replacement animation.

- Don't overuse animations. A few can draw attention to key elements on important slides; too many can turn a presentation into a carnival.

Organizing the Slides

Working in Slide Sorter view (**Figure 15.5**), you can rearrange the slides to match their final order. You can also delete unwanted slides, as well as hide ones you want to keep but won't be using in the presentation.

To organize the slides:

1. Switch to Slide Sorter view. (Click its icon in the Presentation Views group on the Views tab or at the bottom of the document window.)

2. Adjust the magnification controls to clearly display the slide thumbnails.

3. *Do any of the following:*
   - ▲ To change a slide's order in the presentation, drag its thumbnail to a new position.
   - ▲ To delete a slide, right-click its thumbnail and choose Delete Slide from the pop-up menu (**Figure 15.6**).
   - ▲ To hide a slide, right-click its thumbnail and choose Hide Slide from the pop-up menu. The slide number indicates the hidden status (**Figure 15.7**).

✔ Tips

- ■ You can also organize slides in Normal view. To change a slide's position, drag its thumbnail to a new location in the list. To delete or hide a slide, right-click the thumbnail and choose Delete Slide or Hide Slide from the pop-up menu.

- ■ If you need to modify a slide, double-click its thumbnail. The slide appears in Normal view, ready for editing.

- ■ You can play a slide's animations in Slide Sorter view by clicking the animation indicator beneath the lower-left corner of the thumbnail (see Figure 15.7).

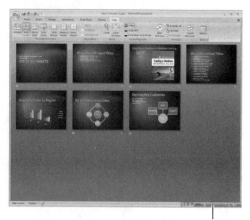

Magnification controls

Figure 15.5 Slide Sorter view.

Figure 15.6 Right-click a thumbnail to delete or hide a slide.

Play animations   Hidden slide indicator

Figure 15.7 When a slide is hidden, its number is surrounded by a shaded box.

No Transition

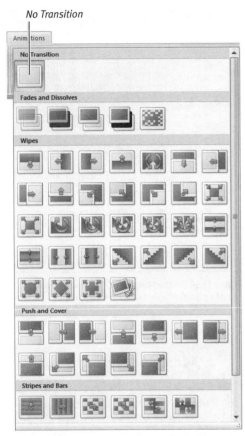

Figure 15.8 Choose a transition effect from the drop-down gallery.

Adding Transitions

When presenting a slide show, a *transition* is an effect that appears when switching between slides. You can use the same transition for every slide change, different transitions between different slides, or no transitions at all (when presenting real slides or using an overhead projector, for example). When setting transitions, note that they are applied to the current slide's *entrance*—not its exit.

To specify a transition:

1. In Normal or Slide Sorter view, select the slide thumbnail to which you want to add a transition.

2. Click the Animations tab.

3. Choose a transition effect from the Transition to this Slide gallery (**Figure 15.8**).

   A live preview is presented for any transition over which you hover the cursor.

4. *Optional:* To add a sound effect to the transition or to change the transition's speed, choose options from the drop-down menus in the Transition to this Slide group (**Figure 15.9**).

5. Select an Advance Slide option (see Figure 15.9) to determine whether the slide will advance manually (under presenter control) or automatically (based on time).

6. *Optional:* To apply the transition to every slide in the presentation, click Apply To All.

Sound and speed settings   *Advance Slide options*

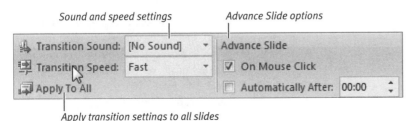

Apply transition settings to all slides

Figure 15.9 You can set additional options in the Transition to this Slide group.

✔ Tips

■ Transitions can be skipped if you won't be presenting on a computer.

■ To change a transition effect, sound, or speed for a slide, select the slide and choose new options and settings from the Transition to this Slide group (see Figures 15.8 and 15.9).

■ To remove a transition, choose the No Transition effect for the slide (see Figure 15.8). To remove transitions from *all* slides, set any slide's transition to No Transition and then click Apply to All.

Figure 15.10 On the Mouse Click or Mouse Over tab, specify a button action and then click OK.

Adding Action Buttons

An *action button* is a shape you can place on a slide that performs a function when clicked, such as returning to the first slide, playing a sound effect, or launching an application.

To add an action button to a slide, switch to Normal view, click the Insert or Home tab, and choose a button from those at the bottom of the Shapes gallery. Click and drag to draw the button on the slide. (To keep the button proportional to its original dimensions, press (Shift) as you drag.) Like other objects, you can move, resize, or change the format of an action button.

In the Action Settings dialog box (**Figure 15.10**), specify the action you want the button to perform in response to a mouse click or *mouse over* (moving the mouse over the button). Close the Action Settings dialog box by clicking OK.

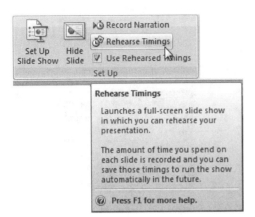

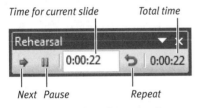

Rehearse Timings

Launches a full-screen slide show in which you can rehearse your presentation.

The amount of time you spend on each slide is recorded and you can save those timings to run the show automatically in the future.

ⓘ Press F1 for more help.

Figure 15.11 If you click Rehearse Timings, the amount of time spent on each slide will be recorded.

Time for current slide *Total time*

Rehearsal

→ ‖ | 0:00:22 | ↺ | 0:00:22 |

Next Pause *Repeat*

Figure 15.12 Use the Rehearsal toolbar to view slide timings, pause the show, or perform the next action.

✔ **Tip**

■ To replay a presentation using the saved timings, switch to the Slide Show tab, click the Use Rehearsed Timings check box (see Figure 15.11), and click From Beginning in the Start Slide Show group. The slide show will play and automatically advance through the animations and slides using the saved timings.

Rehearsing a Presentation

You'll want to rehearse your presentation before giving it to an actual audience. In addition to helping prepare what you'll say for each slide, a rehearsal can record the time spent per slide and on the total presentation. This serves two purposes. First, by reviewing slide timings, you can determine if you're spending too much or too little time on certain slides or the presentation. Second, if the presentation will run in kiosk mode, timings can be used to automatically advance slides.

To rehearse slide timings:

1. On the Slide Show tab, click the Rehearse Timings icon in the Set Up group (**Figure 15.11**).

   The slide show begins.

2. Present the show as you intend to give it to your audience, advancing through the slides by clicking the mouse, pressing a keyboard shortcut (see Chapter 14), or clicking the Next button on the Rehearsal toolbar (**Figure 15.12**).

   As you switch slides, PowerPoint notes the amount of time spent on each one.

3. During the rehearsal, you can also use the Rehearsal toolbar as follows:

   ▲ Click the Pause button if you need to take a break. Click Pause again when you're ready to continue.

   ▲ To restart the timing for the current slide, click the Repeat button.

4. When the show ends, a dialog box displays the total time and asks if you'd like to save the slide timings. Click Yes to save or No if you prefer not to save the timings.

Printing Notes and Handouts

In preparation for the presentation, you can print your notes and audience handouts.

To print notes:

1. Click the Office Button and choose Print > Print Preview.

   Print Preview (**Figure 15.13**) allows you to see the output onscreen prior to routing it to your printer.

2. Choose Notes Pages from the Print What drop-down menu in the Page Setup group.

3. Choose a paper orientation (portrait or landscape) from the Orientation drop-down menu in the Page Setup group.

4. *Optional:* To print the notes in shades of gray (*grayscale*) or black and white rather than in color, choose a setting from the Options drop-down menu in the Print group.

5. *Optional:* To review the slides, click the Next Page or Previous Page icons in the Preview group.

6. *Do one of the following:*

   ▲ When the settings are to your liking, click the Print button.

   ▲ If you aren't ready to print, click the Close Print Preview icon in the Preview group.

   When you print, the notes are printed one slide per page.

Print options

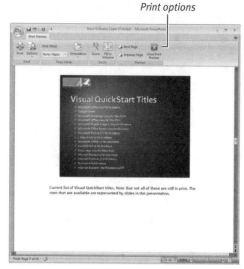

Figure 15.13 All print settings can be chosen and their effects previewed in Print Preview mode.

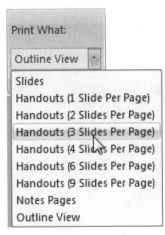

Figure 15.14 Choose a Handouts command from the Print What drop-down menu.

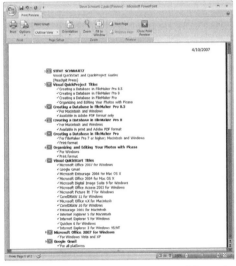

Figure 15.15 Choose Outline View to print slide text in outline form.

To print handouts:

◆ Perform the previous task list. In Step 2, choose a Handouts command from the Print What drop-down menu in the Page Setup group (**Figure 15.14**).

The 3 Slides Per Page option provides lines on which the audience can write notes.

✔ Tips

■ Choose Slides from the Print What drop-down menu to print enlarged versions of the slides (one per page).

■ It can be helpful to choose Outline View from the Print What drop-down menu. The printout (**Figure 15.15**) provides a slide-by-slide listing of the text contained on each slide.

■ You can also set print settings and then print by choosing Print > Print.

Saving a Presentation in Other Formats

If the slide show will be presented or needs to be delivered to recipients in a form other than as a PowerPoint 2007 presentation, you can save an additional copy of it in the necessary format(s).

To save a presentation in an alternate format:

1. Click the Office Button, and choose one of the following formats from the Save As menu (**Figure 15.16**):

   ▲ **PowerPoint Show.** When you open a PowerPoint Show (.ppsx) file, Slide Show view is selected and the show automatically begins.

   ▲ **PowerPoint 97-2003 Presentation.** Choose this file format when you or the recipient will be using an older version of PowerPoint to give the presentation.

   ▲ **PDF or XPS.** Use this option to create a static version of a presentation with one slide per page. PDF output can be viewed with Adobe Reader, Preview (Apple), or a similar utility. XPS output requires a compatible viewing program, such as Internet Explorer 7. (Note that you must install Microsoft's PDF/XPS add-in to use these options.)

   ▲ **Web (HTML) presentation.** Choose Other Formats. When the Save As dialog box appears, choose Web Page or Single File Web Page from the Save as type drop-down list.

2. In the Save As dialog box, select a folder in which to save the presentation.

3. Accept or edit the proposed filename.

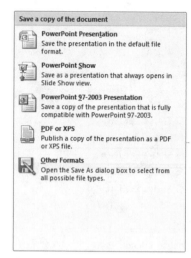

Figure 15.16 Save As choices.

Figure 15.17 When creating a PDF or XPS file, these options are displayed at the bottom of the Save As dialog box.

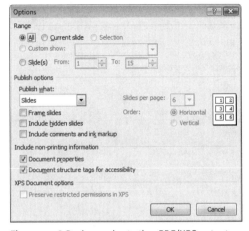

Figure 15.18 Review and set other PDF/XPS output options in the Options dialog box.

Figure 15.19 Other Save As options are also available when you save a Web presentation.

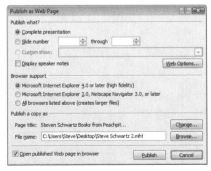

Figure 15.20 Publish as Web Page dialog box.

4. When you save as a PDF or XPS file, additional options appear in the Save As dialog box (**Figure 15.17**):

▲ To automatically display the resulting file (if an appropriate reader application is installed), click the Open file after publishing check box.

▲ Click an Optimize for radio button, depending on whether detail/clarity or file size/download speed are the most important considerations.

▲ Click Options to specify additional output options in the Options dialog box (**Figure 15.18**). Click OK to save your changes, if any.

5. When you create output for the Web, other options are presented in the Save As dialog box (**Figure 15.19**):

▲ To change the page title from the default title, click Change Title, type a new title in the Set Page Title dialog box, and click OK.

▲ To set additional options, such as supported browsers and whether animations will play, click the Publish button. The Publish as Web Page dialog box appears (**Figure 15.20**). Click the Web Options button to review or set advanced Web options.

6. Click Save or Publish to generate the output file(s).

7. *Optional:* In most cases, the Save As output file becomes the active PowerPoint file. To resume editing or viewing the original file, click the Office Button and reopen the presentation.

SAVING A PRESENTATION IN OTHER FORMATS

✔ Tips

- You can copy a presentation to CD to transfer it to a recipient. PowerPoint Viewer is included on the CD, enabling any Windows recipient to run and view the presentation. (On the other hand, if you need to copy it to a *DVD*, you can package the necessary files in a folder and then use any DVD-burning application to create the DVD.)

  Click the Office Button, and choose Publish > Package for CD. Set options in the Package for CD dialog box (**Figure 15.21**), insert a blank CD in your CD burner, and click Copy to CD. (If you'll be creating a DVD, click Copy to Folder.)

- Before running a PowerPoint presentation, it's a good idea to review the current settings in the Set Up Show dialog box (**Figure 15.22**). Options in the dialog box let you create a self-running presentation (*kiosk mode*), specify whether recorded timings will automatically advance slides, and set the screen resolution. To open the dialog box, click the Set Up Show icon in the Set Up group on the Slide Show tab.

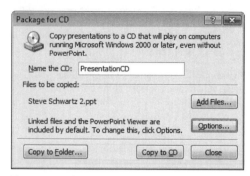

Figure 15.21 Click Copy to CD to burn the files to CD or click Copy to Folder to package the files in preparation for burning a DVD.

Figure 15.22 Review settings in the Set Up Show dialog box before starting a slide show.

Part V: Microsoft Outlook

Chapter 16 Getting Started with Outlook
2007 247

Chapter 17 Using the Address Book.................... 267

Chapter 18 Composing and Sending Mail.......... 281

Chapter 19 Receiving Mail.................................... 303

Chapter 20 Managing the Mail 313

Chapter 21 Tasks and Appointments.................. 329

GETTING STARTED WITH OUTLOOK 2007

Even if you're new to the Internet, you've undoubtedly heard the term *email* bandied about. Short for *electronic mail*, email is a text message sent from one person's Internet account to another's. With most Internet accounts, you must have a computer program known as an *email client* to compose and send messages, as well as receive and read messages from others. In addition to serving as your email client, Outlook can manage your appointments, handle to-do lists, and receive Really Simple Syndication (RSS) Web site feeds.

In this chapter, you'll set up your email accounts for Outlook and learn how to subscribe to RSS feeds. We'll also cover the following essential Outlook topics:

- Creating and using profiles

- Creating groups to schedule automatic send/receive operations

- Understanding the Outlook interface

- Setting options to customize the way Outlook works

- Working online and offline

- Setting preferences

- Getting help while running Outlook 2007

Types of Email Accounts

Outlook supports four Internet mail account types: Post Office Protocol (*POP3*), Internet Message Access Protocol (*IMAP*), Exchange Server, and HTTP. Outlook can send and retrieve email from all of these account types. Your Internet Service Provider (*ISP*), company, or school will let you know which type of account you have.

POP3 accounts

The majority of email accounts are POP3. In fact, unless you're told otherwise, you can usually assume that your email account uses POP3. When Outlook connects with your ISP's mail server to check for new mail, the mail is downloaded to your PC from a POP server. After you've received the new mail, it is automatically deleted from the server. Thus, POP mail servers act only as temporary repositories for both outgoing and incoming email.

IMAP accounts

Unlike a POP3 account, an IMAP account is not a temporary repository for email. The email never actually leaves the IMAP server. Instead, the IMAP server acts like a node on a network to which you can connect. Rather than downloading your new mail to your PC, you're simply *viewing* it on the IMAP server.

Exchange Server accounts

Exchange Server accounts are primarily used by individuals in large companies, educational institutions, and the like.

With many email clients, you must have an active connection to the server in order to read your current messages. However, you can enable Outlook's *Cached Exchange Mode* to store copies of existing messages on your PC, enabling you to view them even when you're offline.

HTTP (Web-based) accounts

With a Web-based account, such as Hotmail, you normally use a Web browser to send and receive email rather than use an email client. However, you can also use Outlook to manage email for many HTTP accounts.

✔ Tips

■ Some ISPs require you to use their proprietary software to send/receive email. You cannot use Outlook for such accounts.

■ Web-based accounts other than Hotmail may be supported by Outlook via POP rather than HTTP. For this to occur, the Web-based email service must also provide auxiliary POP servers to which email clients can connect. Google's free email (Gmail) is handled in this manner, for example. Yahoo! Mail also offers POP support, but only for paying Yahoo! Mail Plus customers.

■ Some email accounts can be accessed in multiple ways. For instance, Apple's .Mac provides both POP and IMAP support. You can configure Outlook to use either account type.

The Case for HTTP Accounts

Why bother with Web-based accounts if you already have an ISP or a company-provided email account? Here are two excellent reasons:

◆ If you ever travel, you can access a Web-based account from anywhere in the world, using a Web browser on any PC or Mac.

◆ Because Web accounts are often free, you can use them to handle email that you'd rather not have cluttering up your ISP email account. When registering at Web sites, for example, you are usually asked for an email address. To avoid receiving volumes of unwanted advertising email (called *spam*) at your primary mail account, you can have it all sent to an HTTP account.

Types of Email Accounts

About Email Addresses

Regardless of the type of account you have, every email account is identified by a unique address, such as jpt417@msn.com or bobp@linetop.net. The address consists of three parts: a user name, the @ (at) symbol, and a domain name (**Figure 16.1**). When you create the account, you normally get to choose your user name. The domain name is the name of the company or organization that is providing access to the Internet.

When people want to send you a message, they address it to your email address. And when you want to send someone else a message, you send it to that person's email address. Because you may know dozens or even hundreds of people, there's little point in attempting to memorize email addresses. Programs such as Outlook generally provide an Address Book (**Figure 16.2**) in which you can record important email addresses. When you want to create a new message, you can select addresses from the Address Book rather than type them from memory.

See Chapter 17 for instructions on using the Address Book.

✔ Tips

- A proper email address cannot include blank spaces. The underscore (_) character is commonly used to represent a space.

- Letter case is irrelevant in an email address. As such, the convention is to type email addresses using all lowercase letters.

- Domains in countries other than the U.S. often end in a country abbreviation, such as .CA (Canada), .UK (United Kingdom), and .JP (Japan).

User name   @ symbol   Domain name

james47@ispworld.com

Figure 16.1 Every email address consists of these three components.

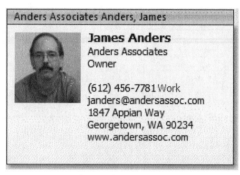

Figure 16.2 In addition to a name and an email address, an Outlook contact record can store mailing and telephone information (for both work and home), a Web site, and a picture.

Click New to add an account

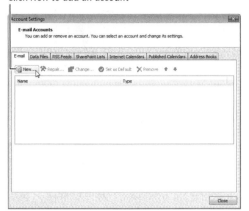

Figure 16.3 You create, delete, and manage email accounts on the E-mail tab of the Account Settings dialog box.

Figure 16.4 To automatically configure an account, enter the name to display when your sent messages are received by others, the full email address, and the account's password.

Outlook's First Launch

The first time you run Outlook or when you first use a new user *profile* (see page 256), the Outlook 2007 Startup wizard runs. You can use the wizard to add your main email account or follow the procedures in "Adding Email Accounts."

Adding Email Accounts

If a previous version of Outlook is on your PC, Outlook 2007 will automatically use the old version's data: all email accounts, messages, contacts, appointments, and so on. However, if no previous version of Outlook is on your PC, you must add the email accounts that you want Outlook to manage.

New accounts can be added *automatically* (with Outlook attempting to discern settings from your address and password) or *manually* (by hand-entering the necessary information).

To automatically add an account:

1. Choose Tools > Account Settings.

   The Account Settings dialog box appears (**Figure 16.3**).

2. Click the E-mail tab, if it isn't selected.

3. Click the New button.

   The Choose E-mail Service screen appears.

4. Select the Microsoft Exchange, POP3, IMAP, or HTTP radio button. Click Next to continue.

   The Auto Account Setup screen appears.

5. Enter the requested information (**Figure 16.4**) and click Next.

   Outlook contacts the domain's mail server, tries to configure the account, and then sends a test email message.

6. *Do one of the following:*

   ▲ If successful, the final screen appears. Click Finish to add the new account.

   ▲ If Outlook can't contact the server, the user name and password aren't recognized, or the server can't handle encrypted messages, instructions for correcting the problem appear. Follow them to retry or click Cancel.

7. Click Close to dismiss the Account Settings dialog box.

To manually add a POP, IMAP, or HTTP account:

1. Choose Tools > Account Settings.

   The Account Settings dialog box appears (see Figure 16.3).

2. Click the E-mail tab, if it isn't selected.

3. Click the New button.

   The Choose E-mail Service screen appears.

4. Select the Microsoft Exchange, POP3, IMAP, or HTTP radio button, and click Next to continue.

   The Auto Account Setup screen appears (see Figure 16.4).

5. *Optional:* Enter the requested information.

   If entered on this screen, the display name and email address will be carried forward to a subsequent screen.

6. Click the Manually configure server settings or additional server types check box, and then click Next.

   The Choose E-mail Service screen appears.

7. Select Internet E-mail and click Next.

   The Internet E-mail Settings screen appears (**Figure 16.5**).

8. Enter the requested account information.

9. *Optional:* If available, click the Test Account Settings button to send a test email message using the current settings. A successful test ensures that the basic settings are correct and you'll be able to send and receive mail.

10. Click Next and then click Finish. Click Close to dismiss the Account Settings dialog box.

✔ Tip

■ Outlook supports all older, free Hotmail accounts. *New* Hotmail accounts, however, must be paid subscriptions.

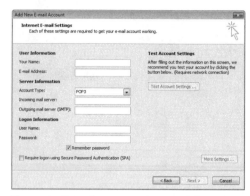

Figure 16.5 Enter the requested account information.

Multiple Exchange Server Accounts

A user profile can handle multiple email accounts. For example, my profile contains two POP3 accounts (both with my ISP), an IMAP account, a Gmail (Google) account, and several Hotmail accounts.

However, a user profile may contain only *one* Exchange Server account. If you already have such an account in the current profile, you must create a second profile to accommodate the additional Exchange Server account. You can do so in the Profiles section of the Mail Control Panel (see Figure 16.6).

Figure 16.6 The Mail Setup - Outlook dialog box.

Use Cached Exchange Mode

Figure 16.7 The Microsoft Exchange Settings screen.

Email from Anywhere

You don't have to restrict email activities to your home or work computer. In fact, odds are excellent that you can interact with your ISP's mail servers from anywhere you can get Internet access.

Simply create a new account in the current computer's email client using the same settings used when you created the account in Outlook 2007. (You'll probably want to delete the account when you're done using the computer.)

To manually add an Exchange Server account:

1. Quit Outlook 2007, and open the Mail Control Panel (a Windows component). The Mail Setup - Outlook dialog box appears (**Figure 16.6**).

2. Click the E-mail Accounts button. The Account Settings dialog box appears.

3. Perform Steps 2–5 from the previous task.

4. Select Microsoft Exchange and click Next. The Microsoft Exchange Settings screen appears (**Figure 16.7**).

5. Enter the information provided to you by the Exchange Server administrator. Click Next to move to subsequent screens.

6. When you're done creating the account, click Close on both the Account Settings and the Mail Setup - Outlook dialog boxes.

✔ Tips

- Try the automatic approach first. If it doesn't work at all, you can then use the manual method. If the automatic method works but not perfectly, you can modify the settings by selecting the account in the Account Settings dialog box and then clicking Edit.

- Messages in an Exchange Server account are normally readable only when you're online. To automatically download copies of all messages so they can also be read when you're offline, click the Use Cached Exchange Mode check box (see Figure 16.7).

- Unless told by your ISP or network administrator that your email account uses Secure Password Authentication (see Figure 16.5), you can assume that it is neither required nor supported.

ADDING EMAIL ACCOUNTS

Changing Account Settings

After adding an email account automatically or working with the account for a while, you may want to modify the account's settings to make it behave in a different manner.

You can also specify a *default account* (from which all outgoing mail will be sent unless another account is specified), change an account's position in the Account Settings list, test an account, and delete accounts.

To edit an account's settings:

1. Choose Tools > Account Settings.
   The Account Settings dialog box appears (**Figure 16.8**).

2. *Do either of the following:*
   ▲ Select the account and click Change.
   ▲ Double-click the account's name.
   The Change E-mail Account screen appears (refer to Figure 16.5).

3. *Optional:* Make any desired changes to the settings, such as the name used to identify messages from you or the mail server names.

4. *Optional:* To view other account-specific settings, click More Settings. The Internet E-mail Settings dialog box appears (**Figure 16.9**). Settings you might wish to alter include the following:
   ▲ **General tab, Mail Account:** Enter a descriptive name for the account, such as Home or the ISP's name.
   ▲ **General tab, Reply E-mail:** When someone replies to a message from you, the reply is addressed to the account from which you sent the message. To direct replies to a *different* account (your main work account, for example), enter that email address here.

Selected account

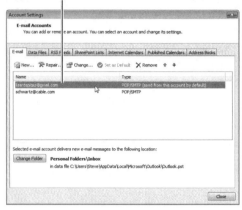

Figure 16.8 In the Account Settings dialog box, select an account to modify.

Figure 16.9 The General tab of the Internet E-mail Settings dialog box.

Figure 16.10 The Advanced tab of the Internet E-mail Settings dialog box.

✔ Tips

■ If you use a particular account only with this PC, do *not* set the option to Leave a copy of messages on the server. Doing so will only clutter the mail server with messages you've already retrieved.

■ If you add more than one email account to Outlook, be sure the correct default account is set. For most users, this will be your main ISP, corporate, or educational account.

■ Even though every user has a default email account, you can send any new message from any account you've added to the Account Settings list.

■ You cannot edit the *account type* (switching from POP to IMAP, for example). If you or the automatic setup sets the wrong type for an account, delete the account and then manually add it again using the correct account type.

▲ **Advanced tab, Leave a copy of messages on the server:** Normally, when you retrieve a message from a POP mail server, the message is automatically deleted from the server. If you are retrieving this account's email from multiple computers (work and home, for example), you can enable this option (**Figure 16.10**) on the secondary computers. Doing so ensures that all messages retrieved on a secondary computer will also be downloaded to your main PC before being deleted from the server.

Click OK to save all changes made in the Internet E-mail Settings dialog box, or click Cancel to ignore all changes.

5. To save the changes to the current account, click Next and then Finish. Or click Cancel to leave without saving changes.

6. Click Close to close the Account Settings dialog box (see Figure 16.8).

To change the default email account:

◆ In the Account Settings dialog box (see Figure 16.8), select an account and click Set as Default.

To change an account's position in the Account Settings list:

◆ In the Account Settings dialog box, select the account and click the up- or down-arrow button.

To check a malfunctioning account:

◆ In the Account Settings dialog box, select the account and click Repair.

To delete an account:

◆ In the Account Settings dialog box, select the account and click Remove. Confirm the deletion.

Working with Profiles

Outlook uses *profiles* to determine which email accounts should be displayed in an Outlook session. When you install Outlook, a single profile is created for all your accounts. However, if several people use the PC, each will need their own profile. Similarly, if you want to keep your work and home email accounts separate, you can create another profile. (Note that on most single-user PCs, a single profile will suffice.)

To create a new profile:

1. Quit Outlook 2007, and then open the Mail Control Panel.

   The Mail Setup - Outlook dialog box appears (see Figure 16.6).

2. Click the Show Profiles button.

   The Mail dialog box appears (**Figure 16.11**).

3. Click Add.

   The New Profile dialog box appears (**Figure 16.12**).

4. Name the new profile and click OK.

   The Add New E-mail Account dialog box appears (see Figure 16.4).

5. *Do either of the following:*

   ▲ Record the first email account for the new profile (described in "Adding Email Accounts," earlier in this chapter).

   ▲ Click Cancel to create the profile without specifying the first email account.

✔ Tip

■ Additional email accounts can be added at any time in Outlook or in the Mail Control Panel.

Figure 16.11 You create, delete, and set startup options for profiles in the Mail dialog box.

Figure 16.12 Enter a name for the profile and click OK.

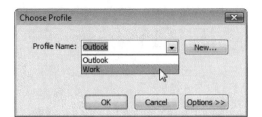

Figure 16.13 You can configure Outlook to prompt for a profile to use each time it's run. Select a profile from the drop-down list and click OK.

To set a startup profile:

1. Quit Outlook 2007, and then open the Mail Control Panel.

The Mail Setup - Outlook dialog box appears (see Figure 16.6).

2. Click the Show Profiles button.

The Mail dialog box appears (see Figure 16.11).

3. *Do either of the following:*

▲ To automatically use a certain profile, click Always use this profile and select the profile from the drop-down list.

▲ To be prompted to select a profile at the start of every Outlook session (**Figure 16.13**), select Prompt for a profile to be used.

4. Click OK.

✔ Tips

■ You cannot switch profiles from within Outlook 2007. If the wrong profile is active, you must quit Outlook and do one of the following:

▲ If Outlook is set to Prompt for a profile to be used, relaunch Outlook and choose the desired profile.

▲ If Outlook is set to Always use this profile, open the Mail Control Panel, click Show Profiles, select the desired profile from the drop-down list (see Figure 16.11), and click OK.

■ Outlook profiles are not password protected. While profiles are convenient for keeping your mail, appointments, and contacts separate from those of other Outlook users, there is nothing to prevent a user from viewing other users' material. If security and privacy are a concern, a better approach is to create a separate password-protected Windows user account for each person.

Working with Send/Receive Groups

Outlook automatically sends and receives email every so many minutes. By creating send/receive groups (each containing one or multiple email accounts), you can specify a different schedule for each group. (When you initially set up Outlook, it creates a default group named All Accounts that consists of all defined email accounts and RSS feeds.)

To modify a group's settings:

1. Choose Tools > Options.

2. Click the Mail Setup tab at the top of the Option dialog box, and click Send/Receive. The Send/Receive Groups screen appears (**Figure 16.14**).

3. Select the name of the group whose settings you wish to modify.

4. Change any of the top three settings (**Figure 16.15**):

   ▲ **Include this group in send/receive (F9):** When checked, all accounts and RSS feeds in the group will perform a send/receive when you press F9 or click the Send/Receive toolbar icon.

   ▲ **Schedule an automatic send/receive every X minutes:** When checked, all accounts and RSS feeds in the group will automatically perform a send/receive at the specified interval. To change the interval, type it in the text box or click the up or down arrow.

   ▲ **Perform an automatic send/receive when exiting:** When checked, a final send/receive will automatically be performed for the accounts in the group each time you quit Outlook.

5. Click Close.

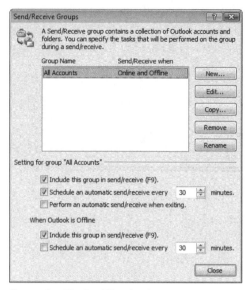

Figure 16.14 The Send/Receive Groups screen.

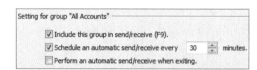

Figure 16.15 These top three settings govern online send/receive behavior for the selected group.

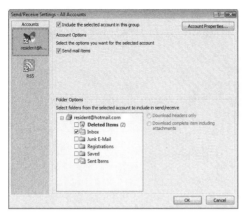

Figure 16.16 Change group membership and individual account settings on the Send/Receive screen.

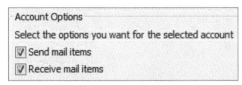

Figure 16.17 These are the options for a POP account. (Each account type has different options.)

Figure 16.18 To set or view options for a folder, select the folder name in the Folder Options area of the dialog box.

To change a group's membership:

1. On the Send/Receive Groups screen (see Figure 16.14), select the group you want to change and click Edit.

   The Send/Receive Settings screen for the selected group appears (**Figure 16.16**). On the left side of the screen, group members' icons contain blue "refresh" arrows, while non-members' icons contain a red X.

2. *Do any of the following:*
   - ▲ To add an account to the group, select its icon and then click the Include the selected account in this group check box (to add a check mark).
   - ▲ To remove an account from the group, select its icon and then click the Include the selected account in this group check box (to remove the check mark).

3. When you're done making changes to the group's membership, click OK to return to the Send/Receive Groups screen.

To view or edit send/receive options for an account:

1. On the Send/Receive Groups screen (see Figure 16.14), select the group that contains the desired account and click Edit.

   The Send/Receive screen for the group appears (see Figure 16.16).

2. On the left side of the screen, click the account's icon.

   Two option sets are displayed for the account: Account Options (**Figure 16.17**) and Folder Options (**Figure 16.18**).

3. Make any desired changes to the settings.

4. *Do either of the following:*
   - ▲ Select and make changes to other accounts in the group.
   - ▲ Click OK to record the changes.

✔ Tips

- You may wish to group accounts by server (all ISP accounts or all Hotmail accounts) or send/receive interval (all accounts to be checked every half hour).

- A group can consist of only one account.

- All RSS feeds—regardless of whether they have one or many sources—are treated as a single account.

- An account doesn't have to belong to *any* group. In general, an account that you check only sporadically (such as a seldom-used HTTP account) can be checked manually by choosing its name from the Tools > Send/Receive submenu.

- If you have a dial-up connection, you may want to set the group that includes your ISP account to perform a send/receive every few minutes. Doing so ensures regular line activity and can prevent disconnects.

- Broadband connections can usually manage a send/receive interval of 1 minute. On the other hand, send/receives on HTTP accounts may fail if performed too frequently. Set the interval to 5 minutes or more.

- If friends routinely send huge, unwanted attachments to your POP account, you may wish to enable the option to Download only headers for items larger than *X* (see Figure 16.18) and set the size to 100 KB or less.

Figure 16.19 Type or paste the feed's URL into this box.

Include this feed (checked)

Exclude this feed (unchecked)

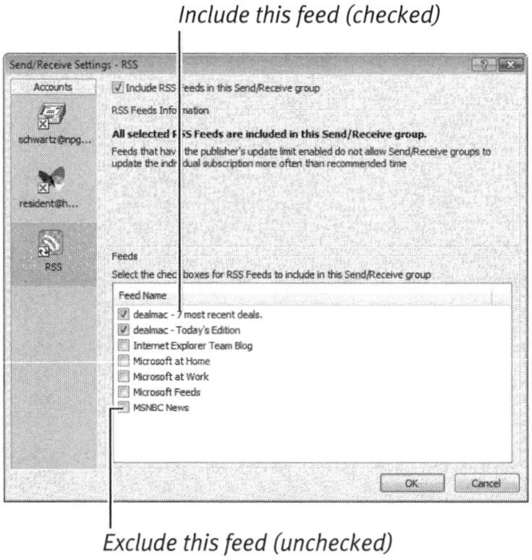

Figure 16.20 To exclude a feed from automatic updates, remove its check mark.

Figure 16.21 The bottom of the RSS Feed Options dialog box shows the update limit for the selected feed.

Subscribing to RSS Feeds

Many Web sites now offer to deliver their latest information to you via Really Simple Syndication (*RSS*) feeds. Subscribed-to feeds can be received by and viewed in Outlook 2007.

To subscribe to a feed:

1. Choose Tools > Account Settings.

   The Account Settings dialog box appears (see Figure 16.3).

2. Click the RSS Feeds tab, and then Click the New button.

   The New RSS Feed dialog box appears (**Figure 16.19**).

3. Enter or paste the address of the feed (obtained from the Web site's instructions) into the text box and click Add.

   The new feed is added to the list in the Account Settings dialog box.

4. Click Close to dismiss the Account Settings dialog box.

✔ Tips

- Many Web sites simplify the process of subscribing to feeds by providing links you can click. For an example, visit http://dealmac.com/rss.html.

- If you want to receive feeds on a schedule, make sure that the RSS account is in a send/receive group. (See the previous section for details.) You can also use the Send/Receive Settings dialog box to selectively include and exclude certain feeds (**Figure 16.20**). To *delete* a feed, select it on the RSS Feeds tab of the Account Settings dialog box and click Remove.

- Feed publishers may set an *update limit* (a minimum time between updates). To view this limit, double-click the feed's name in the Account Settings dialog box (**Figure 16.21**).

The Outlook 2007 Window

Now that you've set up at least one account, it's time to familiarize yourself with the parts of the Outlook window (**Figure 16.22**), what they're for, and how they work.

Note that the screens shown here and throughout the book are based on Vista, Microsoft's newest operating system. If you're using another operating system (such as Windows XP), their appearance may be different.

❶ **Menu bar.** Menus from which you choose Outlook commands.

❷ **Toolbar.** Icons and controls you can use to perform common commands.

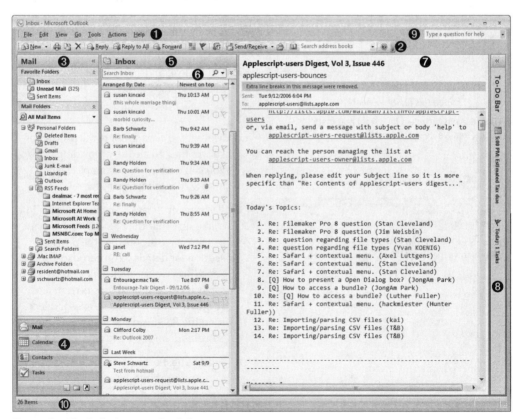

Figure 16.22 The Outlook 2007 main window.

THE OUTLOOK 2007 WINDOW

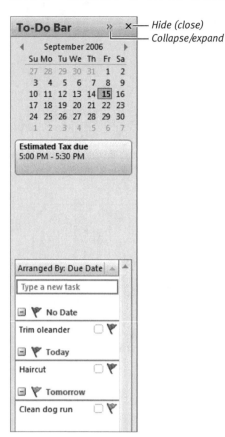

Hide (close)
Collapse/expand

Figure 16.23 The To-Do Bar can be collapsed (see Figure 16.22), expanded (shown here), or completely hidden.

❸ **Navigation Pane.** When the Mail button is at the top of this pane, all of your email accounts, RSS feeds, and their folders are listed. Messages from the currently selected folder are displayed in the message list (❺).

❹ **Navigation Pane buttons.** Click a button to view another Outlook component.

❺ **Message list.** Displays headers of the messages in the currently selected folder. The name of the selected folder is shown at the top of the message list.

❻ **Instant Search box.** Type here to search the current folder (or all folders) for matching text in a message or item.

❼ **Reading Pane.** The text of the selected email message or RSS feed is shown here.

❽ **To-Do Bar.** Displays to-do items and upcoming appointments (**Figure 16.23**).

❾ **Help search box.** Type here to search Outlook Help for relevant help topics.

❿ **Status bar.** Bar at the bottom of the window that displays messages about Outlook's state (Offline, for example) and current activity (such as performing a send/receive).

Detailed instructions for using these Outlook interface components will be presented in later chapters.

Where's the Ribbon?

Other than the new color scheme, the Instant Search box, and the To-Do Bar, the Outlook 2007 window looks very much like the Outlook 2003 window.

The Ribbon is a feature of Office 2007 *documents*. Thus, it is visible only when creating a document (a new email message, task, contact, or appointment) or viewing an existing document (such as a received email message) in its own window.

THE OUTLOOK 2007 WINDOW

Working Online and Offline

In addition to working with Outlook interactively by reading and replying to email messages while online, you can work while you are *offline* (not connected to the Internet).

Why would you want to work offline? Here are a few common reasons:

◆ If you have a dial-up account and use your phone line for both voice calls and Internet access, you can work offline to free up the phone line.

◆ If you're traveling and have a portable computer, you can read previously received email messages as well as compose new messages that will be sent the next time you connect to the Internet.

◆ If the Internet account you're currently using (such as one at an Internet cafe) doesn't provide unlimited access, you can save on time-based connect charges by doing much of your work offline.

In a nutshell, here's how it works. To go offline, choose File > Work Offline (**Figure 16.24**). A check mark appears to the left of the command and the right side of the status bar displays the word *Offline*.

While offline, you can read previously downloaded email and RSS feeds. You can also compose new email messages. When you click the Send button, Outlook stores them in your Outbox until you're next online.

To resume working online, choose File > Work Offline again (to remove the check mark). If you've also disconnected from the Internet, you'll have to reconnect.

✔ Tip

■ Quitting Outlook or going offline does *not* disconnect you from the Internet. To do so and free up your phone line, you'll also have to disconnect.

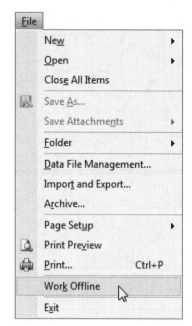

Figure 16.24 Choose Work Offline to work in Outlook without using an Internet connection.

Figure 16.25 Outlook can use Office's spelling checker to prevent embarrassing mistakes in your messages.

Figure 16.26 The Other tab of the Options dialog box.

Setting Preferences

You were introduced to the Options dialog box in "Creating Send/Receive Groups." You also use this dialog box to set preferences for all Outlook components.

The default settings are initially fine for most email users. However, after using Outlook for a bit, it's worth exploring the options. Here are some of the more useful ones:

◆ **Preferences, Junk E-mail:** Set the sensitivity to junk mail and how it is handled.

◆ **Preferences, E-mail Options:** Specify whether original text is quoted in replies and forwards and how it is formatted.

◆ **Preferences, E-mail Options, Advanced E-mail Options:** Specify how you're notified when new mail is received.

◆ **Mail Format:** Set the default format for new messages.

◆ **Mail Format, Signatures:** Create *signatures* to append to outgoing messages. A signature can be your full name, a Web address, additional contact information, or a witty saying, for example.

◆ **Spelling:** Determine whether an automatic spell check occurs before you send each message and whether quoted text is also examined (**Figure 16.25**).

◆ **Other, General (Figure 16.26):** Make Outlook the default email program and specify whether the Deleted Items folder is automatically emptied at the end of each session.

◆ **Other, AutoArchive:** Set options for archiving or deleting old mail.

◆ **Other, Outlook Panes:** Specify buttons displayed in the Navigation Pane, when messages are marked as read, and the contents of the To-Do Bar.

Getting Help

Help in Outlook 2007 is often only a button-click away. Help text is provided in Microsoft Office Outlook Help.

To view help information:

◆ To view a list of related help topics, enter search text in the Help search box (**Figure 16.27**).

◆ To open Outlook Help to its start page, click the Help icon on the Standard toolbar (**Figure 16.27**), choose Help > Microsoft Office Outlook Help, or press F1.

◆ To view help text for the current dialog box, click the *?* button in the upper-right corner of the dialog box (**Figure 16.28**).

To use the Outlook Help window:

◆ To view Outlook Help's start page, click the Home icon at the top of the window (**Figure 16.29**).

◆ To view a help topic (shown as blue under-lined text), click the topic.

◆ To go back or forward to previously viewed help pages, click the arrow icons at the top of the Outlook Help window.

◆ To search for help on a subject, enter search text in the box at the top of the window and click the Search button.

◆ To print the current help page, click the Print icon.

◆ To dismiss the Outlook Help window, click its close button.

◆ You view help from the Help file stored on your hard disk or from Office Online (requires an active Internet connection). Choose a help source by clicking the text in the bottom-right corner of the window (**Figure 16.30**).

Open the Help file   *Search for help*

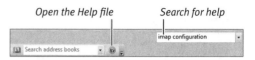

Figure 16.27 At the top of the Outlook window, there are two options for summoning help.

Provide help for this dialog box

Figure 16.28 You can also request help for many dialog boxes.

Search box Home   *Help topic   Close window*

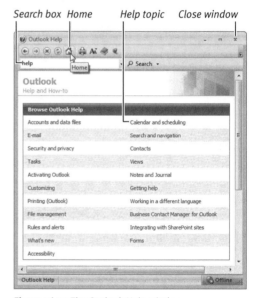

Figure 16.29 The Outlook Help window.

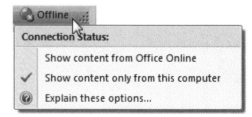

Figure 16.30 Select a help source.

USING THE ADDRESS BOOK

The Address Book (Contacts) is the repository of your contact information for people, companies, institutions, and organizations. After you create records for your contacts, you can address email simply by typing part of the recipient's name.

In addition to standard address information (such as name, home and work addresses, phone numbers, and email addresses), a contact record can store other information, such as a Web page address and a photo.

You can also do the following in the Address Book:

◆ Record multiple email addresses, mailing addresses, and phone numbers for each contact

◆ Browse through and search for contacts

◆ Import contact information from older versions of Outlook, as well as other email, database, and address applications

◆ Create an Electronic Business Card, enabling you to easily share your contact information with others

◆ Create distribution lists to simplify mass mailings

The Contacts Window

To view or work with the Address Book, click the Contacts button in the Navigation Pane, choose Go > Contacts, or press Ctrl 3. In the Contacts window that appears (**Figure 17.1**), you can set a viewing method, view and edit contact records, and locate specific contacts by scrolling, clicking buttons, or searching.

✔ Tip

■ To quickly find an email address without displaying the Contacts window, choose Tools > Address Book. You can address a new message to a selected contact record by pressing Ctrl N.

Set a view   Search for contacts   Go to page

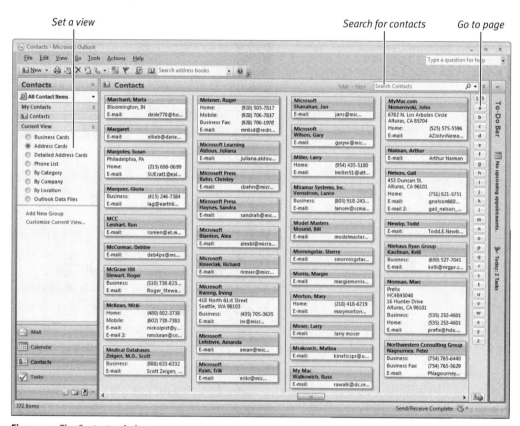

Figure 17.1 The Contacts window.

Figure 17.2 To change the format used to display contact records, click a radio button.

Figure 17.3 After opening a record, you can edit it or select and copy text (such as an email or Web address) for pasting elsewhere.

Viewing Contact Records

Rather than searching for a specific record using the Instant Search box, you'll often find yourself just flipping through contacts to find the one you want. Outlook provides several ways to simplify browsing for contacts.

To browse through contact records:

1. *Optional:* Select a record display format by clicking a radio button in the Current View section of the Navigation Pane (**Figure 17.2**).

2. *Do any of the following:*
   ▲ Click the scroll arrows, click in the scroll bar, or drag the scroll box to a new position. (Depending on the current view, the scroll bar will be on the right or bottom of the screen.)
   ▲ In the first three views (Business Cards, Address Cards, and Detailed Address Cards), click a letter button (see Figure 17.1) to view contacts beginning with that letter.

3. *Optional:* To view the complete contact record, double-click the record, or select the record and press Ctrl O.
   The record opens in a separate window (**Figure 17.3**).

✔ Tips

■ You can change the view at any time. (Outlook remembers the most recent Contacts view you've set.)

■ In Business Cards, Address Cards, and Detailed Address Cards view, the File as information for each record determines how it is alphabetized. See "Creating Contact Records" for details.

■ When working in any columnar list view, you can change the sort order by clicking a column heading, such as Company.

Creating Contact Records

There are several means of creating new contact records when the need arises. You can:

◆ Manually create new records from scratch

◆ Create a new contact record from a received email message

◆ Import contact records from another copy of Outlook 2007, a prior version of Outlook, or another email program or database

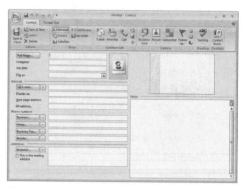

Figure 17.4 In addition to a name and email address, an Outlook contact record can store a wealth of data.

To manually create a new contact:

1. *Do either of the following:*

   ▲ From any window, choose File > New > Contact, click the down arrow beside the New toolbar button and choose Contact, or press Shift Ctrl C.

   ▲ From the Contacts window, click the New toolbar button, choose File > New > Contact, or press Ctrl N.

   An Untitled - Contact window appears (**Figure 17.4**).

2. Fill in as much information for the contact as desired.

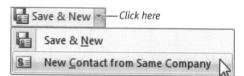

Figure 17.5 If you want to create several contact records for the same company, choose this command to avoid a bit of repetitive typing.

3. *Do one of the following:*

   ▲ To save the new record and close its window, click the Save & Close icon.

   ▲ To save the current contact record and immediately create another one, click the Save & New icon.

   ▲ To save the current contact record and immediately create another one using the same company information, click the down arrow beside the Save & New icon, and choose New Contact from Same Company (**Figure 17.5**).

   ▲ If you decide not to save the record, click the close box (X) or the Delete button, and then confirm this action.

CREATING CONTACT RECORDS

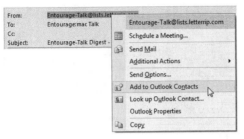

Figure 17.6 To create a contact record from a received message, open the message in its own window, right-click the sender's name or email address, and choose Add to Outlook Contacts.

Handling options

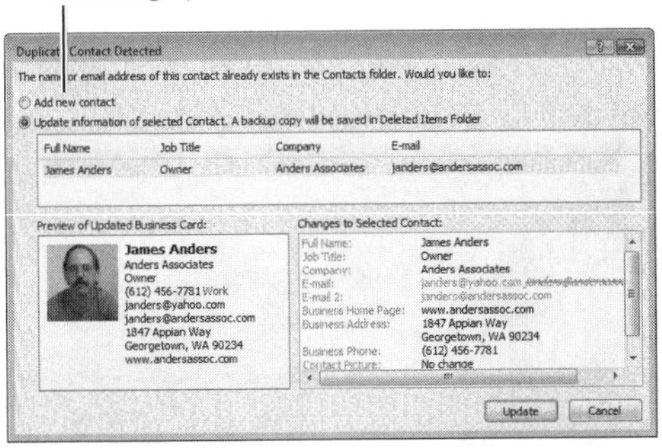

Figure 17.7 This dialog box appears when your new record is believed to already exist.

To create a new contact record from a received email message:

1. Double-click the message header to open the message in its own window.

2. Right-click the sender's name/address, and choose Add to Outlook Contacts from the pop-up menu that appears (**Figure 17.6**).

   A new, partially completed contact card for the person or organization appears.

3. *Optional:* Enter additional information for the contact.

4. Click the Save & Close icon to save the record and close its window.

   If this is a new, unique record, the record is saved and its window closes.

5. However, if a record for this person or organization already exists, a Duplicate Contact Detected dialog box appears (**Figure 17.7**).

   Do one of the following:

   ▲ To avoid creating a duplicate record (discarding the new record), click Cancel.

   ▲ To modify the existing record for this person or organization using the new data, ensure that the Update information... radio button is selected, and click Update.

   ▲ To save the new record (creating a duplicate), click the Add new contact radio button and then click Add.

CREATING CONTACT RECORDS

To import contact data from another copy or prior version of Outlook:

1. In your other copy or version of Outlook, choose File > Import or Export. *Do the following (in order):*

   ▲ Select Export to a file.

   ▲ Select Personal Folder File (.pst) as the output format.

   ▲ Select Contacts as the folder from which to export data.

   ▲ Set a location for the export file by clicking the Browse button. Select Do not export duplicate items.

   ▲ Click Finish to create the export file.

2. In Outlook 2007, choose File > Import and Export.

   The Import and Export Wizard appears (**Figure 17.8**).

3. Select Import from another program or file. Click Next.

4. On the new screen, select Personal Folder File (.pst). Click Next.

5. On the new screen (**Figure 17.9**), click Browse to locate the export file created in Step 1. Specify how duplicates are to be handled, and then click Next.

6. On the final screen (**Figure 17.10**), select Contacts as the import folder, and elect to Import items into the same folder in: Personal Folders. Click Finish to import the data.

✔ Tips

- When creating or editing contact data, you should note that each record can store multiple email addresses and phone numbers. To add other email addresses, click the E-mail down arrow, and choose E-mail 2 or E-mail 3. When adding each phone number, select a phone type from the drop-down list beside the phone field.

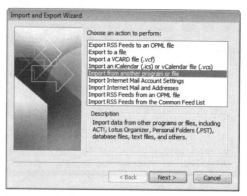

Figure 17.8 In the Import and Export Wizard, begin by selecting the type of data you want to import.

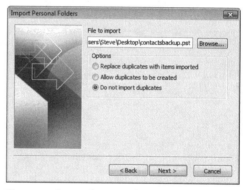

Figure 17.9 Locate the export file you created, and indicate how duplicate records should be handled.

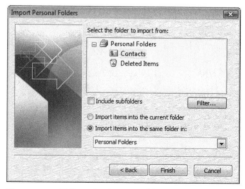

Figure 17.10 Select the Contacts folder, and direct the new data into the same folder in this copy of Outlook.

Figure 17.11 You can add a photo to a record by clicking the Picture menu icon on the Ribbon.

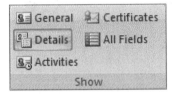

Figure 17.12 To examine a contact record's other tabs, click an icon in the Show group.

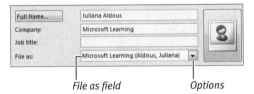

File as field   *Options*

Figure 17.13 To change the contents of a record's File as field, click the down arrow to the right of the field.

- If the contact records you're importing are from Outlook Express or Eudora, you can import your email at the same time by selecting Import Internet Mail and Addresses in the Import and Export Wizard. This is extremely useful if you're replacing Outlook Express or Eudora with Outlook 2007.

- To display a photo for a contact, double-click the picture placeholder, or click Picture in the Options group and choose Add Picture (**Figure 17.11**). To change or remove a picture, choose the appropriate command from the Picture menu.

- In addition to the General tab, there are four other tabs you can select from the Ribbon (**Figure 17.12**). On the Details tab, for example, you can record a person's department, profession, supervisor, and assistant.

- The File as field (**Figure 17.13**) on the General tab is critical because the records are sorted by it in most views. It is important to use a consistent naming convention to enable you to easily browse through your contacts. For corporate contacts, I always ensure that File as displays as *Company (Person)*.

- To edit a contact record, double-click it in the Contacts window, make any necessary changes, and click Save & Close.

- To delete a contact record, select it in the Contacts window and click the Delete toolbar icon, choose Edit > Delete, or press [Ctrl][D] or [Del].

- To restore an accidentally deleted record, select the record in Mail's Deleted Items folder and drag it onto the Contacts button in the Navigation Pane.

- Outlook 2007 can also import contact data from other email programs and databases. The process is similar to the one on the previous page. Export the contact data to an Outlook-compatible file format, such as Personal File Folder, tab-delimited, or Excel. Then import the data into Outlook 2007. (Note that you may have to instruct Outlook 2007 on how fields from the export file map to the ones in Outlook.)

Searching for a Contact

If you want to quickly find a contact without browsing through records, Outlook provides several tools you can use.

To perform a search from the toolbar:

1. Enter a search string in the box at the end of the Standard toolbar (**Figure 17.14**).

   Such a search can be performed in any Outlook component: Mail, Calendar, Contacts, or Tasks.

2. Press (Enter) to execute the search.

3. *One of the following results:*
   - ▲ If only one match is found, its contact record opens.
   - ▲ If no match is found, a dialog box appears (**Figure 17.15**). Click OK to dismiss it.
   - ▲ If multiple matches are identified, the Choose Contact window appears (**Figure 17.16**). Select a contact and click OK to open it, or click Cancel if the desired record isn't shown.

To perform an Instant Search from the Contacts window:

1. Enter a search string in the box at the right edge of the Contacts window.

   Potential matches are checked and displayed as you type (**Figure 17.17**).

2. *Do any of the following:*
   - ▲ Double-click a found record to open it.
   - ▲ Click the X beside the Instant Search box to clear the search text and resume viewing all contact records.
   - ▲ To repeat a previous search, click the down arrow beside the box and choose a search to repeat.
   - ▲ To perform a more complex or specific search, click the Expand/Minimize arrow beside the box.

Repeat a previous successful search

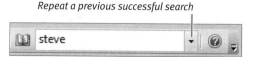

Figure 17.14 You can perform a contact search by typing search text into this box on the Standard toolbar.

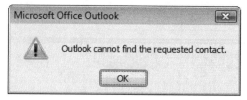

Figure 17.15 If there are no matches, this dialog box appears.

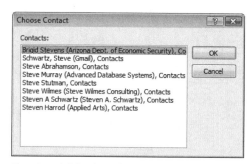

Figure 17.16 If the desired contact is shown, select it and click OK; otherwise, click Cancel.

Expand/Minimize
Search results   Instant Search box

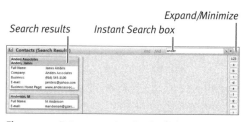

Figure 17.17 Enter a search string in the Instant Search box. Matching records appear as you type.

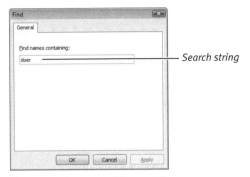

Figure 17.18 Enter part of the name for which you're searching, and click OK.

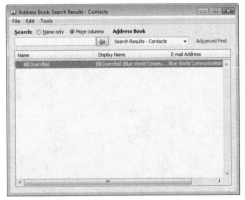

Figure 17.19 The record list is filtered to show only matching contacts.

To perform a search in Address Book:

1. Choose Tools > Address Book.
   The Address Book window appears.

2. Choose Tools > Find.
   The Find window appears (**Figure 17.18**).

3. Enter search text, and click OK.
   All matching records are displayed (**Figure 17.19**).

4. *Optional:* Double-click an entry to open its contact record.

✔ Tips

■ To find a contact you've previously found using the toolbar search box, click the down arrow beside the search box (see Figure 17.14) and select a contact record from the ones listed.

■ When using the expanded query section in the Contacts window (**Figure 17.20**), you can restrict a search to a particular combination of fields or any single field. To use a field that isn't currently shown, click the down arrow beside any unused field and choose the desired field from the drop-down field list.

■ After finding and opening a contact record, you can create a new email message addressed to the person or company by clicking the Email icon in the Communicate group.

Click an arrow to select a different field   *Expand/Minimize*

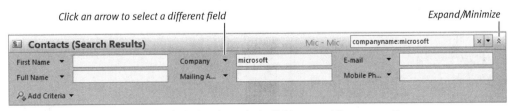

Figure 17.20 To conduct a search that looks in only particular fields, expand the query section.

Using Business Cards

If people often ask for your contact information, Outlook provides a way for you to email your personal contact record as an *Electronic Business Card* (EBC) or *vCard*. If the recipient is an Outlook user, he or she can quickly create a contact record for you.

To create or edit a business card:

1. Open your personal contact record. (Create the record if it doesn't exist.)

2. If you want to display additional elements on the card, complete those fields now.

3. Click the Business Card icon in the Options group.

   The Edit Business Card window appears (**Figure 17.21**).

4. *Do any of the following:*

   ▲ To change the placement of a photo, company logo, or background image, choose an option from the Layout drop-down menu.

   ▲ To use a different image, click the Image: Change button.

   ▲ To change the image's alignment on the card, choose an option from the Image Align drop-down menu.

   ▲ To change a field's formatting, select the field in the Fields list and pick formatting options from the Edit toolbar.

   ▲ To change a field's vertical placement, select the field in the Fields list and click the up arrow or down arrow.

5. Click OK to save the business card.

   The finished business card appears above the Notes area on the contact record (**Figure 17.22**).

6. Click the Save & Close icon in the Actions group.

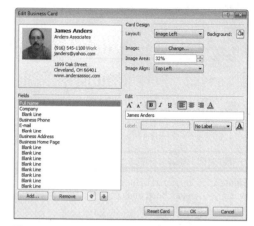

Figure 17.21 Outlook displays the default fields and layout for a new business card. (If the card already exists, the current version is shown.)

Figure 17.22 This finished business card employs a background image aligned as Fit to Edge (to fill the entire card) and white, right-aligned, heavily reorganized fields.

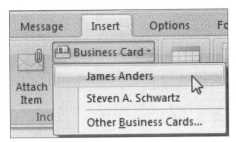

Figure 17.23 Choose a business card to attach to the current email message.

Figure 17.24 To add a received business card as a new contact record, right-click the image ...

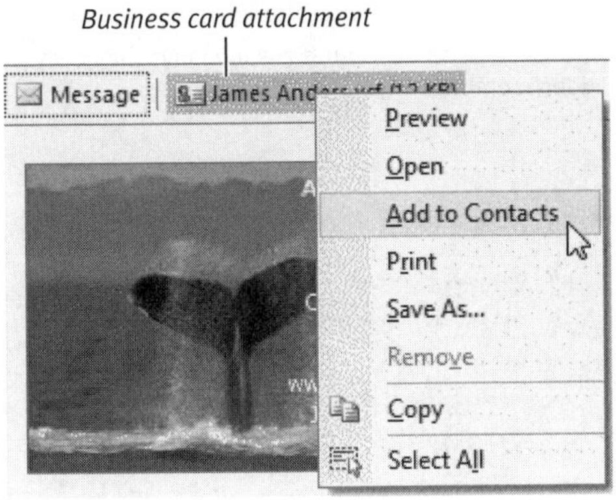

Business card attachment

Figure 17.25 ... or right-click the attachment.

To email a business card:

1. Create a new email message.

2. Click the Insert tab at the top of the Ribbon.

3. *Do either of the following:*

   ▲ Choose the card from the Business Card drop-down menu (**Figure 17.23**).

   ▲ If the card isn't listed, choose Other Business Cards, and select the desired contact record.

   The business card is added to the message as an attached .vcf file.

To save a received business card as an Outlook contact record:

1. Display the received email message in the Reading Pane or open it in its own window.

2. *Do either of the following:*

   ▲ Right-click the business card image and choose Add to Outlook Contacts (**Figure 17.24**).

   ▲ Right-click the .vcf attachment and choose Add to Contacts (**Figure 17.25**).

   A contact record for the business card appears.

3. *Do either of the following:*

   ▲ To save the record, click the Save & Close icon in the Actions group. (If desired, you can edit the information.)

   ▲ If you decide not to save the contact or believe it is a duplicate, click the close box (X) or click the Delete icon in the Actions group.

✔ Tip

■ To quickly save an open record as a .vcf file, click the Office Button and choose Save As > Export to vCard File.

Creating Distribution Lists

Do you ever find yourself repeatedly address-ing email to the same group of people? A project manager, for example, might want a weekly update delivered to all group members. When you need to regularly send messages to a clearly defined group, you can create a *distribution list*.

To create a distribution list:

1. *Do either of the following:*

   ▲ Choose File > New > Distribution List.

   ▲ Click the down arrow beside the New toolbar icon and choose Distribution List.

   An Untitled - Distribution List window appears.

2. Enter a name for the distribution list in the Name text box.

3. To add members with contact records to the distribution list, click the Select Members icon.

   A modified version of the Address Book window appears (**Figure 17.26**). To add a member to the distribution list, select her or his name, and click the Members button. Repeat for each additional new member. Then click the OK button. The new members are added to the distribu-tion list (**Figure 17.27**).

4. To add a member to the distribution list who does not have contact record, click the Add New icon.

   The Add New Member dialog box appears (**Figure 17.28**). Enter the person's name and email address, and then click OK.

5. Click the Save & Close icon.

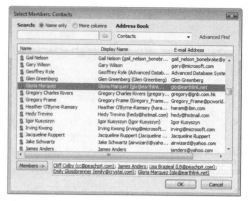

Figure 17.26 You can select group members from your existing Outlook contacts.

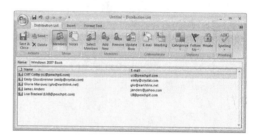

Figure 17.27 The distribution list displays the newly added members.

Figure 17.28 You can also add members who are not stored in your Address Book.

Figure 17.29 Most changes to a distribution list are initiated by clicking an icon in the Members group.

To edit a distribution list:

1. *Do any of the following:*
   - ▲ To remove a member, open the contact record for the distribution list, select the member to be removed, and click the Remove icon (**Figure 17.29**).
   - ▲ To add new members, perform Step 3 or 4 from the previous task.
   - ▲ If the contact records of any of the list members have changed (new email addresses, for example), click Update Now to update their contact data with current information.

2. To save your changes, click the Save & Close icon.

✔ Tips

- ■ A distribution list's contact record is denoted by two faces or the word *Group*, depending on the current view.

- ■ To address a message to the distribution list, enter the list name in the message's To, Cc, or Bcc box.

- ■ To delete a distribution list, select its contact record and click the Delete toolbar icon, choose Edit > Delete, or press Ctrl D or Del. (If the list's contact record is already open, click the Delete icon in the Actions group.)

CREATING DISTRIBUTION LISTS

Composing
and Sending Mail

While much of a new user's email experience will consist of receiving and reading messages from supervisors, mailing list subscriptions, unwanted advertisements, and jokes from friends, most of you will eventually participate in the other part of the process: sending mail to others. You can create new messages, reply to incoming messages, and forward received messages to others.

Whether you are composing a new message, writing a reply, or forwarding email to a co-worker, the process of composing and sending a message consists of these steps:

◆ Open a new, reply, or forward message window.

◆ Specify recipients and enter a Subject.

◆ Select a message format (Plain Text, HTML, or Rich Text).

◆ Compose the message text.

◆ Add optional attachments, such as a photo, text document, or spreadsheet.

◆ Send the message.

In this chapter, you'll learn how to create new messages, reply to and forward received email, and use Outlook tools to ensure that your messages are correct and attractive.

The Message Window

You can create three types of email messages in Outlook 2007:

◆ **New messages.** Messages you compose from scratch.

◆ **Replies.** Responses to received messages.

◆ **Forwarded messages.** Received messages you are sending to someone else.

All messages are composed in a message window (**Figure 18.1**). Window sections include the Ribbon, the message header or address pane (the To, Cc, Bcc, and Subject boxes), the attachments list, and the message body (the text of the message).

The window title differs for each message type, showing *Untitled* for a blank original message, the Subject for a message you're composing, *RE:* for a reply, *FW:* for a forwarded message, and the original Subject for a message you're resending.

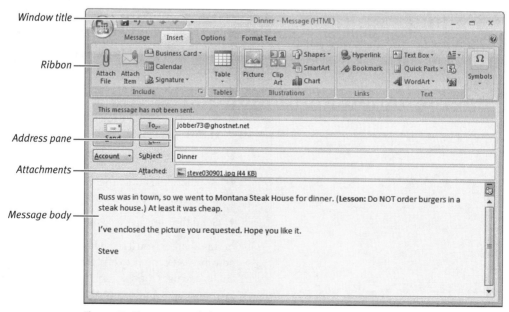

Figure 18.1 The message window.

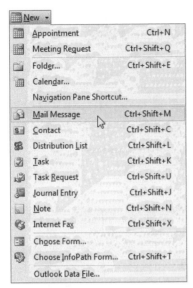

Figure 18.2 You can create a new message by selecting Mail Message from the New toolbar button.

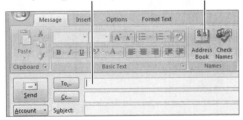

To recipients go here   *Open the Address Book*

Figure 18.3 You enter recipients in the message's address pane.

Figure 18.4 You can type a few letters of a contact's first name or email address, and then select from a list of possible matches.

Creating Messages

To let a relative know what's new, send a Web link or photo to a friend, or tell your supervisor how a project is progressing, you start by creating a new message.

Another way to create email is by replying to or forwarding a received message. You can also resend any previously sent message—either to the same person or someone new.

To create a new message:

1. *Do one of the following:*
   - ▲ When working in Mail, click the New toolbar button, choose File > New > Mail Message, or press Ctrl N.
   - ▲ When working in *any* component (Mail, Calendar, Contacts, or Tasks), click the down arrow beside the New toolbar button and choose Mail Message (**Figure 18.2**), choose File > New > Mail Message, or press Ctrl Shift M.

   A message window opens (see Figure 18.1). The cursor is positioned in the To box (**Figure 18.3**), ready for you to enter the recipients.

2. You enter primary recipients in the To box. Specify the first To email address by doing one of the following:
   - ▲ Start typing the person's name or email address. As you type, a list of matching recipients (drawn from addresses you previously typed into the address pane) is presented (**Figure 18.4**). Select a recipient or continue typing.
   - ▲ To select To recipients from your Address Book, click the To button or the Address Book icon in the Names group (see Figure 18.3). Double-click a contact to add that person to the To list, and then click OK.

continues on next page

3. *Optional:* To enter more To addresses, click in the space following the last address and repeat Step 2.

Note that each pair of addresses must be separated by a semicolon (;).

4. *Optional:* Persons in the Cc (*carbon copy*) box represent secondary recipients. To add Cc recipients, click in the Cc box and follow Steps 2–3.

5. *Optional:* A message can also have Bcc (*blind carbon copy*) recipients. Addresses in the Bcc box are hidden from all recipients. If the Bcc box isn't visible, click the Options tab, and then click the Show Bcc icon in the Fields group (**Figure 18.5**). To add Bcc recipients, click in the Bcc box and follow Steps 2–3.

6. Click or Tab into the Subject box. Enter a subject to identify the message.

7. Press Tab again to move the pointer into the message box, and type the text of the message.

8. Click Send to send the message from your default email account. Or select another account from the Account icon, and then click Send.

✔ Tips

- You can also paste (choose Edit > Paste or press Ctrl V) a copied email address into the To, Cc, or Bcc box.

- You can drag addresses among the To, Cc, and Bcc lines of the address pane.

- The AutoComplete drop-down list does not suggest contacts from your Address Book. However, if you enter a contact's full name, Outlook will email the message to the correct address.

- If you type only a first name, the Check Names dialog box appears (**Figure 18.6**). Select the correct person and click OK.

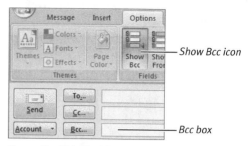

Figure 18.5 Click Show Bcc to expose the normally hidden Bcc box.

Figure 18.6 Select a contact from the Check Names dialog box.

- Outlook remembers the most recent Show Bcc setting. Once enabled, the Bcc box will continue to appear in every new message until you click the Show Bcc icon again.

- You can create a new, preaddressed message by clicking an email address in the body of a received message or an email address (*mailto*) link on a Web page.

- After you send a message, a copy of the message can be found in the Sent Items folder or an account-specific folder.

Type your reply

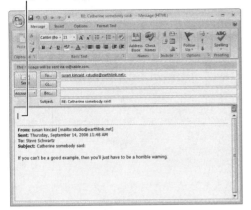

Figure 18.7 When replying to email, enter your reply above the author's quoted text and click Send.

Options for On replies and forwards

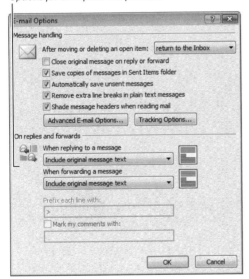

Figure 18.8 You can specify the formatting of quoted text in replies and forwarded messages.

To create a reply:

1. In the message list, select the header of the message to which you are replying or open the message in its own window.

2. *Do one of the following:*
   - ▲ With the message header selected, click the Reply toolbar icon, choose Actions > Reply, or press Ctrl R.
   - ▲ With the message open in its own window, click the Reply icon or press Ctrl R.

   A copy of the message appears in a new window, addressed to the original author as the primary recipient. The author's text is repeated (*quoted*) at the bottom of the message (**Figure 18.7**). The Subject is changed to RE: *original Subject*.

3. *Optional:* You can specify additional recipients in the boxes of the address pane.

4. Type your reply to the message.

   The insertion mark is automatically positioned above the quoted text.

5. Edit the quoted text, if desired (removing extraneous material, for example).

6. Click the Send icon.

   Replies are sent from the account to which the original message was addressed.

✔ Tips

- When writing a reply, you shouldn't edit the automatically generated Subject. The RE: *original Subject* shows the recipient the message to which you're responding.

- Reply and forwarding options are set in the E-mail Options dialog box (**Figure 18.8**). Choose Tools > Options. On the Preferences tab of the Options dialog box, click the E-mail Options button.

- To send a reply to everyone in the To and Cc lines, click Reply to All (Ctrl Shift R).

To forward a received message:

1. Select the header of the message you want to forward or open the message in its own window.

2. *Do one of the following:*

▲ With the message header selected, click the Forward toolbar icon, choose Actions > Forward, or press [Ctrl][F].

▲ With the message open in its own window, click the Forward icon or press [Ctrl][F].

The author's text is repeated (*quoted*) at the bottom of the message. The Subject is automatically changed to FW: *original Subject* (**Figure 18.9**).

3. In the address pane, specify recipients for the forwarded message.

4. *Optional:* You can edit the original text, as well as insert your own comments.

5. Click the Send icon.

Forwarded messages are sent from the account to which the original message was addressed.

✔ Tips

■ In addition to forwarding a message as quoted text, you can forward a message as an attachment. Select the message header and choose Actions > Forward as Attachment.

■ When forwarding jokes, news items, and the like, don't forward multiple layers of attachments; that is, a message within a message within a message, and so on. Open all layers of the received message until you locate the original, and then forward *that* message. Also, you may wish to edit out the email addresses of the current sender and all previous recipients (to ensure their privacy).

New text　　　　　　　　　　*Forwarded text*

Figure 18.9 When forwarding email, you can add your own comments, as well as edit the forwarded text.

Sending Messages from Different Accounts

If you just click the Send icon to send a new message, it is sent from your default email account. When you click the Send icon to send a reply or forwarded message, it is sent from your account that received the original message. To send any message from a *different* Outlook account, click the Account button and select an account from the drop-down list that appears.

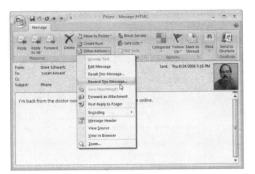

Figure 18.10 Choose Resend This Message from the drop-down menu.

Figure 18.11 If one of your sent messages has yet to be read by an Exchange Server recipient, you can delete the message or replace it with another.

To resend a previously sent message:

1. Open the previously sent message in its own window.

   Previously sent messages can be found in your Sent Items folder(s).

2. Choose Resend This Message from the Other Actions icon in the Actions group (**Figure 18.10**).

   A copy of the original message appears.

3. *Optional:* Change the intended message recipient(s).

4. Click the Send icon (to the left of the address pane).

✔ Tip

■ You can use the Resend This Message command to send the same message to multiple people (one at a time). Simply change the recipient each time.

Recalling a Sent Message

If a message recipient has an Exchange Server account, you can optionally recall a message you've mistakenly sent them or one that contains errors.

1. Open the previously sent message.

2. Choose Recall This Message from the Other Actions icon in the Actions group (see Figure 18.10).

3. Select an option in the Recall This Message dialog box (**Figure 18.11**), and then click OK.

About Message Formats

Every message you create must be in one of three formats: Plain Text, HTML, or Rich Text.

◆ **Plain Text** is a universally readable, single-font format. It provides no support for character formatting (such as boldface, italic, or color) or paragraph formatting.

◆ **HTML** is meant for messages that must contain formatting. You can format text with specific fonts and colors, create bulleted and numbered lists, embed pictures in the message body, insert clickable links, and use stationery backgrounds.

◆ **Rich Text** is a format readable only by Microsoft email clients. Rich Text messages sent over the Internet are automatically converted to HTML format. They are sent unaltered only to other Exchange Server accounts within your network.

Setting the message format

You can set a default format to be used for new messages, as well as change the format of the message you're currently writing.

To specify a default message format:

1. Choose Tools > Options.

2. In the Options dialog box, click the Mail Format tab and choose a format from the drop-down menu in the Message Format section (**Figure 18.12**).

3. Click OK to save your changes and close the Options dialog box.

To set a format for the current message:

◆ In an open message, click the Options tab and select a message format by clicking an icon in the Format group (**Figure 18.13**).

You can set or change the format at any time during the message-creation process.

Choose a message format

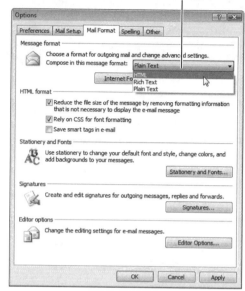

Figure 18.12 By default, all new messages will use the chosen format.

Figure 18.13 Select a format for the current message.

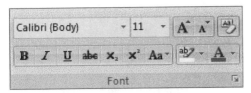

Figure 18.14 Character formatting can be applied or removed by selecting options from the Font group.

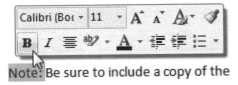

Figure 18.15 The pop-up Mini toolbar contains frequently used character and paragraph formatting commands.

Formatting text and paragraphs

When creating an HTML or Rich Text format message, you can selectively apply character and paragraph formatting. And as in Word, Outlook 2007 includes the Format Painter tool for quickly duplicating character formatting.

To apply character formatting:

1. *Do either of the following:*
   - ▲ Select the text you wish to format. (You can make multiple, noncontiguous selections by holding down Ctrl as you make each selection.)
   - ▲ Position the insertion mark where you want the new character formatting to begin.

2. *Do any of the following:*
   - ▲ Click the Format Text tab and select character formatting options from the Font group on the Ribbon (**Figure 18.14**).
   - ▲ Select the text to be formatted and move the cursor up. The Mini toolbar appears (**Figure 18.15**), containing common formatting commands.
   - ▲ Enter a formatting command's keyboard shortcut, such as Ctrl B for Bold. (To see the keyboard shortcut for a command, rest the cursor over its icon in the Font group.)

ABOUT MESSAGE FORMATS

To apply paragraph formatting:

1. Position the insertion mark in the paragraph you want to format.

   You can also preselect multiple paragraphs or select some text within a paragraph.

2. *Do any of the following:*

   ▲ Click the Format Text tab and select paragraph formatting options from the Paragraph group on the Ribbon (**Figure 18.16**).

   ▲ If you've selected text in the paragraph(s), move the cursor up to display the Mini toolbar (see Figure 18.15). Several paragraph formatting commands are available.

   ▲ Enter a paragraph-formatting command's keyboard shortcut, such as Ctrl J for Justify. (To see the keyboard shortcut for a command, rest the cursor over its icon in the Paragraph group.)

To apply a Quick Style to text:

1. Select the text to be formatted or position the insertion mark in the paragraph to be formatted.

2. Click the Format Text tab on the Ribbon, if it isn't already selected. Then click the Quick Styles icon in the Styles group.

   The Quick Styles palette appears (**Figure 18.17**).

3. As you move the cursor over a style in the palette, a preview of that style is applied to the selected text or paragraph. Click a style to apply it.

   If you decide not to apply any of the styles, click outside the palette.

Figure 18.16 Paragraph formatting options can be set by clicking icons in the Paragraph group.

Quick Styles icon

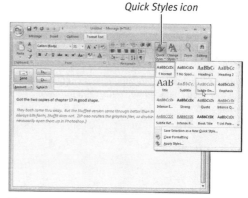

Figure 18.17 To easily apply complex, attractive formatting to text or paragraphs, select a style from the Quick Styles palette.

More Quick Styles

If you don't like the look of the default Quick Styles, there are other style sets from which you can choose. You can also change the colors and fonts used. Click the Change Styles icon to explore the options.

Undo

Format Painter

Format Painter

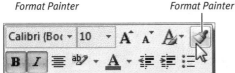

Figure 18.18 Select formatted text that you want to apply elsewhere, and then click the Format Painter tool.

Clear Formatting

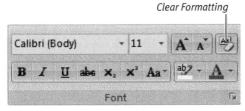

Figure 18.19 To remove all formatting from selected text, click the Clear Formatting icon.

To copy character formatting:

1. Select text containing the formatting you want to copy.

2. Select the Format Painter tool in the Clipboard group of the Ribbon or on the Mini toolbar (**Figure 18.18**).

3. Drag to select the text you wish to format. When you stop dragging, the original formatting is applied to the selected text.

To remove character formatting:

1. Select the text from which you want to remove previously applied formatting.

2. *Do one of the following:*

   ▲ If your most recent action was to apply the character formatting, press Ctrl Z or click the Undo icon in the Quick Access Toolbar (see Figure 18.18).

   ▲ Click the same formatting command in the Ribbon or Mini toolbar.

   ▲ Click the Clear Formatting icon in the Fonts group (**Figure 18.19**) to remove *all* previously applied formatting from the selected text.

✔ Tips

■ When using the Format Painter, you can apply the copied format to a single word by double-clicking the word.

■ You cannot reverse the Text Highlight Color or Font Color of selected text by clicking the same icon again. You can either select the original color or click the Clear Formatting icon.

■ Most paragraph formatting cannot be reversed by clicking an icon again. To restore original formatting, click the appropriate icon in the Paragraph group. (However, you *can* eliminate Bullets and Numbering formatted paragraphs by clicking their respective icons again.)

Adding Attachments

One popular use of email is to transmit documents and photos along with your messages. These files are known as *attachments*.

To add an attachment to a message:

1. On the Message tab or the Insert tab, click the Attach File icon.

   The Insert File dialog box appears (**Figure 18.20**).

2. Navigate to the correct drive and folder, select a file, and click Insert. (You can select multiple files within a folder by ⌈Ctrl⌉-clicking them.)

   The file is added to the Attached list (**Figure 18.21**). You can add more attachments by repeating these steps.

✔ Tips

- You can also add attachments by dragging their file icons from the desktop or any open folder onto the open message.

- To remove an attachment, select it in the Attached list, and then press ⌈Backspace⌉ or ⌈Del⌉. You can also right-click an attachment and choose Remove from the pop-up menu that appears.

- Check the total size of the attachments before sending a message. First, ISPs have a maximum message size, and attachments tend to get larger when encoded for transmission. Second, not everyone has broadband Internet access. If you email a huge video or audio clip to a friend with a dial-up account, you'll tie them up for a very long time.

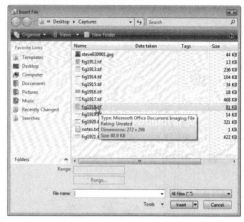

Figure 18.20 Select one or more files and click the Insert button.

Attachments　　　　　　　　*Attach File icon*

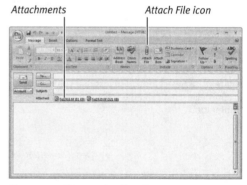

Figure 18.21 The Attached box lists the names and sizes of all attached files.

Picture Tools contextual tab

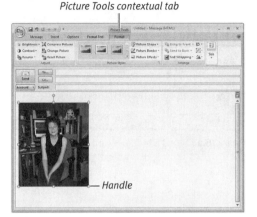

— *Handle*

Figure 18.23 When an inserted image is selected, image editing and enhancement commands appear.

Inserting Items

The Insert tab (**Figure 18.22, bottom**) contains tools for inserting items directly into the body of HTML and Rich Text messages, such as tables, charts, horizontal lines, clip art, and Word Art. In this section, you'll see how to insert three of the most common items: photos and other images, business cards, and hyperlinks.

To insert a photo or other image:

1. Position the insertion mark at the spot in the message body where you want to insert the image.

2. On the Insert tab, click Picture in the Illustration group.

   The Insert Picture dialog box appears.

3. Navigate to the drive/folder that contains the image, select the file, and click Insert.

   The image appears in the message body (**Figure 18.23**).

4. *Optional:* With the image selected (**Figure 18.23**), you can resize it by dragging any corner handle. To rotate the image, drag the green circle. You can also perform advanced image enhancement, editing, and formatting by selecting commands from the Picture Tools contextual tab.

Insert tab

Figure 18.22 In formatted (HTML or Rich Text) messages, click the Insert tab to add items to the message body.

INSERTING ITEMS

To insert a business card image and file:

1. Position the insertion mark at the spot in the message body where you want to insert the business card image.

2. On the Insert tab, click the Business Card icon in the Include group.

3. *Do one of the following:*

   ▲ Choose a business card from those listed in the drop-down menu (**Figure 18.24**).

   ▲ To send contact information for someone whose name *isn't* displayed, choose Other Business Cards.

   A graphic version of the business card is inserted into the message body. The actual business card (vCard) file is also included as a message attachment (**Figure 18.25**).

To insert a clickable Web page link:

1. Position the insertion mark at the spot in the message body where you want to insert the Web link.

2. On the Insert tab, click the Hyperlink icon in the Links group or press Ctrl K.

   The Insert Hyperlink dialog box appears (**Figure 18.26**).

3. Select Existing File or Web Page in the Link to list.

4. Select a recently viewed Web page from the Address drop-down list. Or type or paste a Web address into the Address box.

5. *Optional:* Change the text in the Text to display box.

6. Click OK.

   The link text is inserted into the message. When the recipient clicks the link, the specified page is displayed in the person's default Web browser.

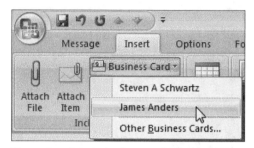

Figure 18.24 Select a business card to insert.

vCard file

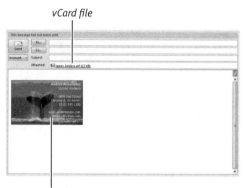

Business card image

Figure 18.25 The business card is added to the message as an image and an attachment.

Display this link text

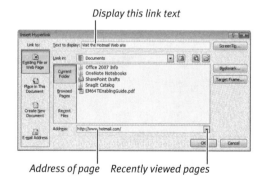

Address of page   Recently viewed pages

Figure 18.26 You can create a Web page hyperlink by specifying the page's URL (address) and the wording for the link text.

INSERTING ITEMS

Figure 18.27 You can also insert a mailto link that generates a new email message to the specified address when clicked.

Selected hyperlink

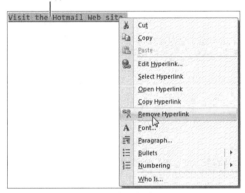

Figure 18.28 To convert a hyperlink to normal text, select and then right-click its text. Choose Remove Hyperlink.

- To convert a hyperlink back to normal text, select the text, right-click it, and choose Remove Hyperlink from the pop-up menu that appears (**Figure 18.28**).

- Outlook supports more than a dozen types of hyperlinks. To see the entire list, open Outlook Help and view this topic: *Outlook Home > E-mail > Creating Messages > Use hyperlinks in Outlook Items.*

To insert a clickable email (mailto) link:

1. Position the insertion mark at the spot in the message body where you want to insert the email (*mailto*) link.

2. On the Insert tab, click the Hyperlink icon in the Links group or press Ctrl K. The Insert Hyperlink dialog box appears (**Figure 18.27**).

3. Select E-mail Address in the Link to list.

4. Type or paste the destination email address in the E-mail address box.

   A *mailto:* prefix is automatically added to the address.

5. *Optional:* Edit the Text to display.

6. *Optional:* Enter a Subject for the message.

7. Click OK.

   The link text is inserted into the message. When the recipient clicks the link, a new email message addressed to the specified recipient appears.

✔ Tips

- You can also create a hyperlink by typing or pasting a complete address into a message. Outlook automatically converts the text into a hyperlink if the text is recognized as a proper link (www.hotmail.com, for example).

- You can also convert existing message text into a hyperlink. Select the text, and then skip to Step 2. The selected text is automatically treated as the Text to display.

- Hyperlinks work best in HTML/Rich Text messages. Although they can also be used in Plain Text messages:

   ▲ The Hyperlink command is unavailable, so you must enter links manually.

   ▲ Long URLs may be broken up, rendering them inoperable.

Correcting Spelling Errors

Unless you're both an exceptional speller and a typist (or you trust that your recipients will simply *know* what you're trying to say, regardless of what you type), it's a good idea to run each outgoing message through Outlook's spelling checker. Outlook offers two spell-checking options:

◆ Outlook can check for and flag potential errors as you type.

◆ You can perform a full spelling check on request or automatically before the message is sent.

To check spelling as you type:

1. This option is enabled by default. If you've disabled it, choose Tools > Options, click the Spelling tab in the Options dialog box, and click the Spelling and Autocorrection button.

   In the Proofing section of the Editor Options dialog box (**Figure 18.29**), click the Check spelling as you type check box, and then click OK.

2. As you type a message, Outlook checks each word. Suspect words are marked with a squiggly red underline.

3. For each flagged word, you can:
   ▲ Ignore the error (because you believe the word is spelled correctly).
   ▲ Edit the word to correct the error.
   ▲ Right-click the word and select from the correction options provided (**Figure 18.30**).

      You can select the correct spelling or choose Ignore to accept this instance, Ignore All to accept all instances of this spelling in the message, or Add to Dictionary to accept the spelling and add it to your spelling dictionary (so it will be recognized in other messages).

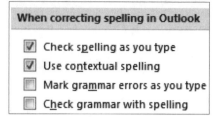

Figure 18.29 The top check box determines whether spelling errors are automatically flagged for you.

Suspect word

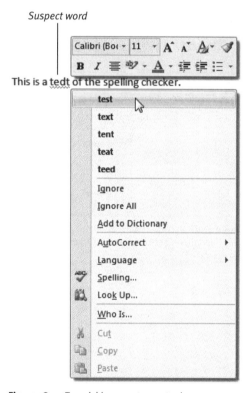

Figure 18.30 To quickly correct an actual error, you can often select the proper spelling from Outlook's suggestions.

Suspect word   Possible replacements   Options

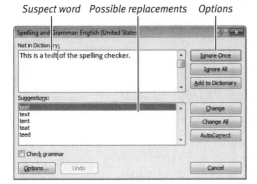

Figure 18.31 When you perform a manual spelling check, Outlook presents each suspect word in this dialog box.

Automatically check spelling before sending

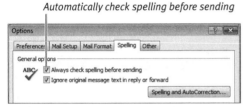

Figure 18.32 Enable this option to automatically request a spelling check of every message you send.

To perform a manual spelling check:

1. Select the Message tab, and then click the Spelling icon (or press F7).

    If any errors are found, the Spelling and Grammar dialog box appears (**Figure 18.31**). Otherwise, you are notified that the spelling check is complete.

2. Each suspect word is displayed in red boldface. Do one of the following:

    ▲ Select a replacement word in the Suggestions list, and click Change to correct this error. (If you think you've made the same mistake elsewhere in the message, click Change All.)

    ▲ Click Ignore Once to ignore this instance of the spelling (leaving the current word unchanged).

    ▲ Click Ignore All to ignore all instances of this spelling (leaving all instances of the word in this message unchanged).

    ▲ If the word is spelled correctly and you want it recognized in future spelling checks, click Add to Dictionary.

3. Repeat Step 2 for each additional suspect word. The spelling check will end when all suspect words have been examined or when you click Cancel.

✔ Tips

■ In addition to selecting a word from the Suggestions list (see Figure 18.31), you can edit the word in the Not in Dictionary box and then click Change.

■ If you'd rather defer spelling checks until you've finished writing each message, choose Tools > Options, click the Spelling tab, check Always check spelling before sending (**Figure 18.32**), and click OK. Whenever you click Send for an outgoing message, a spelling check will automatically be performed.

Using Signatures

Optionally, a message can end with *signature*: text and/or an image that provides your name and mailing address, Web address, electronic business card, or a snappy quote. You can create as many signatures as you like. A signature can be automatically added to every message or manually added to only select messages.

To create a signature:

1. Choose Tools > Options.
   The Options window appears.

2. Click the Mail Format tab, and then click the Signatures button.
   The Signatures and Stationery window appears (**Figure 18.33**).

3. Click New to create a new signature.
   The New Signature dialog box appears.

4. Enter a name to identify this signature and click OK.
   The name is added to the list of defined signatures.

5. Enter one or multiple lines of signature text, formatted as you want them to appear when appended to a message. You can also:
   - ▲ Format selected text by choosing a font, size, and formatting options from the toolbar.
   - ▲ Insert your electronic business card (as an image), a picture, and/or a hyperlink (such as your Web address) by clicking toolbar icons.

6. Click Save to save the new signature (**Figure 18.34**).

7. You can continue creating, editing, and deleting signatures or click OK to close the Signatures and Stationery window.

Defined signatures   *Toolbar*

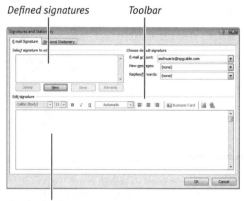

Create the signature

Figure 18.33 You create, edit, and delete signatures in the Signatures and Stationery window.

Signature name

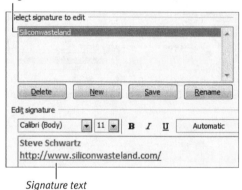

Signature text

Figure 18.34 This simple signature includes my name and a clickable link to my Web site.

Figure 18.35 You can specify a default signature to be used with certain types of messages for a given account.

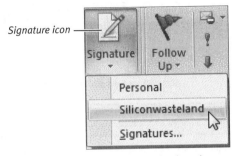

Figure 18.36 Select a signature from the drop-down list.

To specify a default signature for an email account:

1. In the Signatures and Stationery window (**Figure 18.35**), select the email account to which a default signature will be applied.

2. *Do any of the following:*
   - ▲ To set a default signature for new messages from the account, select a signature name from the New messages drop-down list.
   - ▲ To set a default signature for replies and forwarded messages from the account, select a signature name from the Replies/forwards drop-down list.

3. Continue working in the Signatures and Stationery dialog box, or click OK to save your changes.

To add a signature to a message:

1. Click to set the insertion point in your message. Normally, this will be beneath the final message line.

2. Switch to the Message or Insert tab, and select a signature from the Signature icon's drop-down list (**Figure 18.36**).

✔ Tips

- To edit a signature, double-click it in the Select signature to edit list. To delete or rename a signature, select it in the same list and click the appropriate button.

- To replace a message's signature with a different one, select another signature.

- You can also use a signature to store a *complete message*, such as one to notify colleagues that you are out of the office.

- If you create a formatted signature and append it to a Plain Text message, an unformatted version of the signature is automatically used.

Other Message Options

While not essential to most users (or most messages), this section briefly explores some other message-creation options.

Requesting a receipt

If a message is very important, you can request a delivery or read receipt. A *delivery receipt* is an email notification that the message has been delivered to the recipient. A *read receipt* indicates that the recipient has actually opened and read the message.

To request a delivery or read receipt:

◆ Prior to sending the message, click the Options tab. In the Tracking group (**Figure 18.37**), click the appropriate check box or boxes. Then click Send.

If a delivery receipt was requested, email notification will be sent to you when the message is delivered. If a read receipt was requested and the recipient's email client supports this feature, he or she will be asked to verify that the message has been read (**Figure 18.38**).

Setting a message priority

You can set a *priority* for an outgoing message to indicate its level of importance. Setting a priority, however, has no impact on the manner in which it is delivered, and not all email programs recognize priorities.

To set a priority for a message:

◆ Prior to sending a message, click the High Importance or Low Importance icon in the Options group (**Figure 18.39**).

✔ Tip

■ By default, all outgoing messages are sent Normal priority. Unless you want to set a *different* priority, you don't need to click an Importance icon.

Figure 18.37 Click check boxes in the Tracking group to request message receipts.

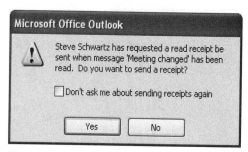

Figure 18.38 In Outlook 2003, this dialog box asks the recipient to verify that the message has been read. (Note that the recipient is not required to respond.)

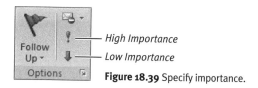

Figure 18.39 Specify importance.

Works in Progress

You aren't required to immediately send each message. If you're still working on a message, you can save it as a *draft*. To save a message in progress, click the Save icon in the Quick Access Toolbar, choose Save from the Microsoft Office Button, press Ctrl S, or close the message and elect to save it when prompted. Saved messages are stored in the Drafts folder, where you can continue working on them at your convenience.

Other Message Options

Theme settings   Page Color

Figure 18.40 To add more formatting and color to an HTML message, select options from the Themes group.

Themes   Preview

Options

Figure 18.41 Select a theme from the Choose a Theme list. Set options for the selected theme by checking or clearing the check boxes.

✔ Tip

■ To remove a default theme, select (No Theme) from the Choose a Theme list in the Theme or Stationery dialog box.

Applying page colors, themes, and stationery

If formatting text with different fonts, sizes, and colors isn't spiffy enough for you, HTML messages can also have a background color or a *theme* (a combination of fonts, bullets, colors, and special effects). These elements can be applied on a message-by-message basis or to all new messages.

To apply a background color or theme to the current message:

1. Create a new message, and set the type to HTML. (On the Options tab, click the HTML icon in the Format group.)

2. *Optional:* Select a background color from the Page Color palette (**Figure 18.40**).

3. *Optional:* To apply a formatting theme to the message, choose options from the other drop-down menus and palettes in the Themes group.

To set a default theme (stationery):

1. Choose Tools > Options.

2. In the Options dialog box that appears, click the Mail Format tab. Then click the Stationery and Fonts button.

   The Signatures and Stationery dialog box appears, open to the Personal Stationery tab.

3. Click the Theme button.

   The Theme or Stationery dialog box appears (**Figure 18.41**).

4. Select a theme.

5. Dismiss all open dialog boxes by clicking OK in each one.

   The selected theme will automatically be applied to every new HTML message you create.

OTHER MESSAGE OPTIONS

19

RECEIVING MAIL

In this chapter, you'll learn how to check for new email (manually and automatically); select and read messages; change your *view*; search for messages in a specific folder or all mail folders; preview, open, and save attachments; and print messages or a list of message headers.

For information on replying to and forwarding received messages, see Chapter 18. To learn about managing your received email (including deleting, copying, and moving messages), see Chapter 20.

✔ Note

- Most information in this chapter applies not only to incoming mail but to *sent* messages, too.

Checking for New Mail

Outlook provides two ways for you to check for new incoming email:

- **Automatically.** While Outlook is running and you are online, all accounts in a given *send/receive group* (see Chapter 16) are automatically checked for new incoming messages every so many minutes, based on the group's schedule.

- **Manually.** To immediately check for new messages in a particular account or an entire send/receive group, you can perform a manual send/receive.

To perform a Send/Receive All:

- *Do one of the following:*
  - ▲ Click the Send/Receive toolbar icon.
  - ▲ Click the down arrow beside the Send/Receive toolbar icon and choose Send/Receive All.
  - ▲ Choose Tools > Send/Receive > Send/Receive All.
  - ▲ Press F9.

To perform a send/receive for a group:

- *Do either of the following:*
  - ▲ Choose Tools > Send/Receive > *group name*.
  - ▲ Click the down arrow beside the Send/Receive toolbar icon and choose the group name (**Figure 19.1**).

To perform a send/receive for a single account:

- *Do either of the following:*
  - ▲ Choose Tools > Send/Receive > *account name* > Inbox.
  - ▲ Click the down arrow beside the Send/Receive toolbar icon and choose *account name* > Inbox.

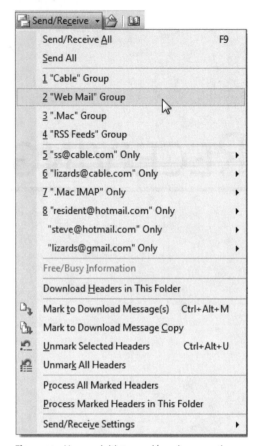

Figure 19.1 You can initiate send/receive operations by choosing commands from the Send/Receive icon's drop-down menu.

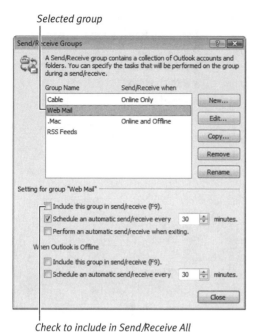

Selected group

Check to include in Send/Receive All

Figure 19.2 Any group can be included in or excluded from Send/Receive All operations.

Mystery of the Missing Images

Some received messages have red Xs where images would ordinarily be. Unlike embedded images that are transmitted as part of a message, the missing ones are actually *links* to images that must be downloaded in order to display. Outlook automatically hides linked images rather than downloading them because spammers often use them to verify that a recipient's email address is real and active.

If you receive such email from a trusted person or company, you can download the images by clicking the colored text box at the top of the message or by right-clicking any missing image and choosing Download Pictures from the pop-up menu.

To perform a send/receive for a single account folder:

1. Select the account folder in the Mail Folders list (in the Navigation Pane).

2. *Do one of the following:*

   ▲ Choose Tools > Send/Receive > This Folder.

   ▲ Click the down arrow beside the Send/Receive toolbar icon and choose This Folder.

   ▲ Press (Shift)(F9).

✔ Tips

■ Even if a given group is set for automatic send/receives, you can still perform manual send/receives whenever you like.

■ By default, the All send/receive group contains every account group you've defined in Outlook. To change a group's inclusion in this group, choose Tools > Options, click the Mail Setup tab, and click the Send/Receive button. Select a group name in the list (**Figure 19.2**), and check or clear the check mark from Include this group in send/receive (F9).

■ When performing a send/receive for a single email account or account folder, you can also choose Download Inbox Headers or Download Headers in This Folder, respectively.

■ The Send/Receive toolbar button is available only when you're in Mail pane view. To perform a send/receive when in another view, choose a command from the Tools > Send/Receive submenu.

Reading Messages

You can read any message that's stored in Outlook, whether it is received email, sent email, or a received RSS feed message. You can even read mail in the Deleted Items folder until the folder is emptied. And unless you have an IMAP or an uncached Microsoft Exchange account, you don't even need an active connection with the mail server to read messages.

To read messages:

1. In the Navigation Pane, select the account folder (**Figure 19.3**) that contains the messages you want to read (Inbox, for example). Expand folders as necessary by clicking the + icon beside a folder's name.

   Message headers for the selected folder are displayed in the message list.

2. *Do either of the following:*

   ▲ In the message list, select the header of the message you want to read. The message is displayed in the Reading Pane (**Figure 19.4**).

   ▲ To read a message in its own window, double-click its header in the message list. (You can also open a selected message by pressing Enter or Ctrl O.)

   After you view a message, it is automatically marked as *read*; that is, the boldface is removed from the message header. (Unread messages are normally denoted by a boldface message header.)

3. If you're reading a message in its own window, close the window by clicking its close box.

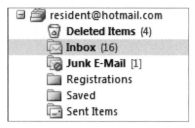

Figure 19.3 Select a message folder in the Navigation Pane.

Selected folder *Reading Pane*

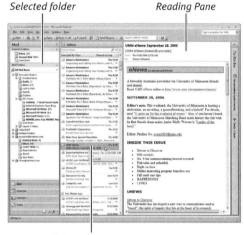

Selected message

Figure 19.4 It's more convenient to read most messages in the Reading Pane than to open them in a separate window.

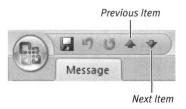

Previous Item

Next Item

Figure 19.5 You can read consecutive messages in an open message window by clicking these icons.

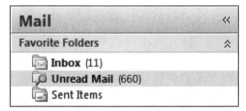

Figure 19.6 To view only unread messages (stored in the folders within Personal Folders), select the Unread Mail folder.

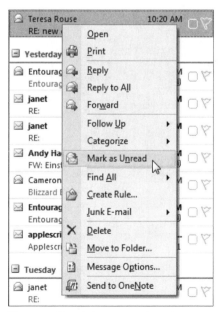

Figure 19.7 To switch a message's read status, choose Mark as Unread or Mark as Read.

✔ Tips

- Whether a message is in the Reading Pane or open in its own window, you can navigate within the message by using the vertical scroll bar. You can drag the scroll box or click the scroll arrow at either end of the bar.

- You can press Spacebar and Shift Spacebar to move forward and backward through any lengthy message.

- With a message open in its own window, you can also use normal navigation keys to move through the message, such as Page Down, Page Up, ↓, and ↑. You can use the keys in the Reading Pane, too, if you first click in the message body.

- If you open a message in its own window, you can read additional messages in the same window. Just click the Next Item or Previous Item icon in the Quick Access Toolbar (**Figure 19.5**) to read the next or previous message in the message list. (Note that if you go past either end of the current message list, the message window will automatically close.)

- If a folder in the Navigation Pane contains at least one unread message, the folder name is displayed in boldface. The number of unread messages is shown in parentheses.

- To limit the message list to only new messages in your Personal Folders, select Unread Mail (**Figure 19.6**) from the Favorite Folders.

- You can change the *status* of a message from unread to read (or vice versa) by right-clicking the message header and choosing the appropriate command (**Figure 19.7**).

Changing the View

To make it easier to read your mail, you can set or change the view whenever you wish. The following are some useful ways you can modify the view.

To change the current view:

◆ *Do any of the following:*

▲ To change the size of the panes, click and drag any dividing line separating a pair of panes.

▲ Choose a new view from the View > Current View submenu (**Figure 19.8**).

▲ Enable or disable AutoPreview for the current folder by choosing View > AutoPreview (**Figure 19.9**).

▲ The Reading Pane can be displayed on the right or the bottom, or it can be hidden by choosing a command from the View > Reading Pane submenu.

Note, however, that if you choose Off, you will only be able to read messages by opening them in their own window.

▲ To reorganize the message list for the current folder, choose a new option from the View > Arrange By submenu.

For example, you could sort your Sent Items folder by To (**Figure 19.10**) in order to alphabetize messages by the recipient's name.

✔ Tips

■ When choosing an Arrange By option, it's often useful to check Show in Groups. Doing so creates separate display groups for each sort unit. For example, if From is the Arrange By field, a separate group will be created for each unique sender.

■ You can also change Arrange By settings for the current folder by clicking the Arrange By text at the top of the message list.

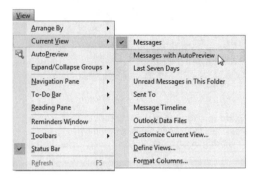

Figure 19.8 You can easily switch to many useful views by choosing one from the Current View submenu.

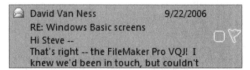

Figure 19.9 When you enable AutoPreview for a folder, a snippet of each message is displayed in the message header.

Figure 19.10 Choose an Arrange By option to reorganize the message list for the current folder.

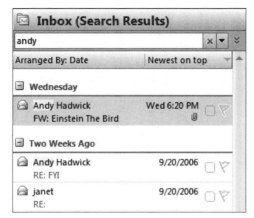

Figure 19.11 As you type the search text, Outlook scans the selected folder and lists matching messages.

Clear Search   Query Builder

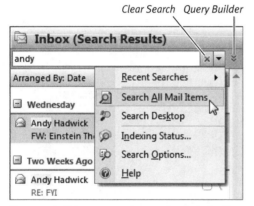

Figure 19.12 You can expand a search to include all mail folders.

- To find a message from someone whose name you've forgotten but whose company or ISP you *do* remember, search for the domain or ISP. For example, enter `microsoft.com` to see all messages from Microsoft employees or `earthlink.net` to find messages from Earthlink users.

- Instant Search is automatically enabled for Windows Vista users. XP users must first install optional software for Desktop Search to enable Instant Search.

Searching for Messages

In many cases, the simplest way to find a particular message in a folder is to sort the message list by choosing a command from the View > Arrange By submenu (as explained in the previous section). For example, to find all messages you received from a particular person, you might sort your Inbox by From.

But if you can't find a message by hunting through folders, Outlook 2007 also provides the Instant Search box, which you can use to quickly find messages that contain a given text string.

To perform an Instant Search:

1. In Mail, select the account folder in the Navigation Pane that you want to search. The message list for the folder is shown.

2. Type a search string in the Instant Search box.

   As you type, Outlook filters the message list to show only matches (**Figure 19.11**). Matches can be anywhere within a message: addresses, Subject, message body, or attachments. The matching text is highlighted in each message.

3. Click the Clear Search box to restore the original message list.

✔ Tips

- To narrow a search's focus and show fewer (but more exact) matches, continue typing. For instance, type `microsoft` rather than just `micro`.

- To expand the search to include all email account folders, choose Search All Mail Items from the Instant Search drop-down menu (**Figure 19.12**).

- To create a more specific or advanced search (such as all messages with attachments), click the Query Builder icon.

Working with Attachments

Attachments (images, documents, and other file types) can be sent to you as part of any email message. In the message list, mail with an attachment is marked with a paper clip icon (**Figure 19.13**). When viewed in the Reading Pane or in their own window, such messages show the attached files under the address information (**Figure 19.14**).

Depending on the attachment's file type and the programs installed on your PC, options for handling an attachment can include previewing it in the message window, opening it in an appropriate program, and saving it to the Desktop or a folder (so it can later be opened without returning to Outlook).

To work with an attachment:

◆ *Do any of the following:*

▲ To preview an attachment in the message window, click its file icon, or right-click the icon and choose Preview from the pop-up menu.

If an appropriate *previewer* is installed (such as the Microsoft Outlook image previewer), the attachment appears in the message window (**Figure 19.15**).

▲ To open an attachment, double-click its file icon, or right-click the icon and choose Open from the pop-up menu.

If a compatible program is on your PC, the attachment opens in that program.

▲ To save an attachment to your hard disk, drag the file icon onto the Desktop or a folder, or right-click the file icon and choose Save As from the pop-up menu.

✔ Tip

■ To save all or selected attachments, choose filenames from the File > Save Attachments submenu (**Figure 19.16**).

Attachment icon

Figure 19.13 Attachments are denoted by a paper clip.

Attached files

Figure 19.14 When you view the message, you can see the specific files that are attached.

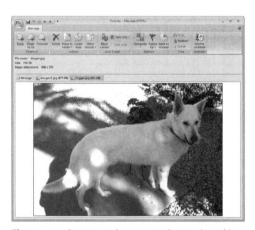

Figure 19.15 Some attachments can be previewed in the message window.

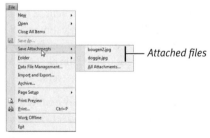

Attached files

Figure 19.16 The File > Save Attachments submenu.

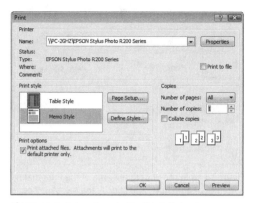

Figure 19.17 Set options in the Print dialog box.

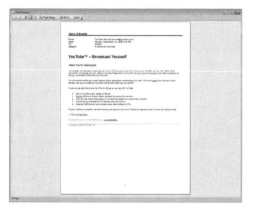

Figure 19.18 You can preview messages prior to printing them.

Figure 19.19 You can also choose a Print command from the Office Button.

Printing Messages

You can print the contents (and the attachments) of selected messages, as well as a list of message headers from the current view.

To print one or more messages:

1. In the message list, select the message or messages you want to print.

   To select multiple contiguous messages, click the first one and (Shift)-click the last one. To select noncontiguous messages, (Ctrl)-click each one.

2. Choose File > Print (or press (Ctrl)(P)). The Print dialog box appears (**Figure 19.17**).

3. Ensure that the correct printer is selected.

4. Select Memo Style as the Print style.

5. *Optional:* To set a specific paper size, fonts, or margins, click Page Setup.

6. *Optional:* To print any attached files, click the check box in the Print options area.

7. *Optional:* To preview the printout before sending it to the printer, click Preview.

   A Print Preview window opens (**Figure 19.18**). Click the Page Down and Page Up toolbar icons, use the vertical scroll bar, or press (Page Down) and (Page Up) to view other pages. If you decide not to print, click the Close icon or close box; otherwise, click Print.

8. Click OK to print the selected message(s).

✔ Tips

■ To bypass the Print dialog box, select messages and click the Print toolbar icon.

■ To go directly to Preview mode for a message, choose File > Print Preview.

■ To print an open message, click the Office Button and choose Print (**Figure 19.19**).

To print a message list:

1. In the Navigation Pane, select the message folder whose headers you want to print.

2. *Optional:* To print only certain message headers from the list, select the ones you want to print.

   To select multiple contiguous headers, click the first one and (Shift)-click the last one. To select noncontiguous headers, (Ctrl)-click each one.

3. Choose File > Print (or press (Ctrl)(P)). The Print dialog box appears.

4. Ensure that the correct printer is selected in the Name box.

5. Select Table Style as the Print style.

6. In the Print range area (**Figure 19.20**), select one of these options:

   ▲ To print all message headers from the selected folder, click All rows.

   ▲ To limit the printout to the currently selected headers, click Only selected rows.

7. *Optional:* To set a specific paper size, fonts, or margins, click Page Setup.

8. *Optional:* To preview the printout before sending it to the printer, click Preview.

   A Print Preview window opens (**Figure 19.21**). Click the Page Down and Page Up toolbar icons, use the vertical scroll bar, or press (Page Down) and (Page Up) to view other pages. If you decide not to print, click the Close icon or close box; otherwise, click Print.

9. Click OK to print the selected message(s).

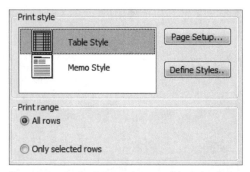

Figure 19.20 In the Print range area of the Print dialog box, click a radio button to specify the message headers to print.

Figure 19.21 Select Table style to print an entire folder of message headers or only selected headers.

20

MANAGING THE MAIL

In addition to sending, receiving, and reading messages, you'll want to spend time organizing and managing your mail. As you'll learn in this chapter, you can:

◆ Manually set the status of messages to unread or read

◆ Delete unneeded messages

◆ Create message folders in which to organize your messages by project, account, and so on

◆ Move or copy messages to other folders

◆ Categorize or flag messages for follow-up

◆ Set options to avoid junk email and phishing attempts

◆ Create rules to automate the handling of certain messages

Marking Messages as Read

One of the simplest ways to manage email is to change a message's read status to read or unread. Unread messages (shown in bold in the message list) stand out and demand attention; read messages (shown in normal type) can be ignored or handled at your leisure.

A message's read status can be changed whenever and as often as you like. For example, to ensure that a previously viewed message will receive additional attention, you can reset it to unread. Similarly, messages you want to ignore can be set to read—even though you've never viewed them. You can change a message's read status *automatically* (via a setting in Reading Pane options or in response to a message rule) or *manually* (by right-clicking the message and choosing a new status).

To set a Reading Pane option:

1. Choose Tools > Options.

   The Options dialog box appears.

2. On the Other tab, click the Reading Pane button.

   The Reading Pane dialog box appears (**Figure 20.1**).

3. To automatically mark new messages as read, click the first or second check box:

   ▲ **Mark items as read when viewed in the Reading Pane.** Any message header that is selected longer than the specified number of seconds will be marked as read.

   ▲ **Mark item as read when selection changes.** Whenever you select a different message, the currently selected message will be marked as read.

4. Click OK to close both the Reading Pane and the Options dialog boxes.

Figure 20.1 Select one of the first two mutually exclusive options to specify how messages will automatically be marked as read.

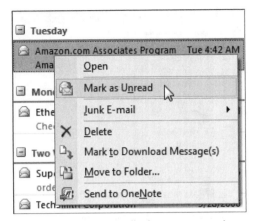

Figure 20.2 You can manually change a message's read status by right-clicking its message header.

To manually change a message's read status:

◆ *Do either of the following:*

▲ Right-click the message header in the message list. In the pop-up menu that appears (**Figure 20.2**), choose Mark as Read or Mark as Unread. (Only the opposite read status is displayed.)

▲ Select a message header in the message list, and choose Edit > Mark as Read ([Ctrl][Q]) or Edit > Mark as Unread ([Ctrl][U]).

✔ Tips

■ You can simultaneously change the status of *multiple* selected messages. After selecting message headers, right-click any one of the headers and choose a new status. (Note that you can set only one read status for all selected messages, even if they are a mixture of read and unread.)

■ To simultaneously mark all messages in the current folder as having been read, choose Edit > Mark All as Read. This command is especially useful for quickly catching up on seldom-read RSS feeds or mailing lists.

■ To automatically set certain incoming messages as read, include the `mark it as read` action in a message rule. I use such rules to mark incoming mailing list messages as read. To learn how to create message rules, see "Creating Message Rules," later in this chapter.

■ You can also mark a message as important by *flagging* it. For instructions, see "Flagging Messages," later in this chapter.

Deleting Messages

To reduce message list clutter and the size of your email account databases, you can delete unwanted messages.

To delete email or RSS messages:

1. Select the headers of one or more messages in the message list.

2. *Do one of the following:*
   ▲ Click the Delete toolbar icon.
   ▲ Choose Edit > Delete.
   ▲ Press ⌈Del⌉ or ⌈Ctrl⌉⌈D⌉.
   ▲ Right-click one of the selected messages and choose Delete from the pop-up menu that appears.

   The selected message(s) are deleted or marked for deletion, depending on the account type.

To restore deleted email or RSS messages:

♦ In a POP, Hotmail, or RSS feed account:
   ▲ Drag the item from the account's Deleted Items folder into the original message folder, such as the Inbox.
   ▲ Select the item in the Deleted Items folder and choose Edit > Move to Folder. In the Move Items dialog box (**Figure 20.3**), select the destination folder and click OK.

♦ In an IMAP account:
   ▲ Select the message marked for deletion and choose Edit > Undelete.
   ▲ Right-click the message marked for deletion and choose Undelete from the pop-up menu (**Figure 20.4**).

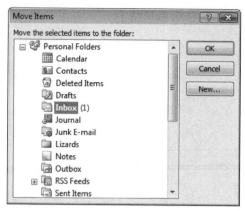

Figure 20.3 To move selected messages from the Deleted Items folder, select a destination folder in the Move Items dialog box and click OK.

Figure 20.4 Use the Undelete command to restore deleted IMAP messages.

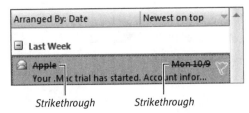

Strikethrough   *Strikethrough*

Figure 20.5 IMAP messages marked for deletion are displayed in strikethrough text.

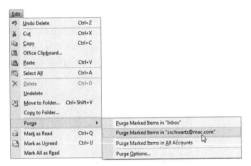

Figure 20.6 To permanently delete IMAP messages, choose a command from the Purge submenu.

Archiving vs. Deleting

If there's a chance you might eventually need an older message, you can *archive* the message rather than delete it. The AutoArchive procedure automatically runs at regular intervals, archiving all messages older than a certain age (such as six months) by moving them into Archive Folders in the Navigation Pane.

◆ To set AutoArchive options, choose Tools > Options, click the Other tab in the Options dialog box, and click the AutoArchive button.

◆ To perform a manual archive, choose File > Archive.

◆ In an Exchange Server account, select the account's Deleted Items folder or the folder in which the message was originally stored, such as the Inbox. Choose Tools > Recover Deleted Items. In the Recover Deleted Items dialog box, select one or more deleted messages and click Recover Selected Items.

✔ Tips

■ When a message is open in its own window, you can delete it by clicking the Delete toolbar icon, choosing File > Delete, or pressing [Ctrl][D].

■ Deleted messages aren't immediately deleted. In fact, what happens to a deleted message depends on its account type:

▲ Most ISP POP and RSS feed messages are moved to the Deleted Items folder where they remain until the folder is emptied or the individual messages are selected and deleted.

▲ Hotmail messages are moved to the account's Deleted Items folder.

▲ An IMAP message is *marked* for deletion by displaying its header in strikethrough type (**Figure 20.5**). When the folder is *purged* by choosing a command from the Edit > Purge submenu (**Figure 20.6**), the message is deleted from the server.

■ The primary Deleted Items folder can be emptied automatically at the end of each Outlook session (click the Other tab in the Options dialog box to see this setting) or by opening the folder, selecting items, and deleting them using any of the procedures discussed in this section.

Copying and Moving Messages

Another way to organize your messages is to move or copy them to other folders. You've already seen how you can move mail out of the Deleted Items folder and back into your Inbox, for example. Similar procedures are used to move or copy messages between almost any pair of folders—including folders in different accounts.

To copy a message to another folder:

◆ *Do either of the following:*

▲ Right-click and drag the message header onto the destination folder in the Navigation Pane. When you release the mouse button, select Copy from the pop-up menu that appears.

▲ Select a message header and choose Edit > Copy to Folder. In the Copy Items dialog box (**Figure 20.7**), select a destination folder and click OK.

A copy of the selected message is stored in the destination folder.

To move a message to another folder:

◆ *Do either of the following:*

▲ Right-click and drag the message header onto the destination folder in the Navigation Pane. When you release the mouse button, select Move from the pop-up menu that appears.

▲ Select a message header and choose Edit > Move to Folder, right-click the message header and choose Move to Folder, or press Ctrl Shift V. In the Move Items dialog box (see Figure 20.3), select a destination folder and click OK.

The message is moved to the destination folder and deleted from the source folder.

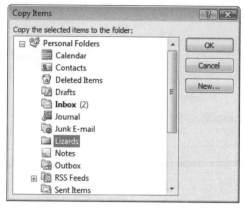

Figure 20.7 You can use the Copy Items dialog box to specify a destination folder for selected messages.

✔ Tip

■ You can also move or copy *multiple* selected messages using these techniques.

Folder name   Parent folder

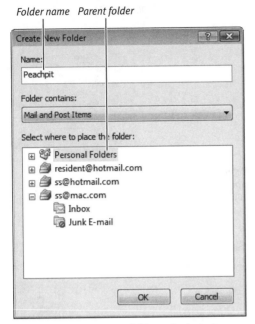

Figure 20.8 Name the new folder and select a location for it.

Creating Message Folders

Although deleting, copying, and moving messages are essential tools for managing your mail, one of the best ways to organize messages is to create additional folders for them. For instance, you can create a folder for project-related messages, to save Web and software registrations, or to store permanent copies of critical messages. You can use any such folder as the target of message moves and copies. And as you'll learn later in this chapter, you can create *message rules* to automatically route incoming messages to particular folders.

To create a new message folder:

1. *Do one of the following:*
   ▲ Choose File > New > Folder.
   ▲ Choose Folder from the New toolbar icon's drop-down menu.
   ▲ Right-click a folder in the Navigation Pane and choose New Folder from the pop-up menu that appears.
   ▲ Press Ctrl Shift E.
   The Create New Folder dialog box appears (**Figure 20.8**).

2. Enter a name for the new folder.

3. Select Mail and Post Items from the Folder contains drop-down list.

4. Select a *parent* (containing) folder from the list in the bottom half of the dialog box. (The new folder will be a subfolder of the selected folder.)

5. Click OK to create the new folder.

✔ Tip

■ Folders can be nested within folders. For example, to handle book-related correspondence, I created a Peachpit folder. Within that folder, I create additional new folders—one for each book.

CREATING MESSAGE FOLDERS

Categorizing Messages

To further help organize your mail, you can assign *categories* (colored labels) to certain messages. Categories can be applied manually or automatically (via message rules). You can use the default categories or create ones of your own, such as Quarterly Report, Work, or Family.

Initially, category names match their color indicators, such as Red Category. For each category, you can specify a name, a color, and a keyboard shortcut. Although you can also create *new* categories, you'll probably start by modifying the default categories.

To modify an existing category:

1. *Do one of the following:*
   - ▲ Click the Categorize toolbar icon and choose All Categories. (The icon is available when you're viewing any folder in the Personal Folders section of the Navigation Pane.)
   - ▲ Choose Edit > Categorize > All Categories.
   - ▲ Right-click the Category box in any message header and choose All Categories (**Figure 20.9**).

   The Color Categories dialog box appears (**Figure 20.10**).

2. To rename a category, select the category and click Rename, or double-click the category name. Enter a new name.

3. To change the color indicator for the selected category, select a color from the Color drop-down palette.

4. To assign a keyboard shortcut to a selected category, select one from the Shortcut Key drop-down list.

5. Click OK to save the changes.

Category box

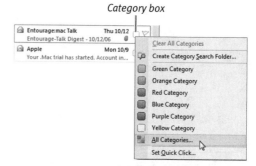

Figure 20.9 To assign a category to a message or open the Color Categories dialog box, you can right-click the Category box in any message header.

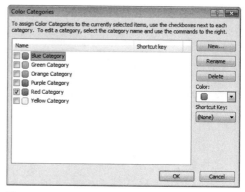

Figure 20.10 You can create, delete, rename, or change options for categories in the Color Categories dialog box.

CATEGORIZING MESSAGES

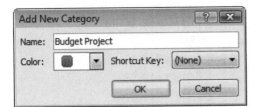

Figure 20.11 Set options for the new category in the Add New Category dialog box.

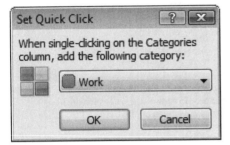

Figure 20.12 Use this dialog box to set your most commonly used category as the Quick Click category.

To create a new category:

1. *Do one of the following:*
   - ▲ Click the Categorize toolbar icon and choose All Categories.
   - ▲ Choose Edit > Categorize > All Categories.
   - ▲ Right-click the Category box in any message header and choose All Categories (see Figure 20.9).

   The Color Categories dialog box appears (see Figure 20.10).

2. Click the New button.

   The Add New Category dialog box appears (**Figure 20.11**).

3. Enter a name for the new category in the Name text box and select a color from the Color drop-down list.

4. *Optional:* To assign a keyboard shortcut to the category, select one from the Shortcut Key drop-down list.

5. Click OK to save the new category.

To set the Quick Click category:

1. *Do one of the following:*
   - ▲ Choose Edit > Categorize > Set Quick Click or Actions > Categorize > Set Quick Click.
   - ▲ Click the Categorize toolbar icon and choose Set Quick Click.
   - ▲ Right-click the Category box in any message header and choose Set Quick Click (see Figure 20.9).

   The Set Quick Click dialog box appears (**Figure 20.12**).

2. Select a category from the drop-down list and click OK.

   The Quick Click category will be applied whenever you click the Category box of a message or other item.

To assign a category to an item:

◆ *Do any of the following:*

   ▲ Click the Category box in any message header to assign the Quick Click category to the message.

   ▲ Select a message header and choose a category from the Categorize toolbar icon's drop-down menu.

   ▲ Select a message header and choose a category from the Edit > Categorize or Actions > Categorize submenu.

   ▲ Right-click a message header and choose a category from the Categorize submenu.

✔ Tips

■ Categories can also be assigned to tasks, calendar events, and contact records. Any item can have zero, one, or many categories assigned to it.

■ To remove a category from an item, choose the same category again. To remove the Quick Click category from an item, click the item's Category box. To remove *all* categories from a selected item, choose the Clear All Categories command.

■ Choose View > Arrange By > Categories to sort and group the current message list by categories.

■ To delete an unwanted category, open the Color Categories dialog box, select the category, click Delete, confirm the deletion, and click OK.

■ To view all messages with categories, select the Categorized Mail folder in the Search Folders (**Figure 20.13**).

■ To create a search folder for a category, find a message header to which the category has been applied, right-click the Category box, and choose Create "*category*" Search Folder from the pop-up menu.

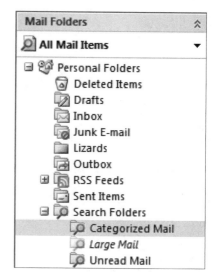

Figure 20.13 To view all messages to which categories have been applied, select the Categorized Mail search folder in the Navigation Pane.

Figure 20.14 Choose a default follow-up flag from this dialog box.

Flagging Messages

If you need to *do* something about a message (such as respond to it at a later date or schedule a meeting about it), you can *flag* the message for follow-up. Flagged messages are denoted by a colored flag in the message header. A flagged message can also have a reminder and/or be marked as completed.

To set the Quick Click flag:

1. *Do one of the following:*
   - ▲ Choose Actions > Follow Up > Set Quick Click.
   - ▲ Click the Follow Up toolbar icon and choose Set Quick Click from the drop-down menu.
   - ▲ Right-click the Follow Up box in any message header and choose Set Quick Click from the pop-up menu.

   The Set Quick Click dialog box appears (**Figure 20.14**).

2. Choose a flag from the drop-down menu and click OK.

   The Quick Click flag will be applied whenever you click the Follow Up box of a message or other item.

To set a follow-up flag for an item:

- ◆ *Do any of the following:*
   - ▲ Click the Follow Up box in any message header to assign the Quick Click flag to the message.
   - ▲ Right-click the Follow Up box in any message header and choose a flag from the Follow Up submenu.
   - ▲ Select a message header and choose a flag from the Follow Up toolbar icon.
   - ▲ Select a message header and choose a flag from the Actions > Follow Up submenu.

✔ Tips

- Flags can also be assigned to tasks, calendar events, and contact records. A given item can have only one flag.

- Flagged items automatically appear in the To-Do Bar and the To-Do List (in Tasks).

- To create a follow-up item without a due date, choose No Date as the flag setting.

- To set a follow-up for a date other than the ones listed, choose Custom Date. Set options in the Custom dialog box (**Figure 20.15**), and then click OK.

- To set a reminder (alarm) for a flagged item, choose Add Reminder. In the Custom dialog box (see Figure 20.15), ensure that the Reminder box is checked, set a date and time for the reminder, and click OK. An alarm icon is added to the item's message header (**Figure 20.16**).

- To remove a flag from an item, choose Clear Flag. You can simultaneously clear a flag and mark the item complete by choosing Mark Complete.

- To toggle between the flag setting for an item and marking the item complete, click the item's Follow Up box.

- To review all flagged messages, select the For Follow Up search folder in the Navigation Pane. (If the folder isn't listed, you can add it by choosing File > New > Search Folder, selecting Mail flagged for follow up (**Figure 20.17**), and clicking OK.)

- Choose View > Arrange By > Flag: Start Date or Flag: Due Date to sort and group the current message list by flagged items.

- To show all flagged messages, expand the Instant Search box, click Add Criteria, choose Flag Status, and set the Flag Status criterion to Completed or Follow Up Flag.

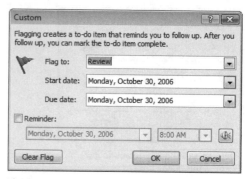

Figure 20.15 Use the Custom dialog box to set a custom follow-up date and/or reminder for an item.

Alarm icon

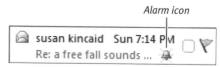

Figure 20.16 A flagged item can also include a reminder.

Figure 20.17 If it isn't displayed in the Navigation Pane, you can add the Search Folder for flagged mail.

Junk mail protection level

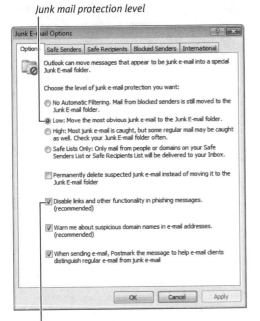

Phishing protection

Figure 20.18 Set junk mail and phishing options on the tabs of the Junk E-mail Options dialog box.

Handling Junk Mail and Phishing

Everyone eventually receives junk mail or *spam*—generally consisting of unwanted advertisements for mortgages, weight loss products, penis and breast enlargers, and the like. If you use your regular email address to register on Web sites or if you send email to corporations, newsgroups, or mailing lists, your volume of received junk mail is liable to increase. Using the Junk E-mail Options feature, you can filter out much of this time-wasting, annoying email.

Outlook 2007 also offers protection against *phishing* (attempts via email to con you into providing important personal data, such as bank account numbers, credit card information, and Web site passwords).

To set junk mail and phishing options:

1. Choose Actions > Junk E-mail > Junk E-mail Options.

   The Junk E-mail Options dialog box appears (**Figure 20.18**).

2. On the Options tab, click a radio button to set the desired protection level.

   When received, suspected junk mail is automatically moved to the Junk E-mail folder or deleted, depending on the settings on the Options tab.

3. To enable phishing protection, check Disable links and other functionality in phishing messages.

4. *Optional:* To automatically delete potential junk mail, check Permanently delete suspected junk e-mail instead of moving it to the Junk E-mail folder.

5. Click OK to save the new settings.

HANDLING JUNK MAIL AND PHISHING

325

✔ Tips

- To automatically classify all new mail from certain addresses as junk, Outlook maintains a Blocked Senders List. To add someone to the list, click the Blocked Senders tab of the Junk E-mail Options dialog box (**Figure 20.19**), click Add, enter the person's email address, and click OK. (To add a person to the list based on a received message, select the message and choose Actions > Junk E-mail > Add Sender to Blocked Senders List.)

- You can also block all email from a *domain*. Doing so is useful when you notice that you're receiving many junk messages from a domain, but each has a different user name. For instance, to block all email from krypton.net, add `krypton.net` or `@krypton.net` to the Blocked Senders List.

- To prevent Outlook from classifying mail from certain individuals as junk, create contact records for them and ensure that Also trust e-mail from my Contacts is checked on the Safe Senders tab of the Junk E-mail Options dialog box. Or you can add their email addresses to the list on the Safe Senders tab.

- Using the International tab of the Junk E-mail Options dialog box, you can classify all email from certain *countries* as junk. Click the Blocked Top-Level Domain List button, select countries to block (**Figure 20.20**), and click OK.

- Outlook will occasionally mark a received message as junk that is actually legitimate mail. To reclassify a selected or open message, click the Not Junk toolbar icon or choose Actions > Junk E-mail > Mark as Not Junk.

- You can specify other actions for junk mail by creating *message rules* (discussed in the next section).

Figure 20.19 You can block future messages from specific users or domains by adding them to the Blocked Senders List.

Figure 20.20 Certain countries are notorious generators of junk mail. To ignore all email from such a country, add it to the list on the International tab.

Defined rules are listed here

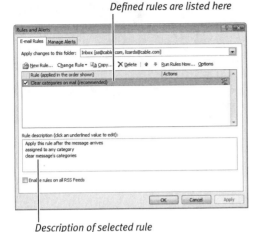

Description of selected rule

Figure 20.21 Rules are created and maintained in the Rules and Alerts dialog box.

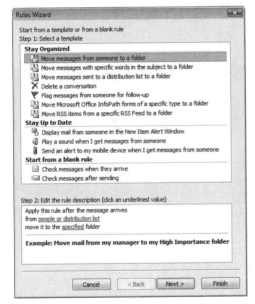

Figure 20.22 Select a template on which to base the rule. On the screens that follow, you can add, remove, and specify rule conditions, actions, and exceptions.

Creating Message Rules

By defining message rules, you can instruct Outlook to automatically perform actions on certain incoming or outgoing email. A message rule could store all incoming email from `Peachpit.com` in a Peachpit folder rather than the Inbox, for example. A rule can be based on a template or created from scratch. Note that rules cannot be applied to HTTP (Web) account email.

To create a rule from a template:

1. Choose Tools > Rules and Alerts.
   The Rules and Alerts dialog box appears (**Figure 20.21**).

2. Click the New Rule icon.
   The Rules Wizard appears (**Figure 20.22**).

3. Select a template on which to base the rule. (If an appropriate template isn't listed, you can create the rule from scratch by selecting a blank rule.) Click Next.

4. Add or remove conditions for the rule by clicking check boxes. Condition place-holders are displayed as blue underlined text in the Step 2 area of the wizard. Click each placeholder and replace it with appropriate data. Click Next to continue.

5. Add or remove actions to be performed by the rule by clicking check boxes. Action placeholders are displayed as blue underlined text in the Step 2 area of the wizard. Click each placeholder and replace it with appropriate data. Click Next to continue.

6. Specify exceptions to the rule by clicking check boxes. Placeholders for exceptions are displayed as blue underlined text in the Step 2 area of the wizard. Click each placeholder and replace it with appropriate data. Click Next to continue.

continues on next page

CREATING MESSAGE RULES

7. On the final wizard screen (**Figure 20.23**), *do the following:*

▲ Name the rule.

▲ Set rule options by clicking check boxes.

8. Click Finish to save the rule. Then click OK to close the Rules and Alerts dialog box.

✔ Tips

■ You can temporarily disable a rule by removing its check mark in the Rules and Alerts dialog box (see Figure 20.21). To permanently eliminate a rule, select it and click the Delete icon.

■ To edit a rule, double-click it in the Rules and Alerts dialog box; or select it, click the Change Rule icon, and choose Edit Rule Settings from the drop-down menu.

■ To alter only a rule's conditions, actions, or exceptions, it isn't necessary to edit the rule. Just select it in the Rules and Alerts dialog box (see Figure 20.21) to display the rule. Then click the placeholder you want to change.

■ Rules are executed in the order in which they're listed in the Rules and Alerts dialog box. To change the order, select a rule and click the Move Up or Move Down icon.

■ To test a rule, click Run Rules Now in the Rules and Alerts dialog box (see Figure 20.21). In the Run Rules Now dialog box (**Figure 20.24**), select the rule to be tested, specify the folder on which to run the rule, and click the Run Now button.

■ Until a message-deletion rule has been successfully tested, don't use the perma-nently delete it action. Instead, use delete it, which merely moves items into the Deleted Items folder rather than instantly deleting them.

Figure 20.23 To complete a rule definition, name and set initial options for the rule.

Figure 20.24 To test a new or revised rule, you can run it on the messages in a selected folder. (Click Browse to select a different test folder.)

Tasks and Appointments

In addition to handling your email and Really Simple Syndication (RSS) feeds, Outlook has exceptional appointment, event, and task management capabilities.

You can use the Calendar pane to schedule one-time appointments (such as a project meeting or dinner with a friend), accompanied by a pop-up reminder an hour before the event. You can also schedule recurring events, such as birthdays, monthly mortgage payments, and weekly staff meetings.

You use the Tasks pane to manage items on your to-do list, such as mowing the lawn, buying a new bathrobe, or picking new office furniture. Unlike Calendar appointments, a task is not required to have a due date or a reminder—although it can optionally have either.

Calendar Basics

To work with the Calendar pane (**Figure 21.1, bottom**), you click the Calendar button and select a viewing option (day, week, or month). *Events* (all-day items) are shown at the top of each day, whereas *appointments* (items with a particular start and end time) are listed by their start times.

To change or view the details for an event or appointment (**Figure 21.2**), you double-click the item on the Calendar.

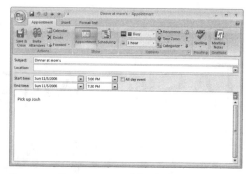

Figure 21.2 You can open a Calendar item to change its start or end time, add or review notes, or set a reminder (alarm) for it.

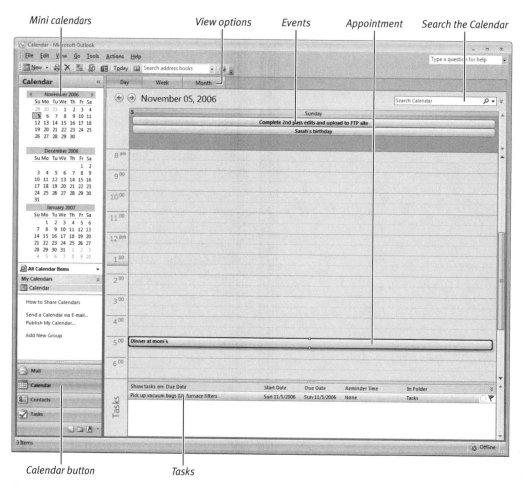

Figure 21.1 The Calendar pane.

Set reminder

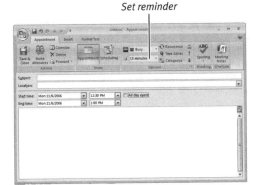

Figure 21.3 You can create a new appointment or event in a window.

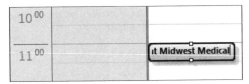

Figure 21.4 Rather than open a window to add an appointment or event, it's often faster to click in a date/time slot and type the item's subject.

Recording an Appointment or Event

To track or be reminded of an appointment or event, you must first add it to the Calendar.

To record an appointment or event:

1. *Do one of the following:*
   - ▲ From any pane, choose File > New > Appointment ([Ctrl][Shift][A]), or choose Appointment from the New toolbar icon's drop-down menu.
   - ▲ From the Calendar pane, choose File > New > Appointment or Actions > New Appointment ([Ctrl][N]).

   An Untitled - Appointment window opens (**Figure 21.3**).

2. Enter a subject (title) for the appointment or event.

3. *Do either of the following:*
   - ▲ To treat this item as an event, click the All day event check box.
   - ▲ To treat this item as an appointment, set start and end dates and times.

4. *Optional:* To set an alarm for this appointment or event , choose a time from the Reminder drop-down menu.

   A reminder will appear the designated number of minutes, hours, or days *before* the appointment or event's scheduled start.

5. Click the Save & Close icon.

✔ Tips

- ■ You can quickly create an appointment or event by selecting a time or event slot on the Calendar and then entering the item's subject (**Figure 21.4**).

- ■ To delete a selected appointment or event (removing it from the Calendar), click the Delete toolbar icon, choose Edit > Delete, or press [Ctrl][D].

RECORDING AN APPOINTMENT OR EVENT

Creating Recurring Events

Not all appointments and events are one-time activities; many recur at regular intervals. For example, you may attend weekly staff meetings or belong to a club that meets at 7 PM every third Tuesday of the month. Birthdays and anniversaries are also examples of recurring events.

To set a recurring schedule for an event or appointment:

1. *Do one of the following:*
   - ▲ From the Calendar pane, choose Actions > New Recurring Event or New Recurring Appointment.
   - ▲ Create a new event or appointment by following Steps 1–4 of the previous task.
   - ▲ Open an existing event or appointment that you want to change into a recurring item.

2. If the Appointment Recurrence dialog box isn't open, click the Recurrence toolbar icon in the appointment or event window.

3. In the Appointment Recurrence dialog box (**Figure 21.5**), set a recurrence pattern. If the event or appointment has a known end date, specify it in the dialog box's Range of recurrence area.

4. Click OK to close the dialog box.

5. In the appointment or event window, click the Save & Close icon.

Recurrence pattern

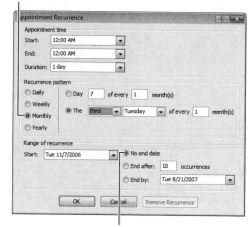

Recurrence end date

Figure 21.5 You can create or modify a recurring schedule for an event or appointment.

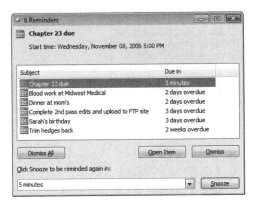

Figure 21.6 Current and overdue reminders are presented as a scrolling list in the Reminders window.

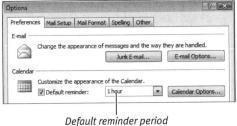

Default reminder period

Figure 21.7 You can set the default reminder period on the Preferences tab of the Options dialog box.

Responding to Reminders

Any event, appointment, or task can have a reminder (alarm) associated with it. If Outlook is running when a reminder is triggered, the Reminders window (**Figure 21.6**) appears. The window can also be opened by choosing View > Reminders Window.

To respond to a reminder:

1. In the Reminders window, select the reminder to which you want to respond.

2. *Do one of the following:*
   ▲ Click the Dismiss button. This turns off the alarm associated with the item. (To disable the alarm for *every* listed item, click Dismiss All.)
   ▲ To repeat the reminder at a later date or time, choose a snooze period from the drop-down menu and click Snooze.
   ▲ To view or edit the item, click Open Item or double-click the item.

3. *Optional:* To respond to other reminders, select the reminder in the list and repeat Step 2.

4. Close the Reminders window by clicking its close box (X).

✔ Tips

■ You can change the default reminder period by choosing Tools > Options. This reminder period (**Figure 21.7**) is automatically set for new events and appointments, unless you specify a different period or disable the item's reminder (see Figure 21.3).

■ Although you won't receive additional reminders for a dismissed item, the item is *not* removed from the Calendar. You must delete an item to remove it from the Calendar.

RESPONDING TO REMINDERS

Modifying Events and Appointments

You can change the subject, start or end time, reminder schedule, or other elements of an existing event or appointment.

To change an event or appointment:

◆ *Do any of the following:*

▲ To edit only the subject, select the appointment or event on any Calendar page, click a second time to set the insertion mark (**Figure 21.8**), and edit the subject as desired.

▲ To delete an appointment or event, select it on any Calendar page and click the Delete toolbar icon, choose Edit > Delete, or press Del or Ctrl D.

▲ To change an appointment or event's starting date or time, you can drag the item to a new Calendar location. (To change only the date while keeping the same start and end times, you can drag the item to a new date on one of the mini calendars.)

▲ To change any aspect of an event or appointment, open the item in its own window. Double-click the item on any Calendar page, right-click the item and choose Open, or select the item and choose File > Open > Selected Items (Ctrl O). When you're done making changes, click the Save & Close icon.

✔ Tips

■ To find old appointments and events, you can flip through the mini calendars. Any date in bold (**Figure 21.9**) indicates at least one appointment or event.

■ When deleting a recurring event or appointment, you can delete only the current occurrence or all occurrences (**Figure 21.10**).

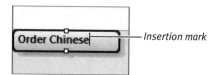

Figure 21.8 Set the insertion mark and edit the subject as you wish.

Figure 21.9 Dates that contain events or appointments (20 and 25) are shown in bold on the mini calendars.

Figure 21.10 When deleting or editing a recurring appointment or event, the deletion or edits can be applied to the selected item or to the entire series.

Expand the Query Builder

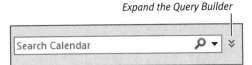

Figure 21.11 To perform a simple search, type search text in this box.

Searching for an Event or Appointment

Scrolling through Calendar pages or mini calendars isn't always an efficient way to find an appointment or event—especially when you have only a vague idea of when the item will occur or happened. You can use the Instant Search box to quickly find most items.

To search the Calendar:

1. *Do either of the following:*

▲ To search all elements of events and appointments, enter search text in the Instant Search box (**Figure 21.11**).

▲ To perform a more specific or complex search, click the Expand the Query Builder icon to the right of the Instant Search box, and then enter the search criteria.

Matches are displayed in a Search Results list (**Figure 21.12**).

2. *Do any of the following:*

▲ Double-click a found item to open it.

▲ To delete an item, select it in the list and click the Delete toolbar icon.

▲ To modify an element of a found item (such as its Subject or Start), click in the appropriate field and make the desired edits.

3. To return to the Calendar, click the Clear Search icon beside the Instant Search box.

Clear Search

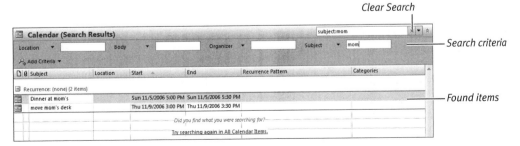

Search criteria

Found items

Figure 21.12 Search Results list.

Emailing a Calendar

While most of your work with the Calendar will be solitary, Outlook also provides ways to share your schedule with others. One of the simplest sharing methods is to email the appointments and events in a date range.

To email a calendar:

1. Create a new email message.

2. Click the Message or Insert tab at the top of the message window.

3. Click in the message area of the window, and then click the Calendar toolbar icon in the Include group.

    The Send a Calendar via E-mail dialog box appears (**Figure 21.13**).

4. Select the dates you wish to include by choosing an option from the Date Range drop-down menu.

    To set a different range or include past dates, choose Specify dates.

5. From the Detail drop-down menu (**Figure 21.14**), specify the amount of appointment information to be included:

    ▲ **Availability only.** Shows only whether you're free or busy (in very general terms).

    ▲ **Limited details.** Shows free times, plus the Subject for booked times.

    ▲ **Full details.** Shows free times, plus full details for booked times.

6. *Optional:* Click the Show button to set Advanced options (**Figure 21.15**):

    ▲ **Include details of items marked private.** Check to share private items; leave unchecked to omit these items. (This option is available only when you have selected Limited details or Full details.)

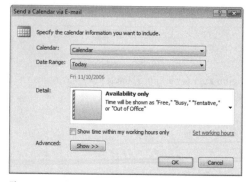

Figure 21.13 Set Calendar-sharing options, and then click OK.

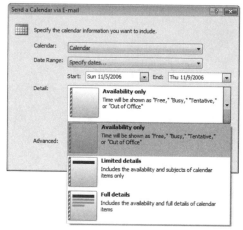

Figure 21.14 Specify the amount of Calendar detail to send to the message recipient.

Figure 21.15 You can customize the Calendar data to be shared.

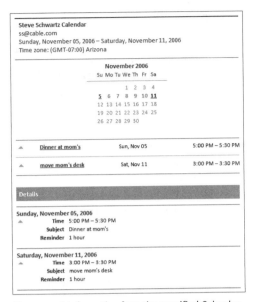

Figure 21.16 Information from the specified Calendar dates is added to the message. This example shows only the list of events scheduled during the period.

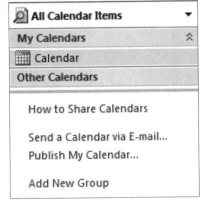

Figure 21.17 Click the Publish My Calendar text to open the wizard.

▲ **Include attachments within calendar items.** When checked, if an appointment or event has an attachment (such as a picture or document), the attachment will also be available to the recipient. (This option is available only when Full details is selected.)

▲ **E-mail Layout.** *Daily schedule* is the standard layout, providing information on both free and booked times. *List of events* shows only booked times.

7. Click OK.

The Calendar information is added to the message body (**Figure 21.16**). It is also included as an attachment that can be opened and viewed—if the recipient also has Outlook 2007.

8. Click Send to send the message.

✔ Tips

■ When an Outlook 2007 user receives an emailed Calendar, he or she can open the attached file in Outlook and view the two Calendars side-by-side. Doing so makes it simple to see times when you're both free. Appointments from the received file can be dragged onto the recipient's Calendar, if desired.

■ Users with a Microsoft Exchange account can share their default Calendar with other users on the server by clicking Share My Calendar in the Navigation Pane.

■ You can also make your Calendar available online. In the Navigation Pane, click Publish My Calendar (**Figure 21.17**) and follow the steps in the Microsoft Office Online Registration wizard.

Task Basics

Click the Tasks button in the Navigation Pane to make the Tasks pane active (**Figure 21.18**). You use the Tasks pane to create, view, and manage a To-Do List. You can change the view of your tasks, delete tasks, mark tasks as complete, or edit any aspect of a task.

✔ Tips

- The distinction between tasks and appointments is up to you. Because a task can occur at a specific time and also have an alarm that appears in the Reminders window, such to-do items can be recorded as tasks *or* as appointments.

- No matter which Outlook component is currently active, your tasks can be viewed in the new To-Do Bar. To change the To-Do Bar display, choose a command from the View > To-Do Bar submenu, or click the double-arrow or X at the top of the To-Do Bar.

Change the view   *To-Do List*   *Search the To-Do List*   *To-Do Bar*

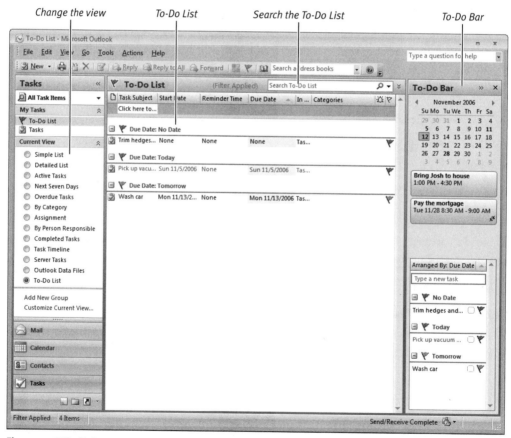

Figure 21.18 The Tasks pane.

TASK BASICS

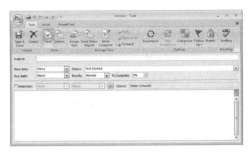

Figure 21.19 Like Calendar appointments and events, tasks are typically created in a special window.

Type here to create a new task

Figure 21.20 Another way to add a task is to type a Subject in this box at the top of the To-Do List. Then change the default settings in the task fields to the right of the Subject.

Creating a Task

Like appointments and events, you can record as many new tasks as you like.

To create a task:

1. *Do one of the following:*
   - ▲ From any pane, choose File > New > Task (Ctrl Shift K).
   - ▲ From any pane, choose Task from the New toolbar icon's drop-down menu.
   - ▲ From the Tasks pane, choose File > New > Task or Actions > New Task (Ctrl N).

   An Untitled - Task window opens (**Figure 21.19**).

2. Enter a Subject for the task.

3. *Optional:* For a time-sensitive task, enter a start and end date.

   For a task with no specific start and/or end date, leave these options set to None.

4. *Optional:* To set an alarm for this task, click the Reminder check box and specify a reminder date and time.

   At the appropriate time, the reminder will appear in the Reminders window (see Figure 21.6).

5. *Optional:* Choose a progress setting from the Status drop-down menu.

   If you choose In Progress, you can also specify the % Complete.

6. *Optional:* Enter task notes or details in the scrolling text area.

7. Click the Save & Close icon.

   The new task is added to the To-Do List.

✔ Tip

- ■ You can also create a new task by typing the Subject directly into the To-Do List (**Figure 21.20**).

Modifying Tasks

When a task is completed or you make progress on a lengthy task, you can mark it as complete or change the % Complete setting. You can also delete any task you no longer wish to track.

To modify a task:

1. In the Current View list (**Figure 21.21**), select a view that displays the task and task fields you want to change.

2. *Do either of the following:*

   ▲ Double-click the task to open it in its own window, make the necessary changes, and click Save & Close.

   ▲ Make the changes by directly modifying the task information displayed in the To-Do List.

✔ Tips

■ To mark a task complete, click the task's check box in the To-Do List (**Figure 21.22**). Click the check box again to reverse the task's completion status.

■ To delete a task you no longer wish to track, select it in the To-Do List. Then click the Delete toolbar icon, choose Edit > Delete, or press Ctrl D or Del . (Note that most task deletions aren't accompanied by a warning dialog box. They are carried out immediately.)

■ Another way to delete a task or change its completion status is to right-click the task in the To-Do Bar and choose a command from the pop-up menu that appears (**Figure 21.23**).

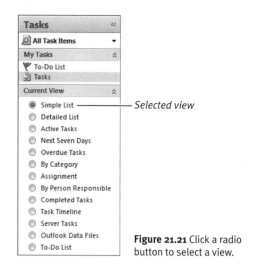

Figure 21.21 Click a radio button to select a view.

Figure 21.22 Click the check box to toggle a task's status from incomplete to complete (and vice versa).

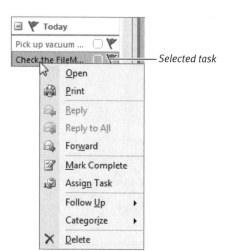

Figure 21.23 You can right-click a task in the To-Do Bar.

MODIFYING TASKS

Part VI:
Microsoft OneNote

Chapter 22 Getting Started with
OneNote 2007 343

Chapter 23 Creating Notes..................................... 353

Chapter 24 Embellishing and Editing Notes..... 363

Chapter 25 Managing and Organizing Notes... 375

GETTING STARTED WITH ONENOTE 2007

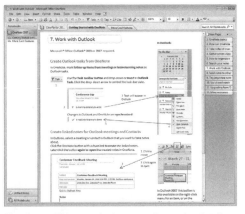

Figure 22.1 This page in the example notebook tells how Outlook can be integrated with OneNote.

OneNote 2007 is a free form note-taking and organizing application, similar to an electronic scrapbook. A note can consist of text, an audio clip, or a video clip and can be positioned anywhere on the page. You can create notes from scratch or move them into OneNote via copy-and-paste, drag-and-drop, or one of OneNote's Insert commands.

The organization of your notes is up to you, but OneNote provides structure to help you. At the top level is the *notebook*. You might start by creating two notebooks: Work and Personal, for example. Each notebook can be divided into *sections*, similar to tabs in a 3-ring binder. And each section can have multiple *pages*. A given page can contain one note or as many notes as you like.

If you check the File menu, you'll note that the traditional Save command is absent. OneNote automatically saves changes in each notebook as you work.

✔ Tip

- Because OneNote is a unique type of application and will be foreign to many users, an example notebook ("OneNote 2007 Guide") is included to introduce the program's many features (**Figure 22.1**). Be sure to thoroughly review this notebook before you delete it.

The OneNote Interface

In order to use OneNote effectively, it helps to understand the workings of its interface (**Figure 22.2**).

Menus and toolbars. Unlike Word, Excel, and PowerPoint 2007, OneNote did not inherit the new Ribbon. Commands are still chosen from menus and by clicking toolbar icons and controls.

Notebook Section   Toolbar   Menus   Section tabs   Pages Search box

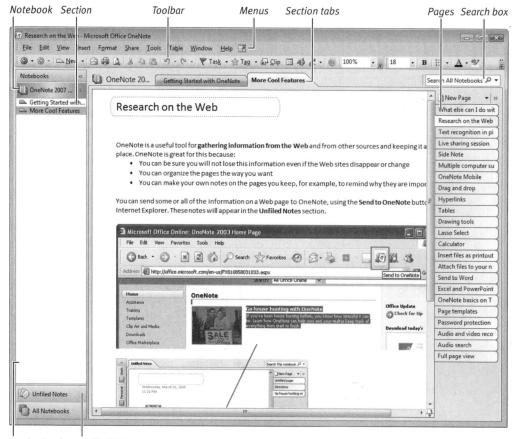

Navigation bar Unfiled Notes

Figure 22.2 The OneNote 2007 interface.

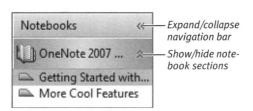

Figure 22.3 Click double arrows to expand/collapse or show/hide material in the navigation bar.

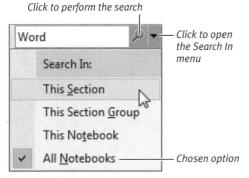

Figure 22.4 You can also click All Notebooks at the bottom of the navigation bar to select a section.

Figure 22.5 Choose the material you wish to search (from the Search In drop-down menu), enter the text string, and click the search icon.

Navigation bar. Click to select material to view, such as a notebook, a section, or Unfiled Notes. Expand/collapse lists as necessary (**Figure 22.3**).

Section tabs. Click a section tab to view or edit pages in that section of the current notebook. A section can also be selected from the list at the top of the navigation bar or from the All Notebooks pop-up menu at the bottom of the navigation bar (**Figure 22.4**).

Pages. This list shows the names of all pages in the selected section of the current notebook. Click a page name to view that page.

Search box. Search for all occurrences of a text string in the specified area of OneNote (**Figure 22.5**).

Unfiled Notes. Click this navigation bar icon to view or work with notes that weren't directly added to a notebook page. New notes are stored in Unfiled Notes if they are created with any of the following tools:

- OneNote screen clipping

- OneNote side note

- Send to OneNote command (found in programs such as Internet Explorer 7 and Outlook 20007)

✔ Tips

■ The title bar (at the top of the OneNote window) displays the name of the notebook page you're currently viewing.

■ To make it easier to concentrate on your notes, press F11. In *full view*, menus, the navigation bar, and page and section lists are hidden until you press F11 again.

THE ONENOTE INTERFACE

Notebooks, Sections, and Pages

OneNote provides a single window in which to view and edit notebooks. To organize your notes, a notebook can be divided into named sections, each of which can contain multiple named pages. Because the creation and deletion of notebooks, sections, and pages are fundamental to using OneNote, we'll cover them here. For additional help with managing and organizing notebooks, see Chapter 25.

To create a new notebook:

1. Choose File > New > Notebook, or click the down arrow beside the New toolbar icon and choose Notebook.

   The New Notebook Wizard appears (**Figure 22.6**).

2. Enter a name for the new notebook in the Name box, and *do one of the following:*

   ▲ To create a notebook from scratch, select Blank in the From Template list.

   ▲ To base the notebook on a OneNote template, select the template in the From Template list. (Templates typically provide predefined notebook sections and page formatting.)

   Click Next to continue.

3. On the second wizard screen (**Figure 22.7**), click a radio button to indicate who will be using the notebook. Click Next to continue.

4. On the final screen (**Figure 22.8**), specify a disk location in which to create the notebook folder. (To set a location other than the proposed one, click Browse.)

5. Click Create.

   The new notebook appears in the navigation bar.

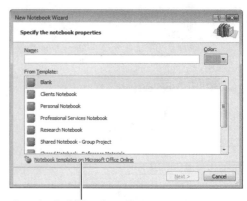

Download additional templates

Figure 22.6 Notebooks are created in the New Notebook Wizard.

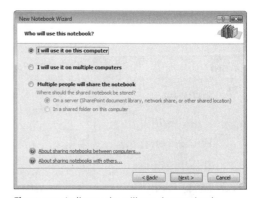

Figure 22.7 Indicate who will use the notebook.

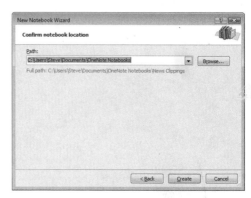

Figure 22.8 Specify a disk location for the notebook.

Documents folder   Close box

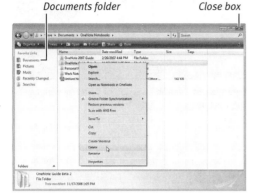

Figure 22.9 Right-click the notebook folder and choose Delete from the pop-up menu.

Downloading OneNote Templates

To download and install additional notebook templates, follow these steps:

1. Click the text link beneath the From Template list (see Figure 22.6).

   Your browser launches and opens to Microsoft Office Online.

2. Select a template, and click its Download Now button.

3. Follow the onscreen instructions to save the template package, unpack it, and install the template. (Accept the default save locations.)

   A new notebook based on the downloaded template is automatically created. In addition, whenever you issue the File > New > Notebook command, the template (and its variations) will appear in the From Template list.

To delete a notebook:

1. If the notebook is currently open, select its tab in the navigation bar and choose File > Close this Notebook.

   You shouldn't delete a notebook that is in use. As an alternative to closing the notebook, you can quit OneNote.

2. Open the OneNote Notebooks folder inside the Documents folder. (In Windows Vista, you can find this folder by opening *any* folder and clicking Documents in the Favorite Links list.)

   OneNote does not provide a command for deleting notebooks, so you must use normal Windows procedures to delete the notebook folder and its contents.

3. Right-click the folder of the notebook you want to delete, and choose Delete from the pop-up menu (**Figure 22.9**).

   The notebook folder and contents are moved to the Recycle Bin.

4. Close the folder window by clicking its close box (X).

To add a section to a notebook:

1. *Do one of the following:*
   - ▲ Choose File > New > Section.
   - ▲ Choose Section from the New toolbar icon's drop-down menu.
   - ▲ Right-click a section tab, and choose New Section from the pop-up menu.

   The new section appears.

2. Type a name for the new section, and press (Enter).

3. *Optional:* Set a color for the section by right-clicking its tab and choosing a color from the Section Color submenu.

4. *Optional:* Change the section's placement among the other sections by dragging its tab to the left or right.

NOTEBOOKS, SECTIONS, AND PAGES

347

To delete a notebook section:

1. Right-click the section's tab, and choose Delete from the pop-up menu.

A confirmation dialog box appears (**Figure 22.10**).

2. Click Yes.

The section and its pages are moved from the notebook into the Recycle Bin.

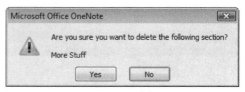

Figure 22.10 Confirm a section deletion by clicking the Yes button.

✔ Tips

■ In addition to right-clicking a section tab at the top of the OneNote window, you can add or delete a section by right-clicking a section name in the navigation bar.

■ If you haven't emptied the Recycle Bin, you can restore a deleted notebook or section. Open the Recycle Bin, right-click the item's icon, and choose Restore from the pop-up menu that appears.

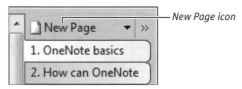
New Page icon

Figure 22.11 Add a page by clicking this icon above the page list.

To add a page to a notebook section:

1. Switch to the section in which you want to add a page.

2. *Do one of the following:*

▲ Choose File > New > Page ((Ctrl)(N)).

▲ Choose Page from the New toolbar icon's drop-down menu.

▲ Click the New Page icon above the page list (**Figure 22.11**) or choose New Page from its drop-down menu.

3. Type a name for the new page in the text box at the top of the page.

To delete a page:

1. Click the page's tab in the page list (on the right side of the window).

2. *Do either of the following:*

▲ Choose Edit > Delete ((Del)).

▲ Right-click the page tab and choose Delete from the pop-up menu.

✔ Tips

■ To rename a page, edit the name in the text box at the top of the page.

■ You can reverse a page deletion by immediately choosing Edit > Undo Delete or by pressing (Ctrl)(Z).

NOTEBOOKS, SECTIONS, AND PAGES

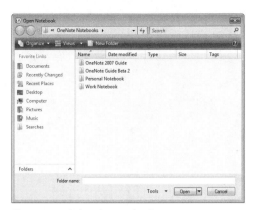

Figure 22.12 Select the notebook you want to open, and then click Open.

Selected notebook

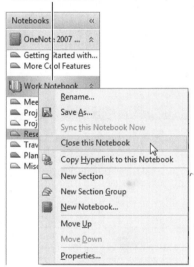

Figure 22.13 Right-click the notebook's name in the navigation bar, and choose Close this Notebook.

Opening and Closing Notebooks

Unlike its predecessor, OneNote 2007 supports multiple notebooks. If you create many of them or if—when expanded—they contain many sections, you may prefer to open and close certain ones as needed in order to minimize navigation bar clutter.

To open a notebook:

1. Choose File > Open > Notebook.

   The Open Notebook dialog box appears (**Figure 22.12**) with the OneNote Notebooks folder displayed.

2. Select a notebook and click Open.

   The notebook is added to the Notebooks list in the navigation bar.

To close an active notebook:

1. Make the notebook active by selecting it or one of its sections.

2. *Do either of the following:*

   ▲ Choose File > Close this Notebook.

   ▲ Right-click the notebook's tab in the navigation bar, and choose Close this Notebook from the pop-up menu (**Figure 22.13**).

   The notebook closes and is removed from the navigation bar.

✔ Tips

■ After you select a notebook in the Open Notebook dialog box, Windows Vista displays the message: "No items match your search." Ignore it, and click Open.

■ You can also select a notebook by clicking the All Notebooks icon at the bottom of the navigation bar.

OneNote Integration

In addition to creating text, audio, and video notes within OneNote, you can use OneNote utilities to extract information from other programs to include as notes and other note page additions. OneNote also integrates well with the other Office components. Each of the integration features in this section will be discussed in depth in the chapters that follow, but here's a brief overview.

Copy-and-paste/Drag-and-drop

The simplest way to incorporate a portion of any document into a OneNote note is to copy ((Ctrl C)) it in the source document and then paste ((Ctrl V)) it into OneNote as a new note. If you select text or a graphic in a drag-and-drop enabled application, such as Internet Explorer, you can drag the material directly into a OneNote page as a new note.

Insert commands

By choosing commands from the Insert menu (**Figure 22.14**), you can place the following materials on a note page:

- Pictures from a file, scanner, or camera
- Clickable links to files on your hard disk
- Images of printouts from any program

Screen clippings

Using OneNote's screen capture tool, you can create a note from a selected portion of any document or the Windows desktop. Right-click the OneNote icon in the system tray and choose Create Screen Clipping (**Figure 22.15**). Drag a rectangle around the material (**Figure 22.16**) to create a new note in the Unfiled Notes section.

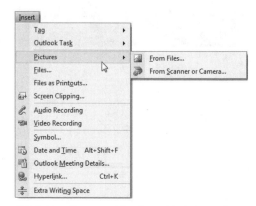

Figure 22.14 You can add various objects to a note page by choosing commands from the Insert menu.

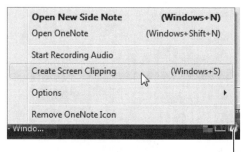

OneNote system tray icon

Figure 22.15 To create a screen clipping, right-click the OneNote icon, and choose Create Screen Clipping or press its keyboard shortcut.

Screen Clipping cursor

Figure 22.16 Drag a rectangle around the material you want to copy. When you release the mouse button, the material is added to OneNote as an unfiled note.

ONENOTE INTEGRATION

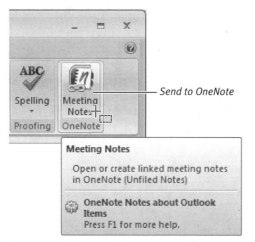

Send to OneNote

Figure 22.17 With an email message, appointment, or contact record open in its own Outlook window, you can click a toolbar icon to send the data to OneNote.

Send to OneNote

Figure 22.18 You can also select an Outlook item without opening it and then click a toolbar icon to send the item to OneNote as a new note.

Integration with Office 2007

In addition to using drag-and-drop or copy-and-paste to move material between OneNote and other Office applications (and vice versa), several commands are provided for this purpose.

OneNote to Outlook. You can use a note as a basis for an Outlook email message, appointment, contact record, task, or meeting request. You can also insert meeting details or edit an Outlook task from within OneNote.

OneNote to Word. You can create a new Word document from a OneNote note or from selected text within a note by choosing File > Send To > Microsoft Office Word.

Outlook to OneNote. Outlook 2007 material can be used to create a new unfiled note in the following ways:

◆ In an open email message, contact record, or appointment, click the appropriate toolbar icon (**Figure 22.17**).

◆ With the Outlook item selected, click an icon in the Standard toolbar (**Figure 22.18**) to create a new unfiled note from the material.

✔ Tip

■ You can also create a note from an email message in Outlook by right-clicking its header in the message list and choosing Send to OneNote from the pop-up menu. The Standard toolbar above the message list also contains a Send to OneNote icon that performs the same function.

ONENOTE INTEGRATION

Getting Help

Microsoft Office OneNote Help (**Figure 22.19**) works the same as help for the other Office applications (see Chapter 2).

To use OneNote Help:

1. To summon help, choose Help > Microsoft Office OneNote Help or press F1 .

2. *Do any of the following:*
   - ▲ Click the Home icon in Help's toolbar to view the main help page.
   - ▲ Click the Table of Contents icon in Help's toolbar to expand the window to show/hide the table of contents.
   - ▲ Click blue text to read help information on that topic.
   - ▲ To search for a help topic, type search text in the box and click the Search icon.
   - ▲ Click the Print icon in Help's toolbar to print the current help page.
   - ▲ To switch between offline and online help information, click the drop-down menu in the lower-right corner of the Help window and choose an option.

3. When you're done using OneNote Help, click the window's close box (X).

✔ Tip

- ■ OneNote Help automatically closes when you quit OneNote.

Figure 22.19 The OneNote Help main page.

CREATING NOTES

In Chapter 22, you learned the OneNote basics: how note information is created, stored, and organized. In this chapter, we'll go over the details of *creating* notes. OneNote supports the following note types:

- ◆ Typed notes
- ◆ Audio notes
- ◆ Video notes
- ◆ Handwritten notes
- ◆ Notes created from Outlook email messages, contact records, or appointments
- ◆ Side notes
- ◆ Screen clippings

Typing a Note

Many notes are created simply by typing your thoughts into a new *note container* (the enclosure for every note).

To create a typed note:

1. Switch to or create the page on which you want to add the note.

2. Click to set the text insertion mark at the spot where you want to create the note.

3. Type the note, pressing (Enter) whenever you want to start a new paragraph.

4. To complete the note (**Figure 23.1**), click anywhere outside the note container.

✔ Tips

■ When you type a new note, the text will not wrap until it bumps into the right page margin or another note container. To force a wrap at a more appropriate note width, resize the note container by moving the cursor over its right edge and dragging to the left or right (**Figure 23.2**). The text rewraps to match the container's width.

■ You can resize a note container after typing the note or at any time after entering the note's first character.

■ You can change a note's position on the page. Move the cursor over the container's top edge, and then click and drag to reposition the note (**Figure 23.3**).

■ To create a note with specific formatting, choose font, size, style, and other options from the Formatting toolbar (**Figure 23.4**) immediately after setting the text insertion mark in Step 2.

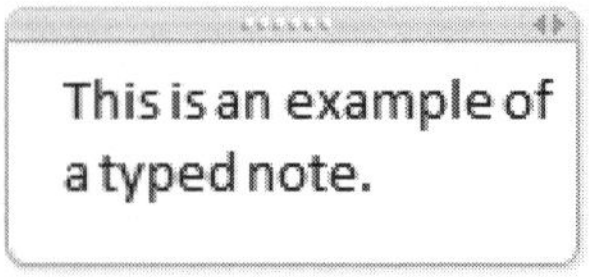

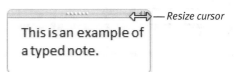

Figure 23.1 This is what a typed note looks like.

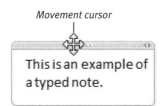

— *Resize cursor*

Figure 23.2 To change the width of a note, click and drag using this cursor.

Movement cursor

Figure 23.3 To change the position of a note, you can drag it to another location on the page.

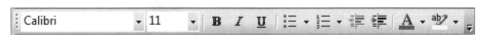

Figure 23.4 The Formatting toolbar.

Record icon

Figure 23.5 To begin recording, choose Record Audio Only from this icon on the Standard toolbar.

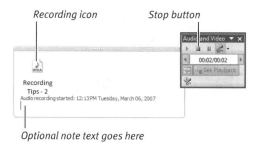

Recording icon   Stop button

Optional note text goes here

Figure 23.6 Record your note, and then click Stop.

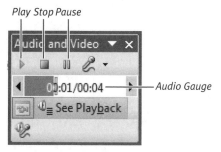

Play Stop Pause

Audio Gauge

Figure 23.7 Click icons in the Audio and Video Recording toolbar to control playback.

■ You can even create audio clips when OneNote isn't running. Right-click the OneNote icon in the notification area of the taskbar, and choose Start Recording Audio from the pop-up menu. When you're done, close the Audio and Video Recording toolbar and the note window. The audio note is added to a new page in Unfiled Notes.

Recording an Audio Note

If you have a microphone connected to your PC, you can add audio notes to any page.

To create an audio note:

1. Click in the spot where you want to place the audio note.

2. On the Standard toolbar, click the Record toolbar icon and choose Record Audio Only from the icon's drop-down menu (**Figure 23.5**).

   The Audio and Video Recording toolbar appears (**Figure 23.6**). Recording begins immediately.

3. Speak into the microphone to record the note. When you're done, click Stop and close the Audio and Video Recording toolbar.

4. *Optional:* You can type explanatory text into the note container.

To play an audio note:

◆ *Do any of the following:*

   ▲ Double-click the recording icon in the note container.

   ▲ Move the cursor over the *Audio recording started* text, and click the tiny Play icon that appears to the left of the note container.

   ▲ Right-click in the note container, and choose Play from the pop-up menu.

   The Audio and Video Recording toolbar appears (**Figure 23.7**) and the note plays. Click Stop to end the playback, and close the Audio and Video Recording toolbar.

✔ Tips

■ To play a note from a point other than the beginning, click in the Audio Gauge where you want to start playback, and then click Play.

RECORDING AN AUDIO NOTE

Recording a Video Note

Use the same procedure to record a video note that you use when creating audio notes. Video notes require a connected desktop camera. If you also have a microphone, the note will include any audio commentary you make at the time of the recording.

To create a video note:

1. Click in the spot where you want to place the video note.

2. On the Standard toolbar, click the Record toolbar icon and choose Record Video from the icon's drop-down menu (see Figure 23.5).

   The Audio and Video Recording toolbar appears, as does a Video window (**Figure 23.8**). Recording begins immediately.

3. When you're done recording, click the Stop button and close the Audio and Video Recording toolbar.

4. *Optional:* As is the case with other types of notes, you can type explanatory text into the note container.

To play a video note:

◆ *Do any of the following:*

   ▲ Double-click the recording icon in the note container.

   ▲ Move the cursor over the *Video recording started* text, and click the Play button that appears to the left of the note container.

   ▲ Right-click in the note container, and choose Play from the pop-up menu.

   The Audio and Video Recording toolbar and the Video window appear, and the note plays. When you're done, click Stop to close the Video window, and close the Audio and Video Recording toolbar.

Audio and Video Recording toolbar

Video window

Figure 23.8 The process of recording a video note is the same as that of recording an audio note.

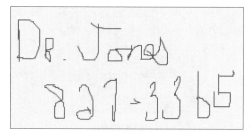

Figure 23.10 You can create text with a Tablet PC's stylus or another pointing device.

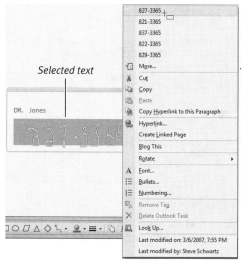

Selected text

Figure 23.11 Right-click selected text and choose the replacement text from the pop-up menu.

Creating Handwritten Notes

If you have a Tablet PC or a drawing tablet, you can add free-form drawings and hand-written text to note pages. (If you like, you can also create such notes using a mouse, a trackball, or another pointing device.)

To create a handwritten note:

1. *Do one of the following:*
   - ▲ On the Standard toolbar, click the Drawing Toolbar icon. The Drawing toolbar appears at the bottom of the window (**Figure 23.9**, page bottom).
   - ▲ Choose View > My Pens Toolbar. A palette of drawing pens appears on the left edge of the window.
   - ▲ From the View > Toolbars submenu, choose Drawing Tools, My Pens, or Writing Tools.

2. From one of these toolbars, choose a pen color and line width.

3. Use your stylus or other drawing/pointing device to write the note (**Figure 23.10**).

4. *Optional:* To convert the handwritten text to normal text, select the Type/Selection Tool (see Figure 23.9). Select each word to convert, right-click it, and then choose the replacement text from the pop-up menu that appears (**Figure 23.11**).

✔ Tips

- ■ To selectively remove handwriting, use the Eraser tool.

- ■ Select shapes from the Drawing toolbar to draw shapes anywhere on the page.

Type/Selection Tool   *Pen*

Eraser

Figure 23.9 The Drawing (or Drawing Tools) toolbar.

Copy-and-Paste and Drag-and-Drop

Text and images from which you want to create notes may occasionally reside in other documents. You can generally use copy-and-paste or drag-and-drop to move a copy of the material onto a note page.

To add material using copy-and-paste:

1. In the document containing the material you want to copy, *do one of the following:*

   ▲ To copy text or an object, select the text or object (**Figure 23.12**), and choose Edit > Copy or press Ctrl C.

   ▲ To copy an image in an image-editing or image-viewing program, choose Edit > Copy or press Ctrl C.

   A copy of the text, object, or image is placed on the Windows Clipboard, making it available for pasting.

2. In OneNote, switch to the page where you want to add the material.

3. Click to set the text insertion mark where you want to paste the new material.

4. Choose Edit > Paste or press Ctrl V.

   The text, object, or image is added to the note page (**Figure 23.13**). Move or resize the material as needed.

✔ Tips

■ When you paste text (see Figure 23.13), a Paste Options icon may appear. Click it to specify how you want the pasted text to be formatted (**Figure 23.14**).

■ You can copy a *portion* of an image in an image-editing program by selecting the portion before issuing the Copy command.

■ You can also use copy-and-paste to add material to existing notes.

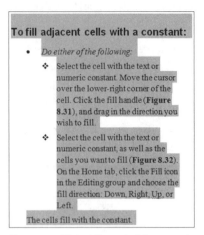

Figure 23.12 Select the material you want to copy, such as this Microsoft Word text.

Paste Options

Figure 23.13 The pasted material appears at the text insertion mark. In the case of pasted text, a new note is created.

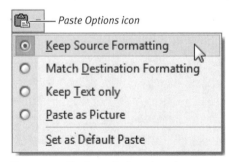

Figure 23.14 The Paste Options drop-down menu.

Note page

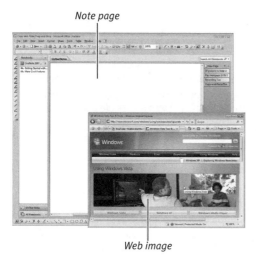

Web image

Figure 23.15 In this example, we'll drag an image from a Web page onto a OneNote note page.

Figure 23.16 If the selected material can be dragged into OneNote, this special cursor appears on the note page.

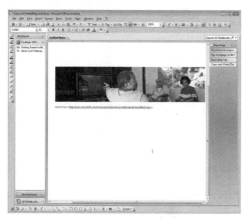

Figure 23.17 The Web image is now part of the note page.

To add material using drag-and-drop:

1. Open a document in any drag-and-drop enabled application.

   Only certain Windows applications, such as Office and Internet Explorer, support drag-and-drop. Refer to the documentation of each application for information.

2. Arrange and resize the document and OneNote window so both are visible (**Figure 23.15**). Make the note page that will receive the material active.

3. Select the material in the document that you want to copy into OneNote.

   Selected items can include text, objects, images, or a combination of material.

4. Using the left mouse button, drag the material onto the note page. If the material can be copied via drag-and-drop, a boxed plus (+) symbol is added to the cursor (**Figure 23.16**).

   The material is added to the note page (**Figure 23.17**).

✔ Tips

- Even if an application doesn't support drag-and-drop, copy-and-paste will often work.

- Web designers sometimes place restrictions on images, preventing them from being copied.

- If you're running Windows Vista and you attempt to drag Web content into OneNote, a permissions dialog box may appear. Click the Allow button to enable Web material to be added to OneNote.

- If you paste or use drag-and-drop to copy a Web page hyperlink onto a note page, the link will be clickable in OneNote, too.

COPY-AND-PASTE AND DRAG-AND-DROP

Creating Notes from Outlook Items

As mentioned in Chapter 22, you can create a note from any Outlook email message, contact record, or appointment. Rather than using copy-and-paste or drag-and-drop, all you have to do is issue the appropriate Outlook command.

To create a new note in Outlook:

◆ *Do one of the following:*

▲ In an open email message, contact record, or appointment window, click the Send to OneNote, Meeting Notes, or Contact Notes toolbar icon (**Figure 23.18**), respectively.

▲ With the Outlook item selected, click the OneNote icon in the Standard toolbar (**Figure 23.19**) to create a note from the material.

If OneNote isn't currently running, it launches. The Outlook material is added to a new page in Unfiled Notes.

✔ Tip

■ You can also create a note from an Outlook email message by right-clicking its header in the message list and choosing Send to OneNote from the pop-up menu (**Figure 23.20**).

Send to OneNote

Figure 23.18 In an open message, appointment, or contact window, you can click the OneNote toolbar icon to create a note from the material.

OneNote icon

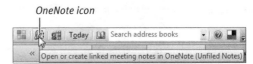

Figure 23.19 With a message, appointment, or contact selected in its list, click the OneNote icon in the Standard toolbar to create a new note.

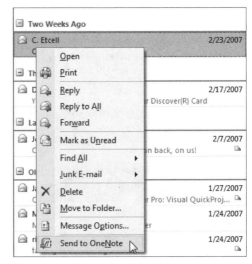

Figure 23.20 You can also right-click a message header and choose Send to OneNote from the pop-up menu that appears.

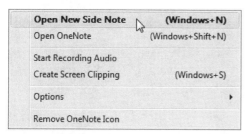

Figure 23.21 You can create side notes, screen clippings, and audio notes by choosing commands from this pop-up menu.

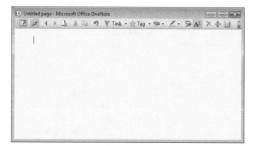

Figure 23.22 Create a new side note in this window.

Toolbar Options icon

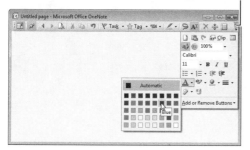

Figure 23.23 Click the Toolbar Options icon to reveal additional toolbar commands.

Notes without OneNote

You can even create notes when OneNote isn't running. Using the OneNote icon in the notification area of the Windows taskbar, you can create *side notes* (typed and other notes made in a special window) or *screen clippings* (graphic notes from screen captures). Each note is appended to the Unfiled Notes list.

To create a side note:

1. *Do one of the following:*
   ▲ Click the OneNote icon in the notification area of the taskbar.
   ▲ Right-click the OneNote icon in the notification area of the taskbar, and choose Open New Side Note from the pop-up menu (**Figure 23.21**).
   ▲ While holding down the Windows key, press $\boxed{\text{N}}$.
   An Untitled page note window appears (**Figure 23.22**).

2. By typing and clicking toolbar icons, create the typed, handwritten, audio, or video note.

3. When you're finished, close the window. The note is added to Unfiled Notes. You'll see it the next time you run OneNote.

✔ Tips

- To view the entire toolbar, widen the note window. As an alternative, you can choose the additional commands by clicking the Toolbar Options icon at the right end of the toolbar (**Figure 23.23**).

- By clicking the Previous Page and Next Page icons, you can view (and, optionally, edit) all other notes that are stored in Unfiled Notes.

NOTES WITHOUT ONENOTE

To create a screen-clipping note:

1. Display the document or window from which to create the screen clipping.

2. *Do either of the following:*
   ▲ Right-click the OneNote icon in the notification area of the taskbar and choose Create Screen Clipping from the pop-up menu (see Figure 23.21).
   ▲ While holding down the Windows key, press Ⓢ.
   The screen turns hazy.

3. Using the screen-clipping cursor, drag a rectangular selection over the material you want to capture (**Figure 23.24**).

   When you release the mouse button, the selected area is made into a screen clipping and is added as a new item in Unfiled Notes (**Figure 23.25**).

✔ Tips

■ To change the behavior of side notes and screen clippings, right-click the OneNote icon and choose a command from the Options submenu (see Figure 23.21).

■ You can initiate a screen clipping from *within* OneNote by clicking the Clip icon on the Standard toolbar. While you're selecting the screen-clipping material, OneNote hides itself to reveal the other items and documents on the Desktop.

Screen-clipping selection

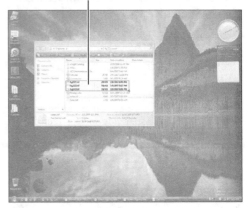

Figure 23.24 Drag-select the material you wish to clip, such as this partial file list.

Figure 23.25 The screen clipping is added as a graphic note on a new Unfiled Notes page.

EMBELLISHING AND EDITING NOTES

Although everyone starts using OneNote in the same basic way, you'll quickly become dissatisfied with unformatted notes presented on stark white pages. In this chapter, you'll learn to improve your notes and pages in these ways:

- ◆ Apply paragraph and character formatting to text notes

- ◆ Apply attractive templates to new pages

- ◆ Insert images from your hard disk

- ◆ Add tables

- ◆ Insert clickable hyperlinks that display Web pages, create new email messages, and open files on your hard disk

- ◆ Edit note text, add date/time stamps, and correct spelling errors

Using Page Templates

OneNote includes a nice assortment of templates from which you can create attractive note pages.

To create a page from a template:

1. *Do one of the following:*

   ▲ Choose File > New > Page from Template.

   ▲ Click the New icon on the Standard toolbar and choose Page from Template from the drop-down menu.

   ▲ Click the New Page icon above the page list and choose More Template Choices and Options.

   The Templates task pane appears to the right of the page list (**Figure 24.1**).

2. Expand template categories as necessary and click the template you want to use.

   A new page appears, formatted with the selected template (**Figure 24.2**).

3. When you're done using the Templates pane, click its close icon (X) to dismiss it.

✔ Tips

■ If you want to create all new pages using a particular template, select the template name from the Choose default template drop-down list (see Figure 24.1).

■ The New Page drop-down menu lists the templates you've recently used, simplifying the process of applying them to other new pages.

■ To view and download additional templates, click the Templates on Office Online text link (see Figure 24.1).

■ You can add a memo-pad background to any page by clicking the Show/Hide Rule Lines icon on the Writing Tools toolbar.

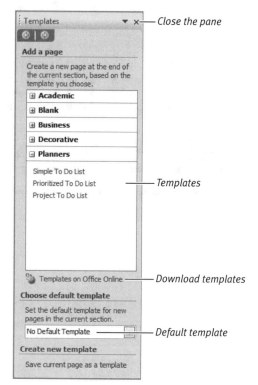

— Close the pane
— Templates
— Download templates
— Default template

Figure 24.1 Templates pane.

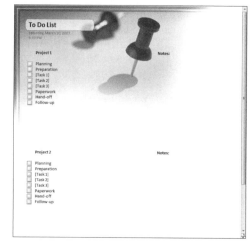

Figure 24.2 This to-do list template features a gradient background, graphics, and clickable check boxes.

USING PAGE TEMPLATES

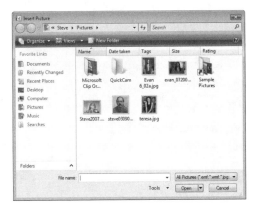

Figure 24.3 Select a picture and click Open.

— Drag cursor

Figure 24.4 Drag a corner handle.

Move handle

Figure 24.5 Drag the move handle.

Inserting Images from Disk

In addition to using copy-and-paste or drag-and-drop to add images to notebook pages, you can insert image files from disk.

To insert an image from disk:

1. Set the text insertion mark where you want to add the image.

   You can also click inside an existing note container to add the image to that note.

2. Choose Insert > Pictures > From Files. The Insert Picture dialog box appears (**Figure 24.3**).

3. Navigate to the folder that contains the desired picture or image file.

4. Select a picture to insert, and click Open. The picture appears on the note page.

5. *Optional:* To change the picture's size proportionately, select the picture and drag a corner handle (**Figure 24.4**).

6. *Optional:* To move the picture to a new location, *do one of the following:*

   ▲ Click the *move handle* to the left of the picture and drag (**Figure 24.5**).

   ▲ When you move the cursor over the edge of an unselected picture (see Figure 24.5) or anywhere over a selected picture, the cursor changes to a plus. Click and drag the picture to its new location.

✔ Tips

■ You can insert images directly from a video camera or scanner. Choose Insert > Pictures > From Scanner or Camera.

■ To delete an image, select it and then choose Edit > Delete ([Del]).

■ The Tag menu contains many useful graphic elements that you can insert.

Inserting and Working with Tables

A *table* (an array of rows and columns) is another type of element you can include in a note container. Like Word tables, a OneNote table can have variable-width columns and contain *nested tables* (tables within tables).

To insert a table onto a note page:

1. Set the text insertion mark at the spot on the page where you want to add the table.

   You can insert a table as a new note container or add it within an existing note.

2. *Do one of the following:*

   ▲ Click the Insert Table icon on the Standard toolbar, and highlight the desired number of rows and columns.

   ▲ Choose Table > Insert Table (**Figure 24.6**). The Insert Table dialog box appears (**Figure 24.7**). Enter numbers in the Number of columns and Number of rows text boxes, and click OK.

   The table appears on the note page (**Figure 24.8**).

✔ Tips

- If you've created a table in Word, you can add it to OneNote via copy-and-paste.

- You can insert an Excel cell range as a OneNote table using copy-and-paste or drag-and-drop.

- To add an Excel *chart* to OneNote, you *must* use copy-and-paste.

- In addition to typed and pasted text, a table cell can contain a picture, a link to a document, or even another table.

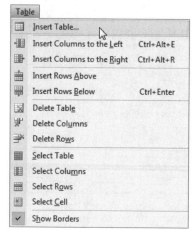

Figure 24.6 Choose table-related commands from the Table menu.

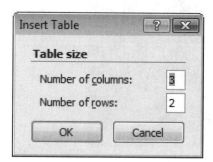

Figure 24.7 Specify the number of rows and columns, and click OK.

Figure 24.8 The new table appears.

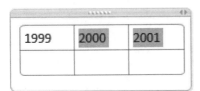

Figure 24.9 To add two columns at the end of this table, I selected two cells to the left of where I wanted the new columns. Then I chose Table > Insert Columns to the Right.

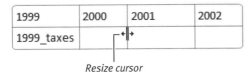

Resize cursor

Figure 24.10 Click and drag a column's right border to change the column's width.

To modify a table:

◆ **Enter data.** Enter data in a table as you would in a Word table or an Excel worksheet. Click in the cell in which you want to enter data or press Tab/Shift Tab to move from cell to cell. (When possible, columns automatically widen to accommodate the entered text.)

◆ **Delete rows or columns.** To delete a single row or column, select a cell in the row or column (or select the entire row or column), and then choose Table > Delete Rows or Table > Delete Columns. To delete multiple rows or columns, select cells in the rows or columns to be deleted prior to choosing the Delete command.

◆ **Delete a table.** Select a cell in the table or nested table that you want to delete, and choose Table > Delete Table.

◆ **Add rows or columns.** To insert a single row or column, select a cell in the row or column (or select the entire row or column), and then choose a Table > Insert Rows or Table > Insert Columns command (see Figure 24.6). To insert multiple rows or columns, select contiguous cells that match the number of rows or columns to insert (**Figure 24.9**) prior to choosing the Insert command.

◆ **Change column widths.** Move the cursor over the right edge of the column whose width you want to change (**Figure 24.10**). Click and drag to the left or right to set the new width. (When widening columns, it may also be necessary to widen the note container.)

continues on next page

✔ Tips

■ To correct an inadvertent row or column deletion, immediately choose Edit > Undo Delete ((Ctrl)(Z)).

■ If you (Tab) out of a table's bottom-right cell, a new row automatically appears.

■ Cell data can be formatted in the same manner as note data. You can selectively apply character and paragraph formatting as you wish. Formatting is discussed later in this chapter.

■ Each table row displays its own move handle to the left of the table (**Figure 24.11**). Click the move handle to select the entire row. (Note that the move handle works in a different manner when a table contains nested tables.)

■ The Table menu (see Figure 24.6) also contains Select commands to help you select table components based on the currently selected cell or cells.

■ To show or hide table borders, select any cell in the table and choose Table > Show Borders. The current border state is indicated by the presence/absence of a check mark beside the command.

■ To insert a date/time stamp into a cell (or anywhere else on a note page), choose Insert > Date and Time.

Move handle

Figure 24.11 Click this move handle to select all cells in the second row.

INSERTING AND WORKING WITH TABLES

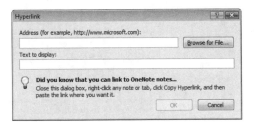

Figure 24.12 Enter a hyperlink (in the proper form) and the text that will represent the link in your note.

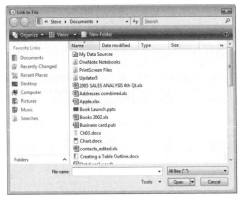

Figure 24.13 Select the document or program to which you want to link.

Ch03: Cannibalizing an Old Computer

Figure 24.14 When clicked, this hyperlink opens a Word document on my computer.

Inserting Hyperlinks

A note can also contain *hyperlinks* that— when clicked—do one of the following:

◆ Open your browser to a specific Web page

◆ Address an email message to a particular recipient

◆ Open a document from your hard disk in the program in which it was created

◆ Launch a program from your hard disk

◆ Go to a notebook, section, or page

To insert a Web, email, document, or program hyperlink:

1. Set the text insertion mark at the spot where you want to insert the hyperlink.

2. Choose Insert > Hyperlink.

   The Hyperlink dialog box appears (**Figure 24.12**).

3. *Do one of the following:*

   ▲ **Web-page link.** Enter the *URL* (Web page address) in the Address box in the form http://*address*, such as http://www.microsoft.com.

   ▲ **Email link.** Enter the recipient's email address in the Address box in the form mailto://*address*, such as mailto://steve762@interworld.net.

   ▲ **Document or program link.** To locate the document or program, click the Browse for File button (see Figure 24.12). In the Link to File dialog box (**Figure 24.13**), select the document or program, and click Open.

4. *Optional:* In the Text to display box of the Hyperlink dialog box, enter the text that will represent the hyperlink in your note.

5. Click OK.

   The hyperlink appears (**Figure 24.14**).

To insert a link to a notebook, section, or page:

1. If the link references a notebook that isn't open, choose File > Open > Notebook. In the Open Notebook dialog box, open the OneNote Notebooks folder, select the notebook, and click Open.

2. Copy the link-to item (notebook, section, or page) by *doing one of the following:*

   ▲ **Notebook.** In the navigation bar or the All Notebooks tab, right-click the notebook name and choose Copy Hyperlink to this Notebook from the pop-up menu (**Figure 24.15**).

   ▲ **Section.** In the navigation bar, select the notebook that contains the section to which you want to link. Right-click the section name in the navigation bar, the All Notebooks tab, or at the top of the OneNote window and choose Copy Hyperlink to this Section from the pop-up menu.

   ▲ **Page.** Switch to the section that contains the page to which you want to link. In the page list, right-click the page name and choose Copy Hyperlink to this Page from the pop-up menu.

3. Switch to the page where you want to insert the hyperlink.

   The link can be placed anywhere in the same or a different notebook.

4. Set the text insertion mark where you want to insert the hyperlink.

   A hyperlink can be created as a new note container or within an existing container.

5. Choose Edit > Paste or press Ctrl V.

   The hyperlink appears (**Figure 24.16**). Clicking a link to a section or page in any open notebook switches to that section or page. Clicking any link to a closed notebook causes the notebook to open.

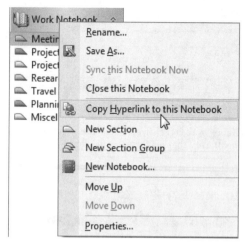

Figure 24.15 To copy the link information to the Clipboard, right-click the element and choose the Copy Hyperlink command from the pop-up menu.

Figure 24.16 When the cursor moves over a hyperlink, it changes to the familiar pointing hand. A ToolTip with link information also appears.

INSERTING HYPERLINKS

Figure 24.17 Link to an Excel worksheet.

To insert a file link as an icon:

1. Set the text insertion mark at the spot where you want to insert the file link.

2. Choose Insert > Files.

   A file dialog box appears, similar to the Link to File dialog box (see Figure 24.13).

3. Select a file and click Insert. (You can also insert *multiple* files by Ctrl-clicking each one prior to clicking Insert.)

   The file icon(s) appear on the page (**Figure 24.17**). To later open a file in the program in which it was created, double-click its icon.

✔ Tips

- Because hyperlinks can be used to launch programs and open documents, you could create a page on which you've added links to all documents related to a project.

- Rather than insert a link to a document, you may want to insert an *image* of the document that you can read in OneNote. Choose Insert > Files as Printouts. In the file dialog box that appears, select the document and click Insert. The creating program opens the document, creates a graphic *print file* from it, and then adds it to OneNote.

INSERTING HYPERLINKS

Editing and Formatting Notes

Like other documents, you can freely change the content or formatting of notes.

To edit note text:

◆ **Insert text.** Click to set the text insertion mark where you want to add the new text and then type.

◆ **Delete text.** Select the text to be deleted and press (Backspace), (Del), or (Delete).

◆ **Replace text.** Select the text to be replaced and then type the new text.

◆ **Move text within a page.** Select the text to be moved and drag it to the new location. You can use this procedure to rearrange text in a note, move it into a different note, or create a new note by dragging the text into an empty area.

◆ **Move or copy text to a different page.** Select the text, and *do one of the following*:

 ▲ To move the text to a new location, choose Edit > Cut, click the Cut icon on the Standard toolbar (**Figure 24.18**), right-click the text and choose Cut from the pop-up menu, or press (Ctrl)(X).

 ▲ To copy the text to a new location, choose Edit > Copy, click the Copy icon on the Standard toolbar, right-click the text and choose Copy from the pop-up menu, or press (Ctrl)(C).

 Switch to the destination page, and set the text insertion mark where you want to add the text. It can be added to an existing note or used to create a new note (by clicking an empty spot on the page). Complete the process by choosing Edit > Paste, clicking the Paste icon on the Standard toolbar, or pressing (Ctrl)(V).

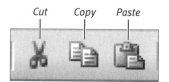

Figure 24.18 You can click an icon on the Standard toolbar to cut, copy, or paste.

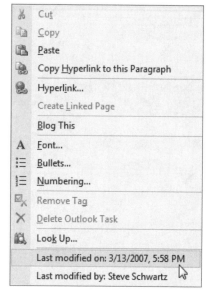

Figure 24.19 You can insert a Last modified stamp by choosing it from the bottom of the pop-up menu.

"Last Modified" Stamps

For important notes or notes in shared notebooks, it's often helpful to show when and by whom a note was last modified. To add this information to a note, right-click in the note and choose the Last modified date/time stamp or author name from the pop-up menu (**Figure 24.19**).

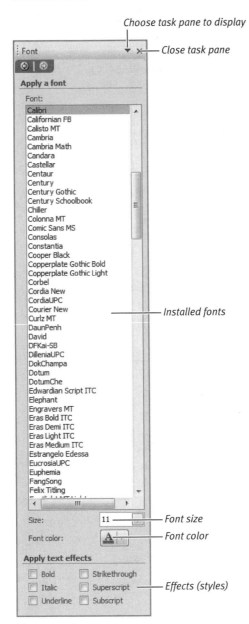

Choose task pane to display

Close task pane

Installed fonts

Font size

Font color

Effects (styles)

Figure 24.21 Font task pane.

To apply paragraph formatting:

1. Within a note, select the paragraph(s) you want to format.

2. *Do either of the following:*

   ▲ Click commands on the Formatting toolbar (**Figure 24.20, bottom**). If the toolbar isn't displayed, choose View > Toolbars > Formatting.

   ▲ Right-click the paragraph selection and choose paragraph-formatting commands from the pop-up menu.

To apply character formatting:

1. Within a note, select the text to format.

2. *Do either of the following:*

   ▲ Click commands on the Formatting toolbar (see Figure 24.20).

   ▲ Choose Format > Font ([Ctrl][D]). The Font task pane appears (**Figure 24.21**). Select character-formatting commands from the task pane.

✔ Tips

■ To add paragraph-alignment commands to the Formatting toolbar, click the Toolbar Options button at the end of the toolbar (see Figure 24.20). Choose Add or Remove Buttons > Formatting, followed by an alignment command. (Checked commands are displayed on the toolbar.)

■ To open *any* task pane, you can choose View > Task Pane ([Ctrl][F1]). With a task pane displayed, choose the specific pane you want to use from the drop-down menu to the right of the pane title.

Toolbar Options

Figure 24.20 The Formatting toolbar.

EDITING AND FORMATTING NOTES

Correcting Spelling Errors

By default, OneNote flags suspected spelling errors as you type, marking them with a wavy red underline (**Figure 24.22**). You can also conduct a normal, full-page spelling check in the Spelling task pane.

Figure 24.22 A suspected error.

To enable/disable automatic spell checking:

1. Choose Tools > Spelling Options.

The Spelling Options dialog box appears.

2. Add or remove the check mark from Check spelling as you type, and click OK.

To correct a flagged spelling error:

◆ Right-click the word (**Figure 24.23**), and *do one of the following:*

▲ Choose the correct word from the suggested replacements.

▲ Choose Ignore if the word is correct.

▲ Choose Add to Dictionary to instruct OneNote to accept the spelling and remember it for other spell checks.

Figure 24.23 Right-click a flagged word and choose a handling option.

To perform a spell check:

1. *Optional:* Select text to restrict the spell check to only the selected text.

2. Choose Tools > Spelling > Spelling, press F7, or right-click a flagged word and choose Spelling (see Figure 24.23).

The Spelling task pane appears (**Figure 24.24**).

3. For each identified error, *do one of the following:*

▲ Select a replacement word and click Change.

▲ Manually correct the error in the text box and click Change.

▲ Click Ignore or Add to Dictionary.

Figure 24.24 Spelling task pane.

✔ Tip

■ By default, AutoCorrect is also enabled, instructing OneNote to instantly correct common typos and misspellings. To view or change AutoCorrect options, click the AutoCorrect Options text link at the bottom of the Spelling task pane.

Managing Notes

In previous chapters, you learned to create sections and pages; create typed, audio, video, and handwritten notes; edit and format note text; and insert images, tables, and hyperlinks.

In this final OneNote chapter, we'll wrap things up by exploring these techniques to help organize and manage your notes:

◆ Rearrange notebooks, sections, and pages

◆ Move sections and notebook pages

◆ Create section groups and page groups

◆ Delete notes and objects from pages

◆ Assign passwords to sections that contain sensitive material

◆ Search open notebooks for text, audio, video, and graphic notes that contain a particular text string

◆ Print select notebook pages

Rearranging Notebooks, Sections, Pages

Normally, section tabs within a notebook and page tabs within a section are arranged in creation order. Notebooks are listed in the in the navigation bar in the order in which they were opened. You are free to change the page, section, or notebook order as you like. Since OneNote remembers the changes, they'll be in effect in future sessions, too.

To rearrange open notebooks:

1. *Do either of the following:*
   - ▲ In the navigation bar, drag the note-book's tab up or down to a new position (**Figure 25.1**).
   - ▲ Click the All Notebooks tab at the bottom of the navigation bar, and drag the notebook's title to a new position.

2. Release the mouse button to complete the move.

To rearrange sections in a notebook:

1. If the notebook isn't open, choose File > Open > Notebook.

2. Select the notebook's tab in the navigation bar or from All Notebooks pop-out list at the bottom of the navigation bar.

3. Drag the section tab at the top of the window (**Figure 25.2**), in the navigation bar, or in the All Notebooks pop-out list to a new position in the tab list. Release the mouse button to complete the move.

To rearrange pages in a section:

1. Switch to the section that contains the pages you want to rearrange.

2. In the page list, click the page you wish to move and drag it up or down to its new location (**Figure 25.3**). Release the mouse button to complete the move.

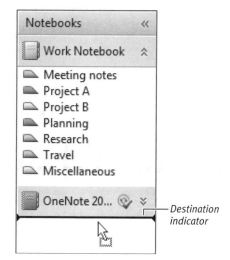

Destination indicator

Figure 25.1 The Work Notebook can be dragged to the bottom of the list in the navigation bar.

Destination indicator

Figure 25.2 You can rearrange sections by dragging a section tab to a new position.

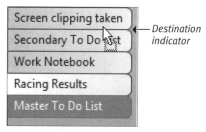

Destination indicator

Figure 25.3 You can drag a page to a new position in the page list.

Page list

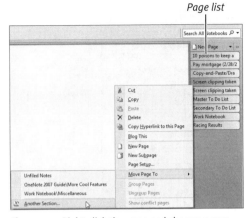

Figure 25.4 Right-click the page and choose a command from the Move Page To submenu.

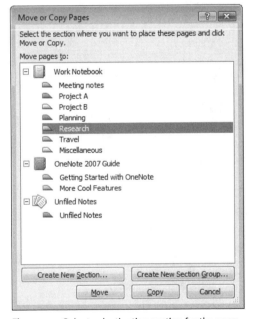

Figure 25.5 Select a destination section for the page.

Moving Notes

Use cut-and-paste to move a note to a different page, section, or notebook.

Moving Pages and Sections

As explained in Chapter 23, whenever you create a side note or screen clipping, it's saved as a new page in Unfiled Notes. Unless these pages are only temporary notes, you'll normally want to move them into other notebooks. Similarly, *any* section or page can be moved into a different notebook or into another section in the current notebook, respectively.

To move an Unfiled Notes page to another section:

1. Select the Unfiled Notes section at the bottom of the navigation bar.

   The pages in Unfiled Notes are displayed in the page list.

2. If the destination notebook isn't listed in the navigation bar, choose File > Open > Notebook and open the notebook.

3. *Do either of the following:*

   ▲ To move pages using drag-and-drop, expand the destination notebook in the navigation bar so its sections are listed. Drag the Unfiled Notes page onto the destination section.

   ▲ Right-click the page, and choose Move Page To from the pop-up menu (**Figure 25.4**). If the destination page is listed among the recently used sections, choose it; otherwise, choose Another Section. In the Move or Copy Pages dialog box (**Figure 25.5**), select the destination section and click Move.

   The page is added to the end of the destination section's page list.

To move a page into a different section:

1. Switch to the section containing the page you want to move.

   The section's pages are displayed in the page list on the right side of the OneNote window.

2. If the destination notebook isn't listed in the navigation bar, choose File > Open > Notebook and open the notebook.

3. *Do either of the following:*

   ▲ To move pages using drag-and-drop, expand the destination notebook in the navigation bar so its sections are listed. Drag the page onto the destination section (**Figure 25.6**).

   ▲ Right-click the page, and choose Move Page To from the pop-up menu. If the destination section is shown among the list of recently used sections, choose it; otherwise, choose Another Section. In the Move or Copy Pages dialog box (see Figure 25.5), select the destination section and click Move.

   The page is added to the end of the destination section's page list.

To move a section into a different notebook:

1. Ensure that both notebooks are listed in the navigation bar.

   If one or both notebooks aren't shown, choose File > Open > Notebook and open the notebook(s).

2. Expand both notebooks in the navigation bar to display their sections.

3. Drag the section from one notebook into the appropriate position in the other notebook (**Figure 25.7**). Release the mouse button to complete the move.

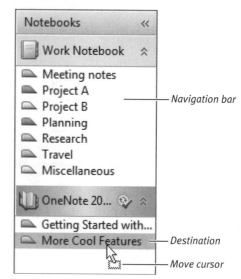

Figure 25.6 Drag the page onto the destination section.

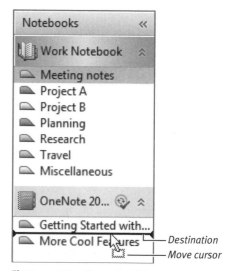

Figure 25.7 Drag the section into position in the other notebook.

✔ Tip

■ To *copy* a note page to a new section, click Copy in the Move or Copy Pages dialog box.

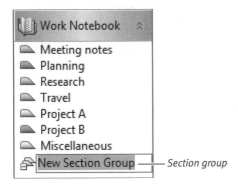

Figure 25.8 The new section group appears at the bottom of the notebook's section list.

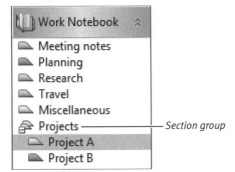

Figure 25.9 I named the section group Projects and dragged the two Project sections into it.

Creating Section Groups

When a notebook is complex or jammed with sections, you can impart additional order to the material by creating section groups. A *section group* is a container for other sections—usually ones with similar or related content.

To create a section group:

1. With the notebook open and active, *do one of the following:*
   - ▲ Choose File > New > Section Group.
   - ▲ Click the New icon in the Standard toolbar and choose Section Group from the drop-down menu.
   - ▲ Right-click the notebook's name or any of its sections and choose New Section Group from the pop-up menu.

   A New Section Group appears at the top of the OneNote window and in the navigation bar (**Figure 25.8**).

2. Name the section group by typing over the temporary name (New Section Group).

3. To add a section to the section group, drag its tab onto the section group name (**Figure 25.9**).

✔ Tips

- ■ Sections within a section group can be reorganized by dragging their tabs to new positions.

- ■ To remove a tab from a section group, drag it into the ungrouped section tabs.

- ■ To delete a section group, right-click its tab in the navigation bar and choose Delete from the pop-up menu. (Note that deleting a section group also deletes all sections contained within it. To avoid deleting the sections, drag them out into the notebook's section list.)

CREATING SECTION GROUPS

Creating Page Groups

Like section groups, you can create *page groups* to organize related pages within a section. The Travel section of the Work notebook (**Figure 25.10**) contains an example of a page group.

To create a page group:

◆ *Do either of the following:*

▲ Rearrange the pages that will form the group, starting with the page that will be the main page and followed by the pages that will become subpages. [Shift]-select the pages, right-click any one of them, and choose Group Pages from the pop-up menu (**Figure 25.11**).

▲ Switch to any normal page (not a subpage). Choose File > New > Subpage ([Ctrl][Shift][N]), click the New toolbar icon and choose Subpage, choose New Subpage from the drop-down menu above the page list, or right-click the page tab and choose New Subpage from the pop-up menu.

✔ Tips

■ To remove a page group, right-click the main page or any of its subpages and choose Ungroup Pages from the pop-up menu that appears.

■ To add new subpages to an existing page group, select the page tab below which you want to add the subpage. *Do one of the following:*

▲ Choose File > New > Subpage ([Ctrl][Shift][N]).

▲ Click the New toolbar icon and choose Subpage.

▲ Choose New Subpage from the drop-down menu above the page list.

▲ Right-click the page tab and choose New Subpage from the pop-up menu.

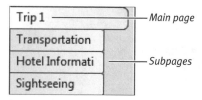

Figure 25.10 A page group consists of a main page and one or more subpages.

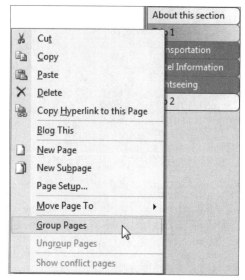

Figure 25.11 Right-click any of the selected pages and choose Group Pages.

Cursor

Figure 25.12 Click a container's top edge to select it.

Cursor

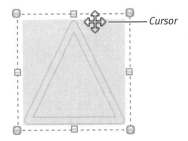

Figure 25.13 Select a floating object by clicking any edge.

Figure 27.14 You can also delete a note container by right-clicking its top edge and choosing Delete.

Combining Notes

Rather than delete a note, you may want to combine its material with that of another note. Drag the note container onto the destination container while pressing Shift. Release the mouse button when the material from the dragged note is in the desired position.

Deleting Notes and Objects

In Chapter 23, you learned how to move and resize note containers. One of the simplest ways to manage your notes and other objects is to *remove* ones you no longer need.

To delete a note container:

1. Select the note container and its material by clicking the container's top edge (**Figure 25.12**).

2. *Do one of the following:*
   ▲ Choose Edit > Delete.
   ▲ Press Del, Delete, or Backspace.
   The note container is removed.

To delete an object:

1. Select the object (an inserted picture or drawn shape, for example) by clicking one of its edges (**Figure 25.13**).

2. *Do one of the following:*
   ▲ Choose Edit > Delete.
   ▲ Press Del, Delete, or Backspace.
   The object is removed.

✔ Tips

■ Another way to delete a note container is to right-click its top edge and choose Delete from the pop-up menu that appears (**Figure 25.14**).

■ To recover from an accidental note or object deletion, immediately choose Edit > Undo Delete (Ctrl Z).

■ See Chapter 22 for instructions on deleting notebooks, sections, and pages.

DELETING NOTES AND OBJECTS

Adding Section Passwords

If a notebook contains sensitive business or personal data, you can add password protection to selected sections.

To password protect a section:

1. Switch to the section to which you want to add password protection.

2. *Do either of the following:*

   ▲ Choose File > Password Protect this Section.

   ▲ Right-click the section tab (at the top of the OneNote window or in the navigation bar) and choose Password Protect this Section from the pop-up menu that appears.

   The Password Protection task pane appears (**Figure 25.15**).

3. Click the Set Password button.

   The Password Protection dialog box appears (**Figure 25.16**).

4. In the Enter Password box, type the password you want to assign to the section. Enter it a second time in the Confirm Password box, and then click OK.

   The Backup Files of Password Protected Section dialog box appears (**Figure 25.17**).

5. Although the current section data and any future backups will be protected, OneNote's *previous* backups of the material are not secure. *Do one of the following:*

   ▲ To delete the old backups, click Delete Existing Backup Files.

   ▲ To retain the unsecured backups, click Keep Existing Backup Files.

✔ Tip

■ OneNote passwords are case sensitive. You'll probably find it simpler if you use all lowercase letters.

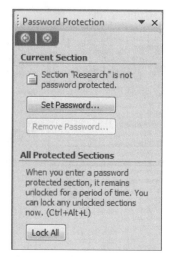

Figure 25.15 Password Protection task pane.

Figure 25.16 Enter the password to use for the selected section.

Figure 25.17 You can delete all backups of the section data that were made prior to password-protecting the material.

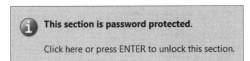

Figure 25.18 This message appears when you try to view a password-protected section.

Figure 25.19 Enter the password for the section and click OK.

Figure 25.20 The Change Password dialog box.

Figure 25.21 The Remove Password dialog box.

To open a protected section:

1. When you click the tab of a password-protected section, a gray page appears (**Figure 25.18**). Click where indicated or press Enter.

   The Protected Section dialog box appears (**Figure 25.19**).

2. Enter the section password and click OK.

   The section remains unprotected until you close the notebook or quit OneNote.

To change the password or remove protection from a section:

1. Open the protected section as described in the previous task list.

2. Choose File > Password Protect this Section.

   The Password Protection task pane opens.

3. *Do one of the following:*

   ▲ **Change password.** Click the Change Password button. In the Change Password dialog box (**Figure 25.20**), enter the current password and the new password. Confirm the change by reentering the new password in the Confirm Password box. Click OK.

   ▲ **Remove password.** To remove protection from the section, click the Remove Password button. Enter the password (**Figure 25.21**) and click OK.

✔ Tips

■ If you're going to be away from your computer for a while and want to secure the OneNote protected sections, click the Lock All button in the Password Protection task pane (see Figure 25.15).

■ To view or change OneNote password preferences, click the Password Options text link at the bottom of the Password Protection task pane.

ADDING SECTION PASSWORDS

Searching for Notes

You can use the Search feature to find notes in any open notebook. If you enable certain options, you can also search for matching text in pictures and audio/video recordings.

To enable/disable text search within pictures:

1. Right-click any picture on a OneNote page.

   A pop-up menu appears (**Figure 25.22**).

2. *Do one of the following:*

   ▲ To enable picture searching, choose a language from the Make Text in Image Searchable submenu.

   ▲ To disable picture searching, choose Disabled from the Make Text in Image Searchable submenu.

To enable/disable text search within audio and video recordings:

1. Choose Tools > Options.

   The Options dialog box appears.

2. Select the Audio and Video category from the list on the left side of the dialog box.

3. In the Audio Search section of the dialog box page (**Figure 25.23**), check or uncheck the option and click OK.

Figure 25.22 Enable or disable the search for text within pictures using this pop-up menu.

Figure 25.23 The state of this check box determines whether OneNote will search recordings for matching spoken text.

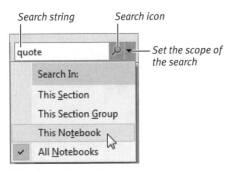

Search string   *Search icon*

Set the scope of the search

Search In:

This **S**ection

This Section **G**roup

This No**t**ebook

✓ All **N**otebooks

Figure 25.24 You perform searches in this component.

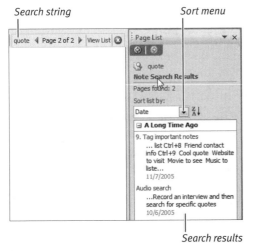

Search string   *Sort menu*

Page List

quote

Note Search Results

Pages found: 2

Sort list by:

Date

☐ **A Long Time Ago**

9. Tag important notes
... list Ctrl+8 Friend contact
info Ctrl+9 Cool quote Website
to visit Movie to see Music to
liste...
11/7/2005

Audio search
...Record an interview and then
search for specific quotes
10/6/2005

Search results

Figure 25.25 Search results appear in the task pane.

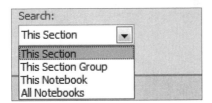

Search:

This Section

This Section
This Section Group
This Notebook
All Notebooks

Figure 25.26 You can change the scope of the current search by choosing an option from this drop-down menu.

To perform a search:

1. *Optional:* To include password-protected sections in the search, unlock them. Otherwise, their material will be excluded.

2. Enter the search string in the Search box at the top of the OneNote window.

3. Set a scope for the search by choosing an option from the Search drop-down menu (**Figure 25.24**).

4. Click the Search icon.

   The results are displayed in the task pane (**Figure 25.25**). The first note page containing a match is displayed. The matching text is highlighted.

5. *Do any of the following:*
   ▲ To sequentially move through the matches, click the Previous Match and Next Match arrows to the right of the search text string.
   ▲ To go directly to a match, click its text in the Page List task pane.

6. *Optional:* Dismiss the task pane by clicking its close box (X).

✔ Tips

■ To change the order of the search results, choose a new option from the Sort list by drop-down menu.

■ To change the scope of the search, choose an option from the Search drop-down menu at the bottom of the Page List (**Figure 25.26**). The search results automatically update to reflect the new scope.

SEARCHING FOR NOTES

Printing Notes

Printing in OneNote is performed one note page at a time. You can optionally preview the output before sending it to the printer.

To print a note page:

1. Switch to the page you want to print.

2. *Optional:* Choose File > Page Setup. The Page Setup task pane appears. Choose a paper size and set other options that you want to apply to the printout.

3. *Do one of the following:*
   ▲ To print to your default printer using the current settings, click the Print toolbar icon. (This option bypasses the Print dialog box.)
   ▲ Choose File > Print. The Print dialog box appears (**Figure 25.27**). Select a printer, review the print options, and click Print.

   The note page prints.

✔ Tip

■ To preview the output before sending it to the printer, choose File > Print Preview. Review options in the Print Preview and Settings dialog box (**Figure 25.28**). Click Print to send the page's data to your printer or click Close to exit from the dialog box without printing.

Selected printer

Figure 25.27 Select a printer, review the options, and click Print.

Preview   Print options

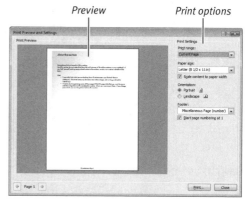

Figure 25.28 As you change settings in the Print Preview and Settings dialog box, the preview changes.

Part VII: Microsoft Publisher

Chapter 26 Getting Started with
Publisher 2007 389

Chapter 27 Distributing and Printing
Publications 409

GETTING STARTED WITH PUBLISHER 2007

26

Publisher is a *desktop publishing* or *layout* program that's used to create *publications*, such as newsletters, flyers, brochures, and business cards. A word-processing document is text-oriented. The text typically extends from the left edge of the page to the right. By contrast, text and images in a publication are *laid out* (arranged) on a page in a manner designed to be visually pleasing. Whereas a word-processing application's emphasis is on making writing as easy as possible, a layout program's emphasis is on simplifying the process of arranging text and graphics.

In Publisher, you can create publications from scratch or by modifying one of the many included templates. Because Publisher users often work *exclusively* with templates, and because modifying a template is the easiest way to learn how to use Publisher, this chapter takes a different approach than the others in this book. Rather than serving as a reference to Publisher essentials, this chapter provides a tutorial in which you'll modify a typical template. In doing so, you'll become comfortable using the basic tools needed to create your own publications.

The Publisher Interface

Unlike the core Office applications, Publisher 2007 more closely resembles the previous Office applications. It relies heavily on menus and toolbars rather than on the new Ribbon. You'll use the components described in this section (**Figure 26.1**) to interact with Publisher and the parts of your publication.

Menus. Choose menu commands or press their keyboard shortcuts to perform program functions and modify selected elements in your publications.

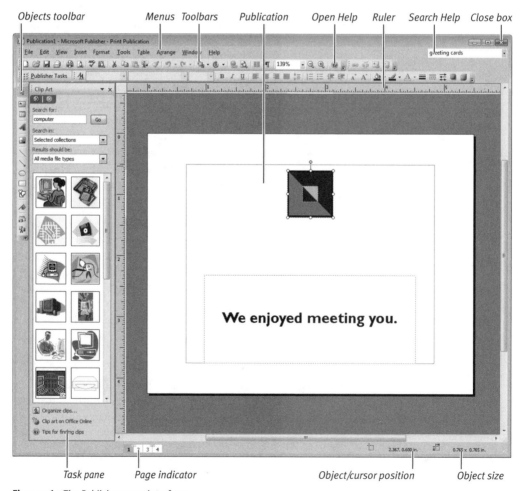

Objects toolbar · Menus · Toolbars · Publication · Open Help · Ruler · Search Help · Close box

Task pane · Page indicator · Object/cursor position · Object size

Figure 26.1 The Publisher 2007 interface.

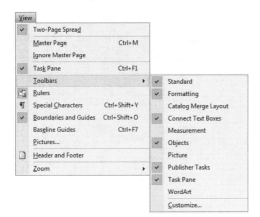

Figure 26.2 Checked toolbar names in the Toolbars submenu are enabled.

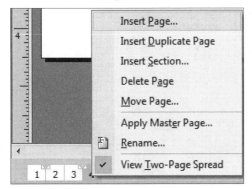

Figure 26.3 To insert new pages, delete pages, or perform other page-related commands, right-click a page icon and choose a command from this pop-up menu.

✔ **Tip**

■ To search Publisher Help for a given topic, type a search text string in the search box above the publication and press Enter.

Toolbars. Toolbars provide ready access to the most common commands, tools, and controls for modifying a publication. To hide or show a toolbar, choose its name from the View > Toolbars submenu (**Figure 26.2**).

Task pane. Performing some actions or choosing certain commands opens a task pane dedicated to the action or command. To switch to a different task pane, select its name from the drop-down list at the top of the pane. To give the publication additional display space, click the task pane's close box (X) to dismiss it.

Publication. A *publication* is a Publisher document. Depending on the type of publication on which you're working, its length can be one or many pages. Every new or opened publication opens in its own window and is represented by a button in the taskbar.

Rulers. To assist with object placement, Publisher provides horizontal and vertical rulers. As you drag an object, you can see the location of its top and left edges on the rulers.

Page indicator. To view a specific page in the current publication, click its icon. You can rearrange pages by dragging the icon representing a page or *spread* (pair of facing pages) to the left or right. Right-click a page icon to access page-related commands (**Figure 26.3**).

Object/cursor position and object size. When an object is selected, these indicators show the object's exact location and size. When nothing is selected, the first indicator shows the cursor's position.

Publisher Help. To open the Publisher Help window, click the Help icon on the Standard toolbar or press F1 . Help works in Publisher as it does in other Office applications.

Close box. Click a publication's close box (X) to close the publication. If it's the only open publication, Publisher quits.

THE PUBLISHER INTERFACE

Creating a Publication

Each time you launch Publisher, you can select a template on which to base a new publication. (To work on an existing publication, choose File > Open or press Ctrl O.)

To create a new publication:

1. To make the templates screen appear (**Figure 26.4**), *do one of the following:*

   ▲ If you just launched Publisher, the templates screen appears.

   ▲ If a publication is already open, choose File > New (Ctrl N).

   The Getting Started category is selected.

2. *Do one of the following:*

   ▲ Select a template category from the Publication Types list.

   ▲ If the desired category is shown among the Popular Publication Types, click its icon.

   In this tutorial, you'll create a postcard to use in a customer mailing. Click the Postcards category or icon. The Postcards templates list appears.

3. Scroll to the We've Moved section of the list and select the Banner Bar template.

4. Select options from the drop-down lists in the Customize and Options pane (**Figure 26.5**):

   ▲ If you've created a *business information set* containing your contact data, select its name from the Business information drop-down list.

   ▲ Choose Address only from the Side 2 information drop-down list.

5. Click Create at the bottom of the pane. The new publication appears.

6. Save the publication. Choose File > Save, click the Save icon (disk) on the Standard toolbar, or press Ctrl S.

Template categories   Popular Publication Types

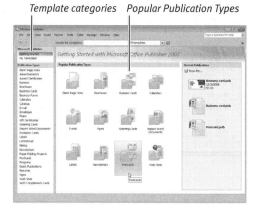

Figure 26.4 You can create a publication based on a template by selecting one from this screen.

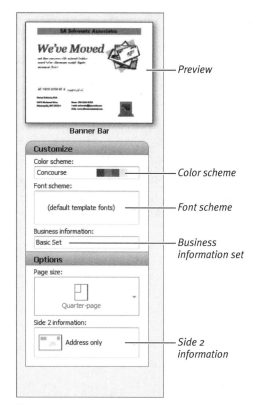

Figure 26.5 You can set options for the publication in this pane.

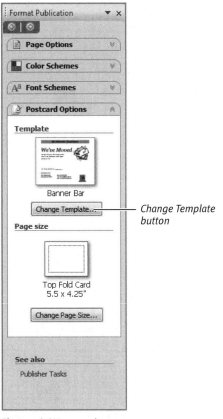

Change Template button

Figure 26.6 You can change templates at any time.

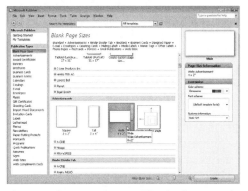

Figure 26.7 You can create a publication from scratch by choosing a paper size.

✔ Tips

■ You can also create a publication by clicking the New icon on the Standard toolbar. However, this creates a publication based on a blank, letter-sized page. To apply a template to the blank publication, click the Change Template button (**Figure 26.6**) in the Format Publication task pane.

  Note that this technique can also be used to apply a different template when you're working on a *non-blank* template.

■ In addition to clicking the New toolbar icon to create a publication from scratch, you can pick a template from the Blank Page Sizes template category (**Figure 26.7**). You can also scroll to the end of any category list and select a blank template that matches your intended paper size.

■ Options in the Customize area (see Figure 26.5) can be set at any time. If you set them before creating the publication, you'll have to rely on the preview to see how they look. Unless you've decided on or standardized on a specific color and font scheme, it's easier to set these options *after* initially creating the publication.

Creating a Business Information Set

Because many templates display your contact information, Publisher allows you to save this data as a *business information set*. You can create different sets to store your work and home data, as well as save variations of a set (with different email addresses, for example).

To create a business information set:

1. Choose Edit > Business Information.

   The Create New Business Information Set dialog box appears (**Figure 26.8**).

2. Type the appropriate data into each text box and remove information that isn't applicable.

3. In the Logo box, *do one of the following:*
   - ▲ If you don't have a logo, click Remove.
   - ▲ To replace the current logo with your organization's logo, click Change. The Insert Picture dialog box appears. Navigate to the folder that contains your logo, select it, and click Insert.

4. Enter a name for this set, and click Save.

   The Business Information dialog box appears (**Figure 26.9**).

5. To enter the saved information into the placeholders in the current publication, click Update Publication.

   The data is copied into the publication (**Figure 26.10**) and the dialog box closes.

✔ Tip

- ■ You can replace the labels in the Phone, fax, and e-mail text box and remove irrelevant ones. As shown in Figure 26.9, I eliminated the Fax line and replaced it with a Web line in order to display the address for my Web site.

Set name   Logo

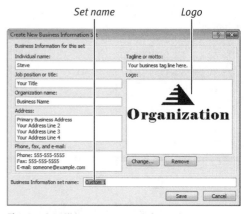

Figure 26.8 Fill in your contact information, enter a name for this set, and click Save.

Defined sets

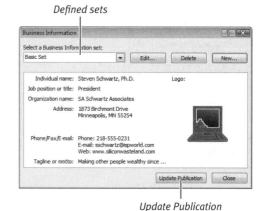

Update Publication

Figure 26.9 The Business Information dialog box shows the data for the current set. To view a different set, choose its name from the drop-down menu.

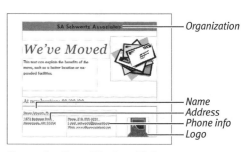

Figure 26.10 The publication with data.

Figure 26.11 To replace placeholder text, start by selecting it.

At new location: 00/00/00

Figure 26.12 Click the date placeholder to select it and then type the actual date.

Replacing Text Placeholders

In addition to the text placeholders that are filled in with your business information data, most templates also contain others that you'll replace with your own text. The techniques explained in this section can be used to modify and format *any* text block.

To replace placeholder text:

1. Click anywhere in the text in the upper placeholder text box (**Figure 26.11**).

   All the placeholder text is selected.

2. Type the replacement text. In this tutorial, type the following:

   To better serve our clients (and take advantage of a massive tax break), we've moved our headquarters to a more modern facility with improved parking.

   The moment you being typing, the placeholder text disappears and is replaced by the new text.

3. Click in the At new location placeholder to select the date (**Figure 26.12**). Replace the date with the following move date: September 1, 2007.

   The placeholder date can be replaced with a date entered in *any* format, such as 09/01/07, 9-1-07, or Sept-01-2007.

Save Often!

It's important to save every publication often or to save multiple copies using the File > Save As command. Because layout work is often experimental ("Let's see what it looks like if I tweak the page by doing these things"), the saves ensure that you can recover if you decide recent changes weren't desirable. Just close the publication without saving and open your most recent save.

To edit business information set text:

1. You can change business information set text in the publication without saving the changes to the set. To see how this works, you can prepare to edit your name text by *doing either of the following:*

   ▲ Click anywhere in the name text.

   ▲ Move the cursor over the name text. An i icon appears above the text. Click the i icon, and choose Convert to Plain Text (**Figure 26.13**).

2. Edit the text. Change the name text by replacing your first name with a nickname or by adding a middle initial, middle name, or salutation/title (Ms., Mr., Dr., or Ph.D., for example).

✔ Tips

■ To save edits made to business information data, choose Save to Business Information Set (see Figure 26.13)

■ When working in publications with larger text blocks, such as a newsletter, you may prefer to edit in Word. Click anywhere in the text block and choose Edit > Edit Story in Microsoft Word. A new Word document opens that contains your text. Make the edits. When you close the Word document window, the changes are transferred to the text block in Publisher.

■ If you've already written text in a text-editing application, you can insert it into the active text block by choosing Insert > Text File. (If you want to *replace* the text in the block with the inserted text, select the text before choosing this command.)

■ To add a new text box to a publication, choose Insert > Text Box or click the Text Box icon on the Objects toolbar. Click and drag to draw the text box (**Figure 26.14**).

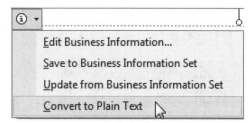

Figure 26.13 You can change business information text to plain text, enabling you to make edits that affect only this publication.

New text box   Drawing cursor

Figure 26.14 To add text to a publication, you can insert additional text boxes. In complex publications, you can link the boxes to one another to flow the text.

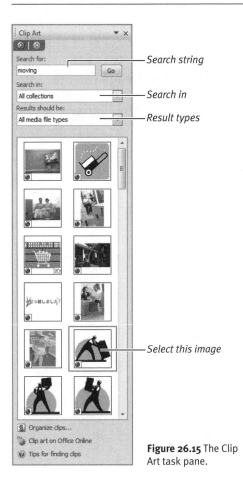

Figure 26.15 The Clip Art task pane.

Replacing and Inserting Artwork

Artwork (photos, clip art, and shapes, for example) figures prominently in most publications. You can insert additional artwork where it's needed, as well as replace images that are included with a given template. As in other Office applications, you can move and resize artwork, too.

To replace artwork:

1. To replace existing artwork, begin by selecting the graphic in your publication.

   In this tutorial, select the stack of letters (see Figure 26.14).

2. Choose an artwork source from the Insert > Picture submenu.

   In this example, choose Clip Art. The Clip Art task pane appears.

3. To locate a suitable clip art image, enter moving in the Search for box, set the Search in box to All collections, and click Go to perform the search.

   Search results are shown as thumbnails in the Clip Art task pane (**Figure 26.15**).

4. Click a clip art image to insert it into your publication.

   The clip art replaces the selected graphic (**Figure 26.16**).

✔ Tip

■ When inserting *additional* artwork, you don't have to select anything. The inserted artwork simply appears on the page. Resize it by dragging a handle, and drag it into position on the page.

Figure 26.16 This is how the postcard should look now.

Previewing the Publication

By default, dotted boundaries surround each object in the publication. Although this enables you to see how objects relate to one another in position and size, the boundaries can make it difficult to envision how the publication will look when printed.

To preview a printed publication:

◆ *Do either of the following:*

   ▲ **Print preview.** Choose File > Print Preview or click the Print Preview icon on the Standard toolbar. A Preview window appears (**Figure 26.17**). When you're done, click the Close toolbar icon.

   ▲ **Hiding/showing boundaries.** To disable or enable boundaries, choose View > Boundaries and Guides or press Ctrl Shift O. Disabling boundaries is visually similar to a print preview.

✔ Tip

■ In Print Preview mode, use toolbar icons (**Figure 26.18**) to do the following:

   ▲ Print the publication.

   ▲ View single or multiple pages.

   ▲ Choose a magnification level from the Zoom drop-down menu.

   ▲ View the publication in color or shades of gray. (Displaying the grayscale version is very useful if you'll be printing on most laser printers.)

   ▲ Close the print preview and restore the normal view of the publication.

Figure 26.17 Issue the Print Preview command to see how a publication will look when printed.

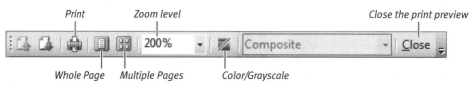

Print   *Zoom level*   *Close the print preview*

Whole Page   *Multiple Pages*   *Color/Grayscale*

Figure 26.18 The Print Preview toolbar.

Handles

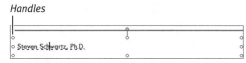

Figure 26.19 The name is in its own text box. To select a text box, click anywhere in its text.

Fill Color

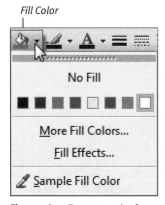

Figure 26.20 To copy a color from an item to the currently selected item, choose Sample Fill Color.

Figure 26.21 The name text box is now filled with the same color as the company name text box.

✔ Tips

- To apply a color to an item without sampling another object, click a color swatch or choose More Fill Colors (see Figure 26.20).

- To remove the fill color from an item, choose No Fill (see Figure 26.20).

Making Minor Changes

The print preview and disabled boundaries suggest several changes you can make to improve the design:

- The space between the name and address looks odd. By filling the name text box with color, the separation won't be so apparent. In addition, because the text box extends above both address components, a colored box will visually tie them together.

- The logo is too low on the page and its color doesn't blend well with the other design elements.

- Some text could benefit from additional formatting.

Coloring the name text box

As you see in the company name text box (see Figure 26.17), adding a fill color to a text box can do a marvelous job of drawing the viewer's eye to important text. To maintain consistency in the design, you'll apply the same fill to the name text box.

To add a fill color to a text box:

1. Click anywhere in the text box's text. (In this instance, click your name in the bottom part of the postcard.)

   Handles appear around the text box to show it's selected (**Figure 26.19**).

2. Click the Fill Color icon on the Formatting toolbar and choose Sample Fill Color from the drop-down menu (**Figure 26.20**).

   An eyedropper cursor appears.

3. Click any blue area in the company name bar near the top of the publication.

   Doing so samples its color and then applies the color to the selected text box (**Figure 26.21**).

Moving the logo

As initially placed, the bottom of this logo is well below the baseline of the adjacent text. It will look better if it's moved up so its top is in line with the top of the name text box.

To move an object:

◆ *Do one of the following:*

▲ Select the name text box and the logo by Shift-clicking the two objects (**Figure 26.22**). Choose Arrange > Align or Distribute > Align Top.

▲ Select the name text box. Note the distance of its top edge from the top of the page (**Figure 26.23**). Shift-drag the logo upward until its distance from the top edge matches that of the name text box. (Pressing Shift as you drag ensures that the object only moves vertically or horizontally, depending on the direction dragged.)

The tops of the two objects are now aligned with each other (**Figure 26.24**).

✔ Tips

■ You can also change the *size* of any object, such as the logo. To resize proportionately, drag a corner handle.

■ To change the rotation of a selected object, click the green rotation handle at the top of the object (**Figure 26.25**) and drag to the left or right. Press Ctrl to restrict changes to 15-degree increments.

Selected name text box   *Selected logo*

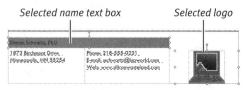

Figure 26.22 When aligning objects, begin by selecting them.

Distance from left edge of object to left side of page

0.500, 3.125 in.

Distance from top of object to top of page

Figure 26.23 Check the distance to the top of the page.

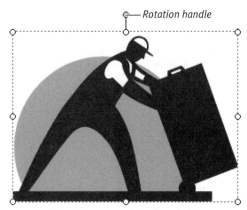

Figure 26.24 The top of the logo and the top of the name text box are now aligned with each other.

Rotation handle

Figure 26.25 You can rotate a selected object by dragging its rotation handle. You can also choose a command from the Arrange > Rotate or Flip submenu.

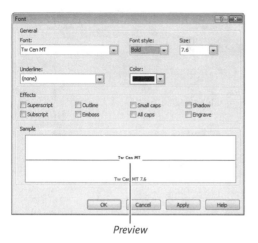

Preview

Figure 26.26 Using the Font dialog box, you can set multiple font attributes at the same time, as well as preview the results.

Steven Schwartz, Ph.D.

Figure 26.27 By applying boldface to the name text in the color-filled box, its formatting matches that of the company name at the top of the postcard.

Formatting text

In a template, the initial font, size, style, and color of placeholder text represent what the designer felt was visually pleasing and complemented the other design elements. However, because this is *your* publication, you can change the character or paragraph formatting of any and all text.

To apply character formatting to text:

1. Select the text to be formatted:
   ▲ Double-click to select a single word or triple-click to select a paragraph.
   ▲ Click and drag to select the text.
   In this example, select your full name.

2. *Do either of the following:*
   ▲ Choose font, size, style, or color settings from the Formatting toolbar. If the toolbar isn't visible, choose its name from the View > Toolbars submenu.
   ▲ Choose Format > Font to open the Font dialog box (**Figure 26.26**). Choose new settings and click OK.

   Apply boldface (Bold) to make the name's formatting match that of the company (**Figure 26.27**).

✔ Tip

■ Fonts which list a Bold or Italic version in the Font dialog box support these styles. If you apply the Bold or Italic style to text, Publisher substitutes the *actual* bold or italic font for the style (such as Times New Roman Bold)—if a version of the stylized font exists.

   If you apply a style to a font that *doesn't* support that style, an algorithm is applied to the base font in an attempt to generate a bold-like or italic-like font on the fly. In most cases, an *actual* bold or italic font will produce superior printed output compared to a generated font.

MAKING MINOR CHANGES

To apply paragraph formatting to text:

1. Select the paragraph(s) to be formatted. (To format one paragraph, click anywhere in the paragraph. ⌜Shift⌟-click or ⌜Shift⌟-drag to select multiple paragraphs.)

   In this example, select the blurb paragraph: "To better serve our clients…".

2. *Do any of the following:*

   ▲ Choose paragraph-formatting options (such as alignment, bullets, number-ing, line spacing, or indent level) from the Formatting toolbar.

   ▲ Choose commands from the Format menu.

   ▲ Choose a defined *style* from the Styles drop-down menu or task pane (**Figure 26.28**).

   In this example, apply justification to the paragraph by clicking the Justify icon on the Formatting toolbar (**Figure 26.29**) or by pressing ⌜Ctrl⌟⌜J⌟. (As shown in **Figure 26.30**, a *justified* paragraph has flush left and right margins.)

✔ Tip

■ Another way to alter paragraph formatting is to choose Format > Paragraph and make changes in the Paragraph dialog box.

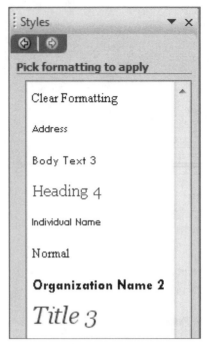

Figure 26.28 The Styles task pane lists all styles for the current publication. To apply a style to selected text, click the style's name.

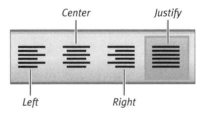

Figure 26.29 Click an alignment icon to set the alignment for selected paragraph(s).

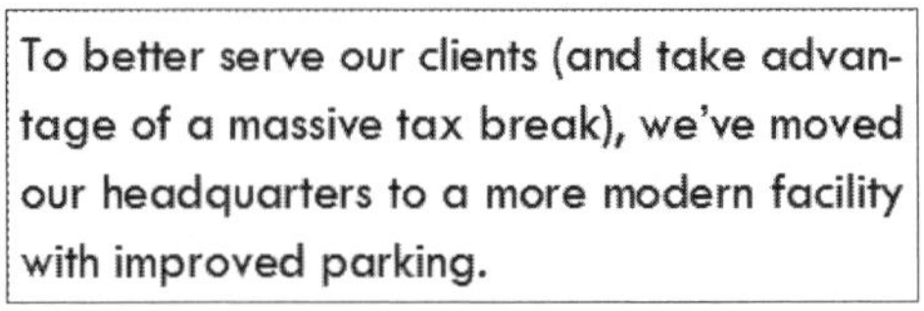

To better serve our clients (and take advan-tage of a massive tax break), we've moved our headquarters to a more modern facility with improved parking.

Figure 26.30 Full justification sometimes looks better than left-aligned text with a ragged right margin.

Figure 26.31 Choose Grayscale to convert color artwork to the equivalent shades of gray.

Figure 26.32 Choose a line color (or No Line) for a selected object from the Color drop-down menu.

Figure 26.33 This is the completed postcard as it appears in Print Preview.

Formatting the logo

If the postcard will be printed on a color printer, the elements' colors are critical. (However, if the postcard will be printed in grayscale, the only requirements of color elements are that they translate well to shades of gray.) Because this color (red) logo draws attention away from the blue bars and the moving-man clip art, the logo will be less distracting if converted to grayscale.

To convert a color image to grayscale:

1. Select the logo.

2. *Do one of the following:*
   ▲ Click the Format Picture icon on the Picture toolbar.
   ▲ Choose Format > Object or Format > Picture.
   ▲ Right-click the logo and choose Format Object or Format Picture from the pop-up menu.

   The Format Object or Format Picture dialog box appears.

3. Click the Picture tab. Choose Grayscale from the Image control: Color drop-down menu (**Figure 26.31**), and then click OK. The logo is converted to grayscale.

4. *Optional:* If the grayscale logo is now surrounded by a box, open the Format Picture/Format Object dialog box again, click the Colors and Lines tab, and choose No Line from the Line: Color drop-down menu (**Figure 26.32**). Click OK.

   This concludes the tinkering with the postcard publication (**Figure 26.33**). The remaining sections describe additional changes you can make to this or any other template-based publication.

Storing and Reusing Items

The new Content Library is a repository for pictures, text, and other material you'd like to reuse in your publications.

To store an item in the Content Library:

1. Select the text or item (a graphic, for example) to add to the Content Library.

   To add only certain text from a text block, select only that text. To add an entire text box and the box's formatting to the Content Library, select the text box.

2. Display the Content Library (**Figure 26.34**) by *doing one of the following:*

   ▲ If a task pane is already open, choose Content Library from the drop-down menu at the top of the task pane.

   ▲ Open the task pane by choosing View > Task Pane ([Ctrl][F1]). Choose Content Library from the drop-down menu at the top of the task pane.

3. *Do one of the following:*

   ▲ Choose Insert > Add to Content Library.

   ▲ Right-click the selected item and choose Add to Content Library from the pop-up menu.

   ▲ At the bottom of the Content Library task pane, click Add selected items to Content Library.

   The Add Item to Content Library dialog box appears (**Figure 26.35**).

4. In the Title box, enter a name for the item or material.

5. *Optional:* Classify the item by clicking one or more of the Categories check boxes.

6. Click OK to add the item to the Content Library.

Figure 26.34 Content Library task pane.

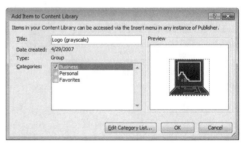

Figure 26.35 Name and assign categories to the Content Library item.

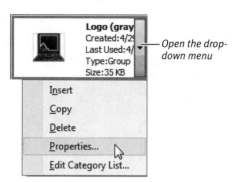

Open the drop-down menu

Figure 26.36 You can edit the properties of any item in the Content Library.

■ If you add many items to the Content Library, it can be hard to find a particular one by simply scrolling through the list. To make it easier to locate an item, choose options from the drop-down menus at the top of the task pane (see Figure 26.34).

✔ Tips

■ You can also add an item you've just selected and copied (Edit > Copy or Ctrl C) to the Clipboard. At the bottom of the Content Library task pane, click Add item on clipboard to Content Library.

■ To create, rename, or delete categories, click the Edit Category List button in the Add Item to Content Library dialog box.

■ To edit a stored item's name or categories, open the item's drop-down menu (**Figure 26.36**), and choose Properties.

To insert a Content Library item into a publication:

1. Display the publication page in which you want to insert the Content Library item.

2. Open the Content Library task pane by *doing one of the following:*
   ▲ Choose Insert > Item from Content Library (Ctrl Shift E).
   ▲ If a task pane is already open, choose Content Library from the drop-down menu at the top of the task pane.
   ▲ Open the task pane by choosing View > Task Pane (Ctrl F1). Choose Content Library from the drop-down menu at the top of the task pane.

3. *Do either of the following:*
   ▲ Click the down arrow beside the item and choose Insert (see Figure 26.36).
   ▲ Drag an item from the Content Library into the publication.

✔ Tips

■ Dragging an item from the Content Library provides better positioning control than using the Insert command.

■ You can drag text into a blank area to create a new text box or drag it into a specific spot within existing text.

STORING AND REUSING ITEMS

Changing the Font or Color Scheme

Every template-based publication provides default *schemes* for the fonts and colors. The fonts are designed to complement each other as are the colors. Rather than manually change fonts or colors in the publication, you can choose new schemes.

To choose a new font or color scheme:

1. Open the Format Publication task pane by *doing one of the following:*

   ▲ If a task pane is already open, choose Format Publication from the drop-down menu at the top of the task pane.

   ▲ From the Format menu, choose Format Publication, Color Schemes, or Font Schemes.

2. **Color scheme.** If necessary, expand the Color Schemes section (**Figure 26.37**) by clicking the arrow icon to the right of its name. The current color scheme is selected. Note its name. To apply a new color scheme, click it.

3. **Font scheme.** If necessary, expand the Font Schemes section (**Figure 26.38**) by clicking the arrow icon to the right of its name. The current font scheme is shown as the first item in the list. To apply a new font scheme, click it.

✔ Tips

■ To restore the default font or color scheme, reapply it by clicking its name in the list.

■ To view or change the way font schemes are applied, click Font scheme options at the bottom of the Font Schemes section (see Figure 26.38).

■ Save before experimenting with new font or color schemes, as well as when trying out different templates (see next page).

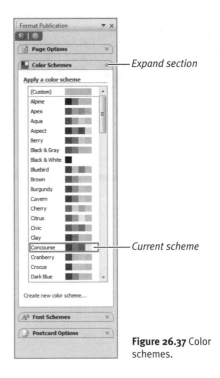

Figure 26.37 Color schemes.

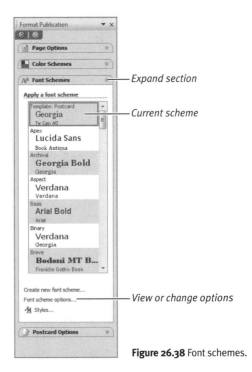

Figure 26.38 Font schemes.

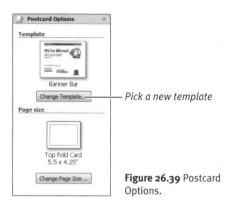

Figure 26.39 Postcard Options.

Figure 26.40 Select an option by clicking a radio button, and then click OK.

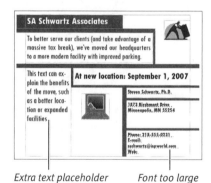

Extra text placeholder   Font too large

Figure 26.41 New template applied.

- If you overlay the current publication with the new template, you can restore the original by choosing Edit > Undo Wizard Action ($\boxed{\text{Ctrl}}\,\boxed{\text{Z}}$). You can also accomplish this by closing the publication without saving.

Changing Templates

If you're curious how the current business information data, replaced placeholder text, and placed text and graphics would look in a *different* template, you can swap the current template for another.

To change templates:

1. Open the Format Publication task pane by *doing one of the following:*
   - ▲ If a task pane is already open, choose Format Publication from the drop-down menu at the top of the task pane.
   - ▲ Choose Format > Format Publication.

2. In the Postcard Options area of the task pane (**Figure 26.39**), click the Change Template button. (The *template* Options area will be named differently for other types of templates.)

   The Change Template screen appears. (The screen is similar to the one from which you selected the first postcard template.)

3. Select a new template and click OK.

   The Change Template dialog box appears (**Figure 26.40**).

4. Click a radio button to indicate whether the selected template will be applied to the current publication or a new publication will be created. Click OK to apply the template (**Figure 26.41**).

✔ Tips

- After you switch templates, a certain amount of cleanup is usually necessary. Additional text placeholders may need to be filled or parts of the initial template may be duplicated.

- Unless you're certain you don't want to keep the initial template, it's usually simpler to create a new publication rather than overlay the original.

CHANGING TEMPLATES

Addressing the Postcards

Your final step in working with the postcard template will depend on how you intend to use the cards.

To address the postcards:

1. Click the 2 icon at the bottom of the screen to view the other side of the postcard (**Figure 26.42**).

2. *Do one of the following:*

   ▲ If you intend to send out individual cards as needed, replace the address placeholder with a client or customer address and print. When you need another postcard, edit the address.

   ▲ If the address list will be printed on labels, remove the address placeholder text box.

   ▲ If you want to perform a mass mailing, use the Mail Merge tool to merge an existing address list with the publication. The mail merge will produce an addressed postcard for each person.

     To perform the merge, choose Tools > Mailings and Catalogs > Mail Merge. Follow the step-by-step instructions in the Mail Merge task pane (**Figure 26.43**).

✔ Tips

■ You can perform a mail merge using addresses stored in Outlook, a database, a spreadsheet, or a typed list.

■ If the postcards will be printed by a print shop and will include a printed address (rather than a label), perform the mail merge prior to giving the publication to the printer.

■ For information on printing and working with print shops, see Chapter 27.

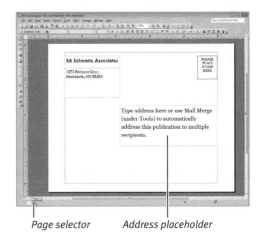

Page selector   Address placeholder

Figure 26.42 The address side of the postcard is on page 2.

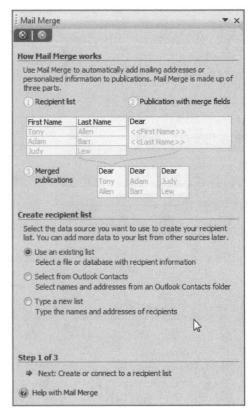

Figure 26.43 The Mail Merge task pane will walk you through the merge process.

DISTRIBUTING AND PRINTING PUBLICATIONS

27

After you finish writing, editing, and laying out a publication, you'll want to use one or more of Publisher's output tools to share it with others. In this chapter, you'll learn to perform these output tasks:

◆ Run a prepress check to correct publication problems.

◆ Create a Portable Document Format (PDF) version of the publication that recipients can read and print with Adobe Reader or Apple's Preview.

◆ Email a publication as the message or an attachment.

◆ Publish publication pages to the Web.

◆ Print a publication on a connected or networked printer, at a local copy shop, or at a commercial printing service.

Running a Prepress Check

You can use the Design Checker to quickly ferret out common design problems in a publication. If you'll be turning the publication over to a commercial printer, you can also check for and eliminate potentially costly printing-related problems. (It's smart to run Design Checker *regardless* of how you intend to print or distribute a publication.)

To use the Design Checker:

1. Open the publication to be checked.

2. Open the Design Checker task pane by *doing one of the following:*

   ▲ If a task pane is already open, choose Design Checker from the drop-down menu at the top of the task pane.

   ▲ Choose Tools > Design Checker.

3. At the top of the Design Checker, click the check boxes of checks to be performed.

   Design Checker performs the checks and displays the results (**Figure 27.1**).

4. Examine the problems in the Select an item to fix area list. For each one, click the down arrow that appears to its right (**Figure 27.2**) and decide whether the problem needs to be corrected.

5. *Optional:* Dismiss the Design Checker task pane by clicking its close box (X) or the Close Design Checker button.

✔ Tip

■ Not all noted problems are *real* problems. For instance, an RGB publication is fine if you intend to print it yourself. But the same publication should be converted to CMYK for commercial printing.

   Moral: Be sure to read each problem's explanation, if one is provided.

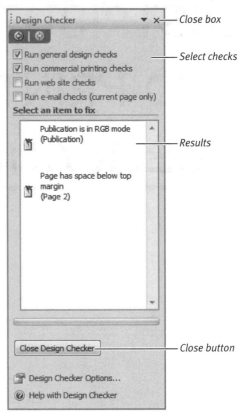

Figure 27.1 The Design Checker.

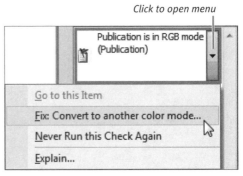

Figure 27.2 For each noted problem, options for viewing or correcting it are presented in a drop-down menu.

Output file type

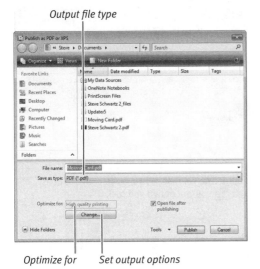

Optimize for   Set output options

Figure 27.3 The Publish as PDF or XPS dialog box.

Creating PDFs

In addition to printing a publication, there are many reasons you might want to create s Portable Document Format (PDF) file:

◆ PDF files can be viewed in most browsers, as well as with Adobe Reader (free) and Apple's Preview (included with OS X). Recipients don't need Publisher to open, view, or print a publication that's in PDF format.

◆ The PDF format was designed to produce output that is visually identical to a printout. You don't have to worry that fonts will be substituted, text will rewrap, or image positions will shift.

◆ When creating a PDF, you have control over its quality. You can produce a high-quality file that is suitable for copy-shop printing or a low-quality file that you can post on a Web site or send as an email attachment.

Note: To create PDF files in any Office 2007 application, you must download and install the Microsoft Save As PDF or XPS add-in (see "New File Formats" in Chapter 1).

To publish a document as a PDF file:

1. Open the publication.

2. Chose File > Publish as PDF or XPS. The Publish as PDF or XPS dialog box appears (**Figure 27.3**).

3. Navigate to the folder in which you want to save the PDF file.

4. Ensure that PDF (*.pdf) is selected in the Save as type drop-down list.

5. *Optional:* Change the output filename. (The proposed name is the publication name with a .pdf extension.)

continues on next page

CREATING PDFS

411

6. The current quality setting is shown in the Optimize for box. Click Change to change the setting or its options.

The Publish Options dialog box appears (**Figure 27.4**).

7. Select one of the following output options from the list at the top of the dialog box:

▲ **Minimum size.** This option creates a file intended for display on a PC. The combination of small file size and low resolution (96 dpi) is suitable for posting on the Web and distributing to people who don't need a printed copy.

▲ **Standard.** With a modest resolution (150 dpi), this option is a compromise between Minimum size and High quality printing. The quality is more than necessary for screen display, but it will produce decent printed output on a desktop printer.

▲ **High quality printing.** With a resolution of 300 dpi, this option is the proper choice when recipients need to print a crisp, clear copy on their or a copy shop's inkjet or laser printer. However, depending on the size and complexity of the publication, the resulting PDF file may be too large for email distribution.

▲ **Commercial Press.** Pick this option when the publication will be printed on a high-end printer and Microsoft Publisher files are not supported.

8. *Optional:* To review or change specific print settings, such as downsampling large graphics, click the Advanced button.

9. Click the Print Options button.

The Print Options dialog box appears, presenting the equivalent of Page Setup options (**Figure 27.5**).

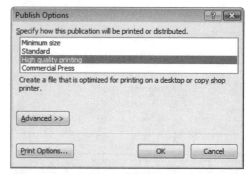

Figure 27.4 For many PDFs, all you have to do is select an output option and click OK.

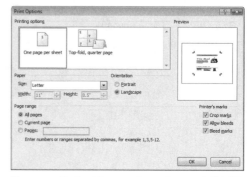

Figure 27.5 Review/change print settings, and click OK.

Figure 27.6 After you generate a PDF, it can be viewed in any compatible program, such as Adobe Reader.

10. Review the options, make any desired changes (such as adding crop marks or printing only selected pages), and click OK. Then click OK in the Publish Options dialog box.

11. To generate the PDF file using the specified settings, click the Publish button in the Publish as PDF or XPS dialog box (see Figure 27.3).

    If Open file after publishing was checked in the Publish as PDF or XPS dialog box, the PDF file opens (**Figure 27.6**).

✔ Tips

■ When using a commercial printer, submit a PDF only if they cannot accept Publisher files and say that a PDF will suffice. Ask them to provide the proper settings for all of the PDF-generation dialog boxes.

■ Submitting a PDF to a commercial printer has one major disadvantage. The PDF must be *perfect*. If there's an error, such as a photo that's too dark, you must make the correction in your publication, create a new PDF, and resubmit. If the printer can accept Publisher files, they're in a position to make simple corrections.

■ One way to determine which PDF output option is best is to try them all. Check the resulting file sizes and the print quality of each one.

■ To open a PDF file on disk, click/double-click its icon. If you have a compatible program, it will launch and open the file.

■ With an appropriate add-in, most Web browsers can also display a PDF file. Use the browser's File > Open command or drag the PDF file's icon into an open browser window.

CREATING PDFS

Emailing a Publication

From within Publisher, you can email a publication in either of the following ways:

◆ Send the publication as a Publisher, PDF, or XPS file attachment.

◆ Convert the publication into a message.

To send a publication as an attachment:

1. Open the publication.

2. Choose an Attachment command from the File > Send E-mail submenu (**Figure 27.7**):

   ▲ **Publisher.** To send the Publisher file, choose Send Publication as Attachment. This is the appropriate choice when the recipient needs to be able to edit the file.

   ▲ **PDF.** Choose Send Publication as PDF Attachment when the recipient needs to view and/or print the file, but not edit it. PDF files can be opened with Adobe Reader, Apple's Preview, and other utilities.

   ▲ **XPS.** Choose Send Publication as XPS Attachment when the recipient needs to view and/or print the file and requests this format. Files in XPS format can be opened with Internet Explorer 7 and other utilities.

   Currently, PDF utilities are commonly installed on most PCs and Macs; XPS utilities are not.

   A new email message is created in which the publication is an attachment of the chosen type (**Figure 27.8**).

3. Address the email message, type the message text, and send the message.

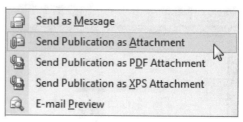

Figure 27.7 You can email a publication as an attached Publisher, PDF, or XPS file.

Attached publication

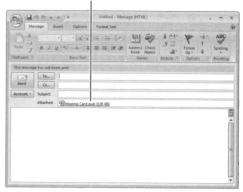

Figure 27.8 The publication is attached to a new email message.

EMAILING A PUBLICATION

Figure 27.9 Click this radio button to send the current publication page.

Email toolbar   Run Design Checker

Figure 27.10 Address the message as you normally do. Click toolbar icons to preview the message, pick an account from which to mail the message, and so on.

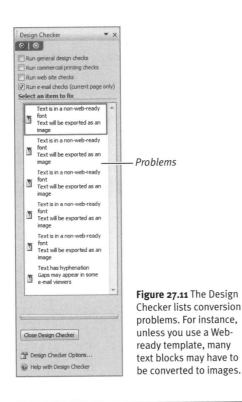

Problems

Figure 27.11 The Design Checker lists conversion problems. For instance, unless you use a Web-ready template, many text blocks may have to be converted to images.

To send a publication page as a message:

1. Switch to the page you want to send.

2. Choose File > Send E-mail > Send as Message.

   The Send as Message dialog box appears (**Figure 27.9**).

3. Click Send current page only. Click OK.

   An email address section appears above the publication (**Figure 27.10**).

4. *Optional:* If conversion problems are noted, click the Design Checker button and review them (**Figure 27.11**).

5. *Optional:* Click the E-Mail Preview toolbar icon (see Figure 27.10) to see how the converted publication page will look.

   The publication is converted and then shown to you in your default browser.

6. Address the message, enter a subject, and click Send.

   The publication is sent to the designated recipients.

✔ Tips

- As explained in the previous section, creating email attachments in PDF or XPS format requires you to install the Microsoft Save As PDF or XPS add-in.

- To send a multipage publication in a format that virtually anyone can open, view, and print, choose the Send Publication as PDF Attachment command.

- If you decide *not* to email a page as a message and want to restore the document window, click the Cancel toolbar icon (see Figure 20.10) or choose File > Send E-Mail > Cancel E-mail Message. To restore a converted multipage publication, click Cancel and then choose Edit > Undo Wizard Action ([Ctrl][Z]).

- When you send *all* pages as a message, a conversion occurs. Pages are combined, and the design elements are placed in an email template—often with unexpected results (**Figure 27.12**):
  - ▲ All elements have been rearranged.
  - ▲ The company slogan (not used in the original postcard) is now present (❶).
  - ▲ The color logo that was converted to grayscale has reverted to color (❷).
  - ▲ All contact information—including the new address—has been omitted.
  - ▲ Page 2 is missing.
  - ▲ Email-relevant text has been added to the bottom of the message (❸).

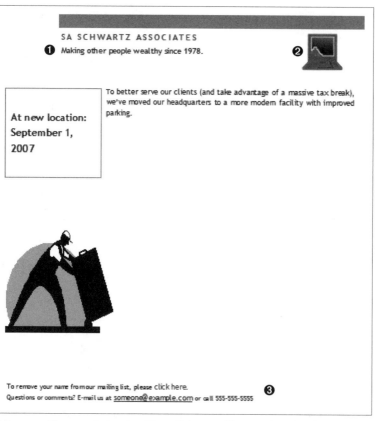

Figure 27.12 The converted postcard bears little resemblance to the original publication.

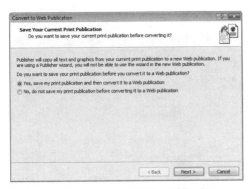

Figure 27.13 If you need to save the publication before converting it, select Yes.

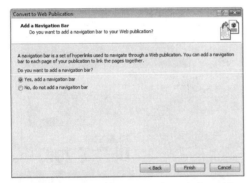

Figure 27.14 To help people move through the publication's pages, add a navigation bar by selecting Yes.

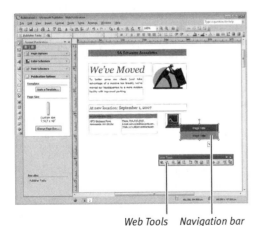

Web Tools   Navigation bar

Figure 27.15 The converted publication appears.

Publishing to the Web

If you have a Web site or free access to a Web server through your *Internet Service Provider* (ISP) or a Web-based email account, you can convert Publisher documents into Web pages for viewing in a browser. Because Publisher is a layout program, you'll find it easy to create basic, appealing pages in which the text and graphics are positioned exactly as you want.

If you didn't create the publication using a template from the Web Sites category, you must start by converting your print publication into a Web publication.

To convert a print publication into a Web publication:

1. Open the publication you want to convert.

2. Choose File > Convert to Web Publication. The Convert to Web Publication dialog box appears (**Figure 27.13**).

3. If you've made changes that haven't been saved, select Yes. Otherwise, select No. Click Next to continue.

   The Add a Navigation Bar screen of the dialog box appears (**Figure 27.14**).

4. To include a page-navigation bar on the pages, select Yes. Otherwise, select No. Click Finish to convert the publication to Web format.

   The converted publication appears (**Figure 27.15**).

✔ Tip

■ If you created a navigation bar, edit the tab name text. (Renaming tabs affects the bar on *every* Web page.) On each page, resize the navigation bar and drag it to the desired page position. To place the bar in the same spot on each page, use the positioning information in the status bar.

To create Web pages from a publication:

1. Open the publication. Choose File >
   Publish to the Web.

   An information dialog box appears.

2. Click OK.

   The Publish to the Web dialog box appears
   (**Figure 27.16**).

3. Navigate to the folder in which you want
   to save the Web files.

4. In the File name box, enter a name for the
   main Web page you're creating.

   If this will be the opening page of your
   Web site, index.htm is fine. Otherwise,
   type a descriptive filename (without
   spaces) that ends with a .htm extension.

5. Click Save.

   The main page and a folder containing
   essential files (the additional Web pages
   and all image files) are created. The folder
   name is derived from the name entered in
   Step 4. For instance, creating moving.htm
   results in a folder named moving_files.

6. To view the generated pages in your
   browser, click (or double-click) the icon
   of the main .htm file.

7. Upload the .htm file and folder to your Web
   server. Test the Web page by entering its
   address in your browser (**Figure 27.17**).

✔ Tips

- Before creating the HTML pages, you can
  preview the publication in Web format by
  choosing File > Web Page Preview or by
  clicking the Web Page Preview icon on
  the Web Tools toolbar (see Figure 27.15).

- If you're creating a site rather than just
  a few pages, explore the options in the
  Web Site Options section of the Format
  Publication task pane.

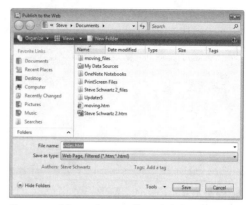

Figure 27.16 Name the .htm file and click Save.

Figure 27.17 This is an example of a page created in
one of the Web Sites templates. To view it online, visit
www.siliconwasteland.com/office2007.htm.

- You can name each Web page, creating
  a title that will appear in a browser's title
  bar. In the Web Tools toolbar (see Figure
  27.15), click the Web Page Options or
  the Rename icon, or choose Tools > Web
  Page Options.

- If you need to make changes to the generated Web pages, modify the converted
  publication and generate the pages again.

Destination printer | Printer-specific settings

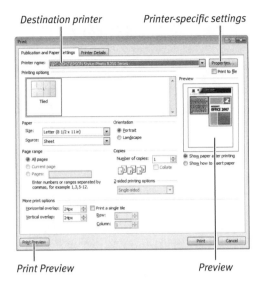

Print Preview | Preview

Figure 27.18 The Print dialog box.

Printing a Publication

When PDF or Web output won't do, you can print your Publisher publication in any of the following ways:

◆ Print to a connected or networked inkjet or laser printer. Print locally when small quantities are needed—when printing a greeting card, for example.

◆ Print the publication at a local copy shop. Use this option when producing large quantities of moderate-quality publications, such as flyers, or when you need to print on an unusual paper stock.

◆ Submit the publication to a commercial printer for printing on a high-end printer. This option is used when publishing a book or printing a magazine, for example.

To print to a local or networked printer:

1. Open the publication you want to print. Ensure that the destination printer is on.

2. *Optional:* Run a prepress check (described earlier in this chapter) and correct errors.

3. Choose File > Print, click the Print icon on the Standard toolbar, or press Ctrl P. The Print dialog box appears (**Figure 27.18**).

4. Select the destination printer from the Printer name drop-down list.

5. *Optional:* To set printer-specific settings, such as print quality and color vs. grayscale printing, click the Properties button.

6. Review other print options, such as paper size, page orientation, number of copies, and the page range to print. Make any necessary changes.

7. Click Print to send the print job to the designated printer.

Proof Before Printing

When you're having a publication commercially printed, request a *proof* of the print job before it's printed. Instead of being stuck with 10,000 brochures featuring people with beet-red faces, it's considerably less expensive to correct problems at the proof stage.

Note: Although a proof printed on your color inkjet can show whether your publication is in the ballpark, it's not a safe substitute for a proof from the commercial printer.

PRINTING A PUBLICATION

To print at a copy shop:

1. Contact the copy shop and ask about their capabilities. Be sure to inquire about the price of printing, collating, and other required services; availability of special paper stocks (if required by the print job); how quickly the job can be completed; and whether they can handle Publisher 2007 files or would prefer a PDF.

2. Follow the steps in the previous task list to print the publication on your own or a network printer. Proof the printout and correct any errors. Reprint, if necessary.

   The printout will ensure that no obvious errors remain in the publication and also let you check the color output (if applicable). In addition, you can give the printout to the copy shop personnel as a guide to the expected output.

3. In preparation for your trip to the copy shop, *do one of the following:*

   ▲ **PDF.** If the copy shop requires a PDF, create one as described earlier in this chapter. Burn the PDF file to a CD or copy it to a USB flash drive that you can take to the copy shop.

   ▲ **Publisher.** If the copy shop supports Publisher 2007, use the Pack and Go Wizard (described in the following task list) to prepare the files needed to print the publication.

Two-Sided Printing

To conserve paper—or because certain publications, such as newsletters, are normally produced this way—Publisher supports *two-sided* (or *duplex*) *printing*. Some advanced printers provide support for duplex printing. However, most can print on both sides of a page only if you manually flip the paper.

To enable two-sided printing, click Show how to insert paper (beneath the Preview area), and click the Run the Two-Sided Printing Setup Wizard text that appears. Run the wizard once for each printer you want to use in this fashion.

Why Embed Fonts?

When you read the task list on the next page, you may wonder why Pack and Go embeds fonts in the material for the printer. You'd think copy shops and commercial printers would already have the common fonts, right?

Pack and Go does this is because there are often several variations of a font. In addition to PostScript and TrueType versions, font designers may have created several newer versions of a given font. Unless a commercial printer uses *your* specific version of a font, there's no guarantee that the text in your expensive print job will match the character-spacing, kerning, and line breaks in the proof you printed. Unless you provide your fonts, there's a chance that your carefully edited and arranged text will contain some unpleasant, expensive-to-fix surprises.

Figure 27.19 Specify a destination drive or device.

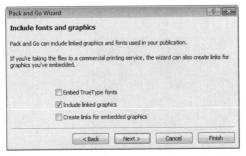

Figure 27.20 Specify whether fonts will be embedded in the publication and how linked graphics will be handled.

Figure 27.21 Review this information. Click Finish to create the archive.

To use the Pack and Go Wizard to prepare for printing (copy shop):

1. If you'll be saving the files to a flash drive, hook it up or insert it now.

2. Open the publication and choose File > Pack and Go > Take to Another Computer.

   The opening screen of the Pack and Go Wizard appears. Click Next to continue.

3. On the Select the location for saving your files screen (**Figure 27.19**), *select one of the following options:*

   ▲ **Burn to disc.** Use this option if you want to copy the files to a CD or DVD in the drive with the specified letter.

   ▲ **Copy to removable storage.** Select this option to copy the files to a connected removable storage device, such as a flash drive.

   ▲ **Copy to floppy disk.** You can select this option if you and the copy shop each have a floppy drive.

   ▲ **Other location.** Select this option to copy the files to your PC's hard drive, an external hard drive, or a network drive. Click Browse to select the drive and destination folder.

   Click Next to continue.

4. Contact the copy shop to determine which boxes you should check on the Include fonts and graphics screen (**Figure 27.20**). Click Next to continue.

5. Read the Pack my publication screen (**Figure 27.21**), and click Finish. Click OK to dismiss the following screen.

   The publication and supporting materials are compacted into a Zip archive and copied to the designated drive or media.

PRINTING A PUBLICATION

To use the Pack and Go Wizard to prepare for printing (commercial):

1. Choose File > Pack and Go > Take to a Commercial Printing Service.

    The Take to a Commercial Printing Service task pane appears (**Figure 27.22**).

2. Ensure that Commercial Press is chosen from the drop-down menu.

3. Review and repair the listed problems.

    For example, RGB graphics should be converted to CMYK. (If you aren't sure which fixes are necessary, contact the commercial printer.)

4. Click the Printing Options button.

    The Print Options dialog box appears (**Figure 27.23**).

5. Ensure that the print settings are correct, and then click OK.

    Check with the printer if you have questions, such as the types of printer's marks that should be added to each page.

6. In the Export area of the task pane, remove check marks from items you do not want to include. Click Save.

    The Select the location for saving your files screen of the Pack and Go Wizard appears (see Figure 27.19).

7. Select a destination for the Zip file (as explained in the previous task list). Click Next to continue.

    The files are compacted and copied to the specified drive or device. The resulting file is *publication name*.zip.

8. On the final screen, check or uncheck the Print a composite proof check box. (If it's checked, make sure your printer is on.) Click OK.

    You or the printer can use the proof to ensure that their results match yours.

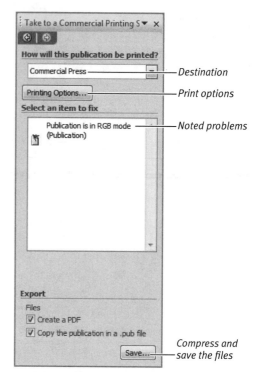

Figure 27.22 Take to a Commercial Printing Service task pane.

Destination — Commercial Press
Print options — Printing Options...
Noted problems — Publication is in RGB mode (Publication)
Compress and save the files — Save...

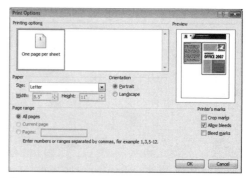

Figure 27.23 Set print options, and click OK.

✔ Tip

- You can use Windows Vista or a Zip utility, such as WinZip (www.winzip.com), to extract the files from the archive.

INDEX

@ (at) symbol, 250
_ (underscore) character, 250
3-D charts, 204
3-D reference style, 174–175
97-2003 format, 7, 114, 115,
    215, 242

A

A1 reference style, 174
absolute cell references, 178
Access, xii, 4
Account Settings dialog box,
    251, 254
action buttons, 238
Action Settings dialog box, 238
active cell, 129
active sheet, 129
Add Effect menu, 235
Add New Category dialog box,
    321
Address Book, 267–279
    accessing, 268
    creating contact records in,
        270–273
    creating distribution lists in,
        278–279
    importing contact records
        into, 270, 272–273
    purpose of, 250, 267
    searching for contact records
        in, 275
    viewing contact records
        in, 269
address list, merging
    publication with, 408
Adobe Acrobat, 114

Adobe Reader, 7, 114, 242, 411
aligning
    objects, 400
    paragraphs, 63, 402
    table data, 98
alignment icons, 63, 402
Analysis group, 206
Animate menu, 234, 235
animations, within-slide, 211,
    216, 234–235, 236
Apple .Mac accounts, 249
Apple Preview utility, 242, 411
appointments, 329–335
    defined, 330
    deleting, 331, 334
    modifying, 334
    recording, 331
    responding to reminders
        about, 333
    searching for, 335
    setting recurring schedule
        for, 332
    vs. tasks, 329, 338
Archive command, 317
arguments, function, 179
arithmetic operators, 176
Arrange All command, 17
artwork, 397
at (@) symbol, 250
attachments, email, 115, 292,
    310, 414
audio notes, 355, 384
Auto Fill Options menu, 143
AutoComplete feature, 134
AutoCorrect feature, 44, 66, 374
automatic page breaks, 55
AutoSum formula, 181

AVERAGE function, 175
axes, chart, 207

B

background color, 52
Background group, 198
backgrounds, chart, 198
Basic suite, xii
Bcc box, message window, 284
Blank Page icon, 58
Blocked Senders List, 326
Blogger, 116
blogs, 116–117
borders, 54, 97, 169
Borders and Shading dialog box,
    54, 93
Borders menu, 97
Breaks menu, 56
browsers. See Web browsers
bulleted lists, 66–69
business cards, 277, 294
Business Contact Manager, xii
Business Information dialog
    box, 394
business information sets,
    394, 396

C

Cached Exchange Mode, 248,
    253
calculated columns, 185, 188
calculations, in Word tables, 99
calendar appointments. See
    appointments
calendar events. See events
Calendar pane, 329, 330–332

calendars, 329–337
    creating recurring items
        in, 332
    deleting items in, 331
    emailing, 336–337
    modifying items in, 334
    publishing online, 337
    recording items in, 331
    responding to reminders
        from, 333
    searching for items in, 335
    viewing items in, 330
Cascade command, 17
case, in email addresses, 250
categories, message, 320–322
Categorized Mail folder, 322
Cc box, message window, 284
CD, copying presentations
    to, 244
cell addresses, 174
cell references, 174–175, 178
cells
    adding borders to, 169
    applying color to, 168
    applying Number format
        to, 165
    copying, 138
    deleting, 139
    editing contents of, 136
    enabling text wrap for, 164
    entering data in, 134–135
    filling, 142–143
    fitting text within, 164
    formatting, 162
    inserting, 138
    moving, 137
    naming, 154–155
    removing formatting
        from, 170
    replacing formatting in, 171
    reusing formatting in, 171
    selecting, 132–133
Center alignment icon, 63
Change Styles icon, 75
Change Template screen, 407
character formatting
    in email messages, 289, 291
    in Excel worksheets, 163
    in OneNote notes, 373
    in Word documents, 49, 66,
        72–74
Chart Layouts group, 202
chart placeholders, 223
Chart Styles group, 202

charts, 195–208
    adding gridlines to, 204
    adding legends to, 205
    adding text items to, 199
    adding trendlines to, 206
    changing background for, 198
    changing layout/style for, 202
    changing type of, 197
    creating, 197
    customizing, 195
    deleting, 197
    displaying data tables on, 203
    elements of, 196
    embedding, 195
    formatting text in, 200
    linking, 195
    modifying axes for, 207
    modifying data in, 208
    switching rows/columns
        in, 201
    ways of using, 195
    in Word documents, 101
Check Name dialog box, 284
circular references, 183
Clear Formats command,
    170, 171
click-and-type feature, 38
clip art, 104
Clip Art icon, 104
clip-art placeholders, 222
Clip Art task pane, 397
Clipboard
    Office, 20–21, 25, 31, 40
    Windows, 20, 21, 358
close box, 16, 29, 129, 213, 391
Close this Notebook command,
    349
Color Categories dialog
    box, 320
Color Scales submenu, 166
color schemes, 220, 263, 392, 406
Colors drop-down list, 220
column breaks, 56
columns
    adding/deleting, 140, 141,
        192–193
    calculated, 185, 188
    setting width of, 160–161
    switching to rows, 201
Columns menu, 50, 51
Combine command, 121
comma-separated value
    files, 148

commercial printers, 412, 413,
    419, 422
company logos, 400, 403
Compare Side by Side dialog
    box, 36
comparison operators, 176
Compatibility Pack, Microsoft
    Office, 7
conditional formatting, 166–167
constants, 176
contact information, 265, 267,
    276, 294, 394
contact records, 267–279. See
    also Address Book
    adding to distribution lists,
        278–279
    creating, 270–273
    deleting, 273
    displaying photos for, 273
    editing, 273
    importing, 270, 272–273
    information included in, 267
    saving business cards as, 277
    searching for, 274–275
    viewing, 269
Contacts window, 268
Content Library, 404–405
context menus, 6
contextual tabs, 6
Convert Text to Table dialog
    box, 93
converters, file, 7
copy-and-paste
    in Excel, 94, 101, 138, 145, 171
    in Internet Explorer, 102
    in OneNote, 343, 350, 351,
        358–359, 366
    in Word, 31, 38, 40, 48, 104
Copy Items dialog box, 318
copy shops, 419, 420–421
Copy to CD command, 244
Copy to Folder command, 244
copyright symbol, 48
COUNT function, 175
country abbreviations, 250
Cover Page icon, 57
Create New Folder dialog
    box, 319
Create Screen Clipping
    command, 350
CSV files, 148
currency format, 165
Custom Animation task pane,
    234, 235

cut-and-paste
  in Excel, 136, 137, 193
  in OneNote, 377
  in Word, 40, 89

D

data
  editing, 136, 182
  entering, 134–135
  exporting from Excel,
    146–148
  filtering, 190, 191
  finding/replacing, 149–151
  formatting, 162, 166–167
  importing to Excel, 144–145
  presenting large quantities
    of, 195
  protecting, 156–158
  sorting, 152–153, 190
Data Bars submenu, 166
Data group, 101
data tables, 203
database application, xii
databases, 185. *See also* data
Decrease Indent icon, 64, 69
default email account, 254, 255
definitions, 41
Delete Sheet commands, 193
Delete Table commands, 192
Deleted Items folder,
    316–317, 318
delivery receipts, message, 300
Depth Gridlines submenu, 204
Design Checker, 410, 415
Desktop, opening documents
    from, 14
desktop publishing program,
    xiv, 389
dictionary, Word, 41
Different First Page check
    box, 61
Different Odd & Even Pages
    check box, 61
digital signatures, 124
distribution lists, email,
    278–279
.doc file extension, 7, 114
.docm file extension, 7
document formatting, 49, 50–51
Document Inspector, 122
Document Map option, 37
Document Views group, 33

documents
  adding background color
    to, 52
  adding blank page to, 58
  adding cover page to, 57
  adding graphics/objects to,
    102–109
  adding headers/footers to,
    59–61
  adding page borders to, 54
  applying watermarks to, 53
  cascading, 17
  changing line spacing for,
    70–71
  checking spelling/grammar
    in, 42–44
  closing, 16, 29, 32
  combining, 121
  comparing two versions of,
    36, 120
  correcting errors in, 39–40
  creating, 13
  encrypting, 124
  entering/editing text in,
    38–40
  entering special characters
    in, 48
  formatting, 49–83
  inserting breaks in, 55–56
  inserting charts in, 101
  inserting tables in, 92–93
  marking as final, 123
  merging, 78–83
  moving objects in, 111
  opening, 14, 29, 32
  printing, 22, 419–422
  publishing as PDF files,
    411–413
  removing invisible data
    from, 122
  resizing objects in, 111, 112
  rotating objects in, 111, 112
  saving, 15
  sending via email, 114, 115
  setting magnification for, 19
  specifying page settings for,
    50–51
  splitting into halves, 17
  switching among open, 16, 35
  tracking changes to, 118–119
.docx file extension, 7, 114
domain names, 250
domains, blocking email from
    specific, 326

double-clicking, 13
double-spaced text, 70
Draft view, 34
drag-and-drop
  in Excel, 145, 193
  in Internet Explorer, 145
  in OneNote, 343, 350, 358–
    359, 365–366, 377–378
  in Word, 40, 102
Draw Borders group, 97
Draw Table icon, 93
drawing canvas, 106
drawing tablets, 357
duplex printing, 420
DVD, copying presentations
    to, 244

E

E-mail Options dialog box, 285
EBCs, 276
Edit Name dialog box, 155
Electronic Business Cards, 276
electronic mail, 247. *See also*
    email
electronic scrapbooks, 343
email. *See also* Outlook
  accounts. *See* email accounts
  addresses. *See* email
    addresses
  attachments, 115, 292, 310,
    337, 414
  clients, xiv, 247, 273
  distribution lists, 278–279
  junk, 265, 325–326
  links, 284, 295
  messages. *See* email messages
  reminders, 324
  sending calendars via,
    336–337
  sending Word documents
    via, 114, 115
email accounts
  accessing with Web
    browsers, 250
  adding to Outlook, 251–253
  addresses for, 250
  changing settings for,
    254–255
  checking new mail for,
    304–305
  creating message rules for,
    327–328
  deleting, 255

email accounts *(continued)*
  sending messages from
    different, 286
  specifying default, 254, 255
  specifying signature for, 299
  types of, 248–249
  working with send/receive
    groups for, 258–260
email addresses, 250, 268,
  278–279. *See also* Address
  Book
email messages
  adding signatures to, 265,
    298–299
  applying colors to, 301
  applying themes to, 301
  archiving, 265, 317
  categorizing, 320–322
  changing read/unread status
    of, 307, 314–315
  checking for new, 304–305
  copying, 318
  creating, 281, 283–285
  creating contact records
    from, 271
  creating folders for, 319
  creating message rules for,
    326, 327–328
  defined, 247
  deleting, 316–317
  entering recipients for,
    283–284
  flagging, 315, 323–324
  formats for, 288
  formatting, 288–291
  forwarding, 286
  inserting items into, 293–295
  junk, 265, 325–326
  managing, 313–328
  missing images in, 305
  moving, 318
  printing, 311–312
  reading, 306–307
  recalling sent, 287
  red Xs in, 305
  replying to, 285
  requesting receipts for, 300
  resending, 287
  saving, 15, 300
  searching for, 309
  sending, 281
  setting default format for, 288
  setting preferences for, 265
  setting priority for, 300

sorting, 309
spell checking, 265, 296–297
types of, 282
working with attachments to,
  292, 310
embedded fonts, 420
embedded objects, 195
Encrypt Document command,
  124
Enterprise suite, xii
Eudora, 273
Evaluate Formula dialog
  box, 183
events, 330–335
  defined, 330
  deleting, 331, 334
  modifying, 334
  recording, 331
  responding to reminders
    about, 333
  searching for, 335
  setting recurring schedule
    for, 332
Excel, 125–208. *See also*
  worksheets
  AutoComplete feature, 134
  changing default font for, 162
  closing documents in, 16
  compatibility issues, 7
  creating charts in, 195–208.
    See also charts
  and CSV files, 148
  editing data in, 136
  entering data in, 134–135
  file extensions, 7
  finding/replacing data in,
    149–151
  and fixed-width fields, 148
  formatting features, 159–171
  functions, 173, 175
  getting help with, 24
  importing data into, 144–148
  interface, 128–129
  list-related features, 173, 185
  macros, 175
  naming cells/ranges in,
    154–155
  new features, 8
  opening documents in, 14
  printing documents in, 22–23
  protecting data in, 156–158
  purpose of, xiii, 127
  quitting, 26
  saving documents in, 15

scripts, 175
selecting cells/ranges in,
  132–133
setting column/row size in,
  160–161
setting magnification in, 19
setting preferences for, 26,
  128, 130
sorting data in, 152–153
using Office Clipboard in,
  20–21
window management
  commands, 17
working with formulas in,
  143, 146, 173–183, 188
working with tables in,
  185–193. *See also* tables
  (Excel)
exceptions, 188
Exchange Server accounts, 248,
  252, 253, 287
Exit command, 26
Exit Word command, 29
exporting data, 146–148
Extensible Markup Language, 7.
  See also XML

F

fields
  adding/deleting, 192–193
  defined, 185
  fixed-width, 148
  mail merge, 78, 81, 83
  sorting, 190
file converters, 7
file extensions, 7
file formats, 7, 114, 288
Fill Color icon, 399
Fill Effects dialog box, 52, 168
Find and Replace dialog box,
  45–47, 149–151
flagging messages, 315, 323–324
floating objects, 195
Folder Options setting, 13
Font dialog box, 72, 73, 200, 401
font schemes, 406
fonts, 72–73, 200, 401, 420
footers, 59–61
form letters, 78–81
Format Cells dialog box, 165,
  168, 169
Format Painter tool, 74, 171,
  289, 291

formatting
  character. *See* character
    formatting
  conditional, 166–167
  data, 159–171
  documents, 49–83
  duplicating, 74
  email messages, 289–291
  merge fields, 83
  notes, 373
  numbers, 165
  paragraph. *See* paragraph
    formatting
  table data, 98
  text, 401–402
  worksheets, 159–171
Formula Auditing group, 183
formula bar, 129
Formula dialog box, 99
Formula icon, 99
formulas, 173–183
  anatomy of, 176
  cell references in,
    174–175, 178
  copying/moving, 178
  creating/editing, 180–182
  in Excel tables, 188
  in Excel worksheets, 143
  exporting from Excel, 146
  operator precedence in, 177
  troubleshooting, 183
  ways of using, 173
  in Word tables, 99
Full Screen Reading view, 33–34
Function Arguments dialog
  box, 179
Function Library group, 179, 182
functions
  3-D reference style, 175
  arguments for, 179
  creating formulas with, 180
  Excel's built-in, 173
  getting help with, 179
  nested, 181
  purpose of, 179

G

Gmail, 249, 252
Google, 249, 252
grammar checker, 42–44
graphic placeholders, 222
graphs, 195. *See also* charts

grayscale, converting color
  image to, 403
gridlines, 37, 204

H

handwritten notes, 357
hanging indents, 64, 65, 66
headers, 59–61
Help features
  Office, 24–25
  OneNote, 24, 352
  Outlook, 263, 266
  Publisher, 391
  Word, 31
Highlight Cell Rules submenu,
  167
Home & Student suite, xii
horizontal ruler, 31
Hotmail, 249, 252
.htm file extension, 418
HTML format, 288, 289, 293, 418
HTTP accounts, 249, 251, 252
hyperlinks, xiv, 284, 294–295,
  369–371

I

Icon Sets submenu, 166
IMAP accounts/servers, 248,
  251, 252
Import and Export Wizard, 272,
  273
Import Data dialog box, 144
Import Text File dialog box, 147
importing data, 144–145
Increase Indent icon, 64, 69
indents, 64–65
InDesign, xiv
index.htm, 418
Insert Alignment Tab icon, 61
Insert Caption command, 103
Insert Function dialog box, 179
Insert Greeting Line dialog
  box, 81
Insert Hyperlink dialog box, 295
Insert Merge Field dialog box, 82
Insert Picture dialog box, 103
Insert Table command, 92
Instant Search box, 263, 309
interface
  Excel, 128–129
  Office, 4–6
  OneNote, 344–345

Outlook, 262–263
PowerPoint, 212–213
Publisher, 390–391
Word, 30–32
International tab, Junk E-mail
  Options dialog box, 326
Internet
  domain names, 250
  mail account types, 248–249
  Service Providers, 417
Internet E-mail Settings dialog
  box, 255
Internet Explorer, 102, 145
ISPs, 417

J

Junk E-mail Options dialog box,
  325–326
junk mail, 265, 325–326. *See also*
  spam
Justify alignment icon, 63

K

keyboard shortcuts
  character-formatting, 74, 98
  PowerPoint, 231
  Publisher, 390
kiosk-mode presentations, 244

L

layout program, 389
Left alignment icon, 63
legends, chart, 205
letter case, in email addresses,
  250
levels, outline, 87, 88
Line Spacing icon, 70
linked objects, 195
links, xiv, 284, 294–295, 369–371
lists
  bulleted, 66–69
  email address, 278–279, 408
  multilevel, 66, 69
  numbered, 66–69
  vs. tables, 185
  to-do, 338–340
live preview, 6
logos, 400, 403

M

.Mac accounts, 249
macros, xiii, 175
magnification, 19
Mail dialog box, 256
mail merge fields, 78, 81, 83
Mail Merge tool, 408
Mail Merge Wizard, 78–81
Mail Message command, 283
Mail Setup - Outlook dialog
    box, 253
mailing labels, 83
mailto links, 284, 295
manual breaks, 55–56
MAPI, 83
Margins menu, 50
Mark All as Read command, 315
Mark as Final command, 123
Mark as Not Junk command, 326
Mark as Read command, 315
Mark as Unread command, 315
mass mailings, 408
MAX function, 175
Maximize/Restore Down
    button, 18
menu bar, Outlook, 262
merging documents, 78–81, 408
message folders, 319
message formats, 288
message list, Outlook, 263
message rules, 326, 327–328
message window, Outlook, 282
messages. See email messages
Messaging Application
    Programming Interface, 83
Microsoft
    Access, xiii
    Excel. See Excel
    Exchange, 251, 253
    Office. See Office
    OneNote. See OneNote
    Outlook. See Outlook
    PowerPoint. See PowerPoint
    Publisher. See Publisher
    Visual Basic, xiii
    Word. See Word
Microsoft Office Access 2003 for
    Windows, xii
Microsoft Save As PDF or XPS
    add-in, 411, 415
MIN function, 175
Mini toolbar, 6, 72, 98
Minimize button, 18

misspelled words. See spelling
    checker
mixed cell references, 178
multilevel lists, 66, 69

N

Name Manager dialog box, 155
navigation bars, 417
Navigation Pane, 263, 265
nested functions, 181
nested tables, 366
New Blog Account dialog
    box, 116
New Name dialog box, 154
New Notebook Wizard, 346
New Photo Album command,
    229
New Presentation dialog
    box, 218
New Profile dialog box, 256
New Slide icon, 221
New Window command, 17
no-print zone, 51
note containers, 354, 381
notebook application, xiv, 343.
    See also OneNote
notebooks, 346–349
    adding sections to, 347
    closing, 349
    creating, 346
    creating page/section groups
        in, 379–380
    deleting, 347
    deleting sections from, 348
    downloading templates
        for, 347
    moving pages/sections in,
        377–378
    opening, 349
    organization of, 343
    password-protecting, 382–383
    rearranging, 376
    saving, 343
    searching for notes in,
        384–385
notes
    adding to presentations,
        213, 216
    combining, 381
    copying/pasting material
        into, 358
    creating, 343, 353–362
    deleting, 381

dragging/dropping material
    into, 359
editing, 372
formatting, 373
inserting hyperlinks in,
    369–371
inserting images in, 365
inserting tables in, 366–368
managing, 375–386
organizing, 343, 346
printing, 240–241, 386
recording, 355–356
searching for, 384–385
spell-checking, 374
templates for, 364
types of, 353
typing, 354
viewing unfiled, 345
Number Format menu,
    Excel, 135
numbered lists, 66–69

O

objects
    animating, 234–235
    moving, 111
    resizing, 111, 112
    rotating, 111, 112
    wrapping text around, 110
Office
    applications. See Office
        applications
    basics, 11–26
    Clipboard, 20–21, 25, 31, 40
    Compatibility Pack, 7
    file extensions/formats, 7
    Help options, 24–25
    interface, 4–6
    new features, 3–10
    personalizing, 123
    suites, xii
    templates, 13
    window management
        commands, 17–18
Office applications. See also
    specific applications
    closing documents in, 16
    creating documents in, 13
    getting help with, 24–25
    integration of OneNote with,
        350, 351
    launching, 12
    opening documents in, 14

Office applications *(continued)*
  printing documents in, 22–23
  quitting, 26
  saving documents in, 15
  setting magnification in, 19
  setting preferences for, 26
  similarities among, 11
  using Office Clipboard in,
    20–21
  working with windows in,
    17–18
Office Button, 4–5, 29, 30,
    128, 212
Office Online, 24
OneNote, 341–386
  creating notebooks in, 346.
    See also notebooks
  creating notes in, 353–362
  creating page/section groups
    in, 379–380
  deleting notes/objects in, 381
  editing notes in, 372
  embellishing notes in,
    363–374
  formatting notes in, 373
  getting help with, 24, 352
  integration with other
    programs, 350–352
  interface, 344–345
  managing notes in, 375–386
  moving pages/sections in,
    377–378
  new features, 10
  note types supported by, 353
  and Office Clipboard, 21
  opening/closing notebooks
    in, 349
  passwords, 382–383
  printing in, 22–23, 386
  purpose of, xiv, 343
  quitting, 26
  rearranging notebooks in, 376
  saving notebooks in, 343
  Search feature, 384–385
  setting magnification in, 19
  setting preferences for,
    26, 383
  spelling checker, 374
  tables, 366–368
  templates, 347, 364
  window management
    commands, 18
Open dialog box, 14
Open Notebook dialog box, 349

operators, 176–177
Options group, 61
Orientation menu, 50
Origin Letter template, 79, 80
orphans, 55
outdents, 65
Outline Level menu, 87
Outline view, 34, 85, 86, 241
outlines, 85–90
  adding/deleting points in, 88
  changing display settings
    for, 90
  creating, 87
  defined, 85
  formatting, 88
  moving points in, 89
  printing, 90
  reorganizing, 88–89
  selecting points in, 88
  setting/changing levels in, 87
  undoing changes to, 89
  ways of using, 85
Outlining tab, 86
Outlook, 245–340
  adding email accounts to,
    251–253
  Address Book, 250, 267–279.
    See also Address Book
  Blocked Senders List, 326
  Cached Exchange Mode,
    248, 253
  categorizing messages in,
    320–322
  changing account settings in,
    254–255
  changing view in, 308
  checking for new mail in,
    304–305
  composing/sending mail in,
    281–301
  copying messages in, 318
  creating message folders
    in, 319
  creating message rules in,
    327–328
  creating notes in, 360
  deleting messages in, 316–317
  email account types
    supported by, 248–249
  flagging messages in, 323–324
  Format Painter tool, 289, 291
  getting help with, 24, 263, 266
  handling junk mail/phishing
    in, 325–326

Import and Export Wizard,
    272, 273
  main window, 262–263
  managing mail in, 313–328
  managing tasks/
    appointments in,
    329–340
  message window, 282
  moving messages in, 318
  new features, 9
  and OneNote, 351
  printing messages in, 22–23,
    311–312
  purpose of, xiv
  Quick Styles palette, 290
  quitting, 26
  reading messages in, 306–307
  Rules Wizard, 327–328
  saving messages in, 15
  searching for messages
    in, 309
  setting magnification in, 19
  setting preferences for, 26,
    265, 285, 333
  spelling checker, 295
  Startup Wizard, 251
  using Office Clipboard in,
    20–21
  viewing RSS feeds in, 261
  working offline in, 264
  working with attachments in,
    292, 310
  working with profiles in,
    256–257
  working with send/receive
    groups in, 258–260
Outlook Express, 273

P

Pack and Go Wizard, 420,
    421–422
Package a Presentation for CD
    feature, 211
Package for CD dialog box, 244
Page Background group, 52
Page Borders icon, 54
Page Break icon, 55
page breaks, 55–56
page groups, 380
Page indicator, 32, 390, 391
Page Setup dialog box, 50–51
Page Setup Dialog Box
    Launcher, 50, 51

Page Setup group, 50, 56
paper size, 50
Paragraph dialog box, 63, 64–65
Paragraph Dialog Box Launcher
    icon, 62
paragraph formatting
    in email messages, 290
    in Excel worksheets, 163
    in OneNote notes, 373
    in Publisher publications, 402
    in Word documents, 49,
        62, 66
paragraph styles, 62
paragraphs
    aligning, 63
    changing line spacing for, 70
    changing spacing before/
        after, 71
    indenting, 64–65
Password dialog box, 124
passwords
    for Excel workbooks, 156–158
    for OneNote notebooks,
        382–383
    for Outlook profiles, 257
Paste Options icon/menu, 40
Paste Special dialog box, 171
PDF files
    burning to CD, 420
    emailing, 115, 414
    meaning of acronym, 409
    publishing documents as,
        411–413
    saving documents as, 7, 114
    saving presentations as,
        242, 243
    viewing, 114
permissions, document, 124
personalized letters, 78–81
phishing, 325–326
phone numbers, 165
photo albums, 229–230
Picture Options dialog box, 116
Picture tools, Word, 102
Picture Tools tab, 6
picture watermarks, 53
placeholders, 213, 222–224,
    395–396
Plain Text format, 114, 288
points, 71
POP servers, 249
POP3 accounts, 248, 251, 252, 260
Portable Document Format. See
    PDF files

Post Office Protocol accounts.
    See POP3 accounts
postcards
    adding contact information
        to, 394
    addressing, 408
    changing template for, 407
    creating, 392–393
    making minor changes to,
        399–403
    previewing, 398
    printing, 408
    replacing artwork in, 397
    replacing text placeholders
        in, 395–396
    sending as email message,
        416
    templates for, 392
PostScript fonts, 420
PowerPoint, 209–244
    adding/deleting slides in, 221
    closing documents in, 16
    compatibility issues, 7
    creating charts in, 195
    creating photo albums in,
        229–230
    creating presentations in,
        215–216, 217–231
    file extensions, 7
    getting help with, 24
    interface, 212–213
    new features, 9
    opening documents in, 14
    printing documents in, 22–23
    purpose of, xiii, 211
    quitting, 26
    replacing placeholders in,
        222–224
    Save As options, 242–243
    saving documents in, 15
    setting magnification in, 19
    setting preferences for,
        26, 212
    setting themes in, 220
    using Office Clipboard in,
        20–21
    views, 214
    window management
        commands, 17
PowerPoint 97-2003
    Presentation format, 242
PowerPoint Show files, 242
PowerPoint Viewer, 211, 244

.ppsx file extension, 242
.ppt file extension, 7
.pptm file extension, 7
.pptx file extension, 7
preferences
    Excel, 26, 128, 130
    Office, 26
    OneNote, 26, 383
    Outlook, 26, 265, 285, 333
    PowerPoint, 26, 212
    Publisher, 26
    Word, 26, 30, 42, 44
prepress checks, 409, 410
presentations. See also
        PowerPoint; slide shows
    adding animations to, 216,
        234–235
    adding/deleting slides in, 221
    adding notes to, 213, 216
    adding transitions to, 216,
        237–238
    applying themes to, 215,
        218–219, 220
    closing, 213
    copying to CD/DVD, 244
    creating, 211, 215–216,
        217–231
    distributing, 211
    organizing slides in, 236
    playing, 216
    printing notes/handouts for,
        240–241
    putting finishing touches
        on, 233
    rehearsing, 216, 239
    removing transitions
        from, 238
    replacing placeholders in,
        222–224
    saving, 219, 242–244
    selecting template for, 218
    self-running, 244
Preview utility, 242, 411
Print command, 22
Print dialog box, 22, 311, 419
Print Layout view, 33
Print Options dialog box, 412
Print Preview command, 22, 23,
        240, 311, 386, 398
Print Preview toolbar, 398
Printed Watermark dialog
        box, 53
printers, 23, 412, 413, 419, 422

printing
    documents, 22–23
    email messages, 311–312
    handouts, 241
    Help topics, 25
    message headers, 312
    OneNote notes, 386
    outlines, 90
    PDF files, 412, 413
    postcards, 408
    presentation notes, 240
    previewing prior to, 22, 23
    proofing before, 419
    publications, 419–422
    two-sided, 420
priority, message, 300
PRODUCT function, 175
Professional Plus suite, xii
Professional suite, xii
profiles, email account, 252, 256–257
Proofing indicator, Word, 32
proofing tools, Word, 41–44
proofs, 419
publication templates, 389, 392–393, 407
publications. *See also* Publisher
    changing font/color scheme for, 406
    converting from print to Web, 417–418
    creating, 392–393
    creating PDF versions of, 411–413
    defined, 391
    emailing, 414–416
    finding/fixing problems in, 410
    formatting text in, 401–402
    making minor changes to, 399–403
    merging address lists with, 408
    previewing, 398
    printing, 419–422
    replacing artwork in, 397
    replacing text placeholders in, 395–396
    running prepress check on, 410
    saving, 395
    storing/reusing items for, 404–405

Publish as PDF or XPS dialog box, 411
Publish as Web Page dialog box, 243
Publish Options dialog box, 412
Publish to the Web dialog box, 418
Publisher, 387–422. *See also* publications
    changing font/color scheme in, 406
    closing publications in, 16
    creating business information sets in, 394
    creating PDFs in, 411–413
    creating publications in, 392–393
    emailing publications from within, 414–416
    formatting text in, 401–402
    getting help with, 24, 391
    interface, 390–391
    modifying publications in, 399–403
    new features, 10
    previewing publications in, 398
    printing publications in, 22–23, 419
    publishing to Web in, 417–418
    purpose of, xiv, 389
    quitting, 26
    replacing artwork in, 397
    replacing text placeholders in, 395–396
    running prepress check in, 410
    saving publications in, 15
    setting magnification in, 19
    setting preferences for, 26
    storing/reusing items in, 404–405
    using Office Clipboard in, 20–21
    window management commands, 18
publishing
    blog entries, 116–117
    calendars, 337
    Web pages, 417–418

Q

QuarkXPress, xiv
Quick Access Toolbar, 4, 5, 30, 128, 213
Quick Click categories, 321, 322
Quick Click flags, 323
Quick Style sets, 75
Quick Styles gallery, 75
Quick Styles palette, 290
Quick Table feature, 93, 94

R

R1C1 reference style, 175
ranges, 132–133, 154–155, 174
Reading Pane, 263, 314
Really Simple Syndication feeds, xiv, 247. *See also* RSS feeds
Recall This Message command, 287
receipts, message delivery, 300
Recent Items submenu, 12
records, 185, 190, 191, 192–193
reference operators, 176, 177
Register a Blog Account dialog box, 116
Rehearse Timings icon, 239
relative cell references, 178
reminders, 324, 333
reports, 57
Research task pane, 41
Resend This Message command, 287
Resize Table dialog box, 193
resolution, 244, 412
Reviewing Pane, 119, 121
Ribbon
    and Excel, 129
    how to use, 5
    illustrated, 4
    and Outlook, 263, 282
    and PowerPoint, 213
    purpose of, 5
    and Word, 31
Rich Text Format, 114, 288, 289, 293
Right alignment icon, 63
rows
    adding/deleting, 139, 140, 192–193
    setting height of, 160–161
    switching to columns, 201
    totaling, 189

INDEX

RSS feeds, xiv, 247, 260, 261
.rtf file extension, 114. *See also*
    Rich Text Format
rulers, 31, 37, 391
Rules and Alerts dialog box,
    327, 328
Rules Wizard, 327–328
Run Rules Now dialog box, 328

S

Safe Senders tab, Junk E-mail
    Options dialog box, 326
Sample Fill Color command, 399
Save As dialog box, 15
Save As PDF or XPS add-in,
    411, 415
Save Workspace command, 18
screen clippings, 350, 361, 362
scroll bars/box, 31
searching
    for appointments, 335
    for contact records, 274–275
    for email messages, 309
    for events, 335
    for OneNote notes, 384–385
section breaks, 56
section groups, 379
Send a Calendar via E-mail
    dialog box, 336
Send as Message dialog
    box, 415
send/receive groups, 258–260
Send/Receive icon, 304
Send to Mail Recipient
    command, 114
Set Quick Click dialog box,
    321, 323
Set Up Show dialog box, 244
Shading menu, 97
Shape Fill icon, 105
Shape Styles group, 225
Shapes gallery, 225
Shapes icon, 105, 225
Sheet tab bar, 129, 130
shortcut menus, 6
shortcuts, keyboard. *See*
    keyboard shortcuts
Show Document Text check
    box, 61
Show/Hide options, Word, 37,
    120, 121
side notes, 361, 362, 377

signatures
    digital, 124
    email, 265, 298–299
single-clicking, 13
slide shows. *See also*
    presentations
    adding transitions to,
        237–238
    distributing, 214
    organizing slides in, 236
    of personal/business photos,
        229–230
    previewing, 231
    rehearsing, 239
    removing transitions
        from, 238
    saving in other formats,
        242–244
    ways of using, 211
Slide Sorter view, 214, 216,
    221, 236
slide timings, rehearsing, 239
slides. *See also* slide shows
    adding action buttons to, 238
    adding/deleting, 221, 236
    applying themes to, 230
    duplicating, 226
    hiding, 236
    inserting date/time in, 227
    inserting items in, 225–228
    inserting shapes in, 225, 228
    inserting text boxes in, 226
    numbering, 227
    organizing, 236
    previewing, 231
Slides/Outline tab, 213
Small Business suite, xii
SmartArt, 107, 110, 224
Social Security numbers, 165
Sort & Filter icon, 191
Sort dialog box, 100
Sort Text dialog box, 68
sorting
    email messages, 309
    Excel tables, 190
    Word lists, 68
    Word tables, 100
spam, 249, 325–326. *See also*
    junk mail
special characters, 48
spelling checker
    OneNote, 374
    Outlook, 265, 296–297
    Word, 42–44

Split command, 17
spreads, 391
spreadsheet programs, xiii, 127,
    165. *See also* Excel
spreadsheets, 185. *See also*
    worksheets
Standard suite, xii
Start button, 12
Start menu, Windows, 12
Startup wizard, Outlook, 251
stationery, message, 301
status bar
    Outlook, 263, 264
    Publisher, 417
    Word, 32, 33
STDEV function, 175
STDEVP function, 175
stock charts, 206
structured references, 175, 188
styles
    adding to sets, 76
    chart, 202
    defined, 75
    modifying, 76–77
    naming, 76
    paragraph, 62
    purpose of, 49
    shape, 225
    WordArt, 225
Styles pane, Word, 31
suites, Office, xii
SUM function, 175, 179
Switch Windows menu, 16, 35
Symbol dialog box, 48
Synchronous Scrolling icon, 36

T

tab stops, 31, 37, 59, 65, 92
Table icon, 92
table placeholders, 223
Table Tools tab, 6, 94
tables (Excel), 185–193
    adding total rows to, 189
    changing size of, 192–193
    creating, 186
    cutting/pasting, 193
    dragging/dropping, 193
    filtering, 190, 191
    formatting, 187
    moving, 193
    sorting, 190
    using formulas in, 188
tables (OneNote), 366–368

tables (Word), 91–100
  applying cell shading in, 97
  applying table styles in, 97
  changing line properties
      in, 97
  deleting rows/columns
      in, 96
  entering data into, 94
  formatting cells in, 98
  inserting in documents,
      92–93
  inserting rows/columns
      in, 96
  merging/splitting cells in, 96
  modifying grid for, 95–97
  sorting, 100
  using formulas in, 99
Tablet PCs, 357
tabs, contextual, 6
tasks, 338–340
Tasks pane, 329, 338
templates
  cover page, 57
  message rule, 327–328
  notebook, 347
  Office, 13
  OneNote, 364
  presentation, 218
  publication, 389, 392–393, 407
text
  animating, 234–235
  in charts, 199–200
  deleting, 39
  finding/replacing, 45–47
  formatting, 401–402
  outlining. See outlines
  in Word documents, 38–40
  wrapping, 110, 164
text boxes, 109, 110, 226, 399
text color, 52
text concatenation
      operators, 176
Text Import Wizard, 147–148
text insertion mark, 38
text placeholders, 222, 395–396
text watermarks, 53
themes
  message, 301
  presentation, 215, 218–219,
      220
  slide, 230
thesaurus, 41
thumbnails, 37
To box, message window, 283

To-Do Bar, 263, 338, 340
To-Do Lists, 338–340
toolbars
  Excel, 128
  Office, 4
  OneNote, 344
  Outlook, 262
  PowerPoint, 212
  Publisher, 390, 391
  Word, 30
ToolTips, 4, 5, 24
Top/Bottom Rules
      submenu, 167
Total Row check box, 189
Track Changes Options dialog
      box, 118
Transition to this Slide
      gallery, 237
transitions, between-slide, 211,
      216, 237–238
trendlines, 206
TrueType fonts, 420
two-sided printing, 420
.txt file extension, 114
typed notes, 354

U

Ultimate suite, xii
underscore (_) character, 250
Unfiled Notes page, 355, 360,
      361, 362, 377
Use Rehearsed Timings check
      box, 239
user interface. See interface
user profiles, email account, 252,
      256–257

V

VAR/VARP functions, 175
vCards, 276–277, 294
.vcf file extension, 277
vertical ruler, 31
video notes, 356, 384
View controls
  Excel, 129
  PowerPoint, 213, 214
  Word, 32, 33–34
View Ruler icon, 31
View Side by Side mode, 36
Vista. See Windows Vista
Visual Basic, xiii
Visual QuickStart series, xi

W

watermarks, 52, 53, 110
Web-based accounts, 249
Web browsers
  accessing email accounts
      with, 249
  viewing Publisher documents
      in, 417
Web (HTML) presentation
      format, 242
Web Layout view, 34
Web logs, 116–117
Web pages, converting
      Publisher documents to,
      417–418
Web Query Options dialog
      box, 145
Webdings, 48
Widow/Orphan control, 55
wildcards, 150
Window group, Ribbon, 17
window management
      commands, 17–18
Window menu, 17
Windows applications,
      launching, 12
Windows Clipboard, 20, 21, 358
Windows Live Spaces, 116
Windows Vista, 12, 23, 262,
      309, 422
Windows XP, 12, 23, 262, 309
WinZip, 422
Word, 27–124
  adding blank page in, 58
  adding cover page in, 57
  adding headers/footers in,
      59–61
  adding page borders in, 54
  applying character
      formatting in, 72–74
  change tracking features,
      118–119
  changing default font in, 73
  changing line spacing in,
      70–71
  click-and-type feature, 38
  closing documents in, 16,
      29, 32
  combining documents in, 121
  comparing documents in,
      36, 120
  compatibility issues, 7
  creating charts in, 101, 195

INDEX

Word *(continued)*
　creating lists in, 66–69
　Document Inspector, 122
　emailing documents from,
　　114, 115
　entering/editing text in,
　　38–40
　entering special characters
　　in, 48
　file extensions/formats, 7, 114
　finding/replacing text in,
　　45–47
　formatting documents in,
　　49–83
　getting help with, 24
　graphics tools, 102
　inserting breaks in, 55–56
　interface, 30–32
　managing windows in, 35–36
　modifying page background
　　in, 52–54
　new features, 8
　and OneNote, 351
　opening documents in, 14,
　　29, 32
　Outline View, 85, 86. *See also*
　　outlines
　popularity of, 29
　printing documents in, 22–23
　proofing tools, 41–44
　protecting documents in,
　　123–124
　publishing blog entries via,
　　116–117
　purpose of, xiii, 29
　quitting, 26
　saving documents in, 15
　setting indents in, 64–65
　setting magnification in, 19
　setting paragraph alignment
　　in, 63
　setting preferences for, 26
　setting Show/Hide options
　　in, 37
　setting tabs in, 65
　sorting lists in, 68
　specifying page settings in,
　　50–51

spelling/grammar checker,
　42–44
tables, 91–100. *See also* tables
　(Word)
using Office Clipboard in,
　20–21, 31
View controls, 32, 33–34
ways of using, xiii
window management
　commands, 17
working with multiple
　documents in, 35–36
working with styles in,
　75–77
Word 97-2003 format, 7, 114
Word Count dialog box, 32
Word Options dialog box, 39,
　40, 66
word-processing application,
　xiii, 29, 38, 389. *See also*
　Word
WordArt, 108, 110
WordArt Styles group, 225
words
　finding/replacing, 45–47
　finding synonyms for, 41
　looking up definitions for, 41
Words indicator, Word, 32
Work Offline command, 264
workbooks
　creating new, 131
　defined, 127
　numbering of worksheets
　　in, 130
　password-protecting,
　　156–158
　types of information included
　　in, 127
worksheets
　changing default font for, 162
　changing order of, 131
　components of, 130
　as databases, 185
　deleting, 131
　editing contents of, 136
　filling cells in, 142–143
　finding/replacing data in,
　　149–151

formatting, 159, 162, 166–167
importing data into, 144–148
inserting new, 131
merging with Word
　documents, 78–81
removing formatting
　from, 170
renaming, 130
reorganizing data in, 137–141
replacing formatting in, 171
reusing formatting in, 171
setting column/row size in,
　160–161
showing/hiding gridlines
　in, 162
sorting data in, 152–153
ways of using, 185
Wrap Text icon, 164
WYSIWYG, xiii

X

.xls file extension, 7
.xlsm file extension, 7
.xlsx file extension, 7
XML files, 7
XML Paper Specification files,
　115. *See also* XPS files
XP. *See* Windows XP
XPS files, 115, 242, 411, 414, 415
XY axes, chart, 207

Y

Yahoo! Mail, 249
yellow dot, 106

Z

ZIP codes, 135, 152, 165
.zip file extension, 422
Zip utilities, 422
Zoom controls
　Word, 32
zoom controls
　Excel, 129
　PowerPoint, 213
Zoom dialog box, 19